AYATOLLAHS, SUFIS AND IDEOLOGUES

AYATOLLAHS, SUFIS AND IDEOLOGUES

State, religion and Social Movements in Iraq

Edited by
Faleh Abdul-Jabar

Saqi Books

To the memory of Marion Farouk-Sluglett,
the scholar, the friend, the person

British Library Cataloguing-in-Publication Data
A catalogue record for this book is available from the
British Library

ISBN 0 86356 912 9 (hb)

This edition published 2002

Saqi Books
26 Westbourne Grove
London W2 5RH
www.saqibooks.com

Contents

Glossary

'adala	justice
adilla	inference (plural of *dalil*), or evidence
agha	kurdish notable or landlord
aghlabiyya	majority
ahkam (plural of *hukum*)	imperatives, injunctions, rulings
ahl al-bayt	the prophet's household
akthariyya	majority
a'imma (plural of *imam*)	religious leaders, legitimate rulers
'alim	the most knowledgeable, doctor of religion, cleric
'alamiyya	best knowledge
'am	general, absolute
aqalliyya	minority
'aql	reason, mind
ashab (see *sahib*)	
'ashura	ten days of mourning
'atabat (plural of *'ataba*)	shrines
atba' (plural of *tabi'*)	followers
a'waj	crooked
'aza'	(literally, condolence) mourning assembly for Husayn
bab	gate
barnamaj	programme
Barnamajuna	*Our Programme* (Da'wa Party)
batini	esoteric, mystic or sufists
bazar	market place
bayt al-mal	central treasury
bedoon	nationals without nationality
bid'a	heresy
bulogh	coming of age

dars	lesson
dars al–karij	higest level of education at the religious *madrasa*
da'wa	call
darwish (dervish)	sufi
du'at	missionaries, activists
dustur	constitution
faqih (plural *fuqaha'*)	jurist, jurisconsult
faqih-wali	ruling jurist (as for Khomeini)
fiqh	jurisprudence
fitna	chaos, civil strife
fursan (plural of *faris*)	knights, horsemen, warriors
hadd (plural *hudud*)	punishment
hadith	oral tradition
hammam	public bath
haras	guards
hashiyya	entourage
hawza	collectivity of senior *'ulama*
hawza 'ilmiyya	college of religious schools
hiss	sensibility
hurriyya	freedom (as in not being a slave)
idariyya	administrative
ijma'	unanimity, consensus
ijtihad	free religious judgement
imam	religious leader, legitimate ruler
imami	Twelver Shi'i
imamiyya	Twelver Shi'ism
iman	belief
intifada	uprising
iqamat	enforcement
jihad	holy war, exertion
jood	generosity
Juz'i	partial
kafir	infidel
kalam	theology
kashf	uncover revelation

Khalifa (plural *khulafa'*)	caliph(s)
khan	caravan lodging
khass	particular, limited
khilafa(t)	caliphate
khums	fifth, religious taxes
lughat	language
majlis	council
manaqib	prophet's exemplary deeds, eulogy
marad al-ras	return of the head (of slain Imam Husayn), the 40th day after the death of Husayn
marja' (plural *maraji'*)	religious authority (specific persons)
marja'ism (also *marja'iyya*)	religious authority (in collective or in the abstract)
mashruta	constitutional monarchy (revolution in Iran 1906)
ma'sum (plural *ma'sumin*)	infallible
mawakib	processions
mawlid	birth, lineage
mawlid	Sunni ceremony on the Prophet's birthday
Muharram	first lunar month
mujahid	warrior for God, militant
mujtahid	high ranking Shi'i jurists
multazem	tax farmer
muqaddas	sacred, divine, holy
muqallid	emulator
murshid	guide, leader
mustabida	absolute monarchy
mutlaq	absolute, supreme
mutasarrif	district governor in monarchic Iraq
Murabitun	North African dynasty
nahiya	county in Iraq administrative units.
na'ib	deputy
nahwu	grammar
nas	people at large
nawa'i	mourning verse and melody
niyaba	deputation
mustafti	person seeking religious opinion (*fatwa*)
peshmarga	Kurdish partisan

qabila (plural *qaba'il*)	tribe
qismat	division
rahbar (Persian)	leader
riyasa	headship
ruhani (plural *ruhaniyoon*)	spiritualist
rujolah	manhood, being masculine
sahib (plural *ashab*)	companions
sahm (*sahmi*)	share of
shura	consultation
sayyid	noble, descendant from the household of Ali
shabana	local police
shabih	passion play
shahada	martyrdom
shahid	witness
shaheed	martyr
shar'	law
Shari'a	Islamic law
shart	condition
shaykh	non-sayyid jurists, elder, tribal chief, Sufi leader
salat	prayer
Shmurt	Najaf clan of fighters
shu'ur	feeling
siyanet	protection
siyasa	politics, policy
sufi	mystic, member of sufi orders
suk	market place
shu'ubiyya	anti-Arab Persian hatred
Sufar	lunar month
sufiyya	Sufism
tabligh	admonition, indoctrination
Taff	Karbala battle
ta'ifiyya	communalism, communal discrimination
taharat	purity
takya (plural *takaya*)	Sufi lodging
tariqa	order (Sufi)
tasawuf	Sufism
tatbeer	head-cutting in *'ashura*

tanfith	implementation, enforcement
tasrif	syntax
thatiyya	subjective, individualistic
thawra	revolution
Thiker	Sufi ceremony
ta'ziya (see *majlas 'aza'*)	lamentation assembly
'ulama	doctors of religion, clerics
uli-al-amr	those in charge
umma	community, nation
usul	methodology
uzma	grand (rank of Ayatollah)
wakil (plural *wukala*)	representative
wali(s)	regional governor(s)
wali	religious ruler
waqf (plural *awqaf*)	religious endowment
wilaya(t)	province(s)
wilayat al-faqih	the guardianship (rulership) of the jurisconsult
yawm al-ghadir	anniversary of Imam's Ali nomination
yawmi	daily
zann	probable knowledge (assumption)
Zghurt	Najaf clan

Introduction

Faleh Abdul-Jabar

The rise of modern Islamic social movements across the Middle East and beyond has been a noted phenomenon since at least 1967. That year marked the 'appearance' of Mary the Virgin in Cairo, following the defeat in the June 1967 Arab-Israeli war. A thin line runs from the Virgin Mary episode to the anti-Ba'th Shi'i Islamist mass demonstrations in Iraq, in February 1977, to the phenomenal success of the Iranian revolution in February 1979, the assassination of Sadat at the hands of a small, clandestine Islamist group led by Khalid al-Islamboli in October 1981, down to the verge of the Algerian Islamic Salvation Front (FIS) on power in 1990–91 through the ballot, or the Islamist military takeover in the Sudan a year earlier, or the seizure of the Afghani capital, Kabul in 1996 by the fundamentalist Taliban.

The clear thread running through these developments appeared to question, or even disprove the modernist, lineal notion that 'advance' in society towards modernity encourages the decline of all traditional patterns of social structures, including religion. The resurgence of Islamism seemed to suggest that Islam is of a 'different' essence. When similar trends were observed among the Sikhs of India, or, as Gilles Kepel has amply shown, within Judaic traditions, the difference assumed a wider validity, that of Orient-Occident dichotomy. And sooner rather than later, the Weberian polar Orient-Occident dichotomy was brought into full force. This is based on a cultural polarity of two different, opposing essences. Essence, in this tradition, is an Aristotelian fixed determinant of the dynamic or stagnant 'nature' of society. Yet a scrutiny of the very concepts of fundamentalism as a fixed cultural essence, gave rise to a more fruitful conjunctural method, to study the role of Islam in modern societies. The works of N. Keddie, Juan Cole, Kepel, Sami Zubaida, E.Mortimer, to name but a few, stand in bold relief.

While a plethora of works on the inter-relationship of state, society and religion has covered a multitude of countries, such as Iran, Pakistan, Turkey, Algeria, Egypt and the Sudan, no comprehensive research on religion-state-society in Iraq has ever been carried out. With the exception of a few papers and essays (Hanna Batatu, John Thomas Cummings, Sylvia Haim, Ofra Bengio, Amatzia Baram, Peter Sluglett and others), Islam and Islamism in the Iraqi context has remained an understudied phenomenon. Thus a glaring gap in our knowledge of the social and political roles of religion in Iraq is too obvious to ignore.

Little attention has been given to Islamism in Iraq, which preceded the Iranian Revolution; even less has been focused on its nature, origins, the social movements that developed as a result of it, the social actors it involved and the ideological responses it gave rise to. These aspects remain relatively obscure.

As well as 'filling the gap', this book was motivated by an attempt to go beyond the oversimplified, totalizing conceptions of Islam; beyond the schematic representation of Iraqi society within the customary trilogy of Sunnis, Shi'is and Kurds, and beyond the narrow, communal conception of contemporary Islamist social movements in Iraq.

Islam provides a multitude of forms, structures, doctrines, schools and social actors, which are too complex and intricate to confine within a holistic 'essence'. Institutionalized religion, in the form of the Shi'i *marja'iyya*, or the Sunni institution of Shaykh al-Islam or Mufti, is an ethical, literate pattern of religiosity, anchored in the sacred text, the legalities of the divine law, with an emphasis on the norms and canons of purity, in terms of social and private contracts and rituals, as embodied in the jurisprudence of rituals (*fiqh al-'ibadat*) and jurisprudence of contracts (*fiqh al-mu'amalat*), or the theology, relating to the nature of God, and the divine designs for the past, present and future of human kind. It resembles the ideal type Weber termed as 'ethical prophecy'. While the Shi'i institution is decentralized and informal, the Sunni institution is blended with the state bureaucracy, lacking the former's organizational and financial autonomy.

A second set of institutions in Islam is the religious *madrasa*, the transmitter and producer of religious knowledge. In the *madrasa*, much of the renewal of modern Islamic thought takes place, and many of the 'ideological brains' and 'militant hands' come out of it. However, the *madrasa* is also the bastion of rigid conservatism.

The pattern of headship, or social networks among the bureaucratized or autonomous clerical class, or in the *madrasa*, vary from country to country. These patterns have played, and continue to play, crucial social, political and cultural roles. Khomeini's first cells originated in the networks of his own novices and emulators; four decades on, the Taliban (literally novices of a religious school) movement in Afghanistan thrived on such master-novice associations as well.

A third level is the myriad patterns of popular religion, like the Sufi orders, organized on the basis of the guilds in urban neighbourhoods, or blended with tribal structures in rural settings, as seen, for example in the Naqshabandiyya Sufi order prevailing in west Kurdistan and the Qadiriyya Sufi order in the east; another example might be the *hay'at hussaynia* (Husayn rituals bodies), which organize the 'ashura and other rituals in the city neighbourhoods or rural villages. Patterns of popular religion stand in contrast with canonical-ethical religion of the literate clerical class. The Sufi *thikr* (ceremony), or the Shi'i passion plays (*tashabih*), or Husayn assembly (*majlis ta'ziya*), the Sunni visitation to tombs of saints, or the Shi'i pilgrimage to holy shrines (*ziyarat*), provide examples of community-based organizations of religion which may function as conduits of media of salvation, mediation with saintly figures, moral catharsis, social solidarity, and, most importantly, tools for mass politics.

The relations between the high religious culture of the clerical class and the low, popular culture of the communities, are fluid and varied, involving sub-national solidarities of the extended family, guild and city affiliation or even regional allegiances, or supra-national networks of emulators, or national, ethnic belonging.

The relations between high and low cultures involve tensions, constraints, clashes and cooperation of every imaginable sort, ranging from social to cultural and other factors.

By the same token, the realm of modern Islamist, or militant Islam, contains a myriad of Islamic social movements of every conceivable structure, ideology, strategy, or course of action. In the case of Iraq, there are at least three Shi'i political movements, five Shi'i institutions, two major Kurdish Islamist groups and two Sunni Arab organizations.

In summing up these points, it might be noted that the wider literature on Islam and Islamism across the Middle East, including Shi'i Islamism, has provided ample evidence attesting to the fact that religion has a range of institutionalized forms, various social actors, different cultural forms, and diverse modalities operating within distinct and changing national contexts (G. Kepel, E. Sivan, S. Akhavi, E. Abrahamian, E. Mortimer, H. Enayat and R. Mottahedeh offer some examples).

The complexities relevant to Islam and Islamism also apply to Iraqi society, the national space where these patterns have originated and have been operating. Nowhere has this complexity intrigued scholars more than in the realm of studying Islamism in Iraq. Three distinct approaches underpin the meagre literature on Islamist activism in Iraq: a) communal; b) cultural-essentialist; and c) conjunctural. The basic concepts of the communal pattern revolve around the classical German community versus society dichotomy (Gemeinschäfte *vis-a-vis* Gesellschaft) as developed by Ferdinand Tönnies. Projected onto the Iraq reality, they centre on the Sunni minority-dominated state *vis-à-vis* the Shi'i majority-oppressed community. Hence Islamist militancy is, firstly, confined to Shi'ism, and, secondly, is seen as an expression of grievances arising from this tense, communal dichotomy.

Within this approach, the community is almost treated as a homogenous monolithic socio-cultural entity. This lends a fixed essence to communal spaces and structures and the identity (or identities), sometimes imbued even with a mono-dimensional social or political activism, as if religious culture in and for itself creates a unifying space of social and political nature under any circumstances. This interpretation overlooks the rich social and cultural diversity within the Shi'i.

Gemeinschäfte, which, as clearly demonstrated in Batatu's voluminous work, have constantly been caught in the process of transformation to modern forms of social organization and culture in such a way that old forms existed in different levels of transformed symbiosis with new ones, that their reality is far more complex and rich in terms of social organization and culture: the tribe, the clan, extended families, urban guilds, status groups, city neighbourhood and city solidarities, splitting religious spaces and cutting across such totalizing categories as Sunnis, Shi'is or Kurds. As these traditional patterns have been, and continue to be, in a process of transformation (a set of erosion, modification and mutation of various elements), modern diverging social, economic and cultural interests have added to the complexity. The trilogy of Shi'is, Sunnis and Kurds is theoretically thin. In the words of Peter Sluglett, 'The notion of the heterogeneity of Iraqi society is another theme that needs further definition and refinement, The facts are that the population of Iraq, now about 18 million, is divided on both ethnic and sectarian lines. Of course, neither the communities nor the sect constitute homogeneous or monolithic single entities.'

'A simplistic image of Iraqi society has emerged, largely under the influence of Middle Eastern "experts" of the U.S. defence establishment, of "their Arab Sunnis" supporting the "Sunni" regime of Saddam Hussain and the allegedly "somewhat less Arab" Shi'is (a sort of Iranian fifth column) bitterly opposed to it.' (*The Historiography of Modern Iraq*, 1991, pp. 1412–3, italics added).

Cultural essentialism attributes the rise of Islamism to the incompatibility of Islam with modernity or lack of sufficient separation of the secular from the sacred. A variety of this approach is the notion that Shi'ism as such is a radically anti-modern-state doctrine. The concept of the hidden Imam which denies legitimacy to worldly powers is claimed to have been the source of cultural rejection of modernity of which the ruling elites in the Middle East were part. Or Shi'ism is held radical by dint of the logical structure of the theo-jurisitic doctrine itself; its social and political activism and action is deduced from this source with no due consideration to socio-political, economic and other factors. Both communal and cultural approaches share common reductionist grounds.

The conjunctural approach, by contrast, has provided a comparative study of Islamist social movements (Batatu, Zubaida, Cole and Keddie, among others). Accordingly Islamist militancy could be typified into various different patterns, among which is the social pattern where Islamist protest is caused and stimulated by many catalysts and factors among which 'factors of economic and social change that are common to many Muslim countries, and sometimes Third World countries' (N. Keddie and Juan Cole). Another general pattern is local, where activism is spurred by protest against group-discrimination under authoritarian regimes in specific nation-states. A third variety may also be seen in protests anchored in social disparities, economic exclusion and political disfranchisement resulting from the disturbance of the processes of modern nation-building.

This book is the result of a two-day academic seminar on State, Society, Religion and Social Movements in Iraq which was organized by the Iraqi Cultural Forum, a London-based research group active since 1993, in conjunction with the Department of Politics and Sociology at Birkbeck College, University of London, in 1997. Prominent academic researchers, political writers and social activists with academic training gathered together to examine various aspects of the topic. Whether or not the contributors in this volume may agree with my views in this introduction, their chapters focused on the unique nature of religion and state-religion tensions in Iraq, common features with other Middle Eastern societies notwithstanding. The collection may well contribute to widen the perspectives of our observation and help bring forth hitherto undiscussed major issues.

Part One examines the role of religion in defining community and its relation to the state.

Professor Y. Nakkash lucidly shows that compared to Iran, Shi'ism in Iraq is a *sui generis* in cultural and other terms. In his opinion, part of Shi'i protest, or militancy, stems from their response against state attack on their identity as Iraqis. His conclusions defy any schematic conceptualizing of Shi'ism as a homogeneous cultural space, presumably transcending national and historical contexts. Professor Peter Heine arrives at a complementary conclusion. By examining the structure of traditional society in Najaf in the second half of the nineteenth century and early twentieth century, he deduces that, while Shi'is in general were divided along ethnic lines (Turks, Persians, Arabs), Arab Shi'is of Iraq were socially divided into Bedouin/town dwellers; Shi'i cities competed against each other, whereas city dwellers in turn were, sociologically speaking, segmented. Among the various groups ('*ulama*, non-clerical notables, merchants, artisans and armed groups in charge of violence), Heine examines the role of the monopolizers of means of violence, the neighbourhood gangs who have sundry interests dictating their cooperation with or rebellion against state authorities (the Ottomans).

Helkot Hakim examines a linguistic-cultural battle between Arabist, secular state elites and nationalist Kurds. Paradoxically, Islam is thrown into the clash to blur the linguistic-ethnic character of the Kurds.

Part Two examines the high and low culture of Shi'i and Sunni Islam. In Chapter 4, I study the genesis and development of the informal institution of *marja'ism*. My conclusion is that while centralization forces were at work on all levels as from the mid-nineteenth century, triggering similar tendencies within the Shi'i institution, a decentralized religious turn was, paradoxically set in motion when centralization of the state itself peaked in the 20th century, a fact which reveals the tensions between an authoritarian state and an autonomous religious institution.

Pierre Jean Luizard examines the tension between the state and the institution of *marja'ism*, he concentrates his analysis, however, on a single episode, that of Ayatollah Muhsin al-Hakim versus the Ba'th regime. By contrast, Ibrahim Haydari, Sami Shourush and Helkot Hakim study the popular forms of religion, the functions, structures and actors of the Shi'i 'ashura rituals (Ibrahim Haydari), or the origins of the Naqshabandiyya Sufi order (Hakim), or the multitude of sects, Sufi orders and religions among the Kurds (Shourush). These chapters provide narratives and analysis of the specifics of the Durkheimian nature of these forms of low religious culture as community-based and community self-reflective ceremonial ritualism.

Part Three contains five chapters on various Islamist social movements of Shi'is, Sunnis and Kurds. Abdul-Halim Ruhaimi studies the Da'wa party, Basim al-'Azami the Sunni Muslim Brotherhood, and Sami Shourush the various Islamist Kurds. The three authors focus on the genesis, ideology and actors of these movements, which reveal some common characteristics.

Ali Babakhan, who unfortunately passed away before the publication of this book, and Jens-Uwe Rahe, follow the line and move on to examine the Islamist militants in exile, who were acting in and reacting to a new environment. Babakhan's contribution, based on two books of his in French, is the first of its kind on the causes and consequences of the deportation of the Shi'i in the 1970s and 1980s, a phenomenon which, by and large, has been the most well-known topic among academics but the least studied of all.

The last part, dedicated to ideologies, is mainly focused on Shi'i Islamist thinkers. This is all the more natural, since they occupied the intellectual horizon, whereas the Sunni Islamist leaders towards action.

Yousif al-Kho'i writes on the political thought of Grand Ayatollah Abu al-Qassim al-Kho'i, the great *marja'* who was superior to Khomeini in juristic terms. The general view that he is apolitical, even a preacher of acquiescence, is relatively misleading.

Talib Aziz closely examines the political theory of Ayatollah Muhammad Baqir al-Sadr in its entirety, which is composed of three different elements relating to political action, the political system and the Islamist platform of social reform. Sadr was the first *mujtahid* to endorse the creation of a modern political party for the Shi'is.

Jawdat al-Qazwini provides two comparative historical and detailed chapters on the Najaf and the Qum schools, based on his thorough PhD dissertation on the topic, renowned for its first hand information. Like Yousif al-Kho'i, al-Qazwini descends from a notable family which contributed to the Shi'i world of jurisprudence in the mid Euphrates (Hilla) for centuries.

Other contributions were vital: texts in languages other than English were translated by Abdulilah al-Nuaimi, Wendy Christiansen and Nadje al-Ali. Without their dedication this volume would have not materialized in its present shape.

PART I

RELIGION, COMMUNITY AND
STATE

CHAPTER ONE

The Nature of Shiʿism in Iraq

Yitzhak Nakkash

In the wake of the 1991 uprisings against Saddam Hussein, Iraqi army units were engaged in large-scale operations against Shiʿis in the marshes of southern Iraq. This campaign was backed by a massive propaganda effort mounted by Iraqi government officials and the media against the Shiʿi marsh Arabs, portraying them as 'un-Iraqi' and describing their culture as 'primitive and debased'.[1] The Baʿth government's assault on the identity and culture of the marsh Arabs in the aftermath of the Gulf War raises the following two basic questions: Who are the Iraqi Shiʿis? What is the nature of Shiʿism in Iraq? One can approach these questions from various perspectives. The one opted for in this chapter is a comparison between Shiʿism in Iran and Iraq: some aspects of the political development of Shiʿis in modern Iraq will also be highlighted.

The development of Shiʿism in Iran and Iraq in the past few centuries reflected two radically different processes of community formation. Iran's population became by and large Shiʿi in the 16th and 17th centuries, following the establishment of the Safavid state in 1501. Since then, Shiʿi Islam has been the state religion in Iran (save for a short period after the Sunni Afghan occupation of Isfahan in 1722). On the whole, the state supported religion and the ulama well into the 20th century. In contrast with the state sponsored conversion of the Iranian population to Shiʿism, modern Iraqi Shiʿi society was formed from the mid-18th century onwards. This process reflected the rise of Najaf and Karbala as the two strongholds of Shiʿism in a country which was a Sunni Ottoman possession, and the conversion of Iraq's settled tribes to Shiʿism. This large-scale conversion did not pervade the former social values of the tribesmen. Indeed, against the Persian ethnic origin of the large majority of Iranians, the Iraqi Shiʿis have to a great extent been distinguished by their Arab tribal attributes and moral values, which endured long after the establishment of modern Iraq in 1921 under Sunni minority rule.[2]

On another level, Shi'i Islam in Iran and Iraq has differed greatly in the nature of its organization. Iranian Shi'ism has been distinguished by its highly organizational form. Indeed, students have pointed out that it was religion which held Iranian society together for centuries, and that the pressures and sanctions to behave in proper Shi'i Islamic fashion stemmed largely from Iranian public opinion.[3] Thus, the active involvement of ordinary Iranians in shaping religious activity and belief suggests that Shi'ism in modern Iran might be seen as a system of socio-economic and religious values, which, rather than being imposed on social reality, arose from within it. This distinct feature of Iranian Shi'ism is nowhere more apparent than in the contrasts in interaction between religion and economy in Iran and Iraq. These differences may be illustrated by focusing on the relations between the ulama and the bazaaris and on the organization of Shi'i endowments in the two countries.

In modern Iran, ulama and bazaaris shared considerable similarities in lifestyle and values, and viewed the government as only quasi-legitimate. The bazaar and Shi'i Islam interacted to give each other shape and substance. The socio-cultural milieu of the bazaar and its immediate environs provided most of the financial and moral support for the clergymen in Iran. For its part, Shi'i Islam affected the operations of the marketplace. It shaped the social activity of the bazaaris, giving direction to their conduct and binding them to religion.[4] The religious schooling of bazaaris promoted traditional conservative values, which enabled the bazaar to emerge as a major bulwark of Shi'i Islam. Many bazaaris conducted their business within the framework and morality of Islamic economics. In order to succeed, especially in long-term commercial dealings, an Iranian bazaar merchant needed the capital of a good reputation as much as he needed material resources.[5] There were thus pressures within the bazaar to exhibit modesty and piety in one's daily life, to observe Shi'i rituals, and to support religious structures and activity. The bond between the ulama and the bazaaris in Iran lasted throughout the Pahlavi period and proved instrumental in facilitating the 1978–79 Iranian Revolution.

In contrast, Shi'ism in Iraq was marked by the overall lack of community of interest between the Shi'i ulama and the commercial classes. The Iraqi Shi'i merchants made only very few contributions to their ulama even when, following the exodus of the Jews to Israel in the early 1950s, they began to play an important role in the commercial activity of the country The Shi'i merchants in Iraq did not constitute the financial backbone of the Shi'i religious establishment in their country. Likewise, the bazaar in Iraq did not emerge as a stronghold of political protest. This may be attributed to several factors: the lack of close interaction and shared values between the Shi'i religious and commercial sectors; the search of Iraqi Shi'i merchants for individual mobility and accommodation with the

Sunni state; and the success of the Iraqi government in detaching the important Shi'i markets in Baghdad from the effective influence of the Shi'i ulama. The lack of an alliance between the ulama and the merchants in modern Iraq obliged the supreme Shi'i mujtahids to rely on contributions from outside Iraq, mainly from rich Kuwaiti Shi'is. Often, however, a large percentage of these funds could not be kept in Iraq, let alone freely used to finance Shi'i religious or anti-government activities. Consequently, the leading mujtahids in Iraq found it difficult to act as grand patrons and benefactors and to maintain elaborate clientele connections with the local Shi'i population. And as Shi'i Islamic opposition groups suffered from lack of sufficient resources, they were unable to mobilize the merchants against the Ba'th government which has been in power since 1968.[6]

Another major difference in the interaction between religion and economy in Iran and Iraq has been the existence of diverse Shi'i bequests in Iran, contrasted with the lack of significant Shi'i endowment property in Iraq. Both the Safavids and the Qajars established endowments to sustain Shi'i Islam in their country. At the same time, the support of the Iranian private economic sector for religion manifested itself in the rich bequests attached to religious schools, shrines, and mosques, as well as to those devoted to various Muharram observances in Iran. Thus, the shrine of Imam Ridha in Mashhad was reported in both the nineteenth and 20th centuries to be very well supported. In 20th century Yazd, endowments constituted almost one-quarter of bazaar property. There were also considerable bequests for the city in the hinterland of Yazd. In many of the villages there were gardens, agricultural land, and shared water from irrigation canals which had been turned into endowments for the benefit of religious structures in Yazd. As late as the mid-1960s, the religious schools in Iran had enough endowment properties to support the students there. Iran's Pahlavi rulers were not fully successful in absorbing the proceeds of the endowments or changing the purpose for which they had been originally devoted. And when under Mohammed Reza Shah the state tightened its control over the religious deeds, Iranians stopped making endowments and made more contributions directly to their mujtahids.[7]

In contrast to Iran, the bulk of endowment, or *waqf*, property in Iraq has been Sunni and under tight government control. British officials observed early in the 20th century that practically none of the land in Karbala district was *waqf*, and that only a small income was derived from properties, khans, and shops in the town. The welfare of servants of the shrines in Najaf and Karbala depended on the money they received from pilgrims well into the late 1940s, when the Iraqi government fixed their salaries. Clearly, the *waqf* funds of Najaf and Karbala were insufficient to provide for the upkeep of the mosques and other religious structures in those cities. This was also the case in Kufa, Hilla, and other densely populated Shi'i areas. A number of reasons may be adduced for the lack of significant Shi'i *waqf* property in Iraq. Najaf and Karbala emerged as the two strongholds of Shi'ism only from the mid-18th century onwards, following the collapse of the Safavid state and the subsequent migration of Persian ulama to Iraq. Unlike Iran, where the population had become Shi'i by the 18th century, the Shi'is did not constitute the majority of Iraq's population before the settlement and conversion of the bulk of the tribes in the nineteenth century. It may very well be that the domination of the Iraqi countryside by nomadic tribes until the nineteenth century, as well as the large contributions from Iran and India in the 20th century, did not encourage the mujtahids of the shrine cities to push for the establishment of sizeable Shi'i *waqf* property in Iraq. There was also perhaps a calculated attempt on the part of the mujtahids to allow Shi'i property to escape the control of the Ottoman Sunni government.[8] As a result of both the lack of sizeable endowment property and any close interaction between ulama and bazaaris, Shi'i Islam in Iraq failed to develop an economic basis that could sustain an effective Shi'i opposition to Sunni ascendancy in the state in the 20th century.

If the contrasts in interaction between religion and economy help to explain the relative strength of Shi'ism in Iran and its weakness in Iraq, an examination of Shi'i rituals shows that Iranian and Iraqi Shi'is have also differed in their social and cultural attributes. These distinctions are apparent both in the rituals of *'Ashura,* commemorating the martyrdom of Imam Husayn, who died in the battle of Karbala in 680 AD, as well as in the different images that Iraqi and Iranian Shi'is attach to their saints.

The representation of the battle of Karbala in the form of a play is known as the *shabih.* The play is one of five major rituals that developed around the commemoration of Husayn's martyrdom. In Iran the *shabih* developed from the 16th century, after the establishment of Shi'ism as the state religion. The play was transmitted from Iran to Iraq in the late 18th century.[9] Yet there were fundamental differences in the metaphors of the drama between the two countries. In Iran, the texts and theatrical dimensions of the play were highly developed. Under royal patronage during the Qajar period, the straightforward form of the *shabih* gave way to a more theatrical model, known as the *ta'ziya',* which was enacted on stage. It evolved into a complex melodrama, stopping short of becoming an spectacle of Iranian national theatre in the 20th century.[10] In contrast to Iran, the dialogues in the Iraqi play were minimal, and it is doubtful whether any textual format was ever developed, let alone published. Among the rural and tribal communities, the play often took the form of a carnival. The impact on the audience was achieved largely due to the emphasis laid on the use of live metaphors, the movement of the characters, and the participation of a large number of players drawn from the local population.[11]

There were also important differences in the symbolic meaning of the play in Iran and Iraq. In the Iranian play martyrdom is one of the central themes: in Iraq, it exhibits the strong Arab tribal attributes of Iraqi Shi'i society. This point is evident in the images attached in the play to 'Abbas, son of Imam 'Ali and Husayn's half-brother, who participated with Husayn in the battle of Karbala. In the Iranian play 'Abbas is usually portrayed as a man seeking martyrdom. In contrast, the emphasis in Iraq is on the attributes of the ideal manhood of 'Abbas, stressing his strong physical qualities and comparing him to a fearless lion.[12] Indeed, Iraqi Shi'is do not perceive 'Abbas as a symbol of religious piety, but rather as the protector of Husayn and religion.

The different images attached to Shi'i saints in Iran and Iraq demonstrate the negligible influence of Sufism and mysticism among Arab Shi'is in general, as opposed to their strong mass appeal in Iran. The presence of mysticism in Iranian society was very strong for at least half a millennium.[13] In Iraq, however, the influence of Sufism and mysticism among the Shi'i rural and tribal population was insignificant. In fact, Sufism did not gain ground among Shi'is in Iraq and was recognizable more among Sunnis or the numerically marginal Shi'i extremist groups like the Shabbak of Turkish origin. Such Bektashi and Naqshabandi traces as could be found in the shrine cities of Iraq early in the 20th century were the result of Sunni Ottoman influences. Moreover, in their concept of the saints, Iranians sought to lift the imams and saints into a supernatural, divine sphere, and crossed the border between human and divine more easily than the Arab Shi'is. In contrast, the Iraqi Shi'is were not so concerned with the role of the imams and other saints as intercessors for the sinners with God. Their images stressed the worldly and physical attributes of the saints, as well as their role as protectors of property and crops and the avengers of false oaths. These attributes gained the highest precedence among tribesmen in general in Iraq, and thus the visitation of the tombs of some local saints was shared by both Shi'i and Sunni tribesmen. The differences in Shi'i rituals in Iran and Iraq elucidate the strong Arab cultural and social attributes of the Iraqi Shi'is, and the fact that Iraqi Shi'ism is much more sober and down to earth than its Iranian counterpart.[14]

The establishment of the modern state and the rise of nationalism reinforced the differences between Shi'i religion and society in Iran and Iraq, pulling Iranians and Iraqi Shi'is further apart in the 20th century. A striking feature about the development of modern Iranian Shi'ism is that on various occasions in the 20th century the ulama and the government formed alliances, each side thereby seeking to promote its own interests. The need of Iran's Pahlavi rulers to cooperate with the clergy was evident when both Reza Shah and his son, Mohammed Reza, relied on the ulama to establish and consolidate their own rule in Iran. At times the government also called for, and received, the clergy's backing in dealing with other internal opposition groups in exchange for concessions that led to the growth of religious institutions and to an increase in the ulama's influence in Iranian politics. Thus, in its attempt to fight communism, the Iranian government fostered religion, seeking to placate the ulama and turn them against the Iranian Communist Party. The anti-Baha'i campaign, which broke out in 1955, demonstrated the willingness of the government to appease the ulama on issues related to the status of minorities and religious freedom in Iran. In return, the government sought to secure the ulama's acquiescence, if not support, against the nationalists, who objected to the amount of oil revenue that the western consortium of oil companies proposed to pay to Iran. One consequence of the headway given by the state to the clergy in Iran was the growing confidence of the ulama in their ability to influence public policy and lead mass anti-government protests in the latter part of the 20th century, culminating in the Islamic Revolution of 1978–79.[15]

In contrast with Iran, Sunni governments in Iraq have managed to isolate Shi'i Islam and establish clearer boundaries between religion and state, thus preventing Shi'i ulama from emerging as major players in national politics. Iraq's Sunni rulers succeeded in eradicating much of the power traditionally held by the Shi'i religious establishment based in Najaf and Karbala. The Iraqi government undermined the position of the two cities as desert market towns, and curtailed the Shi'i clergy's income from charities and the pilgrimage. The policies of successive Sunni Iraqi governments also hindered the position of Shi'i institutions of higher learning, as many of Najaf's madrasas lost their economic independence and came under government control. The uneasy relations between Baghdad and the shrine cities were not simple conflicts between centre and periphery, but a struggle over the loyalty and focus of identity of the Shi'is in modern Iraq. And in this struggle Baghdad has gained the upper hand.[16]

With the creation of modern Iran and the Arab states in the 20th century, the differences between Iranian and Iraqi Shi'ism became more apparent than in the past. This point becomes evident from the position of the Shi'i madrasa in Iran and Iraq, and the impact of this institution on secular and religious life in the two countries. Unlike the madrasas of Najaf, which had no impact on Iraqi education in the Sunni government school system, those of Qum and Mashhad did influence Iranian educational life. And, unlike leading mujtahids in Iran whose power and esteem stemmed from the laity, most of their counterparts in the Iraqi Shi'i religious centres in Iraq lost their status among, and influence on, Shi'i masses. In part, this was a result of a fundamental difference in attitude towards the practice of preaching in Najaf and Karbala, as opposed to Qum and Mashhad in Iran. In the two Iraqi cities, the prominent mujtahids and teachers in the madrasas distanced themselves from preaching, an activity which they considered detrimental to a mujtahid's academic standing. Against the aloofness of their Iraqi counterparts, the Iranian mujtahids were very aware of the need to train preachers, considering this profession an art in itself. Indeed, prominent mujtahids in Qum and Mashhad, as well as students at all stages of their studies, were said to be very actively engaged in preaching, thereby reaching out to the Iranian masses and increasing their contacts with the laity. Shi'i Islam in Iraq, however, lost much of its potential influence over Iraqi Shi'is, as well as its power *vis-a-vis* the state, because of the attitude of the mujtahids towards preaching.[17]

The development of the Shi'i madrasa in the 20th century shows that the differences between Iranian and Iraqi Shi'is intensified. Early in the 20th century the shrine city of Najaf enjoyed the status of being the most important academic centre in the Shi'i world. The establishment of the modern state put an end to this and led to the rise of Qum in Iran as the important academic centre as far as Iranians were concerned. Arab Shi'is from Lebanon and the Gulf states, however, continued to go to Najaf despite its declining fame and the relatively better economic conditions offered to students in Qum. The Arabic and Persian languages began to play a greater role in fostering the differences between Arab Shi'is and Iranians. The major Shi'i legal works and biographies in Arabic were translated into Persian, thereby reducing the need for Iranian students to consult the original. Early in the 20th century some of the greatest Shi'i mujtahids were Persians who had a command of spoken Arabic and wrote extensively in that language; this was no longer the case in the latter part of the century, when prominent Iranian mujtahids had difficulties in communicating in Arabic.[18] One of the very few Iraqi students who did study in Qum in the 1960s complained that Arabic was a 'dead' language among the Iranian students. Indeed, those few Iraqis who lived in Qum had to comply with socio-cultural customs which were alien to them, and they were not well integrated into the local society.[19]

The ethnic, socio-political, and cultural differences between Iranian and Iraqi Shi'is help to explain why, two decades after the Iranian Islamic Revolution, the large majority of Iraq's Arab Shi'is were not swayed by it. The political development of the Iraqi Shi'is in the 20th century further illustrates this point. In Iraq, there is a tremendous amount of tension between the Shi'is and the Sunni Ba'th government. Yet this apprehension has not surfaced as a result of the attempt of Iraqi Shi'is to separate from the state or to merge with Iran, but rather from their desire to gain access to power in a state which has been dominated by a Sunni minority elite since 1921.

The establishment of modern Iraq posed major dilemmas for the Shi'is and sharpened the problem of their identity. Indeed, one of the most important issues for Shi'is, particularly in the first half of the 20th century, was quite simply: 'Who are we?' Unlike the Kurds, who constitute a distinct ethnic and national group, the Shi'is are by and large Arabs, and their primary identity came to be Iraqi. Although at times they flaunted their sectarianism, they did, on the whole, make attempts to accommodate their dual identity within the framework of the Iraqi state. The challenge which the Iraqi state posed to the Shi'is as participants in the political system obliged them to redefine who they were and to reassess their existing values and practices. Their conscious effort to reconstruct their identity was evidence of Shi'i recognition that support for the idea of Iraqi nationhood would be beneficial to their status within the state. Yet Iraqi Shi'is were perplexed by how many of their old traditions they should maintain and what they should change or discard in order to become a part of modern Iraq. In coping with this identity crisis, Iraqi Shi'is were explicitly and openly concerned with issues of Arab and Persian race, culture and religion, stressing the authenticity of their own Arab culture and their different historical development as compared with their Iranian counterparts.

The following examples illustrate the nature of the tension between Shi'is and the Sunni government in Iraq, the Shi'i search for mobility and power in the state, and the strong national identity which they demonstrate. The Shi'i pursuit of government employment became a major factor in feeding the tension between Shi'is and Sunnis in modern Iraq. Iraq's Sunni rulers usually included only one token Shi'i minister in the governments of the 1920s and were reluctant to appoint Shi'is in the administration and the civil service. In 1930 it was estimated that whereas the Kurds, who constituted 17% of the population, held 22% of high ranking government posts, the Shi'is, who formed the majority of the population, held only 15%.[20] Clearly, the Shi'is experienced difficulties in penetrating the Sunni network of patronage in the state machinery and the military throughout the monarchic period. Shi'is continued to experience difficulties under the Ba'th as well, even after the great increase in the number of young educated Shi'is who were equipped to compete with Sunnis for government positions. Thus, in the 1970s and 1980s the Republican Guard was composed almost entirely of Sunnis and the Iraqi core elite became mainly Sunni-Takriti. Although Shi'is did join the various institutions of the Ba'th after it had established itself in power in the 1970s, their participation mainly reflected a search for individual mobility as well as party co-optation and fear. Indeed, the rise of the Ba'th to power in Iraq did not lead to any real power sharing, since the key state positions came under tight Sunni-Takriti control.[21]

The struggle over the definition of Arab and Iraqi nationalism has also been a major source of tension between Shi'is and successive Sunni governments. While Iraq's rulers adopted Pan-Arabism as their main nationalist ideology, they repeatedly questioned the loyalty and ethnic origin of the Shi'is. Beginning with

Sati' al-Husri, who may be regarded as the founder of Pan-Arabism in Iraq, the proponents of this ideology emphasized the fame of the Arab empire and expressed a desire to restore its glory. Under the rubric of *shu'ubiyya*, they presented Shi'ism as a subversive heresy motivated primarily by Persian hatred for the Arabs, and stressed the Persian threat to the idea of Arab nationalism. Much of the frustration of Iraqi Shi'is over this issue stemmed from the fact that Iraq's Sunni rulers were able to tie *shu'ubiyya* to Shi'i protests against their discrimination by the government, and to present Shi'i grievances as acts which promoted sectarianism in the state. In doing so, the Sunni politicians were able to place the Shi'is on the defensive.[22]

The Iraqi Shi'is, as stressed several times in this chapter, are for the most part Arabs of recent tribal origin. While they acknowledged the existence of religious ties between themselves and their counterparts in Iran, they argued that these links did not extend to the political level and had no bearing on their own Iraqi national identity. The Shi'is felt that the propagation of Pan-Arabism excluded the majority of Iraq's tribal population and included only the ruling Sunni urban minority. They resented the government's narrow definition of Arab nationalism, as well as the need to prove their Arab origin to Sunni politicians and administrators, who, like Husri, were ex-Ottoman officials. On various occasions, Shi'is argued that they were the 'indigenous sons of the country' and that, for centuries, it was Iraq and its tribes that preserved the true spirit of Arabism.[23] Indeed, to the majority of Shi'is, Pan-Arabism had little to offer, for the proponents of this ideology were mainly Sunni urban politicians whose interests differed from those of the Shi'is. Thus, in the 1950s and 1960s the Shi'is perceived the possibility that Iraq would be included in a confederation of Arab states as a threat to their position in the country. Absorbed as they were in the task of trying to win political equality with the Sunnis, the Shi'is feared that if Iraq became a part of an Arab confederation, they would cease to comprise the majority of the population and recede once again into the status of a politically marginal sectarian group.[24]

The distinct identity of the Iraqi Shi'is may also be seen from their attitude toward Islamic ideology. As the Ba'th acted to control all aspects of public life, it further polarized Iraqi society, leading a growing number of lay Shi'is, including ex-communists, to consider Islamic ideology as a vehicle for political change. In joining the Islamic *Da'wa* movement, Shi'is demonstrated a clear preference for a leadership composed of Iraqis of Arab origin in the organization, and they took pride in the Arab Mujtahid, Mohammed Baqir al-Sadr, whom they felt was one of their own. The surge in Islamic radicalism in the 1970s symbolized the response of Shi'is to the assault of the Sunni Ba'thi elite on their very identity as Iraqis. Although the affairs surrounding the 1978–79 Iranian Revolution served as a major catalyst for stimulating Iraqi Shi'i anti-Ba'thi and anti-Saddam Husayn feelings, it is doubtful whether a genuine 'Islamic revolutionary frame of mind' existed among the Iraqi Shi'i masses, let alone the socio-economic infrastructure necessary for carrying out an Islamic revolution. Moreover, the concept of 'the jurist rule' as developed by Ruhallah Khumayni did not gain ground among the large majority of Iraqi Shi'i laymen affiliated with the *Da'wa*. Also, members of the organization expressed allegiance to an Iraqi entity throughout the 1970s and 1980s, and did not support the idea of any merger between Iraq and Iran.[25]

This point was vividly demonstrated during the Iraqi Shi'i insurrection of March 1991 in the wake of the Gulf War. This has already become an important event in shaping the national identity of Iraqi Shi'is and their collective memory. On various occasions, Iraqi Shi'i refugees stressed that the insurrection was spontaneous. They cited the expulsion of thousands of Shi'is to Iran during the Iran-Iraq War, and the desire to get rid of Saddam Husayn and his government, as major factors in their motivation to rebel. Unlike the attacks of organized Kurdish units on Iraqi army positions in the north, the Shi'i rebels in the south were disorganized, and they lacked a blueprint or well defined Islamic ideological goals prior to the insurrection. It was only after rebels in Najaf appeared to be consolidating their control of the city that the Grand Mujtahid, Abu al-Qasim Kho'i, issued a communiqué in which he sanctioned the establishment of a 'Supreme Committee' of nine people under whose leadership Shi'is were called upon to preserve Iraq's security and to stabilize public, religious, and social affairs.[26] While the content of this communiqué suggests that Kho'i sanctioned some form of a Shi'i governing body in Iraq, there is no evidence that he envisaged the establishment of an Islamic government led by the jurist as advocated by Khumayni and implemented in the Islamic Republic of Iran after 1978.

Indeed, the 1991 insurrection in southern Iraq differed greatly from the 1978–79 Iranian Revolution in which the Ayatullahs played a significant leading role, and where much of the action against the Shah took place in the capital, Teheran. The Iraqi Shi'i rebels lacked a clear religious leadership who would inspire and coordinate the insurrection in the south. And in spite of reported discontent and protests in the capital, the Shi'is of Baghdad did not join the insurrection. In 1991 Iran played a role in propaganda and it provided weapons to rebel groups drawn from among Iraqi Shi'i refugees who entered Iraq a few days after the insurrection had started. In training and arming these refugees, Iran demonstrated the continuity of its traditional aspirations to gain leverage over Iraq by influencing Shi'i affairs in the country. Yet five years after the Gulf War, it seems that if Iran did really try to shape the ideological direction of the insurrection, the attempt did not lead anywhere.[27]

The year 2000 marks the 21st anniversary of the establishment of the Islamic Republic of Iran and the opening of a new era in Iranian history. Against this, the overall reluctance thus far of Shi'is in Iraq to follow the Iranian model perhaps symbolizes the extent to which the trajectories of Iranian and Iraqi Shi'is have diverged in the 20th century.

Notes

1. See 'Madha hasala fi awakhir 'am 1990 wa-hadhihi al-ashhur min 'am 1991 wa-limadha hasala alladhi hasala?' A series of articles published in April 1991 in *al-Thawra al-'Iraqiyya*. Reproduced by the Centre of Iraqi Studies, London, 1993.

2. For details see Yitzhak Nakkash, *The Shi'is of Iraq* (Princeton 1994) 6–7, 13–48; idem, 'The Conversion of Iraq's Tribes to Shi'ism', *International Journal of Middle East Studies*, 26, (1994) 443–63.

3. Ann Lambton, 'Social Change in Persia in the Nineteenth Century', *Asian and African Studies*, 15, (1981) 139; Nikki Keddie, 'The Roots of the Ulama's Power in Modern Iran', *Studia Islamica*, 29, (1969); Michael Fischer, *Iran: From Religious Dispute to Revolution*, Cambridge, Mass., 1980, 31; Joanna de Groot, Mulla and Merchants: 'The Basis of Religious Politics in Nineteenth Century Iran', *Mashriq*, 2 (1983): 20.

4. Ahmad Ashraf, 'The Roots of Emerging Dual Class Structure in Nineteenth Century Iran', *Iranian Studies*, 14,(1981):16; *Encyclopaedia Iranica*, s.v. *Bazar*; Howard Rotblat, 'Social Organization and Development in an Iranian Provincial Bazaar', *Economic Development and Cultural Change*, 23,(1975):298; Gustav Thaiss, 'The Bazaar as a Case Study of Religion and Social Change', in, *Iran Faces the Seventies*, ed., Ehsan Yar-Shatar(New York, 1971), 193.

5. Gustav Thaiss, *'Religious Symbolism and Social Change: The Drama of Husayn'* (Ph.D. diss., Washington University, 1973), 26, 52, 158–59; Michael Bonine, *Shops and Shopkeepers: Dynamics of an Iranian Provincial Bazaar*, in *Modern Iran: The Dialectics of Continuity and Change*, eds., Michael Bonine and Nikki Keddie (Albany, NY, 1981), 235; Rorblat, Social Organization, 299–300; Roy Mottahedah, *The Mantle of the Prophet:Religion and Politics in Iran* (New York, 1985), 346.

6. Nakkash, *The Shi'is of Iraq*, 232–35.

7. Ann Lambton, *Landlord and Peasant in Persia*, 2nd ed. (Oxford, 1969), 233–36; idem, 'A Reconsideration of the Position of the Marja' al-Taqlid and the Religious Institution', *Studia Islamica* 20 (1964): 132; Bonnie, Shops, 235; idem, 'Islam and Commerce: Waqf and the Bazzar of Yazd, Iran', *Erkunde* 41 (1987): 187–89, 194; Hamid Algar, *Religion and State in Iran, 1785–1906: The Role of the Ulama in the Qajar Period* (Berkeley, 1969), 14; Muhsin al-Amin, *Rihlat al-sayyid muhsin al-amin fi lubnan wa al-'iraq wa ian wa masr wa al-hijaz*, 2nd ed.,(Beirut, 1985), 219–22; Fischer, op.cit., 117.

8. Administration Reports for 1918, Karbala, CO 696/1; Administration Report for the Baghdad Wilayat, 1917, and Administration Reports for 1918, Najaf, CO 696/1; Administration Report for the Hilla Division for 1919, FO 371/5080/13054; Meir Litvak, *The Shi'i Ulama of Najaf and Karbala, 1791–1904: A Socio-Political Analysis* (Ph.D. diss., Harvard University, 1991), 99, 143–44; Administration Report of the Shamiyya Division and Najaf, 1918, CO 969/1 and CO 696/2.

9. For details see Yitzhak Nakkash, 'An Attempt to Trace the Origin of the Rituals of 'Ashura', *Die Welt des Islams*, 33,(1993): 161–81.

10. Farrokh Gaffary, 'Evolution of Rituals and Theatre in Iran', *Iranian Studies*, 17(1984): 371.

11. Nakkash, *The Shi'is of Iraq*, 146.

12. Colonel Sir Lewis Pelly, *The Miracle Play of Hasan and Husayn*, 2 vols. (London, 1879),1:250–69; Elizabeth Fernea, *Guests of the Sheikh*, 2nd. ed.(New York, 1969), 203–04, 206; Mahmud al-Durra, *Hayat 'iraqi min wara' al-bawwaba al-sawda'*(Cairo, 1976), 23–24.

13. Motahedeh, op.cit. 144; Ignaz Goldziher, 'Veneration of Saints in Islam', in his *Muslim Studies*, ed. S.M. Stern, 2 vols. (London, 1966), 2:294. See also, Amin, Rihlat, 231.

14. Nakkash, *The Shi'is of Iraq*, 175–79.

15. Ervand Abrahamian, *Iran Between Two Revolutions*, 2nd. (Princeton,NJ, 1983), 372–74; Willem Floor, 'The Revolutionary Character of the Ulama: Wishful Thinking or Reality?' in *Religion and Politics in Iran:Shi'ism from Quietism to Revolution*, ed., Nikki Keddie (New Haven, 1983), 73, 75, 93; Shahrough Akhavi, *Religion and Politics in Contemporary Iran: Clergy-State Relations in the Pahlavi Period* (Albany, NY, 1980), 28, 30, 59, 72, 77, 79–80, 90; Mohammad Faghfoory, 'The Ulama-State Relations in Iran', 1921–1941, *International Journal of Middle East Studies*, 19 (1987): 414–423.

16. Nakkash, *The Shi'is of Iraq*, 75–88, 94–100.

17. Mottahedeh, op.cit. 237; Hanna Batatu, 'Shi'i Organizations in Iraq: al-Da'wah al-Islamiyah and al-Mujahidin', in *Shi'ism and Social Protest*, eds. Juan Cole and Nikki Keddie(New Haven, 1986), 193; Ahmad al-Katib, *Tajrubat al-thawra al-islamiya fi al-'iraq*, 1968–1980'(Teheran, 1980), 173; Anon, *al-Haraka al-islamiyya fi al-'iraq*(Beirut, 1985), 196–97; al-Lajna al-thaqafiyya li-=madrasat al-imam amir al-mu'minin al-'ilmiyya, al-Qadiyya al-'iraqiyya min khilal mawaqif al-imam al-shirazi(Mashhad, 1981), 35; Muhammad Mahdi al-Asifi, *Min hadith al-da'wa wa al-du'at*, 2nd. ed.(Najaf, 1966), 5–8, 17; idem, *Madrasat al-najaf wa-tatawwur al-haraka al-islahiyya fi-ha*(Najaf, 1964), 54, 110; Muhammad Jawad Maghniyya *Min dha wa-dhak*(Beirut, 1979), 128–29.

18. Muhsin al-Amin, *Ma'adin al-jawahir wa nuzhat al-khawatir*, 2 vols. (Beirut, 1981), 1:42.

19. 'Isa 'Abd al-Hamid al-Khaqani, al-Majma' al-'arabi fi qumm, *al-'Irfan*, 50(1963): 660, 663, 674.

20. Conversation between the US Consul and King Faysal's Assistant Private Secretary, Dispatch from Sloan, 28 January 1930, United States National Archive, 890G.00/127.

21. Samir al-Khalil, *Republic of Fear: The Inside Story of Saddam's Iraq* (Berkeley, 1989, NY, reprint, 1990) 212–16; Marion-Farouk Sluglett and Peter Sluglett, *Iraq since 1958:From Revolution to Dictatorship* (London, 1987), 194–95, 197; Hanna Batatu, *The Old Social Classes and Revolutionary Movements in Iraq*, 2nd. ed. (Princeton, 1982), 1078–79; Chibli Mallat, Iraq, in *The Politics of Islamic Revivalism, ed. Shireen Hunter* (Bloomington, 1988) 72–73; compare Amatzia Baram, 'The Ruling Political Elite in Ba'thi Iraq, 1968–1986: The Changing Features of a Collective Profile', *International Journal of Middle East Studies*, 21,(1989):447–93.

22. 'Abbas Kelidar, 'The Shi'i Imami Community and Politics in the Arab East', *Middle Eastern Studies*, 19(1983):12; Hasan al-'Alawi, *al-Shi'a wa al-dawla al-qawmiyya fi al-'iraq* (Paris, 1989), 159–63, 235–38, 242–44, 248; idem, *al-ta'thirat al-turkiyya fi al-mashru' al-qawmi fi al-'iraq*(London, 1988) 142–44, 156–57; Nakkash, *The Shi'is of Iraq*, 113.

23. 'Arabi, al-Shi'a fi biladihim: 'ibar wa-'zat li-katib siyasi kabir min aqtab al-Shi'a fi al-'iraq, *al-'Irfan*, 20(1930):564; Ibn al-Rafidayn, al-Shi'a fi al-'iraq, al-'Irfan, 22,(1931):435; 'Ali al-Sharqi, Lawhat al-qawmiyya al-'arabiyya fi al-'iraq, *al-'Irfan*, 26(1936):773. See also Abd al-Karim al-Uzri, *Mushkilat al-hukm fi al-'Iraq*(London, 1991) 231, 260; 'Alawi, *al-Shi'a*, 240–47, 252–53, 258.

24. Situation in Iraq, Memorandum by Sir Kinahan Cornwallis, 26 April 1943, FO 371/35010/2755; Troutbeck to Bevin, 13 December 1950, FO 371/82408/1016–35; From Basra to Foreign Office, 8 January 1959, FO 371/140900/1015–13. See also Batatu, *The Old Social Classes*, 480, 815–18, 832; Albert Hourani, *Minorities in the Arab World*, (Oxford, 1947, N.Y. reprint, 1982), 94–95; Sami Zubaida, 'Community, Class, and Minorities in Iraqi Politics', in, *The Iraqi Revolution of 1958: The Old Social Classes Revisited*, eds., Robert Fernea and Wm. Louis (London, 1991), 199.

25. Battau, Shi'i organizations in Iraq, 199; T.M.Aziz, 'The Role of Muhammad Baqir al-Sadr in Shi'i Political Activism in Iraq from 1958 to 1980', *International Journal of Middle East Studies*, 25 (1993):209, 210, 218–19; Mallat, Iraq, 75; Slugletts, Iraq, 196; Amatzia Baram, *The Radical Shi'ite Opposition Movement in Iraq*, in, *Religious Radicalism and Politics in the Middle East*, eds., Emmanuel Sivan and Menachem Friedman (New York, 1990), 95, 104; idem, 'From Radicalism to Radical Pragmatism: The Shi'ite Fundamentalist Opposition Movements of Iraq', in *Islamic Fundamentalism and the Gulf Crisis*, ed., James Piscatori(Chicago, 1991), 35–36.

26. For its content see Kanan Makkiya, *Cruelty and Silence: War, Tyranny, Uprising and the Arab World* (New York, 1993), 74–75.

27. Nakkash, *The Shi'is of Iraq*, 227.

CHAPTER TWO

Zghurt and Shmurt: Aspects of the Traditional Shiʻi Society

Peter Heine

The question of why, in modern times, the Shiʻi community in Iraq often constituted a majority which was treated by the respective rulers as a minority, necessarily invokes a discussion about the traditional social structures of the Shiʻis. However, it is important to keep in mind that possible weaknesses in social structures do not solely explain the political situation of the Shiʻa in Iraq. It is beyond the scope of this chapter, however, to consider the wide range of economic and political factors which have certainly contributed to the situation of the Shiʻi community in modern Iraq.

Ethnic fracture lines

The social structure of the Iraqi Shiʻa is characterised by various differences – most notably ethnic – between Arabic, Kurdish, Iranian and Turkish Shiʻi groups. There is a common assumption that a strong bond has always existed, which, to a certain degree, forged the different ethnic groups together against Sunni rulers. Yet this 'bond' has not been strong enough to overcome a series of political or traditional differences. Throughout the nineteenth and the first half of the 20th century, Kurdish and Turkish Shiʻis have always been marginalized within their ethnic or national group. They often stood in a patron-client relationship with Sunni notables: such relationships occurred far less often with the chiefs of their own ethnic group, indicating their marginal position within their group. In some cases, this marginalization can also be detected with respect to their traditional occupations, which were held in low esteem by the Iraqi majority and even by other ethnic Shiʻi groups. Kurdish and Turkish Shiʻis were tinkers, musicians or dancers, for example.

Iranians living in Iraq constituted a small national minority. By virtue of their small numbers, they could not be considered an important political force within Iraq. Furthermore, many of the Iranian Shi'a displayed little interest in the political developments within Iraq, as they were much more interested in the political and economic situation in Iran. They kept their Iranian passports along with an Iranian way of life, i.e. they built their houses in Iranian style, used Persian as their main language of communication and maintained close links with their relatives and friends in Iran. Accordingly, in the 'political game' of Iraq, Iranians were not important players.

Among the various ethnic divisions which exist among the Iraqi Shi'a, the Arab population remains to be considered. It may be argued that, once again, it is possible to detect sociological aspects which tended to weaken the position of this particular Shi'a group within the political framework of Iraq. Of course, Arabs were and are the ethnic majority of the Iraqi population; and the Shi'a Arabs exceeded the Sunni Arabs in number. However, the Shi'a Arabs were divided into town dwellers and Bedouins, e.g. between the population of the Shi'a shrine cities, 'atabat, of Karbala, Najaf, Kazimiya and Samara on the one side, and the Shi'a Bedouin tribes of southern Iraq on the other. The relationship between these two groups was marked by tension: this increased the level of fragmentation among the Iraqi Shi'a.

Ethnic and national differences were enforced and sustained by a specific phenomenon typical of the religious organisation of the Shi'a. It is a long and well-established fact that the Shi'a, unlike the Sunni, are supposed to follow and obey the rulings (fatwa) of their religious authorities (ulama): the rulings of a specific cleric, mujtahid, are binding for a believer, normally for his or her lifetime and the life span of the religious authority. These relationships lead to a hierarchical system of religious authorities that could be called 'clergy'. At the top of this hierarchy stands the Marja' al-Taqlid, the highest authority within Shi'i Islam.

Because of the lack of prescribed regulations concerning the choice of the highest authority, a permanent 'jockeying' for position among the Shi'a religious elite can be observed. The competition and struggle for the position of the Marja' al-Taqlid does not only take place in the realm of religious learning or law, but is also significant with respect to ethnic, national and even regional political contests. The latter became obvious when Iranian and Arabic as well as Indian and Caucasian Shi'a students engaged in fierce struggles.[1] The Sunni Iraqi politician, 'Abd al-Aziz al-Qassab, also noted in his memoirs that' before the First World War, pilgrims from Karbala and Samara engaged in fist fights during a religious holiday in Najaf. The confrontations flared up because of disputes over the position and hierarchy of their respective religious authorities (*mujtahids*).[2]

There was also continual rivalry between the important Shi'i cities, the 'atabat. The mujtahids of Najaf saw themselves as a little higher in the hierarchy of religious scholars than their counterparts from the cities of Karbala, Kazimiya or Samara. The mujtahids of Kazimiya, on the other hand, stressed their political influence. The rivalry between the 'atabat is difficult to document: existing tensions can by deduced from information given, for example, by Mohammed Mahdi Kubba, who reported that fighting between pilgrims from different Shi'i cities were normal at festivals such as *yawm al-ghadir*.[3] Since the 18th century, if not earlier, significant Shi'a religious scholars have gathered young men as bodyguards, who could also be used to pursue political goals.[4] The political aspect of the struggle for the position of the Marja' al-Taqlid is exemplified in the story of the 'Zghurt', a group of young men in Najaf, one of the centres of Shi'ism in Iraq.

Shi'i Islam in Iraq is a religion greatly influenced by urban aspects of life, although there have been strong links between Iraqi cities and the countryside. In political and economic relations, the countryside could even obtain the upper hand. In religious matters, however, it was the city which was the leading force. Islamic cities — Sunni and Shi'a alike — are marked by a series of specific buildings and institutions, such as the Friday-mosque, the public bath (*hammam*) and a political-administrative centre.[5] Certain city structures are also worth mention: a strict separation between markets and places of production on the one side, and residential areas on the other. The co-operation between craftsmen and merchants is one of the most important institutions within the economic sphere of Islamic cities.

Another typical feature of the Islamic city is the separation of different quarters according to religious or ethnic affiliation. Ira Lapidus uses the word 'sub-communities' and states that: 'Muslim cities are cities by virtue of social processes which are not peculiar to any given culture, but they are Muslim by virtue of the predominance of sub-communities which embodied Muslim beliefs and a Muslim way of life'.[6] The different quarters of the cities had a certain autonomy and a rudimentary form of administration. To enforce the command of the quarter-authorities, groups of young men were used as a kind of police force. It becomes obvious that the border between protecting and terrorising the inhabitants of the quarters was not always clear-cut. During the nineteenth century and up until the beginning of the 20th century, these youth organisations played an important role in the Shi'i cities of Iran and Mesopotamia. In this context, Bert Fragner speaks about a: 'co-operate, almost lumpen proletarian male sub-culture, which consisted of young men belonging to the cities' quarters and factions who became part of a rough community life by engaging in continuous gang fights, tests of courage, violent and even criminal acts'.[7]

Quarters were established on ethnic or national bases, but also according to groups following a certain theological position. Particularly interesting in this context are the aforementioned groups of rowdy young men, since they reflect the tendency for segmentation to occur within traditional Shi'i society. Cole and Momen have analysed these youth groups in Karbala, and have traced the roots of these structures back to the times of the famous Muslim traveller, Ibn Battuta, who reported on Karbala: 'The inhabitants of this city are composed of two parties, the Banu Rakhik and the Banu Fayiz. Between them there is uninterrupted fighting, although they all belong to the Imamiya [i.e twelver Shi'is] and trace themselves back to a common father. That is why the city is lying in ruins'.[8]

This situation did not change until the beginning of the 20th century. In fact, youth groups were acting in the same way as they had done during the time of Ibn Battuta, although they did not find the same interest among foreign travellers. The phenomenon described by Cole and Momen in Karbala could also be found in Najaf and other Shi'i cities in Iraq. In Najaf, the eminent *'alim* Shaykh Ja'far Kashif al-Ghita' founded a group of young men in 1806 to defend the city against the attacks of Wahhabi Bedouin warriors. Ja'far Baqir Al Mahbuba describes the foundation of the group as follows: 'The shaykh [Ja'far Kashif al-Ghita'] resorted to appoint several young men from Najaf. He fixed a regular pay for them, bought enough weapons and then placed them as guards (murabitun) at the border of Najaf, miles away from the city'.[9] In time, this paramilitary group, called 'Zghurt', was able to gain significant influence even within the city. In comparison to other youth groups of this kind, no age limit existed, and men could remain members of the group even after marriage. Consequently, the group continued to gain power as federations of families came into existence, joined by common interests rather than the fiction of a common ancestor. Nevertheless, Iraqi historians refer to *'qaba'il'* (tribalism) when it comes to groups like Zghurt and Shmurt.

Only ten years after their foundation, a leader of the Zghurt, 'Abbas al-Haddad was chosen by the Ottoman authorities for the official governance (*riyasa*) of the city. The increased power of the Zghurt led to the emergence of a civil, secular authority parallel to the existing authority of the important religious scholars (mujtahids) in Najaf. Even if appointed by the central Ottoman government, this new secular authority possessed a great deal of autonomy and freedom of action

For many years, the Zghurt continued to play a significant role in the social and political life of Najaf. They imposed protective and custom duties on the different quarters of the city, and at the same time defended it against the various attacking Bedouin forces. During the time of Najaf's autonomy (1916–1918), the Zghurt even negotiated on the future of the city with the commanders of the

British invasion-troops. Moreover, the group was the most important military force during the uprisings of the city against the British in 1918 and 1920. During the siege of Najaf by British troops in 1918, the British took particular care to shell those areas where they suspected Zghurt members were resident or in control.[10]

The importance of the Zghurt can also be established in the context of theological controversies in which the leaders of the Zghurt were often involved. Al-Haj Abu Gulal acted as an intermediary when discussions about the flagellation-processions during 'Ashura and other important occasions arose.[11] When the religious scholar, Salih al-Hilli, declared his adversary Ali al-Ya'qubi to be an apostate, it was Abu Gulal who intervened and forced al-Hilli to apologise.

However, the Zghurt control of the city was not undisputed. In 1813, when the Zghurt were suspected to be responsible for the deaths of several people, an opposition group named 'Shmurt' was founded. The previously mentioned chronicler, Al Mahbuba, writes: 'When Mullah Mohammed Tahir was killed, his relatives asked for blood revenge. One used to call them 'al-Shmurdil'. Those who asked revenge for Sayyid Mahmud [another victim] joined them. They took up arms and occupied fortified positions in high places, such as mosques, minarets and high houses. They started to shoot the Zghurt with rifles. They, in turn, answered the shooting'.[12] The clashes lasted until the Ottoman governor in Baghdad sent troops to stop the fighting. The chroniclers described the conflict between the Zghurt and Shmurt as *fitna'* (chaos or rebellion), a term which has well known historical and theological connotations: 'The fitna continues until today. Sometimes the fire is extinct, then it flares up again. Uncountable is the number of those who lost their lives as well as the values, which were stolen; how often the markets were closed down and how many houses were demolished. During those days, chaos prevailed in Najaf, as the evildoers of both groups played their game. The fitna consisted of a chain of terrible criminal incidents, which were worse than one could imagine. It is not possible to recount them'.[13] The clashes between the two groups were always triggered by struggles over the political control of the city. The Zghurt perceived themselves to be in the dominant position. In 1905 the Ottoman administration gave the riyasa of Najaf to a certain Ahmad 'Ajina, who was suspected of having sympathies towards the Shmurt: this immediately led to an uprising among the Zghurt, during the course of which the appointed man was killed. There are also reports of long lasting fights between the two groups in 1909.[14]

Yet it is important to mention that on some very specific occasions the two groups co-operated: at the very least some of their members worked together. For example, the famous politician and editor of the newspaper *al-'Ilm*, Hibat al-

Din al-Shahrastani, reports on the most significant opponent towards any form of constitution, Marja' al-Taqlid al-Sayyid Muhammad Kazim al-Yazdi al-Tabataba'i (d. 1920): 'Al-Yazdi linked up with a group of Zghurt and Shmurt, men of action who were paid by him. Some of them were well known bandits. These people used to surround al-Yazdi constantly and, wherever he went, protect him with their arms, while shouting the name of the Marja'.[15]

Another documented instance of collaboration is the attack on the city of Kufa by Bedouin groups. The inhabitants of Kufa were unable to defend themselves and asked the experienced warriors of the Zghurt and Shmurt to come to their assistance. They came with their weapons by tramway from Najaf to Kufa. Within a few days of armed clashes – which chroniclers described as a classic case of traditional Bedouin fighting with the hurling of insults, individual and group fights and final mediating attempts by religious authorities – the Zghurt and Shmurt had defeated the Bedouins and returned to Najaf. Even if not explicitly stated in the various sources, one might conclude that the men were paid for their assistance before returning back to Najaf by tram.

The usual clashes between the Zghurt and Shmurt continued more or less openly until the period after World War I. Occasionally, as described earlier, the two groups co-operated in common action. These actions could have crucial political consequences, as, for example, in the year 1916: According to British records, the Zghurt and Shmurt together drove out the Ottomans from Najaf. The role of religious authorities during this event remains difficult to establish. However, there were close ties between the Marja' al-Taqlid al-Yazdi, (known to have been generally reticent where politics are concerned) and the leader of the Zghurt, 'Atiyya Abu Gulal. It is hard to imagine that the Zghurt and Shmurt acted against the will of the religious authorities against the Ottomans.[16]

At such times as when a central government was lacking, for example during the period of 1916–18, both groups controlled the city. They protected it and kept it secure, but also collected taxes and duties, thereby often crossing the boundary to Mafia-like behaviour.[17] Yet the leaders of the Zghurt and Shmurt tried to ensure the autonomy of the holy city by establishing contacts with the invading British troops. The rather diplomatic answer of the British was misunderstood to mean a guarantee for the autonomy of the city.[18]

Muhammad al-Asadi, a chronicler of the Iraqi revolution in 1920, describes the power relations between the two groups and states that three-quarters of the city were controlled by the Zghurt, while the Shmurt controlled only the remainder. After the breakdown of the uprising in 1920, the Zghurt and Shmurt engaged in a number of clashes based on old grievances between the groups, which only worked to the advantage of the occupying forces.[19]

Within social structures characterised by a great level of segmentation, it is generally the case that the levels of fragmentation increase as soon as the size of a particular group grows. This phenomenon is certainly discernible among the Zghurt, who struggled over the leadership of the group. During the second part of the nineteenth century, an outstanding leader, Mahdi al-Sayyid Salman, had presented himself to the Ottomans as the leader of the Zghurt. Tensions arose within the group, even leading to armed conflicts, when he tried to monopolise his contacts with the Ottomans.[20] The Ottoman administration, and later also the British colonial authorities, allegedly tried to profit from the conflicts among the various groupings within the Zghurt. To this end they are said to have attempted to play the various groups off against each other. Similar internal conflicts and tensions have not been reported with respect to the Shmurt. Possibly, the group had not reached the size critical for the development of internal struggles, especially as the pressure from outside was too high to risk internal friction.

It is not necessary to highlight the fact that the tendency for segmentation to occur – which Christian Siegrist called 'regulated anarchy'[21] – constitutes one of the characteristics of almost all oriental societies and ethnic groups. Within ethnology the term 'segmentary society' has become a widely accepted concept and has been applied to the most diverse societies. It was the British social anthropologist, Evans-Pritchard, in his book 'The Sanusi Of Cyrenaica' (1949), who first applied the concept to an Islamic society, but it has now been noted among most ethnic groups within the Near and Middle East. Exceptions can only be found among some special religious sects, such as the Yezidi in the border area between Iraq, Syria and Turkey.

Keeping this broader picture in mind, it is hardly surprising to find a great level of segmentation among the Iraqi Shi'a; however, their clear political and social disadvantages do not appear to be an inevitable consequence of this. Other ethnic and religious groupings in Iraq have also been characterised by similar structures. In the social context of Iraqi Sunnis, who are also characterised by their segmentary tendencies, we find that the family constitutes the main framework with respect to identity, and economic and social security. Accordingly, family or tribal structures emerged which still exist in present-day Iraq, and also among the political elite in various other countries of the Near and Middle East.

What distinguishes the Shi'a, however, is their religiously prescribed subordination to a mujtahid (religious scholar). This affinity might play a more significant role than family affiliation, as close relatives might submit themselves to the authority of different mujtahids. These scholars, as I have described earlier, are continuously contesting each other's rank within the hierarchy of the Shi'i clergy, thereby involving their followers in the competition over religious authority. This, in turn, has accentuated the already existing segmentary tendencies found in most Near Eastern societies.

The occasional cooperation between the Zghurt and Shmurt does not contradict the impression of a strong fragmentation of the Shi'i society in Iraq. On
the contrary, one typical facet of segmentary societies is that antagonistic groups
join together for common actions, only to separate later and resume their earlier
clashes.

The relationship between the high echelons of the Shi'i clergy and the Zghurt
and Shmurt is difficult to assess. We have seen that a mujtahid had founded the
Zghurt group and the Marja' al-Yazdi employed the young men as bodyguards.
On the other hand, one has to bear in mind that the great mujtahids stood apart
from ordinary people: the relationships between them and the youth groups
were therefore rather uneven.

In conclusion, it may be argued that the main problem of the Shi'a in Iraq
has always been their level of segmentation, which, in comparison to that of the
Sunni population, has been more incisive. This is one possible reason for their
political weakness.

Notes

1. The fiercest struggles are supposed to have taken place between students from Turkey, the Caucasus, Turkmenistan and Azerbayjan. See Muhammad Mahdi Al Kubba:
   Mudhakarati fi samim al-ahdath. 1918–1958. Beirut 1965: 11; or Ja'far al-Khalili:
   Hakhadha 'araftuhum; vol. 1, Beirut 1963: 111, 313ff.
2. 'Abd al-Azziz al-Qassab: *Min dhikrayati.* Beirut 1962: 228.
3. Yawm al-Ghadir is a holiday which celebrates the day 'Ali was nominated Imam by
   the Prophet Mohammed
4. Bert G. Fragner: 'Von dem Staatstheologen zum Theologenstaat: Religiöse Führung
   und Historischer Wandel im schi'itischen Persien', in *Wiener Zeitschrift fur die Kunde
   des Morgenlandes* 75 (1983): 73–98; William M. Floor: 'The Political Role of the Lutis
   in Iran', in M.E. Bonine and N. Keddie (eds.) *Modern Iran: the Dialectics of Continuity and Change.* Albany 1981, 83–95.
5. See Baba Johansen: 'The all-Embracing Towns and its Mosques', in *Revue de l'Occident
   Musulman et la Mediterranee* 32 (1981): 139–161.
6. Ira Lapidus: *Muslim Cities in the late Middle Ages.* Cambridge 1967: 47.
7. Bert Fragner (1983): 84.
8. See J.R.I. Cole and Moojan Momen: 'Mafia, Mob, and Shiism in Iraq: The Rebellion of Ottoman Karbala, 1924–1843', in *Past and Present* 112 (1986): 112–143.
9. Ja'far ibn al-Shaykh Baqir Al Mahbuba al-Najafi: *Madhi Najaf wa hadiruha*, vol. 1,
   Sayda 1353 (H):330.
10. Werner Ende: The Flagellations of Muharrram and the Shi'ite 'Ulama', in *Der
    Islam* 55 (1978):19–36.

11. al-Khalili, vol. 2: 151
12. Mahbuba: 334.
13. Ibid.: 336
14. Abbas al-Azzawi: *Tarikh al-'Iraq bayn al-ihtilalayn*, vol. 8, Baghdad 1956.
15. Hasan al-Asadi: *Thawrat al-Najaf 'ala l-Injliz aw al-sharara al-ula li-thawrat al-'ishrin.* Baghdad 1975: 58ff.
16. Fayyad 16; Foreign Office 317/2489/14291 and 317/2771/165592, Arab Bulletin, no. 13; P.Luizard: *La formation de l'Irak contemporain.* Paris 1991: 336.
17. al-Khalili: 46.
18. Foreign Office 371/2489/14291; P. Luizard: 337ff.
19. Asadi 318ff, 330.
20. Asadi 83, 207.
21. Christian Sigrist: *Regulierte Anarchie: Untersuchung zum Fehlen und zur Enstehung politischer Herrschaft in segmentären Gesellschaften Afrikas.* Freiburg, 1967: 21–59.

CHAPTER THREE

Kurds, Islam and State Nationalism

Helkot Hakim

Instrumentalisation of the Kurds' Islamic culture against their own national movements is not a novel policy pursued by some states in the Middle East, be them secular or otherwise. Central governments have consistently tried, one way or another, to manipulate Islam as an ideology to mobilize their citizens against such movements on the one hand and to split the Kurds themselves on the other. The aim has always been to undermine particular movements perceived as a potential danger to central authority and to stem or weaken the development of nationalist consciousness among the Kurdish people as a whole.

Such instrumentalisation of Islam has been blunted as national thinking has grown stronger, and the role of religion itself in public life has declined: nevertheless it has not quite disappeared altogether. In recent years, Kurdish politics has witnessed the dramatic resilience of political Islam. Kurdish Islamic movements have asserted themselves as second to nationalist movements, displacing leftist parties that had remained the second most powerful trend among the Kurds since the early 1960s. This resilience revived the opportunity to instrumentalize Islam once again against Kurdish nationalist drive.

In this chapter, the role of Islam in Iraqi state policy towards the Kurdish national movement will be examined, along with the influence this has had on Kurdish political thinking and action. Emphasis will also be laid on the Kurds' response to Islamic revivalism among themselves. The term 'Iraqi state' will be used as a synonym for 'Iraqi government', since the policy pursued by different governments *vis-à-vis* the Kurds has been institutionalized into patterned security, military and civil structures, some of which date back some 40 years or so. Almost all Iraqi governments have, to varying degrees, adopted a policy of instrumentalisation of Islam in their struggle against the Kurds.

Specific forms of religiosity

The Kurdish version of Islam had its own social and political role to play in the Ottoman Empire's policy, as from the 16th century, initially towards Persia, later towards the Christian communities in the region, and then towards the Kurds themselves. The sacred Ottoman Empire was embedded in the Sunni-Hanafi school of Islam. Like the Ottomans, Kurds were Muslims, in contrast to such ethnic minorities as the Armenians, Chaldeans, Assyrians and Greeks. And like the Ottomans, they embraced Sunni Islam in the face of the Shi'i Islam officially adopted by the Persian Safavid and later Qajar dynasties.[1]

The Ottomans seized the Kurdish region in 1514, following agreement with the local lords. They took advantage of the fact that the Kurds shared their faith to play them off against the rival Shi'i Persian Empire. In the war that broke out between the two sacred empires in that year, the Kurds fought with their Ottoman co-religionists. Hostilities ended with a Persian defeat which involved considerable territorial loss.

The Ottomans pursued a policy of inciting religious zeal among the Kurds, involving them in Turkish moves against the Christian Armenians during the second half of the nineteenth century: this culminated in the infamous attempt to exterminate the Armenians in 1915. This policy resulted in getting the Kurds actively involved in massacring the Armenians. What the Kurds themselves did and could not conceive was that the Ottomans would soon turn against them as an ethnic group, the moment ethnicity and nationalism developed. While engaged in killing Armenians, the Ottomans were energetically fanning Kurdish religious intolerance and portraying the Kurds, to the west in particular, as the culprits in these massacres.[2]

Judging by the last five centuries, the Ottoman Empire was apparently more successful than any other central authority in manipulating the Kurds' religious culture against their own rebellions – be they revolts by traditional tribal chieftains or defiant activity by modern nationalist movements.[3] In both cases, the Ottomans supported more solid central control. The most striking accounts in this connection date back to the first half of the nineteenth century. However, this approach was a key element in the Ottoman policy towards all non-Turkish ethnicities, including the Kurds. And the Ottomans conferred lasting privileges on collaborators and their heirs from one generation to another.

The nascent Iraqi state partially inherited the Ottoman's policy of deploying Islam against the Kurds and Kurdish national movement. It is paradoxical that the first person to instrumentalize Kurdish national feelings against the demands raised by Kurdish nationalists was Sati al-Husri, the well-known theorist of Arab nationalism and the pedagogue who held key positions in both the Ottoman and Iraqi administrations.[4]

The importance of Sati al-Husri (1880–1968) and his thought may be explained by his stature as one of the most prominent theoreticians of Arab nationalism, the 'father' or 'philosopher' of Pan-Arabism, as his disciples called him. As a high official in charge of the educational system in Iraq, he had ample opportunities to put his ideology in practice. He had a direct influence on the country's political culture and orientation. Among his disciples were figures who assumed the highest positions in the Iraqi state. It was al-Husri who modelled the educational system and determined the content of school curricula in post-Ottoman Iraq. As Albert Horani noted, al-Husri 'had great influence in the shaping of Arab nationalist consciousness in Iraq'.[5]

Al-Husri's attitude towards the Kurds can be seen in numerous state decisions and practices concerning public and educational policies. His conscious manipulation of Islamic feelings and values among enlightened Kurds to impose linguistic barriers against the Kurdish language was particularly important. For example, he blocked the use of certain signs and diacriticals on the Arabic print letters which the Kurds added in order to denote Kurdish phonetics which did not exist in Arabic. This seemingly minor technical problem had significant political meaning in the late 1920s.

Education in Kurdish was introduced in Iraq for the first time in 1918 in a number of primary schools in Kirkuk, Sulaymaniya and Arbil. Later, Britain and the Iraqi government promised to meet Kurdish administrative and cultural demands. There was an agreement to develop and extend Kurdish schooling to all Kurdish areas and all levels of education. In its report to the League of Nations on 16 July 1925, the commission of inquiry into the Mosul issue laid emphasis on the need to delegate administration, law enforcement and education in the Kurdish region to the Kurds themselves, using Kurdish as the official language there.[6] In February 1926 the Iraqi Prime-Minister declared: 'We should give the Kurds their rights. Civil servants in the Kurdish areas should be Kurds; their language should be an official language learned by their children at school'.[7]

At this formative phase in the history of Iraqi state formation and nation-building, Sati al-Husri took up his key position in the state apparatus. He had a decisive role to play in directing the educational policy of the newly established, multi-national and multi-cultural nation-state. To implement teaching in the Kurdish language, a four-man committee was set up comprising learned Kurds to oversee translation of text-books.[8] Al-Husri, with his statist and centralizing ideas, was of the opinion that the best way to teach the Kurdish language was to translate Arabic text-books taught at primary schools.[9] The committee proposed that certain signs and diacriticals should be added to some Arabic print letters to represent Kurdish characters as distinct vowels and consonants. According to al-Husri, this demand required 'the creation of 15 new letters by adding dots and signs to 11 known Arabic letters'.[10] He voiced his doubt on the wisdom of such modifications or innovations. A committee member tried to convince Husri using examples from the Kurdish language, such as the existence of two distinct sounds for the letter L. But the director general of education, Husri, who had his own axe to grind, dismissed the difference without having any knowledge of the Kurdish language.[11]

In the face of the ensuing deadlock caused by the committee insisting on the inclusion of these proposed diactricals and signs, a Kurdish minister, together with the Prime-Minister himself, intervened. As a result of this counter pressure, al-Husri proposed seeking a second opinion from other enlightened Kurds.[12] This move by Husri denoted a *de facto* lack of confidence in a committee set up by the government and gave room for manoeuvre. At this point the committee asked the Kurdish minister, Mohammed Amin Zeki, to intercede by referring the dispute to the Prime-Minister, Mohsen al-Sa'doun. In the latter's presence, a 'compromise' was reached, according to which further consultations were to be held with Kurdish intellectuals. Al-Husri addressed an official letter to Kurdish clergymen and learned personalities who were part of the Kurdish intelligentsia. Informing them of the Kurdish committee's proposals, he concluded by asking them to communicate their opinions on the proposals deliberately adding, as he admitted himself, the suggestive note that they should consider the question of 'how to reconcile reading of the holy Qur'an with reading the Kurdish writing'.[13] When the committee read al-Husri's letter, they objected to his concluding remark. The committee members approached the Kurdish minister and appealed to the head of government.[14] But the Director General of Education saw to it that his official letter reached the people concerned before the Prime-Minister's objection to drawing the Qur'an into a purely technical matter that had nothing to do with religion.[15]

Al-Husri had thus confronted 'everybody with a *fait accompli*'.[16] It was too late to retrieve the dispatched letter. Al-Husri defended his action by claiming the right to add a clarifying remark to an official letter in his capacity as Director of Education.[17] The remark, however, was not innocuous. Most of the Kurdish intellectuals who were consulted on the matter approved only some of the proposed modifications, and eventually no more than six new letters were adopted.[18] Thus al-Husri had his way by taking advantage of the Kurds' religious sensibilities.

This incident was only one among many known to all Kurdish politicians and intellectuals familiar with that period in Iraq's history. A Kurdish member of the Iraqi parliament at the time found it necessary to express his apprehensions, pointing out during a parliamentary debate that 'many here agree with me that Sati al-Husri has inflicted considerable damage on the Kurds'.[19]

This was the first significant manifestation of the role played by Islam in Iraqi state policy towards Kurdish cultural and national aspirations. However, playing the Kurds' religious feelings against Kurdish movements was admittedly less virulent under the monarchy for various reasons. But the practice became more explicit and violent in republican Iraq. With the rise of nationalist authoritarian regimes on the one hand, and the development of Kurdish national consciousness on the other, the Kurdish national movement acquired a clearer perspective and put forward more radical demands in terms of national rights.

When the Kurdish nationalist movement took up arms in 1961, the Iraqi government formed Kurdish mercenary militias named *Fursan Salahudin*, i.e., 'Warriors of Salahudin' after the medieval Fatimide leader, Salahudin al-Ayubi, who was also a Kurd. It recruited militias from Arab tribes called the 'Warriors of Khalid Ibn al-Walid' after the leading commander of Islamic armies under Prophet Mohammed who bestowed on him the title 'the Sword of God'. The task of these militias was to fight alongside the Iraqi army against Kurdish nationalist guerrillas. These two out-fits are still active, although their role has greatly diminished. Even in peace time, no Iraqi government has thought of demobilizing them.

Khalid Ibn al-Walid and Salahudin al-Ayubi led the Islamic armies to fight non-Muslims, the former mainly against the Byzantine and Persian Empires, and the latter against the Christian Crusaders. In Islamic terms, they symbolize the drive of Islam against Infidels and Kafirs. The implication is that even under secular governments, Kurdish nationalist guerrillas and activists were portrayed as godless heathens. And this provoked and invoked Islamic sentiments of both Iraqis and non-Iraqis against militant Kurds. Devastating military operations mounted by the Iraqi army against the Kurdish bases and strongholds, or even against civilians, were given religious code-names, mostly borrowed from the Qur'an or derived from terms commonly used by Muslims in their everyday life. The 1966 campaign was coded *Tawakalt 'ala Allah*: Upon God We Rely! The name of the Syrian unit which fought in 1963 with the Iraqi army was the 'Yarmouk regiment':[20] it was named after the battle won by the Early Arab Muslims over the Byzantines in the year 636. Perhaps the most notorious among these is the 1988 campaign of *al-Anfal*, code-named after the title of Chapter Eight of the Qur'an. As this chapter determines the distribution of war spoils seized by Muslim warriors from conquered heathens,[21] the name becomes all the more horrible when we remember that the Anfal was a genocide operation against civilian, defenceless Kurds.

In addition, the Iraqi authorities engaged Iraqi and non-Iraqi clerical dignitaries in issuing fatwas endorsing the government's crusades against the Kurds, or elevating the soldiers killed in combat to the rank of martyrs. In these edicts, the Kurds were depicted as being godless. They were similarly described in various government publications on the Kurdish nationalist movement: the first pages of these books were adorned with Qur'anic' verses implicitly branding supporters of the movement as heathens. To quote but one example: 'The Kurds as Viewed by Science', by Mohammed Rasheed al-Fil, an Iraqi historian, opens with a Qur'anic' verse to the effect that he who kills a believer is doomed to eternal hell. This book, published in 1965, was subsidized by the Iraqi government.

Differentiating between the believer and the killer in the on-going war between central government and the Kurdish national movement is a question which is bound to arise. All writings about the Kurds at that time were directly or indirectly designed to discredit and smear Kurdish nationalists.

This policy continued well into the 1970s and 1980s. Following the chemical bombing of the town of Halabje in 1988, the Iraqi government dispatched three Kurdish clerics to Europe to hold a press conference and propagate the myth, vowing on Qur'anic' verses, that the town was bombed by Iranian, not Iraqi, aircraft.[22]

In its instrumentalisation of Islam against the Kurds, the Iraqi state pursued three goals: Firstly, to win Arab and non-Arab Islamic support for its oppression of the Kurds; secondly, to invoke the religious feelings of both Sunni and Shi'i Arabs against the Kurdish movement; thirdly, to split the Kurds and divide them into Islamic and non-Islamic camps.

In dealing with Islamic groups beyond the border, and even among ordinary religious people, Iraqi state policy has been remarkably successful in attaining its aims. Since the late 1960s, Islamic organizations and their splinter offshoots have viewed the Iraqi Kurdish national movement with hostility or, at the very least, scepticism. It should be remembered, however, that the policies of Arab and non-Arab governments in this context are rooted in geopolitical considerations in which religion counts little.

With the exception of the left and democratic forces or those groups who question the state's religious pretensions, Arab Sunnis have been generally influenced by the state policy of instrumentalizing Islam in this area. A number of Sunni 'ulama, for example, issued fatwas on the martyrdom of the soldier who died in Northern Iraq, and the godlessness of their adversaries, the Kurdish nationalist militants. Some Sunni clerics were even used as a cover to stage a would-be attempt on the life of the Kurdish leader, Mustafa Barzani, in 1972.

However, Iraqi Shi'i response to state pleas to stigmatize the Kurds as godless has a different bent. Grand Ayatollah Mohsen al-Hakim, the highest religious authority of the Shi'i community, constantly declined to issue any fatwas against the Kurds. On the contrary, he issued a fatwa disapproving of the war against

Kurds in the late 1960s. Other Shi'i clerics, of lesser rank and status than Hakim, had pro-government leanings and issued their anti-Kurd fatwas accordingly.

The Islamic factor is more interesting when it comes to state efforts to play the Kurds' Islamic values and tenets against the Kurdish national movement and split them into two pro-Islamic and anti-Islamic camps. This policy, in fact, triggered a deep Kurdish reaction against Islam that is still felt at present. This reaction may have served the Iraqi state in its pursuit of the first two goals mentioned earlier: accordingly, it may be concluded that the Iraqi state has scored some success in this regard.

Kurdish Reactions

Over time, modern nationalist Kurds developed a hostility towards Islam. This response may be construed as mainly, though not exclusively, a hastily-formed attitude bereft of intellectual maturity or sound secular concepts. It was in fact an emotive, subjective reaction lacking any concrete historical or political basis. The resistance among the Kurds towards Islam was, in this case, the outcome of governmental manipulation of religious symbols and values for non-religious ends. This tendency was further accentuated by the fierce inter-struggle between traditional and modernist forces in the Kurdish society.

There were other factors which intensified the hostile view of Islam. First, the inclusion of Islam in the theorization of Arab ethnic nationalism was problematic to the Kurds in the framework of the newly emerging Iraq nation-state. As may be recalled, Arab scholars and historians, especially after the First World War, tried to solve the intrinsic problem through focusing on the question: Who is the Arab? In his definition of the Arab, Sati al-Husri included all those who speak Arabic and live within the borders of Arab lands.[23] This linguistic-cultural and territorial approach to ethnictiy can potentially force the Kurds, the Copts, the Turkoman, the Assyrians and other ethnic minorities into full-blooded Arabhood. Another theoretician, Naji Ma'rouf, a historian and an influential figure in the Iraqi educational system, tried to repudiate al-Husri by lumping the Iranians, the Pakistanis and the Turks together with the Arabs under one and the same ethnic or national identity.[24] His unifying marker was religion. Thus a Kurdish pupil learnt from the history books that Salahudin al-Ayubi, for instance, was an Arab, and that classical thinkers and poets like al-Athir, Ibn Khalakan and al-Zahawi were presumably Arabs. In other words, those who were known from the social and family experiences of the student to be genuine Kurds by descent and lineage would turn up at school with a different ethnic cloth on them. If Naji Ma'rouf's criteria for the definition of an Arab is carried to its extreme limits, the same Kurdish pupil would find himself or herself an Arab, even though he or she would have extreme difficulty in memorizing two lines of Arab poetry or uttering even a few words in Arabic. His or her case would be similar to an Algerian or an African in a French colony who was entitled to refer to 'our Gaullish forefathers' albeit these were the forefathers of the French, not of the Africans.

Apart from text-books usually authored by Arab nationalists, there is a vast volume of literature in circulation which is geared towards serving the purpose of obliterating ethnic markers. The already mentioned historian, Mohammed Rasheed al-Fil, for instance, allegedly attempts to offer 'scientific proof' that the Kurds are in fact Arabs who had originally migrated from Arabia to the mountains of Kurdistan in search of pasture and water sources.[25]

It was Arab nationalists who first manufactured an Arab ethnic identity for Salahudin and other Muslim commanders, scholars and men of letters who used Arabic as their lingua franca and embraced Islam as their world view. When literary-historical nationalism was being churned out by countless Arab writers and historians in the nineteenth century in order to construct the 'Arab hero', Kurdish writing had not even been invented: such assertions could therefore not be repudiated. This was a cause for understandable frustration among the more educated Kurds at a time when the national question was overwhelming the horizons of intellectuals and politicians in the region.

But the Kurds' hostile view of Islam is not solely embedded in their rejection of the Arabising Islam; their position also has roots in other contributory factors. First, Kurdish modernists had a cultural approach that viewed past events from a contemporary perspective, neglecting the historical context of past peculiarities and limitations. This is a common flaw found among followers of nationalist ideologies. The schematic nature of such conceptions explains their widespread popularity. The second factor is the influence of Marxist and other leftist ideas on which many intellectuals and educated people have been weaned: these view religion as an opium for the masses, with the effect of lulling people into self-complacency and holding back any efforts at self-emancipation. Kurds subscribing to the proposition that religion has a stupefying effect would inevitably apply it to their people. Kurdish history abounds with examples and cases which, in their view, provide sufficient grounds to justify their hostile attitude to Islam. The first historical example cited as an obstacle to the Kurds' realizing their national aspirations is none other than the instance of Salahudin al-Ayubi himself. Kurdish nationalists argue that Salahudin did not serve his 'own people' as he never sought to build a Kurdish polity, although conditions were favourable and such an enterprise was within easy grasp.[26] In nationalist conceptions of history, Salahudin figured as the epitome of those Kurds who had betrayed their national identity in the name of religion. Some modern Kurdish nationalists have gone so far as to put Salahudin on trial through dramas performed on stage. This nationalist imagining presumes that Salahudin should have thought and acted in nationalist idiom in the middle ages, i.e at a time when the very concept of nationalism had not come into existence, even in its birth-place, Europe. This approach denies the medieval hero his natural right to personal and military ambition, a fact which does not in the least affect his merits and achievements.

In contrast, traditional Kurdish nationalists never criticised the Islamic history of the Kurds; in fact, they tried to harness the religious culture and values among the Kurds to the national cause. The most vigorous and rigorous defence of the Islamic heritage of the Kurds has come from Islamist Kurds who, at least since the 1980s, have developed a keen nationalist drive hitherto alien to them. Their Kurdish nationalist bent is so entrenched that it advocates full Kurdish stastehood, be it Islamic or otherwise; understandably they would prefer an Islamic polity.[27]

The other example is that of Shaykh Idris al-Badlisi, a high functionary in the Ottoman Empire, who was an administrator rather than a cleric. This Kurd was instrumental in the agreement reached in the early 16th century between Kurdish local lords and the Ottomans to cooperate against the Safavid dynasty. In the eyes of modern Kurdish nationalists, this clergy-administrator became a symbol of religious fanaticism, egoism, and betrayal of one's own people.[28] Al-Badlisi devotedly served the Ottoman Sultans and fought against the Shi'i Persians. He did that for religious and political reasons. He had also a desire to organize the Kurdish region under more effective and efficient administration, although this subsequently led to the imposition of centralized Ottoman authority. In his assessment, the Kurdish historian Mohammed Amin Zeki says: 'There is no doubt that the administrative division worked out by the ingenuity of our master Idris al-Badlisi was in complete harmony with local conditions and regional circumstances. A rugged land like Kurdistan with its inhabitants who are disposed to war and fighting, always rebellious and independent-minded would not and could not have been run by any form other than this kind of administration and structures of governance'.[29]

Acknowledging al-Badlisi's administrative efficiency, the author adds, without explaining why and how, that 'this administrative structuring has virtually and actually wiped out most of the 46 Kurdish principalities that existed before the reign of this successful Sultan [Saleem the second]'.[30]

The al-Badlisi experience, according to Zeki's assessment, has two aspects: one is the modernization of governance, the other the termination of Kurdish principalities. Of these two, only the second was taken up and attacked by modern Kurdish nationalists. They deployed an ideological, rather than a historical, examination of whether or not these local dynasties could have kept out of reach of the Ottoman or Safavid or Qajar hegemony and conquest. And their ideological answer was fraught with fantasy.

Idris al-Badlisi, however, was more fortunate than his counterpart, Mullah al-Khatti, three centuries later. The Ottomans' exploitation of the Kurds' religious feelings is historically associated by modern nationalists with Mullah al- Khatti. His episode merits closer examination, the more so when it is still controversial a century or so later. In nationalist records, Mullah al- Khatti's name is a synonym for national treason motivated by religious zeal, and a striking illustration of the damage inflicted by Islam on the Kurds. Some Kurdish writers have found it necessary to defend al-Khatti in an attempt to rehabilitate him in the face of the Kurdish nationalists' one-sided, harsh and ahistorical assessment of his words and deeds.

In the 1820s and 1830s, Mullah al-Khatti was the mufti of the Suran principality, east of the Mosul province and west of the town of Sulaymaniya. He was on good terms with both its Prince, Pasha Mahmood al-A'war, and the Ottoman governors (walis) of Baghdad, who had concerns over the growing power of Kurdish local lords. In the 1830s Pasha Mahmood posed a serious challenge to the Ottomans who were under pressure from the Egyptian armies. In this context, the Ottomans saw the autonomy of the Suran principality as a menace that should be removed. In the ensuing battles between the Ottoman army and Kurdish forces, the former, surprisingly, scored considerable success. When the Ottoman army resumed its march to seize the town of Rawandouz, the capital of the Suran dynasty, the mufti, Mullah al-Khatti, discouraged Kurdish warriors who were prepared to fight. His appeal was anchored in the belief that the Ottoman Sultan was the Caliph of all Muslims and thus he should not be resisted. He further claimed that he whoever fell in battle against the Ottomans would die a blasphemer, and go to hell; if he survived he would lose his marital rights until Doomsday.[31] Fighters were so demoralized by his speech that the episode ended with unconditional surrender, and the Kurdish Prince was taken to Constantinople and executed. With his elimination, the autonomous Kurdish principality in Suran met its final demise.

Some accounts suggest that al-Khatti delivered his frustrating fatwa on the request of the Ottoman commander of the campaign, who had sent the mufti and the Kurdish Prince a faked order from the Sultan to desist fighting. Al-Khatti is also said to have been rewarded by the Ottomans for his services. Although these accounts still need to be verified, a son of Mullah al-Khatti confirmed that the Ottoman state continued to pay his sons and grandsons allowances until early this century.[32]

Mullah Khatti's fatwa and the motives behind it were the subject of open debate. But a century later, in the 1920s and 1930s, the controversy became particularly heated when Kurdish nationalists started to look for evidence of the damage caused by Islam to Kurdish national aspirations. Mullah al-Khatti has become the archetype of this perceived damage. Kurdish nationalists, it seems, believe that the forces of the Kurdish Prince might have won the battle, kept the principality intact, and developed it into a solid core for the formation of a feasible Kurdish nation.[33]

Historical facts do not support such a hypothesis. However, the nationalist presentation of this episode has acquired such dominance that Mullah al-Khatti is perceived as guilty of high treason. At the beginning of the Kurdish national movement in Iraq, nationalists needed a Kurdish anti-hero. Over a century after his death, Mullah al-Khatti continues to fulfil this function. Attempts by some writers and historians to rehabilitate him have made few advances.

Notes

1. When the Safavids embraced Shi'ism and tried to spread it among the Persian population of their empire, they met stiff resistance. Frequently, they had to use force. The Kurds were among those who resisted the new faith, and the Safavids could only impose it on some of them. The majority of Kurds under Persian control have kept their Sunni leanings to this very day. The collective memory is still scarred by this sectarian conflict.

2. There is ample evidence on how the Ottomans manipulated Kurdish Islamic values against the Armenians. For a detailed account see Kamal Muzhir, *Kurdistan fi sanawat al-harb al-'alamiya al-ula*, (Kurdistan in the Years of the First World War), translated into Arabic by Mohammed Mulla Abdul-Kareem, the Kurdish Academy of Sciences, Baghdad 1977. The author devotes a chapter to Kurdish involvement in massacres against Armenians.

3. Since the adoption of Shi'i Islam by Persia and the Kurdish alliance with the Ottomans in 1514, relations between the central authority and Sunni Kurds have been marred by suspicion. Some Kurds remained part of Persia and others became part of the Ottoman Empire. Wars between the Ottoman and Persian empires in the following four centuries were marked by the use of sectarianism as a weapon for mobilizing people and fighters. Persia, however, could not count on the religious sentiments of its Sunni Kurds whether in its struggle against Kurdish movements or in its wars with the Ottomans, because they were of a different faith. Instrumentalisation of religion was therefore confined to Shi'i Kurds in the south

of Iranian Kurdistan and in the region of Kermanshah. For instance, Persia would frequently rely on armies of the Kermanshah dynasty in its military campaigns to control the Kurdish dynasty of Ardalan in Persia or to install a pro-Persian prince in the Baban dynasty within the Ottoman domain. This state of affairs may still be detected at present although not in such clear-cut terms as before. Political consciousness among Shi'i Kurds is steadily acquiring a nationalist character – slowly in Iran and rapidly in Iraq – at the expense of their religious sectarian affiliations. However, Shi'i Kurds, especially in Iran, are still torn between their religious-sectarian affiliation and national- ethnic identity.

4. Sati' al-Husri held high positions in the Ottoman Ministry of Education in the Balkans. With the decline of the Ottoman Empire he espoused Pan-Arabism after he had been a staunch Ottoman advocate. He worked with King Faisal I in Syria first and later in Iraq. From August 1921 to March 1922 he was the King's education adviser. He then became an aide to the education minister until January 1923, Director of Education until 1927, lecturer at the teachers' training college until September 1931, and General Inspector of Education until the end of 1930. After that he held many positions outside the sphere of education until he was expelled from Iraq in 1941 because of his support for the aborted coup led by Rasheed Aali al-Gaylani.

5. Alias Marcus, *Naqd al-fikr al-qawmi, Sati' al-Husri* (Critique of National Thought, Sati' al-Husri), Beirut, Dar al-Tali'a, 1966, p. 12.

6. The Kurdish historian, Muhammad Amin Zaki (1880–1948), who held several ministerial posts in the cabinet under the monarchy, says that out of 120 Iraqi students who were sent abroad for academic study only 3 were Kurds: in proportion to the Kurdish population, there should have been 21. See his book, *Dawoo teh qah lai bi swood* (Two Futile Attempts), edited and introduced by Sabah Ghalib, London, 1984, p. 73. Zaki also confirms that for the Kurds in Kirkuk, comprising 51% of population, there were only five schools, while there were 18 Turkish schools for the Turkomans who accounted for 12% of the populace. Ibid, p. 76.

7. Basile Nikitine, *Les Kurdes, etudes sociologique et historique*, Librairi C. Klincksieck, Paris 1956, 'e'ed. Ed. D'Aujord'hui, Paris, 1975, p. 197. For instance, in 1932 the Iraqi government enacted the 'Local Languages Law' which granted Kurds the right to use their language in publication, the courts and administration in predominantly Kurdish areas. However, it remained a dead letter in most areas.

8. They are Tawfiq Wahbi, Abdul-Rahman Saleh, Shukri al-Fadhli and Nouri al-Barzanchi. See Sati al-Husri, *Muthakarati fil 'iraq* (My Memoirs in Iraq), vol.I, Beirut 1967, p. 457.

9. The basic details may be drawn from al-Husri's own memoirs, ibid, and the part he devotes to 'the question of writing the Kurdish language', pp. 457–74.

10. Sati al-Husri, ibid, p. 459. There was no need for entirely new letters to be invented. A mere sign on each of the respective Arab print letters would have been enough to solve the problem. These innovations would have overcome difficulties still faced in reading and writing Arabic letters in the Kurdish language.

11. When the Prime-Minister, Mohsen al-Sadoun, was drawn into the dispute between Sati al-Husri and the Kurdish committee, he reprimanded al-Husri, saying: 'You

do not know Kurdish. Why are you raising questions related to Kurdish writing?' Ibid, p. 461. The Minister, Sabih Nashaat, told al-Husri: 'Is it not enough that you have antagonized the Shi'is? Why do you want to antagonize the Kurds as well?' Ibid.

12. In the face of the committee rejecting his proposal, al-Husri replied with typical demagogy: 'You have no right to impose your own opinion on the Kurdish people without putting it to discussion and debate by a committee of enlightened Kurds and scholars from all Kurdish towns', al-Husri, ibid, p. 461.

13. Ibid, p. 463.

14. The stance taken by the committee members on involving the Qur'an in a purely technical matter stems from the fact that many educated Kurds consulted on the issue were clergymen. It was obvious that they would be influenced by al-Husri's remark. Until that time most educated Kurds, as well as students of the Kurdish language and literature, were graduates of religious schools. The poet, Jameel Sidqi al-Zahawi, was one of the enlightened Kurds who was consulted. He rejected the proposed letters and offered letters of his own creation that would be suitable 'for correctly and easily writing any language'.

15. Sati al-Husri, op.cit, p. 463.

16. Sati al-Husri, op.cit, p. 464.

17. When asked about drawing the Qur'an into the dispute, he replied: 'Because teaching the Qur'an is part of the curriculum for Muslims'. Sati al-Husri, op.cit, p. 463.

18. The six proposed letters were not sufficient for the correct writing and reading of the Kurdish language. al-Husri may have succeeded in shelving the added letters for some time, but the changes proposed by the committee served as the basis for the modifications later introduced into the Kurdish language, and have been adopted in printing for over thirty years. They did not make 'reading and writing extremely difficult' as claimed by al-Husri at the time. On the contrary, they have facilitated even the reading of ancient manuscripts written in a mixture of Arabic, Persian and Turkish.

19. Gamaladin al-Alusi, *Sati al-Husri, Ra'id al-qawmiya al-'arabiya* (Husri, the Pioneer of Arab Nationalism), Baghdad, 1986, p. 57.

20. Munthir al-Mosuli, *Arab wa akrad, ru'ya 'arabiya lil qadhiya al-kurdiya* (Arabs and Kurds, an Arab View of the Kurdish Question), Dar al-Ghusoun, Beirut, 1986, p. 30.

21. On the al-Anfal Chapter in the Qur'an Abdullah Mahmood Shahaata says: 'it contains many rules of peace and war, rules on booty and captives'. See Abdullah Mahmood Shahaata, *Ahdaf surat al-anfal*, (The Aims of al-Anfal Chapter in the Holy Qur'an), Egyptian Public Book Enterprise, 1981, p. 102. This chapter is complex and ramified. It is one of the harshest Qur'anic chapters towards the heathens and one of the most expressive in this regard. War spoils, together with the battle of Badr, are the central theme of this chapter. It is difficult to single out one reason for choosing this particular chapter as the code-name of a military campaign mounted by the Iraqi government against the Kurdish people resulting in over 150,000 Kurds killed. The choice, however, is a continuation of the policy of instrumentalizing religion against the Kurdish movement.

22. Those three Imams were prominent clergymen in the towns of Arbil, Sulaymaniya and Dehok.

23. Sati al-Husri holds that the Arab world 'extends from Ragros mountains to the Atlantic coast'. See Sati al-Husri, *al-'Uruba awalan*, (Arabism First), Beirut, Centre of Arab Unity Studies, 1985, p. 79.

24. See as one example Naji Ma'rouf, *'Ualma' yunsabun ila mudun 'ajamiya wa hum min aruma 'arabiya*, (Scholars of Arab Origin Ascribed to Alien Cities), Baghdad, 1965. See also Abbas al-Azawi, *'Asha'ir al-'iraq al-kurdiya* (The Kurdish Tribes of Iraq), al-Najaf Press, 1947.

25. Mohammed Rasheed al-Fil, *al-Akrad fi nazar al-'ilm* (The Kurds as Viewed by Science), al-Aadab Press, Najaf, 1965, p. 24.

26. Kurds narrate a story to the effect that Salahudin and his daughter had once visited Mount Himreen. Seizing the opportunity, the girl said, 'Father, look north. This is the homeland of your people, and you have great possibilities and powers. Build a kingdom for your people where they can live in dignity'. Salahudin was furious with his daughter and ordered her to be cut up into pieces. This story cannot possibly date back farther than early this century. It has many implications and does not justify Salahudin's outburst. It simply serves to understand a present-day view of history. Salahudin as such has nothing to do with it.

27. In the 1980s the Iraqi government had supported the Islamic movements in the hope of undermining the Kurdish national movement.

28. See Muhammed Amin Zeki, *Khulasat tarikh al-kurd wa kurdustan* (Concise History of the Kurds and Kurdistan) translated into Arabic by Mohammed Ali Awni, vol. I, 2nd edition, Baghdad, 1961, pp. 163–77, Jamal Nabaz, *al-mir al-kurdi mir Muhammad al-rawanduzi, al-mulaqab bi miri kura*, (The Kurdish Prince Mir Mohammed al-Rawandouzi, Alias 'Miri Kura'), Kurdish Academy of Sciences and Arts, Stockholm, 1994, pp. 226–27.

29. Zaki, op.cit, p. 176.

30. Zaki op.cit.

31. For details see Jamal Nabaz, op.cit, pp. 124–31, Zubair Bilal Ismael, Muhammed al-Khatti and wa nihayat imarat Suran, *al-Hukm al-Thati Review* – the Autonomy Journal – no. 4, Arbil, 1983, pp. 13–26. This article was reproduced in Jamal Nabaz, op.cit, pp. 269–82, Masoud Muhammed, Tathniyat al-haj ila 'atab al-'allama al-Khatti, *Karwan*, no. 71, Arbil, 1989, pp. 145–51 and no.72, Arbil, 1989, pp. 139–51. This article was also reproduced in Jamal Nabaz, op.cit, pp. 305–25.

32. Jamal Nabaz, op.cit, pp. 126–27.

33. The first to refer to accounts of the discredited role played by al-Khatti in the decline of the Suran dynasty was the Kurdish historian, Mohammed Amin Zakiki, in the Concise History of the Kurds and Kurdistan, vol.I, op.cit. Published in Baghdad, 1931 in Kurdish, and translated into Arabic by Mohammed Ali Awni, 1st edition, Egypt, 1939, 2nd edition, Baghdad, 1961 (see footnote 28). Hussein Hazni Mokiriani, a political commentator (1893–1947), quoted this episode as an incontrovertible fact in his book, *Tarikh Umara' Suran* (History of the Suran Princes) published first in Kurdish, Rawandouz, 1935, translated by Mohammed Mulla Kareem into Arabic and published in Baghdad in 1968.

PART II

INSTITUTIONALIZED AND POPULAR RELIGION VERSUS THE STATE

CHAPTER FOUR

The Genesis and Development of *Marja'ism* versus the State

Faleh Abdul-Jabar

The notion that *marja'ism* as an institution has existed since the time of Kulayni (d. 940) or even earlier, is as widespread among the clerical class and their lay emulators as it is challenged.[1] Ayatollah Muhammad Baqir al-Sadr, for example, postulates that *marja'ism* dates from the time of early Shi'ism (*ashab al-a'imma al-ma'sumin*) through to the present. In his belief, there were four successive stages in the history of *marja'ism*.

1. The subjective *marja'ism* (*al-marja'iyya al-thatiyya*) starting with the deputies of the Imams (the last died in 939) down to 'Allama Hilli (d. 1325).
2. The administrative *marja'ism* (*idariyya*) instituted by al-Shahid al-Awal, Abu Abdullah Muhammad bin Jamal al-Din al-'Amili (d. 1374).
3. The central *marja'ism* established by Shaykh Ja'far bin shaykh Khidr al-Janagi an-Najafi Kashif al-Ghita' (d. 1813).
4. The popular *marja'ism* which emerged against western colonization of the Muslim world.[2]

Whether or not this conceptualizing is historically sound, it clearly underlines a line of development in which religious authority assumed different forms and functions. Yet the present reality of *marja'ism* is projected onto the past, lending all these forms of authority a centralized and institutionalized nature.

This conceptual projection, however, is challenged by some Shi'i jurists and most students of Shi'i Islam. Ayatollah Muhammad Husayn Fadhl Allah of Lebanon, for example, maintains that, 'In past history, there had been no supreme, central *marja'ism* because long distances did not allow scattered communities [of Shi'is] to refer themselves to religious authorities [residing] in remote locations [presumably in Najaf] although there was a degree of contacts...That is why communities consulted the religious authority in their vicinity'.[3]

The idea that *marja'ism* existed from the time of Kulayni or even earlier is clearly a myth. No less romantic is the idea that the institution of *marja' mutlaq* emerged almost ready made.[4] Students of Shi'i Islam agree that the institution of *marja'ism* appeared in the mid or early nineteenth century. Some refer to Kashif al-Ghita (d. 1813), others to Muhammad al-Najafi, the author of *Jawahir al-Kalam* (d. 1849); most, however, single out his disciple, Murtadha al-Ansari (d. 1865), as the first *marja' mutlaq*.[5]

The establishment of this novel, religious institution denoted the growing, autonomous power, wealth and social networks of the *'ulama* embedded in a widely recognised juristic-theological legitimacy. This recognition was also supported by state patronage and popular allegiance.

This chapter will focus on the formative process of this institution in juristic-theological, social, economic and political terms, along with an examination of the inner segmentary structures and external forces which kept this institution in a state of constant flux towards centralisation or decentralisation, and order and disorder, right up until the present day. The major aspects of this process took place over two centuries or so.

There are five major features which require clarification:

1. The juristic-theological concepts of knowledge and power which paved the way for the inception of *marja' taqlid mutlaq*.
2. The relevance of the 17th–18th century Usuli-Akhbari juristic, social, theological and cultural conflict.
3. The drive to centralization in the mid nineteenth century.
4. The characteristic disorder of the informal order of *marja'ism*.
5. Modern attempts at formal institutionalisation and modernisation of *marja'ism*.

Power and knowledge: Major concepts

Legitimisation of the authority of *'ulama* or *mujtahids* revolves, in juristic-theological terms, around the nature of knowledge.[6] Hence concepts of knowledge precede those of power.

Concepts of knowledge

Knowledge is one of the cornerstones of Shi'ism. The infallibility of the Imams as heirs of worldly and spiritual leadership forms the basis of legitimacy of the God-chosen Imam, source of learning, jurisdiction and saintly mediation with the divine. The infallibility of the Imams appears to have two origins. One is the nature of God as all knowing and all good. From this Mu'tazalite premise, a theo-political theory was derived, arguing that if the ruler is not infallible, the community of believers would be led astray: this contradicts divine grace, for God can not command humans to do evil.[7]

The *'ulama* inherited their high status, community leadership and other roles, firstly in their capacity as transmitters and codifies of tradition, Akhbar, from the infallible Imams. Early Shi'i *fuqaha'* in the age of occultation focused on codification and collection: Kulayni (d. 941), al-Sadduq (d. 991), or al-Tusi (d. 1067).[8]

Knowledge has a duality: the sacred infallible versus the mundane and fallible. The former is absolute and in harmony with heavenly justice and grace; the latter lies in probability and is liable to go astray.

The boundaries between these two realms of knowledge were debated, challenged, reinterpreted and modified throughout centuries of turmoil and transformation. Three major changes are discernable:

Reason and ijtihad

A gnosiological domain was created for the *'ulama* to share the power of the Imams in interpreting texts and traditions by means of reason, *'aql*, and *ijtihad*.

The concept of *'aql*, reason, as a fundamental step towards *ijtihad*, was first developed in a very limited form by Shaykh al-Mufid (d. 1022).[9] Like Akhbaris, al-Mufid specified three fundamental sources of Islamic law: the Qur'an, the Sunna and the Hadith of Imams. The investigative methods leading to what is contained in these sources are: language [*lisan*], traditions [*akhbar*] and reason [*'aql*].[10]

Hence the concept of *'aql* was not seen by the Akhbaris as a *source* of *Shari'a* but as a *method* of investigation. Muhaqiqi al-Hilli (d. 1277) took the concept another step forward, but stopped short of accepting *ijtihad*. It was left to al-'Allama al-Hilli (d. 1325) who represented the second wave of Shi'i jurisprudence, that of medieval Shi'ism under the Mongol era, to establish the concept of *ijtihad* with reason as a *source* as opposed to a method.[11]

The concept of *ijtihad* constituted 'a crucial step in the enhancement of the juristic authority of the *'ulama'*.[12]

From an epistemological point of departure, this led to the division of knowledge into two realms: absolute (the sacred text, infallibility of the Imams) and the presumptive or probable (*zann*), based on the human (i.e limited and fallible) exertions of powers of reason by the *'ulama*. It was centuries on that *ijtihad* was extended to stand on an equal footing with absolute knowledge.[13]

Emulation

The superiority of clerical knowledge over that of the lay was established through the concept of emulation, *taqlid*.

It seems that the notion of emulation appeared independently of *ijtihad* in the 11th century. In a cautious and qualified manner, al-Murtadha (a disciple of al-Mufid) expressed the desirability of *taqlid*, in the sense that laymen should seek legal advice from the jurist.[14] Three centuries on, al-'Allama al-Hilli (d. 1325, buried in Najaf) would reiterate the argument of *taqlid*, premising it on practical needs. He identifies a differentiation in knowledge with the division of labour: the lack of legal expertise on the part of laymen is seen as due to their lack of time for acquiring this knowledge, as they have to earn a living.[15]

The incumbency of *ijtihad/taqlid* was not conceptually defined and refined until well into the 16th century. According to J. Cooper, it was the Muqaddas al-Ardabili (d. 1585), in his *Zubdat al-Bayan*, who refuted

> the arguments against *taqlid* and [he] formally conjoin[ed] the ideas of *ijtihad* and *taqlid*. This conjunction greatly enhanced clerical authority in Shi'ism. If *ijtihad* legitimized the juristic authority of the *'ulama*, *taqlid* made compliance with their injunctions and opinions an ethical obligation for the laity. Thus, a new trend has set in. The layman is no longer the voluntary seeker of legal advice (*mustafti*) of medieval Shi'ite literature, and is gradually assigned the *fixed legal status of 'follower'* (*muqallid*) as *subject to clerical authority* [italics added].[16]

Stratified knowledge: 'alamiyya

'Ulama's knowledge itself was differentiated through the concept of *'alamiyya*, the most knowledgable, creating a hierarchy of junior, medium and supreme *mujtahid*. The concept of *'alamiyya* derives from the nineteenth century: 'The jurists of the Qajar period, after having established the principle of *taqlid* in its broad sense, started to accept the *marja' taqlid* as being of the *same superior level of knowledge ('ilm) as the Imam*' (italics added).[17]

The term *'alam* 'first appeared in *Ma'alim al-Usul* by 'Amili. But he seems essentially to have been concerned with the quality of being more precise in reporting tradition.

In the mid-nineteenth century, Ansari 'claimed *ijma'* [unanimity] on the *necessity of emulating the most learned mujtahid*' (italics added).[18]

The principle of *'alamiyya* was clearly defined by Ayatollah Tabataba'i Yazdi (d. 1920) only in the late nineteenth century.[19] He claimed that 'it is *obligatory* to follow the most learned *mujtahid* of the time The most learned *mujtahid* . . . is he who is most informed about the rules and sources of jurisprudence and is most capable of deducing religious ordinances' (italics added).[20]

Knowledge, by its very nature, is cumulative and capable of quantitative comparison and qualitative differentiation. The new *usuli* concept of *'alamiyya* enhanced the confidence in the human mind. The elite of *'ulama* turned into *mujtahids* is, accordingly, stratified into grand, medium and low clerics. In this context, the system of knowledge-related concepts reflects and reinforces the hierarchical grading within the *'ulama* class. *Mujtahids* were ranked into *mujtahid mutlaq, mujtahid juz'i* and apprentice *'ulama* whose *ijtihad* is still short of both, i.e cautious *ijtihad*. The validity of specialized and cautious *ijtihad* was depressed and restricted.[21]

Concepts of power

As concepts of knowledge were endorsed, they took on a life of their own, penetrating the religious culture of both clerics and laymen, binding them in mutual covenant. Through this social bond, knowledge becomes power, and those who control it generate a system which coexists, in uneasy tension, with the worldly centres of political power.

The notion that *'ulama* or *fuqaha'* have some sort of authority is as old as the time of Tusi (d. 1067). According to Bahr al-'Ulum, a debate on their authority was triggered among Shi'i *fuqaha'* when discussing the meaning of *uli al-amr*. In Sura IV, verse 59, we read:

> O ye who believe !
> Obey God,and obey the apostle,
> And those charged
> With authority among you [*uli al-amr minkum*].[22]

Three sources of authority command obedience: God, the apostle, and *uli al-amr*. The last term is interpreted as those charged with 1) authority; 2) responsibility; 3) decision; and 4) the settlement of affairs.[23]

The nature of *uli al-amr* is as ambiguous as any term could be. The above interpretation never states what sort of decision, responsibility or settlement is denoted, or what areas these terms cover.

Classical Shi'i scholars interpreted *uli al-amr* as designating the *imams*, since to obey them means to obey the canons of God, and this obedience should, by definition, be based on the correct, non-deviant comprehension of the divine law: therefore, those obeyed should be infallible, and those are the Imams. Otherwise, it would have been contradictory of God to ask believers to follow a deviant path.[24]

In contrast, the Sunni reformer, Muhammad 'Abdu (d. 1903), interpreted *uli al-amr* as 'princes, rulers, *'ulama*, commanders of the soldiery and all chieftains and leaders to whom people [*al-nas*] resort for their needs and public interests.'[25] In fact, this is the general understanding.

As early as the days of Tusi, Shi'i *'ulama* argued that *uli al-amr* are the *'ulama* themselves. Refuting this concept, Tusi retorted: 'Those who argued that the term denotes the *'ulama* have gone astray, because His saying "*uli al-amr*" means to obey those who have control [*al-amr*], and the *'ulama* are not of this category'.[26]

This internal Shi'i debate conducted some nine centuries ago was perhaps among the earliest manifestations of the *'ulama*'s drive to assert concepts of power supporting their authority. The functions attributed to the Imam are:

1. Leading the Holy War (*jihad*)
2. Division of the booty (*qismat al-fay'*)
3. Leading the Friday Prayer (*salat al-jum'a*)
4. Putting judicial decisions into effect (*tanfith al-ahkam*)
5. Imposing legal penalties (*iqamat al-hudud*)
6. Receiving the religious taxes of *zakat* and *khums*.[27]

Gradually, these duties were performed by the *'ulama* on a de facto basis in their capacity as community leaders. Two major concepts were contrived to justify the expanding role of the *'ulama* on behalf of the hidden Imam: one is Na'ib al-Imam, vice-regent of the Imam; the other is *wilayat al-faqih*, the governance of the jurisprudent. Vice-regency of the Imam is an older term, attributed to al-Muhaqiq al-Hilli (d. 1277). Both al-Karki (d. 1533) and Shahid al-Thani (1558) took up the concept. In the first case it was related to certain functions such as the collection of *zakat*, *khums*, arbitration and the like .In the case of Karki it was expanded to cover the legitimation of the Friday prayers and kharaj farming under the Safavid Shah Abbas.[28] The other term, *wilayat al-faqih*, was coined by Mulla Ahmad al-Naraqi (d. 1828), who developed this 'obscure notion ...

into a doctrine. He argued forcefully for the right of the *mujtahid* to act as a successor to the Imam and vested him with all the power of the Imam.'[29]

Wilayat al-faqih was not a new concept which differed from *niyabat al-Imam*, but an elaboration of the powers the latter denotes.[30] These powers were either limited *(khas)* or general *('amm)*. It is only with Khomeini in the twentieth century that the concept reaches its full development and encompasses political leadership, moving from the old, segmentary community to the modern nation-state.

The social, cultural and juristic-theological divide: Usuli *versus* akhbari

The development of Shi'i concepts outlined in the previous sections resulted from the Usuli-Akhbari conflict, in as much as they were the product of a constant adaptation and accommodation with changing realities on the part of Shi'i *'ulama*. In the words of Juan Cole: 'Schools of thought should be seen as ideologies supporting the position or aspirations of differing groups of *'ulama*.'[31] In other words, the *'ulama*, as a social group, acted in and reacted to changing social, political and economic conditions. They also operated within a given set of doctrines which at times hindered their abilities to cope with the new realities. Reinterpretation, modification and new readings of old tenets and principles were all the more imperative.

Usuli *challenged*

The Usuli school dominated the scene in Persia from the beginning of the Safavid era in 1501. The recruitment of Karki by Ismail, and his appointment as the 'seal of *mujtahids*' by Shah Tuhmasib, was unprecedented in the Shi'i history of ruler-*mujtahid* recognition. This novelty faced two challenges, one explicit, the other implicit. Ibrahim Qutaifi, a Shi'i *mujtahid* who opposed the appointment of Karki, was the first to show dissent. Rivalry was at the root of this defiance.[32] Karki was keen on enjoying the favours of the royal Safavid court himself. Qutaifi's attacks against Karki's authorization of the Friday prayers were a means of discrediting him. His dashing criticism would have been unthinkable were it not for the Shi'i communities, notably of Syria, Bahrain and Iraq, which existed beyond the reach of Safavid power. This geographical extension contributed towards theological pluralism. Qutaifi's opposition of clerical alliance with worldly powers was significant, and might well be interpreted as being an expression of discontent on the part of the disadvantaged section of Shi'i *'ulama* in the Arab lands, those who gained no patronage in the Safavid era or simply rejected Safavid.[33]

The other challenge against Karki's and other Arab-speaking Shi'i *'ulama*'s inclusion into Persian political, social and cultural life, came from a different quarter, what Arjomand termed the Persian 'clerical estate'.[34]

The differences between the Arab *'ulama* and the indigenous noble 'clerical estate' formed the basis of fierce competition between two social groups over posts in the administration, religious services, awqaf revenues, and religious-tax collection. They were split by cultural differences, language (Arabic versus Persian), culture (theology-jurisprudence versus theosophy), and status (learning versus noble lineage). As Arjomand noted, 'In fact, the clerical notables bitterly resented both the intrusion of the Shi'ite religious professionals under the protection and patronage of the ruler, and their pree[m]ption of the term *'ulama* – the learned'.[35] The Arab-*mujtahid* class from Iraq,Bahrain and Syria 'displaced, to some extent, the indigenous "clerical estate" of landed notables who had held official religious office'.[36]

It seems that these two reactions against the alliance of the Usuli School represented by the Karki and his entourage, with the Safavid dynasty, formed the basis of the revival of the Akhbari School as a protest movement in the 17th century. This renaissance took a hundred years or so, during which the Persian 'clerical estate' moved from Sunnism and theosophism to Twelver Shi'ism, gaining enough confidence in their belief that they had 'countered the Shi'ite doctors' bid for hierocratic domination with a radically different interpretation of Shi'ism and a counter-ideology of their own'. So,

> once the intellectual representatives of the clerical estate set forth to create their distinct variant of Shi'ism, they rediscovered the rich heritage of the pietistic traditionalism of Qum and reconciled it with the gnostic philosophy. In reviving Akhbari traditionalism, they discarded the legalistic exoteric rationalism of the *mujtahids* in favour of a gnostic rationalism that advocated innerworldly salvation through the hermeneutic comprehension of the sacred texts.[37]

It would appear that this onslaught was assisted by political factors, particularly the desire of the Safavid dynasty in the late 17th century to weaken the growing influence of the Usuli School: the Ottomans, as has been suggested by al-Qazwini, were intent on sustaining the schism within the Shi'i school.[38]

The theological–methodological onslaught, Astrabadi and the rise of neo-Akhbarism

The rejuvenation of the Akhbari School in the seventeenth century is associated with the name of Mirza Muhamad Amin al-Astrabadi (d. 1626–7), a descendant of the Persian clerical estate.[39] The Akhbari current was present in the Shi'i school from its early days.[40] The oldest reference to Akhabrism and Usulism came in *Nihayat al-Usool fi 'Ilm al-Usool* from al-'Allama al-Hilli, when it was asserted that Abi Ja'far al-Tusi was an Usuli who had been challenged by the Murtadha and his associates on certain issues.[41] Differences, however, were mostly methodological in terms of sources and methods of law-giving.[42]

With Astrabadi, Akhbarism 'crystalized in a separate movement' elevating the theological-methodological differences to the level of excommunication.[43] The animosity between the two reached such a point that Akhbaris would not touch any Usuli textbook without using a handkerchief to avoid impurity.[44] The clash became an acute power struggle, with deep cultural/social rifts extending beyond juristic issues.

Astrabadi started his onslaught on the Safavid-allied Usulism from Hijaz, Arabia. Living in Mecca, he could act freely, supported by notable Shi'i figures in Jabal 'Amil, such as al-Hurr al-'Amili, and Sheikh al-Islam, for example, in Mashhad. The movement soon flourished in Bahrain, Ottoman Iraq and pockets of Persia.[45] In his *Fawa'id al-Madaniyya*, Astrabadi rejected the concepts of *ijtihad*, *'aql* and the probable (*zann*) knowledge, stressing the importance of Akhbar (traditions) transmitted through the infallible Imams and restricting the sources of doctrine and law to two sources, the Qur'an and traditions. There was no place to him for *'aql* and *ijma'*, which he viewed as Sunni traditions and Sunni deviation. He also believed that *mujtahids* are, like their lay-followers, muqalids of the Imams. No human has the right to be emulated.[46] The differences between the two schools expanded to 29 points: some sources give a figure of 43, or even 86.[47]

The Akhbari doctrine aimed at shaking the very basis of Usuli clerical authority rooted in knowledge. The clerical-lay duality and the right of the *mujtahids* as vice-regents of the Imam were abolished. The Akhbaris, in Arjomand's view, served the interests of the Persian clerical estate against the Arab-Usuli jurists by challenging their 'hierocratic dominion'. Placing emphasis on the charisma of lineage, the Akhbaris stressed their importance as sayyids and reduced the status of *'ulama* based on knowledge. They also attracted the mass of ordinary believers through 'devotional piety'.[48]

Prior to and parallel to this line of development, the Akhbari trend was strengthened in Ottoman Iraq, Bahrain and Hijaz from the time of

Qutaifi who, in his challenge to the Karki's alliance with Ismail and Tuhmasib Safavid shahs, based his criticism and opposition on Akhbari lines: a rejection of Friday prayers, of tax collection, of kharaj farming, of deputyship to the Imam by the *faqih*, and of other duties performed by the Shi'i *fuqaha'* under the unjust ruler.[49] Qutaifi's position symbolized an Iraqi (and beyond) Akhbari-based opposition to the Karki.[50] The two trends met and enhanced the influence of each other. The final triumph of Akhbarism was brought about by other factors.

Loss and transformation

The Shi'i world in the seventeenth century was now split into three circles: a pro-Safavid Usuli domain in Persia; an independent Arab Usuli School in Jabal 'Amil; and an Akhbari realm in Ottoman Iraq, Bahrain and Hijaz. The sudden downfall of the first circle under the Sunni Afghan conquering tribes in 1722 demolished the solid, state-patronized base of the Usuli School in Persia. The endowments supporting the clerical class were confiscated, the patronage networks destroyed, and hundreds of scholarly families displaced. This situation led to 'a relative impoverishment and a decline in the influence of this group' of *'ulama* class, and 'great numbers of clergymen and merchants fled Iran for the shrine cities of Ottoman Iraq'.[51]

Migrant *'ulama* arrived in shrine cities as penniless refugees with no social contacts and networks, and converted to Akhbarism.

The other section which remained in the realm of Persia sustained a social change. They no longer sought their sole means of living within the royal court. This group moved now to foster links with the 'richer classes of the bazaar, seeking new forms of economic security'.[52] Some members of the *'ulama* families even tied themselves to the Bazaar merchants and artisans through intermarriage, viewing them as possessing powerful, autonomous guilds and social networks. Some also took on new, non-clerical functions, becoming moneychangers, money coiners, landowners and administrators; others retained religious careers. Paradoxically, this change led the *'ulama* to create an *independent financial base* delivering them from state-patronage and fostering their power and influence in later periods.[53]

Resurgence of neo-usulism

Usuli migrants in the shrine cities of Najaf, Karbala and Kazimiyya staged a comeback later in the century, first during the Zand period (1763–1779), and later in the Qajar period. Their revival is associated with the name of Muhammad Baqir Akmal al-Bihbahani (1704–1791). In Karbala, Bihbahani started his anti-Akhbarism crusade with the utmost caution and secrecy. Usulism was not only excommunicated, but the Akhbari *'ulama* had the Luti gangs at their disposal, who were used in dealing with any dissent.[54] The first clandestine cells organized by Bihbahani were confined to his family; his links with merchant and artisan networks secured the needed resources.[55] The movement gained supporters amid favourable circumstances. Shrine cities in Iraq succumbed to a plague which led to considerable casualties among Arab-Akhbari *'ulama* who, unlike their Persian peers, could not flee to Iran. The ensuing vacuum was soon filled by the rising Usulis.[56] Political developments enhanced the group. The Mamluk rule grew weaker and proved unable to control the emerging Shi'i city-states in Najaf and Karbala, which were prone to asserting their own authority. A powerful social alliance of Arab landowners, merchants, artisans (mostly Iranians) and mixed Arab and Persian powerfully-armed gangsters, formed the backbone of this autonomy. The formation of Shi'i states in Qajar Iran and Oudh (India) further entrenched the trend. The Usuli School was a legitimizing force for both newly emerging Shi'i dynasties.[57]

During the eighteenth–nineteenth centuries, neo-Usulism prospered under unusual circumstance. It was now in firm alliance with productive wealthy classes, such as the Bazzaris, the artisans and landlords, had vast social networks, and sources of income independent of state patronage. The leading core of the clerical class, together with their madrasas, were in the shrine cities of Ottoman Iraq. The new Shi'i states, the Qajar and of Oudh, were either very weak or too remote to have any direct influence on the centres of *ijtihad*. And for the first time, the *'ulama* had an instrument of coercion, the Lutis, i.e the urban gangsters in the Shrine cities who traded their security services through the monopoly of the means of violence with both the mercantile and clerical classes for money.

Centralization tendencies developed in this period, leading to the emergence of the *marja' taqlid mutlaq*, as the supreme source of religious authority. Neo-usulism reasserted the categories of knowledge, the competence of reason, *'aql, ijtihad,* the probable knowledge, together with the power categories, the necessity of emulation of living rather than deceased scholars, the payment of *zakat* and *khums* to the *mujtahids* in their capacity as vice regents of the Imam. These innovations redefined the inner structure of the Shi'i world, and laid down the cornerstone for the emergence of *marja' taqlid*, and its centralization.[58]

Tendencies towards the centralization of marja'ism

There is a general view that the first *marja' taqlid mutlaq* was Murtadha al-Ansari (d. 1864), or, possibly, his predecessor, Muhammad Hassan al-Najafi (d. 1849).[59] Informal arrangements to organize a leading core in the shrine cities preceded the inception of Ansari as the supreme learned (*al-'alam*) faqih. It is presumed[60] that the oldest forms of such leadership arrangements date back to Sayyid Muhammad Mahdi Bahr al-'Ulum (d. 1797), the disciple of Bahbahani. A division of labour was organized in which one *mujtahid* assumed prayer leadership *(salat)*, another took over judiciary functions (*qada'*), a third practised teaching (*tadris*) and a fourth issued *fatwa* and commanded emulation *(fatawa wa taqlid)*. It is not clear whether or not this design was spontaneous, but it indicates one of the persistent features characterizing the elite core of the clerical class: division.[61] A single *marja' mutlaq* as it is known today crystalized with Ansari. The term used to designate the *marja'* was clear and simple: Riyasat, meaning headship or leadership. Although the term conveys the meaning of power over subordinates, it nevertheless falls short of other terms of political power, such as *hakim* (ruler), *sultan* (monarch), or *amir* (prince).[62]

Unlike the institution of *mujtahid* of the age or sadr or sheikh al-Islam under the Safavid, the *marja' taqlid mutlaq* during the Qajar period was informally institutionalized separately from any state (Shi'i or otherwise) by the clerical class in Najaf. This disassociation freed the institution from direct bureaucratic control, but deprived it of order. The process revealed two contradicting, antagonistic, centrifugal and centripetal tendencies. Conflicting processes of integration and fragmentation ensured that *marja'ism* remained an informal, amorphously, structure-less institution.

Centralization was promoted by political, social and economic factors. To begin with, the second half of the nineteenth century was an era of political centralization which was generated by western-influenced reforms of polities: reorganization of the military (standing armies), centralized bureaucracies, state-sponsored educational systems. It was also a period of hectic commercial activity, when telegraph lines, steamboats, and other modern communication systems gradually eroded the hitherto antediluvian segmentary borders. Centralization was a social tendency of which the religious class was only a part.

The *'ulama* class was ethnically and geographically divided: Arabs, Turks, Indians and Persians. The latter were again split into two wings, with one residing in the *'atabat*, shrine cities in Memluk-Ottoman Iraq , and the other in Iran proper.

'*Ulama* in Iran wielded socioeconomic power in provincial towns. They exploited the 'political vacuum'[63] and benefited from the flow of sahmi Imam, *zakat* and other religious payments. They were directly involved in market economic activities, such as investments, landowning, and money lending;[64] they also controlled the judiciary. This caused tensions between the state and the local *mujtahids*. The Qajar state, once seeing diversity of the clerical centres of power as desirable, became more prone to bypasssing local *mujtahids* and seeking alliances with the '*atabat*-based supreme *mujtahids*, who were able to inhibit the power of the locals. Disputes between the local *mujtahids* and their clients, the merchants, over the registration of contracts, and over the injunctions by local '*ulama* of contradictory resolutions in financial and property related disputes,[65] led the merchants and various owners of goods and property to seek higher authority for arbitration. The growing state-merchants tensions increased the need of the mercantile class to attract the support of the '*ulama* in the shrine cities as a counterweight to the absolute monarchy. These factors fed into a drive towards centralization. Other aspects were also important: 'The willingness of the pro-Shi'ite Mamluks of Iraq ... to extend their patronage to Usuli '*ulama*'.[66] The attacks by the Wahabi desert warriors against Karbala also furthered the drive towards more centralization. The trend was so marked that the local *mujtahids* in Iran were turned into mere clients of the grand *mujtahid* at the centre.[67]

The disorder of the marja' system

The institution of the post *marja's taqlid mutlaq* was a 'transformation of the *mujtahids*' function from mere teachers of the madrasa to powerful figures in the life of urban centres.'[68] This lacked the creation of any sustained order of promotion, selection and appointment. Perhaps this is why Amanat calls the 'institution' of *marja'ism* an 'anarchic discipline' or says that 'the order of the clerical community ... is in its disorder'.[69]

Process of selection

The norms, procedures, methods and routine of selection have three major aspects: 1) the subjectively unified normative self-definition of the *marja' mutlaq* as provided by the clerical class itself; 2) the segmentary nature of the clerical class; and 3) the actual selection process as effected by the electoral college, such as mercantile and other urban classes or state functionaries.

1. The idealized norms of the *marja' mutlaq* were subjectively defined by the clerical class. According to al-Shahid al-Thani, the ability of *ijtihad* is based on 'comprehending the six premises which are: theology (*kalam*), methodology (*usul*), grammar (*nahwo*), syntax (*tasrif*), Arabic language (*lughat al-'Arab*) and conditions of inference (*shara'it al-adilla*); and mastering the four sources which are: the holy book, the *sunna* (tradition), *ijma'* (consensus) and the evidence arrived at through reason.'[70]

   The person of *mujtahid*, however, is restricted by ten major conditions. He should meet the following criteria: 1) adulthood (*bulogh*); 2) sanity (*'aql*); 3) belief *(iman)*; 4) justice (*'adala*); 5) freedom (*hurriyya*, i.e not being a slave); 6) masculinity *(rujolah,* being a man — women are allowed by only a few scholars to be *mujtahids* and issue a *fatwa*); 7) being alive (no emulation for deceased *mujtahids*); 8) being the most knowledgeable *mujtahid* (*al-'alamiyya*); 9) purity of birth (*taharat al-mawlid*, i.e being of legitimate parenthood); and 10) not being a lover of worldly wealth (*an la yakona muqbilan 'ala al-dunya*).[71]

   These ramified criteria are reduced by some contemporary scholars to three major conditions: being alive, being the most knowledgeable, and justice.[72]

   Lacking an institution to measure knowledge or justice, the designation of the supreme *mujtahid* was marked by many uncertainties. A plurality or diversity of centres of clerical power always existed. Scholarly fame and, coupled with it, the increased number of novices in the madrasa, is another element influencing the choice. The subjective role of the *'ulama* is related to their organizational skills and generosity in recruiting followers. In the words of one cleric, 'open-handedness' is the instrument of leadership [*al-jood 'alat al-riyasa*].

2. This class is highly segmentary. It is divided by family, city or ethnic descent. Organization of webs of wukala and emulators starts from within the family, the town and fellow students (who, again, are attracted by ethnic and town solidarities). For example, Ansari could assume the highest post thanks to the support of Arab, Persian and Turkish lay emulators. Shirazi of the Tobacco Revolt suffered a split among Azeri and Persian emulators and could not command the obedience of both Shi'i communities until the death of his Azeri clerical rival. Recognizing this reality, most *mujtahids* defined their tribal, familial, city and ethnic origins in their names.[73] This ethnic division would develop into nationalism proper with the creation of nation states in the 20th century.

Indeed, the mass of followers are divided in their loyalties along national lines; at the very least there is a general Arab-Persian divide.

3. Lay emulators, above all those with wealth and influence, such as merchants and landowners, are decisive in the selection of a grand *marja'*. Channelling sahmi imam, *zakat* and other taxes towards a certain *mujtahid*, in the event of the death of the previous *marja' mutlaq*, would be tantamount to a popular vote. State patronage, if and when translated into financial backing, would contribute to the choice. The uncontrollable preference of lay emulators remains a decisive factor.

Leadership ambiguities

The informal institution of *marja'ism* charted a zigzag course between integration and fragmentation. It lacked power structures (apart from the employment and deployment of Lutis for brief moments here and there) and was unable to contain divisive tendencies. The integration witnessed in this class during certain periods has come about as the result of pressures and forces acting from without this class itself.

The tables below shed light on these contradictory tendencies.

The period should be divided into three major political phases: the first extends from 1845 to 1920. It is a pre-modern period in which Iran was under an absolute monarchy; Iraq was subject to Ottoman and British occupation.

The second period dates from 1920 to 1960, during which modernized central states were established in Iran and Iraq in a drive to solve the agrarian crisis; the era was also marked by an increase in anti-colonial measures. In Iraq, the monarchy was toppled; in Iran, the white revolution was looming.

Phase three extends from 1960 to the present. This is the era of authoritarian, single-party or military regimes, culminating in the advent of the totalitarian Ba'th regime in Iraq, and the Iranian revolution. In each phase, *marja'ism* was sustaining mounting pressures and constraints.

Table 1
Marja' Mutlaq, mid-1845–1995: Plurality versus Single Headship

Name	Date of accession	Died	City, residence, burial	Status	Remarks
Single headship, 1845–64					
1 Muhammad Hasan al-Najafi	possibly 1945	1850[a]	Najaf	sheikh	author of *Jawahir al-Kalam*
2 Murtadha al-Ansari	1850	1864[b]	Najaf	sheikh	
First period of plurality, 1864–74[c] (diversified centres, among which:)					
3.1 Muhammad Mahdi Qazvini	?	1882	Najaf	sayyid	
3.2 Muhammad al-Irwani	?	1888	Najaf	sheikh	
Single headship, 1874–95					
4 Mirza Hassan Shirazi	1874	1895[d]	Najaf/Samara	sayyid	tobacco revolt
Second period of plurality, 1895–1908[e] (diversified centres, on the ve of the constitutional revolution)					
5.1 Muhammad Fadlullah Sharibyani	1884(5)	1904	?	sheikh	
5.2 Muhammad Hassan Abdullah Mamaqani	1895[f]	1905	Najaf	sheikh	
5.3 Mirza Hassan Khalil Tehrani	1905	1908	Najaf	sheikh	
Single headship, 1908–20					
6 Muhammad Kazim Khurasani	1908	1911	Najaf	sheikh	
7 Muhammad Kazim Yazdi	1911	1919[g]	Najaf	sayyid	under British mandate

	Name	Date of accession	Died	City, residence, burial	Status	Remarks
8	Muhammad Taqi Ha'iri	1919	1920	Karbala	sayyid	
9	Fathallah al-Isfahani (Sheikh al-Shari'a)	1920	1920	Najaf	sheikh	

Third period of plurality, 1920–35[h]

10.1	Abdullah Hassan Mamaqani	?	1932	?	sheikh	
10.2	Mirza Hassan Na'ini	?	1935	Najaf/Qum	sheikh	
10.3	Aqa Dhiaudin al-'Iraqi	?	1945	?	sheikh	
10.4	Hussain Qumi	?	1945	?	sheikh	

Single leadership, 1935–70

11	Abu al-Hassan al-Isfahani	1935[i]	1945	Najaf	sayyid	Iraq
12	Hussain Brujerdi	1945	1961	Qum	sayyid	Iran
13	Muhsin al-Hakim	1961	1970	Najaf	sayyid	Iraq

Permanent multiple centres, 1970–95
A: 1970–79

14.1	M. Abu al-Qasim al-Kho'i	1971	1899–1992	Najaf	sayyid	
14.2	Kazim Shari'atmadari[j]	?	1905–86	Qum of rank in 1982	sayyid	defrocked
14.3	Muhammad Hadi Milani	?	1895–1975	Mashhad	sayyid	
14.4	Abdullah Shirazi	?	1891–1984	Mashhad	sayyid	
14.5	Ahmad Khwansari	?	1891–1985	Qum	sayyid	
14.6	Shihab al-Din Mar'ashi Najafi	?	1900–91	Qum	sayyid	

Name	Date of accession	Died	City, residence, burial	Status	Remarks
14.7 Muhammad Ridha Gulpwayegani	?	1899–1993 Tehran	Qum/Najaf	sayyid	
14.8 Ruhallah Khomeini	1979	1902–89	Qum/Najaf/Tehran	sayyid	accorded his rank in 1963
14.9 Mahmud Taliqani	?	1911–79	Tehran/Qum	sayyid	

B: 1979—88: After the Iranian revolution

15.1 Kho'i					
15.2 Khomeini					
15.3 Muhammad Baqir al-Sadr		1930–80	Najaf	sayyid	executed
15.4 Muhammad Muntazari		1930?–	Qum	sheikh	dismissed from office as deputy leader

C: 1988–92: Post Khomeini

16.1 Kho'i					
16.2 Muhammad Ali Araqi		1994	Qum	sayyid	

D: Post al-Kho'i

17.1 Muhammad Ali Sistani	1992	1930–	Najaf	sayyid	
17.2 Ali Khamenei	1989		Tehran	sayyid	Supreme leader
17.3 Muhammad Shirazi	?	1930–	Qum	sayyid	
17.4 Muhammad Ruhani		?	Qum	sayyid	

Name	Date of accession	Died	City, residence, burial	Status	Remarks
17.5 Muhammad Sadiq Sadr[k]	1992	1999	Najaf	sayyid	nominated by Iraq; assassinated in Najaf

This table has been compiled from Abdul Hadi Ha'iri, *Shi'ism and Constitutionalism*; Fischer, *Iran from Religious Dispute to Revolution*; Abbas Amanat, 'In Between the Madrasa and the Market Place', in S. A. Arjomand (ed.), *Authority and Political Culture in Shi'ism*; M. Momen, *An Introduction to Shi'i Islam*; Elie Kedouri, 'The Iraqi Shi'is and their Fate', in Martin Kramer (ed.), *Shi'ism, Resistance and Revolution*; Mir Basri, *'Alam al-Adab fil 'Iraq al-Hadith*; Joyce N. Wiley, *The Islamic Movement of Iraqi Shi'ites* (see notes below for full bibliographical details).

a. Or 1849 (Ha'iri and Kedouri).
b. Or 1865 (Ha'iri).
c. Kedouri, Ha'iri and Joyce give no details to fill in the 10 year gap between the death of Ansari in 1864(5) and the rise of Shirazi to *marja'ism* in 1874 (Kedouri). Fischer lists both al-Qazwini and Irwani without further details. It was most probably a period of collective leadership.
d. 1894, according to Ha'iri.
e. This was a period of turmoil and inter struggle among the *'ulama*, when they split into two opposing camps pro-and against constitutionalism. Among the names of prominent religious leaders are Mazindarani, Fadhlulah Nuri, Khurasani, Na'ini, Yazdi and others.
f. Fischer gives the year 1895, a year or so after Shirazi's death.
g. Kedouri gives April 1919, Fischer 1918.
h. The names of Kashani, Muhmmad al-Sadr, al-Khalisi and others are prominent in this period.
i. Basri contends that Isfahani enjoyed his higher status for 20 years. This would modify the date of his inception to the year 1925 when he had just returned from exile in Iran.
j. The first ayatollah uzma to be stripped of his title in April 1982 by the Islamic republic in Iran.
k. Nominated by the Iraqi government in their bid for an Arab *marja'* based in Iraq. Sadr was a student of Muhammad Baqir al-Sadr, and also his relative. His nomination by quarters supported by the Iraqi government may indicate that the latter had realized the mistake they had committed with the execution of Baqir al-Sadr in 1980.

Table 2
General ratio of leadership ambiguity

Duration of ambiguity	67 years	44.7
Duration of sole *marja'ism*	83 years	55.3
Total period	150 years	100.0

Table 3
Periodic ratios of leadership ambiguity

Phase	Duration years	Single headship years	Multiple headship years	% of multiplicity
One 1845–1920	76	51	25	32.9
Two 1921–60	39	23	16	41.0
Three 1960–95	35	9	26	74.2

While the state encouraged centralization of *marja'ism* in the nineteenth century, a reverse process was developing as a result of the constant clashes between the centralized state and centralized *marja'ism*. This started under the authoritarian, modernising Reza Shah in the 1920s, as well as under the newly Sunni secularizing Iraqi monarchy. Both regimes tried to check or silence the clerical class. The state, it seems, abhorred any autonomous centre of power. The two regimes in Iran and Iraq were interlocked in bitter rivalry. The Iranian Pahlavi regime was bent on Iranizing rituals and religious teaching: *marja'ism* was brought back to Qum in order to force it into tight state control; visitations were re-routed to Mashhad and Qum, rather than Najaf and Karbala.[74] Under Muhamad Reza Pahlavi, *marja'ism* was distanced; its relocation in Arab Najaf rendered it weaker and ineffective after the Shah's bitter controversy with the *marja' mutlaq* Brujerdi over agrarian reform.[75] In all these cases, *marja'ism* was not tolerated by the state. This intolerance intensified rather than receded under the Islamic republic. Shari'at Madari and Muntaziri are cases in point. The first was stripped of his religious status as a Grand Ayatollah; the latter was dismissed from office and forced to return to his pious lecturing in his madrasa in Qum. The political institutionalization of the post of the *marja' taqlid mutlaq* under the Islamic republic could not end the age-old segmentary, multiple nature of the Shi'i religious establishment; nor could it overcome the boundaries created by nation-states. The national rivalries among the regimes weakened the nineteenth century drive towards centralization of the religious establishment.

Political turmoil exacted a heavy toll. There were four periods of ambiguity (see table 1). The first coincides with the Tobacco Revolt, and the second with the constitutional revolution. The third took place in the first decade or so of the monarchical era in Iraq, when the *mujtahids* took part in the 1920 anti-British rebellion, led the anti-referendum agitation and opposed the British-Iraq treaty; the Iraqi government, under premier Muhsin al-Sa'don, deported Na'ini, Kashani, Muhamad al-Sadr, and al-Khalisi as punishment for their actions.[76] There were ideological divisions among the clerical class, in terms of pro-and anti-constitutional debate; there were also social pressures (by their lay emulator-financers); state intervention (repressive and/or regulatory measures) was another contributory factor.

Moves towards centralization in the religious establishment produced their own dynamic counter-tendencies. As the revenues accruing to the supreme *mujtahid* increased, a clerical career became all the more attractive. This intensified competition among various contenders: the higher the number of high or medium ranking *mujtahids*, the greater the competition.

Town interests and town-based solidarities are forceful ingredients. Becoming a seat of *marja'ism* means a city can attract a greater student population, increase religious tourism, and enjoy better welfare. Noble clerical families promote such solidarities and thrive on them. Karbala, Najaf and Kazimiyya families not only competed against Qum, Mashhad and other Iranian centres of learning and visitation, but also rivalled each other. Between 1845, the time of the first recognized supreme *marja'*, and 1945, Najaf (77 years), Samarra (21 years) and Karbala (2 years) monopolized the centre of *ijtihad* and, by extension, learning. It was only in the 1920s that Qum managed to revive its madrasa system, thanks to the deportation and migration of Persian *mujtahids* from Iraq. Between 1945–1961, Qum occupied the seat of supreme *marja'ism* under Brujerdi. Najaf regained its former status for only ten years under Hakim (1961–1970). After that, the collective centres of *ijtihad* and authority spread to Najaf, Qum, Mashhad and Tehran.

Status is another segmentary feature. The proportion of Shaykhs, i.e non-Sayyid figures, was overwhelming between 1845–1920 (12 out of 16 *marja'*), yet between 1920–1995 the ratio had reduced to only one Shaykh out of 20 prominent *marja'*. This may reveal the crucial role the noble

class of Sayyids, i.e descendants of the Imams, played as a status group in
controlling and preserving hierocratic centres and structures.

Attempts at institutionalization of marja'ism: Musa Sadr, Baqir Sadr, Taliqani and Khomeini

Marja'iyya revolved around the individual or people of influence rather
than institution. Allegiance was based on local, mechanical solidarities of
the guild, the city-quarter, the clan or the tribe. Under these social forms,
Shi'i's had a dual traditional leadership: the guild master, quarter leaders
and notables or tribal chieftains on the one hand, and the sayyid, cleric or
local mullah on the other. The gradual dissolution of primordial solidarities created novel conditions under which the structureless religious
establishment appeared to be an anachronism. Different groups saw the
reformation of this traditional institution as of paramount importance.

Modern lay Shi'i argued for institutionalization in order to establish
procedures for accountability, planning and budgetary control: their aim
was to bring an end to the prevailing chaos and illegal manipulation of
assets.[77] Sensing these pressures, several initiatives came from leading
religious dignitaries.[78] Other clerics also felt the need to avoid the
squandering of resources.[79]

Several modernization attempts were theoretically and/or practically
made by Musa al-Sadr of the Lebanon and Muhammad Baqr al-Sadr of
Iraq. Real efforts were also made in post-1979 Iran.

Musa al-Sadr (1928–1978) launched his project to organize the Shi'i
community on a national, Lebanese basis. He embarked on his modernizing enterprise by establishing a vocational institute in the southern town
of Burj al-Shamali.[80] Sadr's education was originally mixed: half modern
and half clerical. His modernizing attempt was driven by his desire to
unite the three distinct Shi'i regions in the Lebanon: the tribal Biqa' valley
with its clienteles system and notable leading families, the peasant-
landlords, Jabal 'Amil, of the south, and the poor southern suburbs of
Beirut.[81] The Shi'i leadership was characterized by duality and involved
both the lay, notable families of *multazems* and landlords (al-As'ad,
Himada and others), and the weak local clerical leadership. Sadr's efforts
culminated in the institution of the Supreme Shi'i Council (*al-Majlis al-
Shi'i al-'Ala*) and the formation of a social movement, *Harakat al-
Mahrumin* (the movement of the deprived).[82] The assembly, the first
modern Shi'i institution of its kind, enjoyed legal status when it was
endorsed by parliament in 1967, but it actually began to function in
1969.[83] The organization aimed at the creation of an administrative,
bureaucratic structure for leadership, and the building of a pan-

communal assembly which would include every male holder of an academic certificate, from secondary high school upwards in it. This general assembly would become a leadership body.[84] The Supreme Shi'i Council has its bureaucratic apparatus: administration, accountancy, official records, and specialized committees; it also has a clear set disciplinary regulations and accountability. This modern institution combines bureaucratic structures and electoral representation in one.

Muhamad Baqr al-Sadr's second modernization attempt remained purely theoretical. He envisaged the creation of an organized structure to supervise the various functions traditional *marja'* usually administer through a group of protegees (*hashiya or atba'*) and next of kin.[85] In his treatise '*al-Marja'iyya al-Saliha wa al-Marja'iyya al-Mawdhu'iyya*' (The Righteous and Objective Religious Authority)[86] Sadr differentiates *marja'ism* in two ways: purpose and form.

In the interpretation of purpose, *marja'iyya* may be either *saliha*, righteous, or not, depending on the course it takes. It is *saliha* if it: 1) promotes Islam and educates Muslims; 2) creates a wide current of belief in Islam as the valid, universal system; 3) supports Islamic research in different economic, social and philosophical realms and expands the areas of jurisprudence; 4) supervises and appreciates Islamic intellectual and practical works to support the good and rectify the wrong; and 5) enhances the leading role of the *mujtahids* from the highest to the lowest ranks.

In form, *marja'ism* may be subjective, reliant on the *marja'* himself and on his personal entourage,[87] or objective, dependent on institution. The latter should seek 'the creation of an operative, planning, executive apparatus based on efficiency, specialization, division of labour, encompassing all areas of rational *marja'* work in light of the designed targets.'[88] This apparatus should consist of various standing, pedagogical, educational, research, administrative, public relations, pan-islamic and financial committees[89] and should evolve

> a code of religious authority practice. Historically the *marja'* practises his duties in an *individual* manner, hence the forces which are loyal to him do not feel they truly share his responsibilities. If the *marja'* practises his duties through a council which contains the *Shi'i 'ulama* and the *forces which represent him*, and if the *marja'* links himself [probably indicating some sort of consultation and accountability] *to this council*, the practice of religious authority would be *objective*.[90]

Within a collegiate council, the subject (person), and object, (impersonal institution) are united to preserve continuity. '*The person of* the *mujtahid* is the element which *dies whereas the object, the council, remains constant* and provides a guarantee to fill in the vacuum.[91] Hence the new *marja'* would 'not start from zero, but continue the work already commenced by his predecessor.'[92] It is not clear whether the institution should function with one authority at the helm, or if selection is based on ballot; there is also doubt over whether this institution is national or supra-national. The communal balance and political conditions in the Lebanon helped Musa Sadr achieve his aims; the situation in Iraq, however, ensured that the scheme was mere intellectual practice. In his last years, Baqr al-Sadr formed a nuclei of such an apparatus with three of his disciples, Kazim Ha'iri, Muhamad Baqr al-Hakim and Mahmud al-Hashimi, to fill in the vacuum should he be eliminated.[93]

It was in Iran that such a structural organization of religious authority could take place. Without state power, no such centralization is conceivable. Two factors formed the cornerstone of this authority: Khomeini's version of *wilayat al-faqih* and the Iranian revolution. This version is 'simple and novel' in Shi'i thought.[94] It constitutes a break with the original concept, as had been advanced by Naraqi in the nineteenth century, in that *marja' taqlid* is not seen as a counter balance to monarchy but as its substitute;[95] secondly, there 'is the idea of the *people* as a political force which can effect revolution and transformation.'[96] In other words, the concept has been expanded beyond the legal-religious to the political sphere within the context of the modern nation-state.

Thus *marja' taqlid*, the very subject of the *wilayat al-faqih* doctrine, sustained a radical change in conceptualization, function and setting. For the first time in modern Shi'i history, the post has been constitutionalized and institutionalized within the context of the Iranian state. Previously, a legislative-supervisory role was assigned to the *mujtahids* in the 1905–9 Mashruta. A committee of five *mujtahids*, elected by the parliament, was stipulated in the Fundamental Law as the body to carry out this task. Moderate *'ulama* like Shari'at Madari, were calling, in 1979, for the reinstatement of this constitutional right.[97]

After the revolution, the *wali-faqih* was given a pivotal leading role (Article II, 5 and Article V of the Islamic Constitution), and endowed with vast, legislative, executive and judiciary powers (Articles 57 and 110): to appoint or dismiss from office the President of the republic, and the supreme national security council; and to appoint six (half) of the clerical members of the guardians of the constitution; the other six would be elected by the shura assembly (Article 110).[98]

The post of *wali-faqih* is organized on an electoral bureaucratic basis. Article 107 of the constitution stipulates that either one perfect faqih is recognized by the people, or the experts, elected by the people, would identify the person or persons of the *faqih wali* and declare them for the people.

The concept of the *marja'* has also changed radically. Unlike the old *marja' taqlid*, the *faqih* is both a *marja'* (religious authority) and leader (*wali al-amr*). The terminology used to designate Khomeini differs from that used previously: he is the *faqih wali,* rather than merely the *marja' taqlid*.[99] The term *uli al-amr,* as has been noted earlier in the Tusi debate, refers to the infallible Imams and was never applied to *mujtahids* before 1979. Article 5 of the Iranian constitution reasserts this meaning: '*wilayat al-amr* and the Imamate of the *umma* is upon the just and pious . . . jurist.'[100] The supreme *mujtahid* is now declared the imam of the *umma,* the *marja'* and the leader (*rahbar*). His expertise transcends theological-juristic matters to political, administrative leadership (Article 101 of the constitution).

This change was indeed a modernizing step; however, it did not put an end to the traditional informal hierarchies, but created a conflicting duality. Shari'at Madari and Muntaziri are cases in point.[101] Khomeini's followers were well aware of this contradiction and demanded full compliance by all:

> The maintenance of order in society necessitates that when the Leader or Leadership Council is accepted, *all should obey a single authority* in social and general problems of the country within the framework of the Islamic constitution. Such *obedience* is implied in the title of '*vali-ye amr*' [*wali al-amr*] and the 'Imamate of the *umma*' and applies to *all members of society without exception, and in this respect the mojtahed and the non-mojtahid, the marja' and the non-marja' are in an equal situation.*[102]

The prevailing mood among *mujtahids* outside the realm of the *wilayat al-faqih* is best summed up in the words of Ayatollah Sadeq Ruhani: 'My duty is to say that I see Islam in danger, the *marja'iyya* is in danger.'[103] Amanat contends that the *wilayat al-faqih* doctrine was both an 'innovation as much in revolt against the authority of the secular ruler as it is against the hegemony of the emulators', who determine the *marja'* by voting through payment of religious taxes.[104] If this had been envisaged by the author of the doctrine, then the attempt had scored success on the political rather than theological level. The doctrine of *wilayat al-faqih* is held and supported by a minority of *'ulama*. It derives much of its influence from mass-politics, rather than from theological potence. The political division of the Shi'i world among various nation-states renders the institution of the *wali faqih* limited in scope and character. The Iranian *wilayat al-faqih* proponents could gain little influence in both the Iraqi and Lebanese circles: the resistance to their influence is continually growing.

Multiplicity was forced inside Iran: beyond it various leading authorities continued. Al-Kho'i was one, Sistani was another. After al-Kho'i's death in August 1992, four centres of power emerged, sharing popularity and income: Sistani (Najaf) 40 percent, Rohani (Qum) 40 percent, Khamenei (Tehran) 10 percent and Shirazi (Qum) 10 percent.[105]

Notes

1. Ha'iri, A. Hadi, *Shi'ism and Constitutionalism in Iran*, Leiden, Brill, 1977: 62.
2. Ja'far, Mulla, in A Group of Researchers, *Al-Sadr*, Beirut, Dar al-Islam, 1996: 516; Ha'iri, Kazim: 90–4.
3. *Al-Noor* monthly, no. 69, February 1997.
4. Ha'iri, op. cit.: 64–5.
5. Cole, J., in *Iranian Studies*, vol. XVIII, no. 1, winter 1985: 26–7; Cole, J., in Keddie (ed.), *Religion and Politics in Iran*, New Haven, Yale University Press, (1983): 40–6; Ha'iri, Hadi, 1977: 62–5; Arjomand, S. A. (ed.), *The Shadow of God and the Hidden Imam*, Chicago, Chicago University Press, 1984: 242–9; also Arjomand, S. (ed.), *Authority and Political Culture in Shi'ism, Albany, State University of New York Press*, 1988: 8, 305, passim; Moussavi, A. Kazemi, *Iranian Studies*, vol. XVIII, no. 1, winter 1985: 35, 44–6; Abbas Amanat in Arjomand (ed.), 1988: 101–9; Enayat, Hamid, *Modern Islamic Political Thought*, London, Macmillan, 1982 and 1988:162–3.
6. Arjomand, 1984: 122–55; Akhavi, S., *Religion and Politics in Contemporary Iran*, Albany, State University of New York Press, 1980: 10–11; Enayat, op. cit.: 167–8; Bayat, Mongol, in Esposito, John (ed.) *Islam and Development*, New York, Syracuse University Press, 1980: 90–2.
7. On the Mu'tazilite position on this score see Muruwa, Hussain, *al-Naza'at al-madiyya*, Beirut, al-Farabi, 1979: 661, 763, passim.; Fakhry, Majid, *A History of Islamic Philosophy*, London, Longman, 1980 and 1983: 43, 46–7, 49–50; on the hidden Imam, see Sachedina, Abdul Aziz Abdulhussein, *Islamic Mesianism*, Albany, State University of New York Press, 1981.
8. These are: 1) *al-Kafi fi usul al-din* by Muhammad Ibn Ya'qub al-Kulayni (d. 941 and buried in Baghdad); 2) *Man la yahdhuruhu al-faqih*, by Muhammad Ibn Babewayh al-Razi al-Qumi, aka al-Sudooq (d. 991); 3) *Tahthib al-ahkam* by Muhammad Ibn al-Hassan al-Tusi, aka shaykh al-Ta'ifa (d. 1067); 4) *al-Istibsar* by al-Tusi.
9. 'Ulum, Muhammad Bahr, *Masadir al-tashri' fi al-Islam*, Beirut, Dar al-Zahra', 1983: 120–4.
10. Ibid: 123.
11. Ibid: 124–5; See also 'Ulum, M., *al-ijtihad usuluh wa ahkamuh*, Beirut, Dar al-Zahra', 1991; Arjomand, S. A., 1984, par. 5.3.2; Moussavi, A. Kazemi, *Iranian Studies*, vol. XVIII, no. 1, winter 1985: 37.
12. Arjomand, ibid, par 5.3.2.
13. Ibid; and Moussavi, op. cit.: 37.
14. Ibid.

15. Momen, M., *An Introduction to Shi'i Islam*, New Haven, Yale University Press (1985): 87, 89, 94–5.
16. Cooper, John, in Arjomand (ed.), 1988: 263. For conditions of *ijtihad* see also chapter 10: 240–9.
17. Moussavi, op. cit.: 39.
18. Ibid: 39.
19. Ibid: 39.
20. Arjomand, S. A., 1984: 242–3.
21. 'Ulum, M., 1983: 10–14; Enayat, 1982: 167–9.
22. The Qur'an: 198.
23. The Qur'an: 198.
24. 'Ulum, M., 1983: 14–5.
25. Ibid: 15–6.
26. Ibid.
27. Momen, M., op. cit.: 189.
28. On Karki and Shahid Thani, vice-regency of the Imam, see Arjomand, Momen, Newman and others.
29. Mousavvi, A. K., op. cit.: 40.
30. 'Ulum, M. B., 1991: 251–2.
31. Cole, I.S., 1985, op. cit.: 2–32.
32. Newman, A. J., *Die Welt des Islams* 33, 1993: 60–112; also Arjomand, 1984, ch. 5: par., 5.3.1 & 5.3.2.
33. Newman, ibid: 81–9; Arjomand, ibid; also Arjomand (ed.), 1988: 6–7.
34. Arjomand, 1984, ch.5, par. 5.3.1.
35. Ibid, par. 5.3.3.
36. Ibid.
37. Ibid.
38. Al-Qazwini, Jawdat, *al-Fikr al-Jadid*, no. 1, January 1992: 208–10.
39. Mallat in his *The Renewal of Islamic Law*, Cambridge, Cambridge University Press, 1993, gives the years 1617 and 1623: 29; Arjomand, 1984, par. 5.3.3; al-Qazwini, ibid: 209–10; Cole, I. S., 1984, op. cit.; Momen, op. cit.: 117–8, 222–31.
40. Momen, op. cit.: 222.
41. 'Ulum, M., 1991: 169.
42. Cole: 13; Ulum, in Khalili, Ja'far, *Mawsu'at al-'Atabat al-Muqaddasa*,2nd ed., Beirut, Mu'asasat al-'Amili, 1987, vol. 7, part 2, Najaf: 64–71.
43. Momen: 222; Moussavi, op. cit.: 38.
44. Cole, 1985: 19.
45. Arjomand, ibid, par. 5.3.3; Momen, ibid: 222, passim; Cole, *Iranian Studies*, 1985: 6, 13,19, 21, 23.
46. 'Ulum, in Khalili, vol.7, part 2: 67–8; Cole, op. cit.: 13; Arjomand: 145, passim; Newman, *Die Welt des Islams*: 86–88.
47. 'Ulum: 175–81.
48. Arjomand: 145.
49. Newman, op. cit., p. 86–91.
50. Ibid.
51. Cole: 5.
52. Ibid:6.

53. Ibid: 9.
54. Ibid: 112–43.
55. Ibid: 20.
56. Ibid: 21–2.
57. Algar,Hamid, *Religion and State in Iran*, Berkeley, University of California Press, 1980: 33–44; Cole: 26–7; Cole and Momen, *Past and Present*, op. cit.: 117, 119–121, passim; Cole, in Keddie (ed.), 1983: 38–40.
58. Enayat, 1982: 167, passim; Momen: 223–5; Cole: 3–33; 'Ulum, in Khalili, Ja'far, op. cit., vol. 7, part 2; Najaf: 64–71; 'Ulum, 1991: 175–183; Akhavi, op. cit.: 7; Cole, in N. Keddie (ed.): 33–47; Amanat, in Arjomand (ed.), 1988: 98–132.
59. Cole in Keddie (ed.): 40–50; Mussavi, op. cit.: 45; Amanat, op. cit.; Ha'iri: 63, passim.
60. Interview, Muhammad Bahr al-'Ulum.
61. This version provided by Muhammad Bahr al-'Ulum is backed by the analyses presented by Moussavi who contends that under Bihbahani the time was ripe for the emergence of the *marja' taqlid*, but there were a multitude of powerful Shi'i figures whose rivalry prevented and delayed the emergence of this post, Moussavi, op. cit.: 45–6. The dates of the death of the prominent *mujtahids* he presents differ greatly from those dates given by Fischer and other sources, which makes any scrutinizing of these developments all the more difficult.
62. Amanat, Abbas, op. cit. p. 102; Arjomand (ed.), 1988: 8–9; Moussavi, op. cit.: 44–5.
63. Amanat, ibid.: 106.
64. Amanat, ibid.: 107.
65. Ibid.: 118. Reaction against the wealth and power of hometown *mujtahids* in Iran took also another form: anti-clerical sufi and Babi tendencies.
66. Ibid.: 103.
67. Ibid.
68. Ibid.: 102.
69. Ibid.: 98.
70. *Al-Rawdha al-Bahiyya fi Sharh al-Lum'a al-Dimashqiyya*, vol. 1: 236, in 'Ulum, M., 1991, op. cit.: 51.
71. 'Ulum, ibid.: 230–50.
72. Ibid.: 250.
73. See for example the list of Shi'i supreme *mujtahids* from the time of Kulayni in the tenth century, in Fischer, M. J., *Iran: From Religious Dispute to Revolution*, Cambridge, Harvard University Press, 1980: 252–4; see also Mir Basri, *'Alam al-adab fil 'Iraq al-hadith*, Dar al-Kalima, London, 1994.
74. Nakash,Y, *The Shi'is of Iraq*, New Jersey, Princeton University Press, 1994: 200; Akhavi, op. cit.: 30–8.
75. Akhavi, op. cit.: 91–3.
76. Wardi,Ali, *Lamahat ijtima'iyya*, Baghdad, Ma'arif Press, vol. 6, 1976: 218, 221–30. Temimi, Khalid, *Muhammad Ja'far Abu al-Timman, A Study in Political Leadership*, Damascus, Dar al-Warraq, 1996: 194–5.
77. This view has been voiced systematically by modern secular and Shi'i lay writers and activists who look for a Vatican-type of institution.

78. For Musa al-Sadr, see Cole and Keddie (1986): 161–3; also interview with Karim Muruwa.

79. Najaf, A. (pseudonym), *al-Shahid al-Shaheed,* Tehran, April 1981: 32–3.

80. Cole and Keddie, op. cit.: 161.

81. Ibid.: 162–3.

82. On Islamist Shi'is in the Lebanon, see, Picard, Elizabeth, 'The Lebanese Shi'a and Political Violence', UNRISD, Discussion Papers, April 1993; Norton, A, Ritchard and Cobban, Helena, in Cole and Keddie (eds), 1986: 137–55, 155–78.

83. Norton, ibid.: 165.

84. These details were relayed by Karim Muruwah, member of the Political Bureau of the Lebanese Communist Party, who was a member of the general assembly by dint of being a Shi'i post-graduate.

85. For a detailed account of Sadr's scheme see Najaf, A., *Dawr al-'ulama fi Qiyadat al-Umma* (The Role of the *'ulama* in Leading the Community) (n. p.; n. d.): 9–10; Ha'iri, Kazim, op. cit., vol. 2, part 2: 91–102 ; Ja'far, Mulla, op. cit.: 487–8.

86. The text of his treatise is reprinted in Ha'iri, Kazim, op. cit.: 92, passim.

87. Ibid.: 94.

88. Ibid.: 94.

89. Ibid.: 94–5.

90. Ibid.: 96.

91. Ibid.: 96–7.

92. Ibid.: 96.

93. Ibid.

94. Zubaida, Sami, *Islam, The People and the State,* London, Routledge, 1989: 18; Bayat, Mangol, in Esposito, John (ed.), 1980: 103, passim; Enayat, Hamid, in Piscatori, James, (ed.) 1983: 162–7.

95. Mussavi , op. cit.: 46–7.

96. Zubaida, ibid.: 18.

97. Abrhamian, *Iran Between Two Revolutions,* Princeton, Princeton University Press, 1982: 474; Martin, Vanissa, *Islam and Modernism,* London, IB Tauris, 1989: 120.

98. The Constitution of the Islamic Republic of Iran, Arabic Translation, Irshad Ministry,Tehran, 1st edn, 1043 H.

99. For more details on the difference between the two concepts, see Arjomand, 1988: 179, passim.

100. The translation has been reproduced from Arjomand, ibid.: 179.

101. Arjomand, ibid.

102. Arjomand, ibid.: 181 (italics added).

103. Arjomand, ibid.: 181.

104. Amanat, A., in Arjomand (ed.), 1988: 124.

105. Al-Kho'i Foundation; interviewee wishes to remain anonymous.

CHAPTER FIVE

The Nature of the Confrontation Between the State and *Marja'ism*: Grand Ayatollah Muhsin al-Hakim and the Ba'th

Pierre-Jean Luizard

The confrontation between Sayyid Muhsin al-Hakim and the Ba'th government unleashed the first mass deportation of Iraqi Shi'is to Iran by the Ba'th regime, the first arrests, exiles, tortures and executions of *'ulama*: these measures were unprecedented in the modern history of Iraq. As the events which marked this confrontation during the two years 1968–69 are chronologically well-known, this chapter deals with the various aspects which they imply and reveal.

Secularist Sunni Ba'th against Marja'iyya

It appears that the relationship between the Iraqi government and the *marja'* has been determined both by the Ba'th denial of any independent institution in society, such as the *marja'iyya*, and by the strong secularized feelings characteristic of the Ba'th rule in its early phase. Following the regime of the two 'Arif brothers (November 1963–July 1968), who showed some respect towards Islam, albeit with a strong Sunni connotation, the new Ba'th rulers of Iraq quickly demonstrated a real antagonism towards any manifestation of religion. In referring to the printed speeches Saddam Hussain has delivered on various occasions, particularly at the time of the Ba'th party congresses, it may be seen how strongly his views about religion remained influenced by Michel 'Aflaq's outlook until the early 1980s. It is only because of the war against Iran that he came to realise he could no longer ignore the religious factor: religion ceased to be a simple element in the Ba'th conception of the Arab identity and became, at least in rhetoric, a basic topic in Saddam Hussain's propaganda against both Iran and the militant Islamic movement in Iraq. But in the first years under Ahmad Hasan al-Bakr, the Ba'th contempt for religious manifestations and *'ulama* did not differ greatly from the communist stance on the subject. The discourse of the new government stressed 'progressism', 'land reform', 'socialism', and 'social and economic development'. The *'ulama* figured as a social force which was hostile to any degree of progress and attached to reactionary views. This explains why the government proceeded to confiscate religious endowments in Najaf and to ban religious processions. Some Islamic schools were abolished, recitation of the Qur'an on radio and TV was stopped, and the instruction of Islam was removed from the official curriculum in schools. Nevertheless, Islam remained the state religion in the Provisional Constitution of 1968. Article 4 read that: 'Islam . . . is the fundamental principle of the constitution'.

But Ba'th Islam did not appear in the least to be consistent with the Islam of the *'ulama*. The Ba'th party, which had become predominantly Sunni Arab after the November 1963 coup de etat, also looked upon the *marja'iyya* as a Shi'i rival, even though Sayyid Muhsin al-Hakim claimed his *marja'iyya* to be far removed from politics. The Ba'th, with an extremely narrow political and social basis, sought alliances with the Communist Party or with the Kurdistan Democratic Party, but not with the *marja'iyya*, which, although apolitical and weakened, had been the main historic challenger of the political system established by the British, of which the modern Iraqi state is the heir. But the Ba'th was very careful to overshadow this stake under its progressive, nationalist and anti-imperialist propaganda.

The Candidate of the Shah as Marja'

The circumstances under which Sayyid Muhsin al-Hakim was recognized as the absolute religious authority, *marja'* mutlaq, in 1962, soon after the death of Ayatollah Brujerdi, seem to have played a major part in the way the confrontation with the Ba'th government took place. Brujerdi died on 30 March 1961, and no single candidate proved strong enough to qualify for succession as the sole *marja' taqlid*. This vacuum was not due to any shortage of candidates, since many *mujtahids* did their best to assume that position. The most important figures among the competitors were Ayatollahs Milani (Mashhad), Khunsari (Tehran), Shari'at Madari (Qum) and al-Hakim himself (Najaf). Although the al-Hakim family's surname is Tabataba'i, a noble title for descendants of the Prophet which is common in Iran, the family had its roots in Iraq for many generations and has intermarried with Iraqis. Thus, Sayyid al-Hakim was the only Arab among the candidates. He would have been among the prominent *'ulama* opposing the

1962 land reform project in Iran, with Ayatollahs Bahbahani, Gulpayegani (Qum), Khunsari and Mara'shi-Najafi (Qum). The Shah exploited this moment of disunity among the *'ulama* to push his own designs forward.

It is an acknowledged fact that Sayyid Muhsin al-Hakim was the Shah's favoured candidate for the headship of the *marja'iyya*. The Shah, by sending a telegram of condolence to Ayatollah al-Hakim on the occasion of Brujerdi's death, tried to influence the selection of the *marja'* mutlaq in favour of al-Hakim. This choice was actually made to diminish the influence of Qum. From the 1950s, only a few individual *mujtahids* in Najaf, most notably al-Hakim and al-Kho'i, still enjoyed contributions from either the Bazaar in Iran or rich Shi'is in Kuwait. But at that time, the Shah wanted to displace the *marja'iyya* from Iran, and Muhsin al-Hakim, although not the most popular *marja'*, was known for his disapproval of Khomeini's political positions. Muhsin al-Hakim's *marja'iyya* was thus directly manipulated against the rising militant *marja'iyya* of Khomeini and, more generally, against the Islamic political movement, whose revival in Iraq dates back to the late 1950s. Muhsin al-Hakim became the new *marja'*, but he was unable to consolidate his position, especially among the *'ulama* of Qum, to be regarded as *marja'* mutlaq.

A Marja' under some Influence

The Shah's choice of Muhsin al-Hakim was also due to the old relationship between Iran and Hakim himself. Since the July 1958 anti-monarchy revolution, Muhsin al-Hakim had assumed positions in the internal Iraqi political life which ran in line with Iranian interests. During the years of Qassim's regime (almost five years), Muhsin al-Hakim supported Qassim against President Nasser's accusations of persecution against Islam in Iraq. The *marja'* also opposed unity with Egypt and Syria for fear of Sunni domination. Preventing Arab unity, however, was also an Iranian priority. But in all other matters, Muhsin al-Hakim opposed Qassim. In addition to his hostility to Qassim for being too soft on communists, he opposed the attempt by central government to diminish further the *mujtahids'* influence on sensitive issues such as matrimonial and family law. The promulgation of the Personal Status Code was received in Najaf with dismay, even by the well-established and apolitical *'ulama* such as Hakim, who played a paramount role in the opposition to Qassim's Code.

Ten days after the Iraqi Communist Party made an official request to be legalized, Muhsin al-Hakim issued a *fatwa* on 17 Sha'ban 1379/12 February 1960, forbidding affiliation to the ICP. The text of the *fatwa* was published in issue number 5 of the first year of the Najafi review, *al-Adwa' al-Islamiyya* (The Islamic

Lights). It reads: 'Membership of the Communist Party is unlawful. Such membership is in the nature of disbelief and infidelity, or it is supportive to disbelief and infidelity. May God preserve you and all Muslims from it. God may strengthen your faith and Islam. May God's peace, compassion and blessing be upon you'.

The ICP was then at the height of its influence. At that time, the wave of enthusiasm for Arab unity under the umbrella of the United Arab Republic was waning. The ICP had been in the front line in the fight against the supporters of pan-Arabism, a tendency indirectly serving the interests of Iran, but the communist influence in Iraq was also regarded by the Shah as a menace. The *fatwa* of al-Hakim against the communists, as well as his opposition to the Arab union and his hostility to Qassim's internal policy, were not in disharmony with Iranian interests in Iraq. Nevertheless, al-Hakim condemned the Iranian recognition of Israel in 1960.

As is often the case with Iraqi history, the understanding of historical events is marked by political rivalries: while some may conceive of Muhsin al-Hakim's *fatwa* against the ICP as 'new proof of his allegiance to Iran', others may point to the Grand Marja's 'objective collusion with the regime of Qassim', who at that time was trying to reduce the influence of the ICP. They may even allude to Hakim's surprising 'collaboration with the Ba'this' at the same time. The Ba'this, preparing a coup against Qassim, must have wanted to insure against any possible split within the army between soldiers, mainly Shi'is and supporters of Qassim,on the one hand, and officers, mainly Sunnis, on the other. This last assumption is quite plausible, as the Ba'th party was not, at that time, an overwhelmingly Sunni party. Shi'is continued to play an important part in the party until the coup of 'Arif succeeded against the Ba'this on 18 November 1963. This coup was, in a sense, a defeat to the Ba'th party civil wing, which was predominantly Shi'i. The repression which followed was selective in nature, and was harshly directed against Shi'i Ba'this, but lenient towards Sunnis. As a result, the Ba'th party suffered a sudden and final collapse in its internal representation of the Shi'ites.

At the time of the first Ba'th coup on 8 February 1963, the Shi'ites were well represented in the party. In fact, a Shi'i triumvirate, 'Ali Salih al-Sa'di, Hazem Jawad and Taleb Shabib, appeared to rule over the Ba'th destiny. 'Ali Salih al-Sa'di, himself an Arabized Fayli Kurd, was the Iraqi Secretary of the Iraq Regional Command, and had organized the Military Bureau of the Ba'th, which later constituted the core of the fearsome Ba'th National Guard. Shi'i Ba'thi leaders may have had some dealings with Muhsin al-Hakim in order to serve their anticommunist purposes.

Three possible interpretations of the Hakim *fatwa* against the ICP have so far been presented. In fact, all three may hold true at one and the same time, as interdependence of political and confessional (communal) factors makes Iraqi political life appear to be more a composite of overlapping interests.

During the 'Arif brothers' regime, Sayyid al-Hakim was as much opposed to the nationalisation decrees of 1964 as to the government's close links with Nasser of Egypt. The *marja'*, Muhsin al-Hakim, denounced the government's policies, regarding them as marked by a Sunni confessional stance. He refused the government's demand in 1963 to issue a *fatwa* giving permission to Muslims to fight against the Kurds. In response, the government tried to promote a false, pro-government *marja'*, 'Ali Kashif al-Ghita, who actually issued such a *fatwa* against the Kurds. But, contrary to what is sometimes alleged by pro-Hakim advocates (who wish to serve present political purposes), there is no proof that al-Hakim went so far as to issue a *fatwa* in 1966 forbidding Muslims to fight against the Kurds in the North.

Al-Hakim's Hostility to Political Islam in Iraq

As soon as he assumed his role as a *marja'* in the 1960s, Sayyid Muhsin al-Hakim undertook to build networks of agents (*wukala'*), just as he promoted his own school, which grew in importance. A new generation of young *'ulama* studied under him, from Sayyid Muhammad Bahr al-'Ulum and Mahdi al-Hakim, his eldest son, to Sheikh Muhammad Mahdi Shams al-Din, Sayyid Muhammad Husayn Fadhl Allah and Muhammad Baqir al-Sadr. Among them was Musa al-Sadr, who had moved to Najaf in 1954 to study *fiqh* under Muhsin al-Hakim. In 1960 Musa al-Sadr left for the Lebanon with the active support of his tutor and mentor, Muhsin al-Hakim.

In 1958 Muhsin al-Hakim authorized the formation of *Jama'at al-'ulama'* to fight communism. Sheikh Murtaza Al Yasin, the maternal uncle of Muhammad Baqir al-Sadr, became the first leader of the *Jama'at*. The publication of Islamic periodicals and books aimed at filling the void created in religious education by the demise of the madrasa, the traditional Islamic school. A review called *'al-Adwa al-Islamiyya'*, published by the steering committee of *Jama'at al-'ulama*, allowed Muhammad Baqir al-Sadr to publish some leading articles. Hakim's willingness to put resources of the religious establishments at the service of the reform effort helped the organisation and operation of the *Jama'at al-'ulama*. The series of recruitment meetings held in 1962 and 1963 was organized by the clerical establishment. But all these activities did not mean that Muhsin al-Hakim had converted to militant Islam: neither was he a sponsor of the Da'wa Party in Iraq. Contrary to what is generally said, Sayyid Muhsin al-Hakim did not subscribe to militancy. How could it be otherwise when we remember that Hakim owed his high religious position to the strong support rendered in his favour by the Shah of Iran, who was, on his part, challenged by a growing Islamic movement at home? Since the late 1950s and early 1960s, Muhsin al-Hakim had been one of the two senior *marja'* in Iraq. The other was the Najaf based Abu al-Qasim al-Kho'i. In October 1965 they were joined by the exiled Khomeini. When Khomeini arrived in Najaf, he was not welcomed by Muhsin al-Hakim, who demanded that the exiled Ayatollah should not involve himself in Iraqi political life. At this point, Khomeini was digesting the lessons he had learned from the failure of the 1963 uprising in Iran, and was fighting against the apolitical trend of the clerical hierarchy. Just before he left Najaf in 1978, Khomeini expressed his feelings about the period of his stay in the holy city, saying: 'I found help there, in my exile, thanks to my communion with the shrine of the Commander of the Faithful . . . but only God knows what I had to bear in this country!'.[1] By such a statement, he was not only referring to the Iraqi government's ill-treatment.

At the same time, Muhsin al-Hakim did his best to nip the Da'wa Party in the bud. The resilience of political Islam within the Iraqi Shi'i community dates back to the late 1950s, more than thirty years after the crushing defeat the clerical movement sustained in 1923, when the prominent *mujtahids* were deported to Iran by the newly-installed monarchy. High-ranking clerics, like Muhsin al-Hakim or Abu al-Qasim al-Kho'i, professed calm, and did not participate in this emerging militant movement. Their distance from political Islam further highlighted the isolation of the headship of the Shi'i religious hierarchy, together with all those clerics residing in Najaf who took no action at a time when burning issues, such as the proclamation of Israel, the question of independence or aggravating social problems were of overwhelming importance. By contrast, Musaddaq of Iran and Nasser of Egypt stood firm in the face of the western colonial powers, mobilizing people and stirring up their enthusiasm. Muhsin al-Hakim instructed his sons and novices who had been among the founders of the Da'wa Party in 1957 to leave the organization. Mahdi al-Hakim and Muhammad Baqir al-Sadr had no other alternative but to obey the marja's order.[2] Nevertheless, Muhammad Baqir al-Sadr remained in close touch with the party. Those who refused to comply with Hakim's instruction brought the marja's wrath down upon them. Muhsin al-Hakim's rejection of the Da'wa Party was first embedded in his refusal of any Shi'i political activism. But there was also another determinant in this attitude: the Da'wa Party, it seems, emerged as an independent Iraqi movement and Iran did not want to let such a movement have any influence in Iraq. Internally, Iraq was conceived of by Tehran as a natural sphere of influence and the Iraqi Shi'is were seen as the natural vector of this influence. Thus, Iran has always advocated a confessional view [communal approach] of the Shi'i question in Iraq, a method which may allow Iran to preserve its influence over the Shi'ites,. An Islamic movement which might bring Sunnis and Shi'i together in a united front, however, as during the 1920 revolt in Iraq, was abhorred by Iran. From an Iranian perspective, the rise of an Islamic Iraqi political movement, outside the sphere of Iranian influence, posed a danger, particularly when the regime of the Shah itself was challenged by strong Islamic activism from within. Muhsin al-Hakim's fight against communists, pan-Arabists and Qassim, as well as his hostility towards the Da'wa Party, did not run counter to Iran's national interests.

The Marja' as a Victim of its own Weakness

After the events of 1963, the Ba'th had become an overwhelmingly Sunni party. When they seized power in 1968, Shi'i participation had fallen to 6 percent. The Shi'i 'ulama found themselves confronted by a new government strategy, one far more detrimental to their welfare than the secularization of the British or the leftist policies of Qassim had been. Muhsin al-Hakim was involuntarily dragged into the war that the Ba'th government had declared against the marja'iyya. Paradoxically, this confrontation gave a decisive boost to the nascent political Islam that Muhsin al-Hakim had condemned during his life.

The close links between Muhsin al-Hakim and Iran under the Shah seem to have been exploited by the Ba'th government with some opportunism. The first move came in the form of a confrontation between Najaf and Baghdad over the establishment of the university at Kufa. The project had been part of the great expansion of the educational system in Iraq. The leaders of Najaf, who saw the establishment of a university in the neighbouring historic city of Kufa as a worthwhile opportunity, pressed the issue forward and were successful in raising the necessary funds from wealthy Shi'i businessmen. Administrative stalling on the Kufa project was accompanied by an increased curb on political activity throughout the country. In retrospect, it is clear that the central government could not tolerate a project which rendered close control by the repressive apparatus difficult, but its rejection of it could not openly be directed against an educational endeavour. The government started to attack circles of Najaf with the charge of involvement in an 'Americanization conspiracy'. As early as 1969, Muhsin al-Hakim found it necessary to protest to the Ba'th against what he termed its 'degradation of the religious leaders' in the holy cities. Muhsin al-Hakim was understandably angry and efforts to patch up the quarrel between him and the Ba'th proved useless. He was reportedly 'on strike', when the government chose to send an *'alim* from the *Kashif al-Ghita* family as 'a delegation of Najaf' to Lebanon in 1969.

In the spring of 1969, the government was engaged in a diplomatic contest with the Shah of Iran. The Iraqi government conveyed an official letter to the Iranian ambassador in Baghdad on 15 April, notifying Iran that Iranian navy personnel would no longer be allowed on Iranian vessels in the Shatt al-'Arab waterway. On 19 April Iran abrogated the 1937 treaty that set the border on the Iranian side of the Shatt and announced it would cease to pay tolls to Iraq or to fly the Iraqi flag in the Shatt. The Iraqi President, Ahmad Hasan al-Bakr, visited Sayyid al-Hakim and asked for his mediatory efforts with the Shah. In return, the Iraqi government undertook to stop the deportation of Iraqi Shi'is of Iranian origin, a process which had just begun. Muhsin al-Hakim refused what he considered a fool's deal. When Hardan at-Takriti repeated the request for mediation, the *marja'* declared: 'Iranians are not just a community of immigrants. They are authentic Iraqis who have been deprived of their Iraqi nationality in the past'.[3] After al-Hakim's refusal, the government arrested Iranian seminarians in Najaf. Minister of the interior, Salih Mahdi 'Ammash ordered the closure of the Kufa university in Najaf and confiscated the university's operating and endowment funds. Strict censorship was imposed on religious publications. When Hakim intervened on behalf of the seminarians, the government 'allowed' them to leave Iraq. The first wave of deportation of Shi'is to Iran was unleashed at the end of April 1969, only to be followed by others: 13,000 Iraqis of Iranian origin were deported to Qasr Shirin and Khosraw. From Najaf, Muhsin al-Hakim led a protest movement. Nevertheless, some 20,000 Shi'is, accused of being Iranians, were rounded up and dumped at the Iranian border. On 6 May 1969 Hardan al-Takriti visited al-Hakim in Najaf. The meeting occurred in the presence of al-Kho'i and other senior *mujtahids*, with the exception of Khomeini, who was excluded at Muhsin al-Hakim's request.[4] Once again, the government requested al-Hakim's mediation with Iran, on the condition that the deportees would be allowed back into Iraq in return for bringing the 1937 treaty with Iran back into operation. At this point, Khomeini approached Muhsin al-Hakim, urging him not to fall into the trap. Giving the impression that the *marja'* was acting as an Iranian agent in Iraq, argued Khomeini face to face with al-Hakim, would not be in the interests of the *marja'iyya*.[5]

At the beginning of June 1969, Muhsin al-Hakim led a motor procession of *'ulama* and merchants from Najaf to Baghdad in protest to the government's action and against the regime's maltreatment of the Shi'i *'ulama*. It is claimed that Ayatollah al-Hakim forbade membership of the Ba'th party and sent his son, Mahdi, to advise Shi'is across the country of his position. But such a 'prohibition' seems unlikely. No *fatwa* is available to that effect. Al-Hakim's refusal to act as a mediator with the Shah triggered the government's campaign against him. His son was the first target. With Muhammad Bahr al-'Ulum, another close collaborator of his father, Mahdi al-Hakim fled the country before the death penalty could be inflicted upon him.

During Muhsin al-Hakim's extended stay in Baghdad, thousands of Shi'is came to pay homage to him. Khayrallah Tilfah, then governor of Baghdad, also visited al-Hakim to repeat the government requirements once more. On 10 June 1969 large contingents of police surrounded the house of al-Hakim in Baghdad. Sayyid al-Hakim was sent back to Kufa. There, he chose to retire from public life as a sign of protest. On 15 June 1969, Khomeini visited al-Hakim at his house, urging him to put an end to his isolation and to take up the government's challenge.[6]

The government responded by waging a campaign against the Ayatollah's son, Mahdi, and then publicly accusing him of being an Israeli spy. This charge was also used to prevent people from visiting Hasan Shirazi, who delivered a speech critical of the government's actions at Husayniyya Tehraniyya in Karbala. On 18 May 1969, Hasan Shirazi was arrested in Karbala, imprisoned for nine months, tortured and then exiled. On the same day, a famous Sunni 'alim, Sheikh 'Abd al-'Aziz al-Badri, was also arrested in Baghdad: on 15 July he died under torture. Thus, al-Badri, who spoke in Mahdi's defence from the minbar of a Sunni mosque, and was arrested and killed in jail, became the first martyr of the contemporary Islamic movement in Iraq. Al-Badri's death was considered to be a message to those Sunnis who had been inclined to join forces with Shi'is: his tortured body was deposited at the door of his home.

With other 'ulama, Mahdi al-Hakim had submitted a petition to the government, asking for the end of censorship on religious publications and denouncing false accusations. But the government proceeded to confiscate new religious endowments in Najaf. Representatives and associates of al-Hakim were arrested, and all religious processions were prohibited. The Shi'is responded with anti-government demonstrations in Najaf and other cities, including Basrah, where they lasted for three days. A group of Shi'is moved to answer the government's actions with counter violence. On 9 June 1969 there was a meeting between Sayyid al-Hakim and some leaders of the Da'wa Party: in the course of this, the *marja'* prompted them to avoid any confrontation with the government.[7] Late in 1969 government forces raided the homes of 'ulama in Najaf and Karbala. Some of them were arrested and tortured. On 20 January 1970, the government announced it had uncovered a conspiracy involving the Shah of Iran and a group of officers. Some forty-four people were executed. Between 21 January and 8 February 1970, Khomeini delivered a series of seminal lectures in Najaf, later published in English under the title of 'Islamic Government', advocating his concept of *wilayat al-faqih*, and criticising inactive 'ulama.

Muhsin al-Hakim was seriously ill at that time. Back from London, where he had been treated in hospital, he finally died on 2 June 1970. Refusing government transport, a large crowd of half a million mourners accompanied his bier the 110 miles from Baghdad back to Najaf. The procession quickly developed into an anti-government demonstration. President Ahmad Hasan al-Bakr tried to join the mourners, but was obliged to withdraw as the crowd started to chant: '*Esma', ya rayyis, Sayyid Mahdi mu jasus!*' ('Listen, oh President, Sayyid Mahdi is not a spy'). Followers of al-Hakim divided themselves among the two living marja's, Muhammad Baqir al-Sadr and Abu al-Qasim al-Kho'i. But the worst for the al-Hakim family had yet to come. In May 1983, three years into the war with Iran, ninety members of the family, ranging from the ages of nine to seventy-six, were arrested because one member, Muhammad Baqir al-Hakim, was the leader of an Iraqi opposition coalition in exile in Tehran. On 20 May six leading members were executed before the watching eyes of other relatives. Of the remaining eighty-four, only five elders were eventually released. Seventeen sons and grandsons of Muhsin al-Hakim were to be executed. On January 17, 1988, while attending an Islamic conference in Khartoum, Sudan, Mahdi al-Hakim was assassinated by hitmen driving an Iraqi diplomatic vehicle. Thus, the al-Hakim family was the first victim of the war the Iraqi government waged against the *marja'iyya*.

The government of Ahmad Hassan al-Bakr gained all the benefits from the close links between Muhsin al-Hakim and the Shah. The request the Ba'th government made to Sayyid al-Hakim to be a mediator between Iraq and Iran seems to have been a trap the *marja'* could not escape from: had he accepted the request, he would have appeared to be an Iranian agent in Iraq; but when he declined he exposed himself and his family to repression. In both cases, he had no way of avoiding the resolution of the Ba'thi government to defeat the *marja'iyya*.

Notes

1. Harakat al-Mujahidin al-'Iraqiyyin, *al-Imam al-Sadr wa ara'uhu al-siyasiyya* (The Movement of Iraqi Mujahidin, Imam al-Sadr and his political stances), last page, quoted in: Babakhan, Ali, *L'Irak: 1970–1990, Déportation des chiites*, Paris, 1994.

2. *Sawt al-'iraq* (The Voice of Iraq) no. 128, 15 April 1993, *Hiwar shamil ma' Sayyid Murtaza al-'Askari* (A complete dialogue with Sayyid Murtaza al-'Askari): 4.

3. *Mudhakkarat Hardan 'Abdu'l-Ghaffar al-Takriti* (Memoirs of Hardan 'Abdu'l-Ghaffar at-Takriti), Organization of Iraqi Muslim Students: 37, (there is no proof of the authenticity of this text).

4. Al-Mu'min, 'Ali, *Sanawat al-jamr, Masirat al-haraka al-islamiyya fi al-'Iraq 1957–1986* (Years of Ember, History of the Islamic Movement in Iraq 1957–1986), Dar al-Masira, London, 1993: 93.

5. Ibid.

6. Ibid.: 101–102.

7. Ibid.: 99.

CHAPTER SIX

The Rituals of 'Ashura: Genealogy, Functions, Actors and Structures

Ibrahim Haydari

The rites and rituals of 'Ashura to commemorate the death of the third Imam of the Shi'ites, Imam Husayn, are among the oldest and most important religious and folkloric traditions in the Muslim and Arab world. These rituals are the representation of the Tragedy of Karbala, the bloody 'Taf' battle which took place on 10th October 680 between Imam Husayn and his followers and the army of Umayyade caliph, Yazid bin Mu'awiya. The battle ended with Imam Husayn slain, together with a number of his household members and advocates.

These rituals are known as 'aza', a condolence ceremony for the bereaved to share their sorrow and grief. In time, however, the Husayn 'Aza' assumed a very unique meaning and evolved into a fixed ritual, observed annually in both Muharram and Sufar lunar months, to express grief for the death of the Imam, and to pay homage to his tomb forty days after the date of martyrdom.

This is not a transitory tradition: it is closely linked with the prevailing sociopolitical conditions. As a result, these rituals have become deeply rooted across time and space in the popular memory, creating a collective consciousness. In its turn, this collective consciousness would re-emerge in the different forms of rites, rituals and folkloric ceremonies, expressing the depth of the sensibilities of the Muslims towards 'Ashura.

The constituent structure of Arab-Muslim society has been and still is, essentially, religious. Most sociopolitical oppositional movements in Islam have been motivated by and geared towards religiously determined objectives. This also applies to social, economic, political and kinship relations.[1]

Rituals and Rites

Some writers often confuse rites and rituals; others tend to differentiate between them. In this light, rites may be conceived as symbolic practices signifying unique aspect of the religious creed, because their meaning and objects are related to religious procedures. It is a well known fact that many recurrent daily practices become, by dint of their mere repetition, customs and traditions, but some of these may develop into established rites or rituals. Rites include all ceremonies which express certain behavioural patterns and social values, whether or not these patterns and values are religious or mundane. In both cases, they function to constrain practices, verbal communication, social behaviour and individual manners, to achieve certain ends.

In Islam, rites are sacred because they have a religious function to fulfil, such as daily prayers, fasting, pilgrimage to Mecca, or are related to life-passage ceremonies such as marriage, birth, circumcision, or death and burial. These rites may remain outside the empirical realm, beyond the reach of experimentation, since they are related to doctrine and value systems. Rites, however, represent the practical aspect of worship, and are geared towards the other-world, the deity: hence their sacred character.

Rituals, by contrast, are symbols which do not necessarily carry religious signs and meaning. They may have a religious colouring, but they are linked to custom, convention, tradition, myths, legends and folkloric history. Only when such rituals overlap with rites proper do they rise to the level of creed and become sacred.

Rites and rituals comprise both individual and collective behaviour, handed down from one generation to another. They demand the observance of strict regulations which can only be changed slowly and with great difficulty. In fact, without such rigid regulations and controls, rites and rituals lose their religious value or social significance. Most rituals are related to the sacred and practised as such. This is because the sacred is the overwhelming catalyst in both rites and rituals, and it is this relation with the sacred that generates an intimate correlation between what is social and what is religious, or both the mundane and the sacred.

Rites and rituals, in fact, incarnate or revive a sacred experience through which a liaison with the sacred universe is sought, in order to bring back the internal equilibrium to the straying and tormented soul of the human agent, to relieve the soul from anxiety and angst, or to provide answers to fate-related questions. In this context, rites and rituals become defensive methods and mechanisms related to the haram (taboos), used to wash away guilt and evildoing. They develop into instruments of self-purification in the face of menacing existence.[2]

Behind the rituals lurks a psychological catalyst: this has a paramount role to play in directing human action to continue these rituals, particulaly in times of social, economic and spiritual crisis. Thus they express the ideas and emotions of various individuals.

If we examine rituals from a sociological point of view, we need to move away from the religio-dogmatic to the socio-psychological level in order to interpret them, and analyse them as systems of meaning in social, economic, political and juristic terms.

To begin with, rituals are subconscious mechanisms connected with abrupt changes, whether in the self or in the external world; as ceremonies they do not necessarily stem from religious dogmas, but from the need to elevate these ceremonies themselves to the level of creed out of the search for subjective and objective ends. These ends may include defending the ego, protecting it from hazards, emphasizing its threatened or alienated identity; or self-purification from sins and misdeeds, compensation for impotence, regression and failure in conditions of weakness, humiliation, debacle; or rebuilding those socio-cultural fabrics torn or damaged by the creep of modernization.

Cultural anthropology has already established that various traditional peoples and groups resorted to their rituals in the face of colonization in order to defend their culture and combat alien influences, while rituals were instrumental in the resolution of the struggle of value systems stemming from dependency and cultural invasion. All these facts may help to explain the subjective and social factors which have kept rituals alive.[3]

It is interesting to note that most participants in the 'Ashura rituals, notably those who practise self-flagellation and head-cutting, do not usually observe religious rites such as prayers, fasting, or pilgrimage to Mecca; some do not even hesitate to commit what may, in the eyes of religion, count as the worst of sins and crimes, and that is because they are absolutely convinced that their participation in the ceremonial rituals of 'Ashura is sufficient to wash away their sins, since their Imam, Husayn, would intercede with his grandfather, Prophet Muhammad, on their behalf, on Doomsday.

Of course there is always a disparity between the belief in something and its practice in reality. Various actors do not, in point of fact, necessarily commit fully to religious duties and instructions: they even sometimes breach them in the name of religion itself. In other words, Muslims do not uniformly carry out their religious imperatives as required. There is also a divergence between conscious and committed religiosity on the one hand, and popular religiosity on the other. The latter tends to cling to the form, as opposed to the content. This formal bent may exceed the limits of rationality into the realm of 'heresy'. Heresy, or in the Arabic term *bid'a*, is a renovation which, from the point view of orthodox religion, verges on blasphemy: it may involve innovation, development and advancement if and when it is related to social, scientific or literary phenomena. Whatever the case might be, *bid'a* is a religious attitude which does not coincide with the approved texts of the creed, of the Qur'an and the Sunna of the Prophet in Islam. Thus it may be seen to deviate from the main stream. This definition applies to rituals which, by dint of their nature, are so resilient that they may adapt, shift or mutate in accordance with the imperatives of the time. And in this adaptation and mutation rituals prove to be more flexible and resilient than religious rites, and more dense with changing meaning, shifting ends and renewable and innovated social, mythical and other functions.

Functions of the 'Ashura ritual

To specify and examine the various functions inherent in the 'Ashura and other rituals, it is of crucial importance to analyse them as social action imbued with meaning and having different socioeconomic and political dimensions. It is no less important to study the historical conditions under which these rituals emerged, developed, produced and reproduced.

In general, social action is an instrument of interaction with, competition with, struggle against, or identity with other members of a community; it is an instrument of adaptation and harmony with others with which to secure conservation of life and continuity. On the other hand, rituals are cultural responses to human needs, representing suppressed or unfulfilled emotions, desires and expectations. Rituals may also represent man's spiritual realm, his social philosophy, or his deep-rooted values, which are ingrained into the collective imagination. They aim at consolidating the *spirit de corp*, collective solidarity, unity, reciprocal support by means of providing the community with a set of essential, common concepts and a set of socially accepted values, and principles and moral norms. These sets, put together, form an all embracing ethical system which determines the attitude of individuals towards each other, the attitude of the community towards others, harmonizes the relationships with the external environment, and motivates individuals to innovate and create new ways of thinking and novel methods of work and behaviour in their daily life.

Structure of the Rituals

Husayn rituals have different forms and formations. The first among these is visitation, or pilgrimage, to the shrines of the Imams and saints, particularly the shrine of Imam Husayn in Karbala. These visitations are symbolic actions denoting condolence, loyalty and devotion to the Imams. Pilgrims also seek the mediation of the saints with the deity, in order to wash away sins.

The second major ritual is the 'aza' assembly for mourning over the martyrdom of Imam Husayn. Historically, the rituals related to the 'aza go back to the Karbala Battle in which Imam Husayn was slain. The first group to commemorate his death were people from the city of Kufa, who felt great remorse and a deep sense of guilt over the fate of the Imam, the grandson of their Prophet.[4] Supporters of the household of 'Ali, the Shi'ites, met on the day of 'ashura to mourn and weep for Husayn. This custom began late in the 7th century, and it did not materialize into a ritual until the 10th century, when the first 'wailing assembly' was organized, together with a recital of the story of 'The Death of Husayn'.[5] When Buwaides assumed power in Baghdad, their sultan, Mu'iz al-Dawla, supported the Shi'ites. For the first time in history, an official ceremony to commemorate the death of Husayn was organized on 'ashura day in 963 BC. The suk was closed down, and contingents of wailing women marched the streets of Baghdad while beating their cheeks and reciting grief-laden death poetry.[6]

From that moment on, the Shi'ites of Iraq observed this ritual. Similar ceremonies were organized in Egypt under the Akhshidis and the Fatimids,[7] and in Safavid Persia in the 16th century.[8]

Successive dynasties, the Umayyad, the Abbasid and the Ottomans, tried to put a stop to or restrict these Husayni assemblies, yet the ritual developed and spread further. Over time, it took the form of popular, folkloric ceremonies, and assumed various shapes: assemblies of condolence, processions of condolence, and passion plays, particularly in mid and southern Iraq.

During different epochs, Husayni rituals were also instruments of political opposition in Islam, developing into a multitude of oppositional and protest movements against the official ideology. According to circumstances, rituals revealed implicit or explicit forms of resistance. And the more prohibitions, the more radical they tended to be. This has been the case in Iraq since the mid 1960s. Rituals evolved into political forums and mass demonstrations, absorbing various motifs from Islamic, Arabic and world political events, and developing into a significant 'cultural infrastructure'.

Politicizing of Husayni Rituals

Like any folkloric or ceremonial expression, the Husayn assemblies and processions of condolence have been exploited, manipulated, deformed or reformed by various social groups, political movements or religious currents. This manipulation or reform tended to inject slogans and symbols reflecting cultural preferences, views or specific interests into the rituals and ceremonies.

Successive Iraqi governments, concerned with long-term ideological and political issues, intervened in both these rituals and the religious institutions. Cooperation was sought with ritual organizers and clerical dignitaries, to stem any latent potential political opposition in the ceremonies or the institutions.

In 1949 the British embassy in Baghdad, for their own political ends, tried to intervene in the Husayni rituals. The British intelligence officer, Mr.Ray, wrote a letter to the general director of security service in Iraq advising him that the fight against communism could not be won solely through the use of security: other methods were needed, including what the officer called the 'religious approach', which would serve the government and please the Shi'ites, who formed the majority of the population. His advice was to make the utmost use of the Husayni rituals for these ends.[9] In fact, the British embassy did more than simply offer advice. Shortly after the Second World War, when prices were high and provisions were short, the embassy provided some of the organizers of the Husayni rituals, the so-called 'ru'asa' mawakib' (heads of processions), with sufficient quantities of tea and sugar for use during the ceremonies, and a quantity of white sheeting, usually used as 'shroud' for those machete-for-head-cutting-holders in 'Ashura.[10]

The British had specific political ends to promote: these included their desire to win over the Shi'ites, create political differences and social and communal schisms, and to divert the anti-British common national struggle.

Iraqi political parties, in their turn, took part in these Husayni rituals to spread their own political slogans, to distribute clandestine literature and to agitate the masses. Communists and democrats tried, directly or otherwise, to manipulate these occasions. Various mass organizations of the left, such as Peace Advocates, the Students' Union and the Youth Organization managed to exert control over some of the rituals. Communists and socialists were partly motivated by a radical conception of Islam as a 'revolutionary religion with socialist traits'. This interpretation or notion of Islam had various bases: the just nature of Imam 'Ali, the primitive socialism of Abi Dhar al-Ghifari, the rebellion of Imam Husayn and his martyrdom for the sake of justice and freedom. The crucial role played by Shi'i thought in diverse radical social movements in Islam was also reinterpreted in support of modern socialist ideologies.

In fact, the Iraqi communists did their best to avoid igniting religious sentiments or showing any disrespect to religious dogmas. Hence they actively took part in various assemblies and processions. Their participation in the *Mawakib* (procession) *al-'Abbasiyya* in Karbala, for example, led people to describe it as 'The Red Procession'. In fact, this procession was renowned for its leftist slogans and politically charged, emotive folkloric verse.

By the same token, workers' trades unionists and professional association or guild leaders were keen on attending and using the Husayni rituals to further their own political and social ends. In the early 1950s, for example, activists of the peace movement in Iraq not only distributed leaflets for their cause, but collected signatures for their petitions, or organized forums and discussions, coupled with revolutionary poetry and slogans.

The major contributors to the rituals, merchants, tribal sheikhs, notables and influential dignitaries, spend handsomely to finance these ceremonies. They do not do this simply for charitable ends: there are also private interests at stake, such as elevating their social or religious status, or gaining some economic benefits. The contributor donates money on his own behalf, or for the benefit of his corporation or office: this is tantamount to a propaganda exercise or an advertisement for his work and merchandise, enhancing his reputation as a trustworthy person at the same time.

Economic dimensions

During the season of the 'Ashura ceremonies, economic activities are hectic: prices of hotel accommodation, in restaurants and coffee-houses soar. Unemployed wanderers and poor people seize the opportunity to get a temporary job and spend these days attaining relief from social hardship and tensions. Marginal, *lumpen* elements, outcasts and other similar social groups look to this opportunity to attend the 'wealthiest' of assemblies: they stick by the side of the assembly orators, surround the pulpit, or act as chorus/protégées. In time, this marginal, food-seeking group develops into an entourage for the orator, who in turn becomes their patron. With him they secure a sizable amount of provisions: food, drinks and cigarettes. The orator, the poet and the *nawa'i* – singer – who narrate the historical accounts of Imam Husayn's martyrdom, make their living, partly at least, from these assemblies: not in terms of wages, but in gifts, tips and rewards.

The articulate, vocal orator (*rawzakhoon*) gets bigger cash benefits. These may vary from one orator to another, and from one place to another, according to specific standards. Some orators, notably those who carry out services in the Gulf, have become rich; others lead a humble life, especially when they have no other means of subsistence. During the 'ashura ceremonies, some orators and *nawa'i*-singers may receive necklaces of bank notes, donated by the wealthy to express their admiration of the melodic voice or the text of the death-poetry, or both.

A great number of community members volunteer to collect donations by hand from commercial concerns, companies, restaurants and coffee-houses: they also install donation-boxes and use the proceeds to finance processions and assemblies under the auspices of procession chiefs, community notables and other dignitaries. Volunteers carry out this service in order to gain rewards in the afterlife and display their loyalty to Imam Husayn.

Such donations underline a communitarian charitable solidarity which extends over other areas, such as providing various services during the 'ashura period. It is worth noting that since the 1960s, processions and ceremonies have been organized along the lines of the guild, the old professional unions of the artisans and merchants, such as blacksmiths or butchers. Each ceremony has its own mosque or *husayniyya* as its headquarters. Sometimes other places are used for the community ritual.

Attendants of the Husayn ceremony come from from various social, economic and cultural groups. Their common ground is their allegiance to 'Ali's household, and their willingness to convey their condolences; some, however, may come only out of curiosity or for leisure purposes. Accordingly, ceremonies turn into an all-in-one religious, social or entertainment-oriented festival. This applies particularly to merchants and artisans, who work the whole year round and enjoy the ceremony as a holiday. Poor people take part in the rituals for the sake of the Imam. They offer services to members of the community attending the ceremony, such as cold water in the summer, tea and sweets, or perfume.

On the other hand, orators, ceremony organizers, *nawa'i*-singers or poets make the utmost use of these ceremonies to serve their own interests, often making a good living. More often than not, hypocrisy and insincerity characterize such profit-oriented behaviour, be it in the form of material privileges or inflated social status. One way or another, the assembly orators and singers 'promote' the standing of the ceremony organizer. Usually, all supplications at the end of each ceremony are heaped on the organizers, who, by dint of the value these assemblies have in the community, use them to enhance their social status. That is why almost all wealthy and religious-minded Shi'i merchants tend to organize such assemblies or contribute to them handsomely.

Historical Narratives and Reform Attempts

The orators of the Husayni condolence assemblies and processions do not observe the factual, objective realities of history. Their narratives are devoid of concrete facts and are full of legends, myths and incredible and irrational representations. By such reconstruction of the stories, the orators preserve the formalities of the ceremony and reduce it to a dead, spiritless ritual. While such legends and myths are discarded by the educated and enlightened, they are adored and hailed by the common, illiterate people, who prefer painful, tear-jerking legends – even if they are untrue. Pain, sorrow and tears are as important as the melodic voice of the *nawa'i* singer.

Mythical narratives, however, were severely criticised and scrutinized by various thinkers and clerical reformers, who advocated the need to change and purify the Husayni rituals from what they conceived as 'negative and detrimental practices', such as head-cutting with machetes and swords, self-flagellation with iron chains and metahistorical narratives: their aim was to develop the rituals into a refined cultural practice that might match the 'sublime level' of the creed.

As this criticism waned and lapsed, the 'negative' practices revived, spread and increased. The *'ulama* had, in fact, been so weak that they did not issue any *fatwa* to stop the 'negative' aspects. Even today, there is no specific *fatwa* issued by the grand *mujtahids* which endorses or prohibits such practices. The reasons behind the *'ulama*'s timid attitude are broad, ranging from concern for their own interests, to their fear of arousing the ignorant public against them, or their underestimation of the real detrimental effects arising from the mythical traditionalism enveloping the Husayn rituals. The *'ulama*'s reliance on religious taxes, the *khums*, paid by the public to them or their deputies, *wukala*, spread across town and countryside, was behind the fears of the people. Sunni *'ulama*, as is widely known, receive their stipends from the ministry of religious endowments, in their capacity as civil servants or state-employees: that is why their are generally submissive to the wishes of the government; their Shi'i peers, however, are more critical of and oppositional to the government.[11] But while community finances enabled the Shi'i *'ulama* to defy the government, they have become dependent on the public at large

A number of rational *'ulama*, however, stood fast in their scrutinizing of the mythical, superstitious aspects of the rituals. Although they were being attacked and accused of blasphemy and heresy, they nevertheless intensified their efforts for reform. One of the earliest of these was attempted in Najaf in 1935 by the *Jam'iyyat Muntada al-Nashr* (The Society of Publication Club). In 1936, the society launched a school in Najaf. The aim was to teach preaching in rituals and to cleanse them from myths and misconceptions. These efforts were met with stiff resistance, particularly from the assembly orators, and some conservative, orthodox clerics who feared that reform could threaten their own interests.[12]

Earlier, a dashing attempt at reformation was taken by Sayyid Hibat al-Din al-Shihristani (1883–1967). He wanted to eliminate various superstitions and practices, such as the habit of transferring corpses from remote areas for burial in Najaf, which involves health hazards with the decomposition of corpses, particularly in the summer. He also thought that certain ceremonies and rituals of 'ashura contradict the spirit of Islam, and disapproved of those *'ulama* who did not speak their true minds before the public, for fear that mobs, driven by sound and fury, would harm them.[13]

Another reformer, Sayyid Muhsin al-Amin al-'Amili of Lebanon (1865–1952), denounced various aspects of the 'ashura popular rituals, which, in his opinion, are alien to religion, such as head-cutting. He also forbade processions during 'ashura: he believed they involved satanic impiety.[14]

Both reformers of the 1920s were the target of a fierce smear campaign by outraged mobs, who accused Shihristani and al-'Amili of being apostates and heretics. The 'ulama class split over the issues of reformation. Some endorsed the efforts, other opposed the banning of any rituals. Verbal attacks erupted between the two opposing camps, and the assembly orators and mosque preachers incited the public against the prohibition fatwa.[15]

One example of this took place in Najaf. Sayyid Abu al-Hasan al-Isfahani, the grand marja' at the time, issued a fatwa in 1926 prohibiting head-cutting during the 'ashura rituals; he was supported by Sayyid Mahdi al-Qazwini of Basra. Mirza Muhammad Hasan al-Na'ini (1861–1936), in opposition, proclaimed his fatwa endorsing the rituals. He was backed by ten grand 'ulama.[16] The Na'ini fatwa intensified the rage of the general public against the reformer, Muhsin al-Amin. This was also an opportunity for various dignitaries to settle their accounts with their adversaries or smear them.

The issue of head-cutting, tatbeer, was critical. The 'ulama who did not object to this practice did, however, distinguish between hard head-cutting which could cause death, and soft head-cutting leading to minor injuries. They all supported the other aspects of the 'ashura rituals, provided that they were not outrageously farcical, or antagonistic in character, or involving dishonest acts. Yet they did not explicitly mention head-cutting in their fatwas. The head-cutting and self-flagellation rituals were not known in Iraq before the beginning of the twentieth century. The former originated in Turkish Azerbaijan, the latter in India. The Iraqi historian, Kazim Dujaili(1984–1970), maintains that until the early twentieth century, Arabs in Iraq did not practise head-cutting and self-flagellation; and that these acts were carried out by Turkomans, Dervishes and Iranian Kurds.[17] Sayyid Muhammad Bahr al-'Ulum (b. 1931) confirmed that in Najaf there had been only one procession for tatbeer, and that this was the one organized by the Turks.[18] Both practices were only narrowly observed by non-Iraqis.

With the expansion of processions in 'ashura after the Second World War, Sheikh Muhammad Khalisi (1890–1963) launched a crusade in the early 1950s against superstitions and heresy so that Islam could retrieve its original essence. Khalisi's sermons on the Friday prayers enraged conservative 'ulama and Husayni assembly orators, and Husayni procession organizers and their entourages. His campaign led to fierce confrontations between his advocates and adversaries.

Mobs of traditional Shi'is assailed the prominent sociologist, 'Ali al-Wardi (1913–1995), after he had criticized certain rituals and ceremonies during 'ashura: he was particularly concerned with the self-torturing involving iron chains and machetes, and he denounced the superstitions advanced by Husayni assembly orators and preachers in the service of the Sultan.[19] Wardi's writings on these issues triggered varying responses. Conservatives denounced him as a 'heretic and renegade': they said that he should be prosecuted and censored, that his books should be destroyed, and that his very existence should be eliminated. Open-minded people, however, viewed him as a social thinker and reformer: they argued that his writings comprised exciting, critical endeavours to purify 'ashura rituals from superstition, myths, legends and fantasies far removed from historical reality.

In fact, various contemporary *ulama* and *mujtahids* opposed head-cutting and self-flagellation, such as Imam Sayyid Muhsin al-Hakim (1889–1970), Sayyid Muhammad Baqir al-Sadr (1930–80), and Sayyid Muhammad Husayn Fadhl Al-lah, among others. Other Shi'i *ulama* from Iran took a similar stand, including the ' supreme guide', Ayatollah Khamenei, who prohibited head-cutting under severe punishment.[20]

While the 'ashura ceremony is full of sublime religious and legal symbols for the *ulama*, it has evolved into an emotive funeral in popular religion, and signifies nothing save physical violence and masochistic and regressive torture of the self. The legends and fantasies incorporated into the rituals, despite their irrational and illogical nature, have been repeated by the orators of the assemblies. These myths have been imbued with a sacred garb to avoid any discussions and criticism among the Shi'is. Such fantasies involve stories ranging from supernatural events to magical anecdotes and fables. One myth says that the red line of sunset did not appear on the horizon before the death of Imam Husayn on 'ashura, and that it rained blood the moment he was slain. Another claims that when Husayn's severed head was brought to Yazid's palace in Damascus, the walls poured blood, and the blood moved towards Ibn Ziyad, the commander of Ummayade armies, who ran away while the blood shouted at him: Where art thou running, damned![21] In the text of the 'Wonder Stories' (Kitab al-Qisas al-'Ajiba') we come across some of the most bizarre of the fables: a lion shedding tears over the fate of Imam Husayn while watching a Husayni assembly. In another, a herd of animals comprising lions, deer, oxen, tigers, leopards, and jaguars wail in terrified voices to express their sorrow over the fate of Husayn. The animals then roll over and cry until dawn.[22]

Reformers and modernists have attacked these aspects of rituals as stupefying, control mechanisms imposed on the mass of people to ignite the most basic instincts and emotions and gear them towards communal strife and away from important issues. Psychologically, as mentioned earlier, the rituals are emotional defensive mechanisms to relieve social, political and psychic pressures and suppressed emotions. They may also discharge aggressive tendencies and sense of guilt through the collective ritual. They are, in the final analysis, a form of negative and temporary rebellion against the self, society and the powers that be. From this sociological approach, we may conclude that the Husayni discourse, at least in part, is directed towards the 'self' or the 'us', a mechanism which may be used as a form of defence, punishment or avoidance. Self-abasement is an inward rebellion designed to avoid conflict towards others, the external. It is a social process of conformism and restitution.

As the discourse and mechanisms involved in these rituals have penetrated the depths of collective ego and memory, it is hard to eliminate them through political means, because they have attained a sacred status: at the same time, they have become interwoven with socio-political reality.

Notes

1. Al-Haydari, Ibrahim, *Zur Soziologie des Schiitschen Chiliasmus*, Freiburg, Kalus Schwarz Verlag, 1975: 112.
2. Fromm, Erick, *Psychoanalyse et Religion*, Paris, Epi, T.F.: 138.
3. Tawalbah, Nur al-Din, *al-Din Wal Tuqus wal Taghyirat* (Religion, Rituals and Change), Beirut, Dar 'Uwaidat, 1988: 34–40.
4. Ibn Qutaiba, *al-Imama wal Siyasa* (Imamate and Politics), Cairo, Mustafa al-Babi Publishing House, 1949.
5. Shihristani, Hibat al-Din, *Nahdhat al-Husayn* (The Husayn Uprising), Baghdad, 1966: 173.
6. Ibn al-Jawzi, *al-Tarikh al-Muntazam* (The Order of History), vol. 7, Haydar Abad, 1939: 23. Also, Metz, A., *Die Renaissance des Islam*, Heidelberg, Universitat Buchhandlung, 1968: 65; Busse, H., *Chalif und Grosskoenige*, Berlin, Franz Steiner Verlag, 1949: 42.
7. Kahhala, Omar Ridha, *Dirasat Ijtima'iyya fi al-Usur al-Islamiyya* (Social Studies of the Islamic Ages), Damascus, al-Matba'a al-Ta'awuniyya, 1973: 216.
8. Browne, E., *A Literary History of Persia*, Cambridge University Press, 1959: 20.
9. Batatu, Hanna, *Old Social Classes*, Book Two, Arabic edn, Beirut, Mu'asasat al-Abhath al-'Arabiyya, 1990: 361.
10. Al-Haidari, ibid.: 176.
11. Wardi, Ali, *Dirasa fi Tabi'at al-Mujtama' al-'Iraqi* (A Study in the Nature of Iraqi Society), Baghdad, al-'Ani Press: 334–436.
12. Shubbar, Hasan, *Tarikh al-'Iraq al-Siyasi al-Mu'asir* (Contemporary Political History of Iraq), Baghdad, 1990: 334–436.

13. Shahrastani, Hibat al-Din, *'ulamauna wal Tajahur Bil Haqiqa* (Our 'ulama and Truth-Telling), *al-'Ilm* Review, Najaf, 1930: 266.

14. Al-Amin (al-'Amili), Muhsin, *al-Majalis al-Saniyya* (Illuminated Assemblies), vol. 1, Najaf, al-Sadiq Library, 1954: 6–7.

15. Khalili, Ja'far, *Hakatha 'Ariftuhum* (Dignitaries I Knew), vol. 3: 299, Qum, Iran, Manshurat al-Sharif al-Radhi, 1412 H.

16. Al-Hilli, Abdul Hussain, *al-Sha'air al-Hussainiyya fil Mizan al-Fiqhi* (Hussaini Rituals in View of Islamic Jurisprudence), Damascus, al-Taff Library, 1955: 211–14.

17. Dujaili, Kazim, *'Ashura fil Najaf wa Karbala* (Ashura Rituals in Najaf and Karbala), *Lughat al-'Arab* Review, Baghdad, Matba'at al-Adab Press, 1913: 287.

18. Interview with Sayyid Muhammad Bahr al-Ulum, London, June 1997.

19. Wardi, Ali, *Wu'az al-Salatin* (Clerics of the Sultan), Baghdad, Matba'at al-Ma'arif Press, 1954: 254; indem, *Mahzalat al-'Aql al-Bashari* (The Farce of the Human Mind), Baghdad, Matba'at al-Rashid Press, 1955: 299.

20. In June 1994, the Iranian ministry of the interior issued a prohibition of head-cutting during the 'ashura ceremony.

21. Al-Muqarram, Abdul Razzaq, *Maqtal al-Husayn* (Husayn's Demise), Najaf, al-Irshad Press, 1963: 293–5.

22. Dast Ghaib, Abdul Hussain, *al-Qisas al-'Ajiba* (Incredible Narratives), Beirut, Mu'asasat al-Nu'man, 1990: 101 and passim.

CHAPTER SEVEN

The Religious Composition of the Kurdish Society: Sufi Orders, Sects and Religions

Sami Shourush

Kurdish Religion(s)

The Kurds themselves believe that their ancestors were Zoroastrians.[1] Zaki says that the Kurds maintained their adherence to Zoroastrianism until the rise of Islam.[2] We also find today that many Kurdish customs and religious rituals contain elements of the roots which go back to Zoroastrianism or to even earlier religions.[3] Fire, for instance, is accorded special respect among the Kurds, particularly the Yazidis and 'Kaka'is'. Even Muslim Kurds consider it repugnant to spit into fire.

The common religious and spiritual heritage which the Kurds' ancestors shared with other Indo-Iranian tribes has helped to shape some of the patterns of contemporary Kurdish religious observance.

However, many of the sects and the Sufi orders which are widespread among the Kurds conceal some of the more important manifestations of these influences, either for fear of persecution from others, or out of a desire to preserve their religion or sect and to protect it from the distortion and deviation which could result from a more open expression of their religious identity.

After the Emergence of Islam

The first Kurdish contact with Islam goes back to the year 18 AH, after the Muslims captured Takrit and Halwan.[4] It appears that the Kurds were not especially receptive to the new religion. A campaign led by al-Azra bin Qais embarked from Halwan in the direction of Shahrazur. That crusade failed, and was followed by a second under the command of 'Ataba bin Farqad: this was only able to capture those areas after bloody battles and intensive engagements causing many deaths among the population.[5]

During the Islamisation of the area, the Kurds participated in many rebellions and acts of insubordination against the Islamic authorities. For example, they took part in the Khawarij movement, in the rebellion of 'Abd al-Rahman bin Ash'ath during the reign of the Caliph Marwan bin 'Abd al-Malik, and in the disturbances which erupted during the reign of the Caliph Abu Ja'far al-Mansur.[6] However, as Islam became entrenched throughout the Middle East, a majority of Kurds came to accept it as their religion. This, however, does not mean that they totally abandoned their earlier beliefs.

Most Kurds in Iraq (approximately 80% of the total) adhere to the Sunni sect and follow the Shafi'i theological school. A minority, following the Hanafi theological school, is concentrated in parts of the Kifri and Klar areas of the Kirkuk plain; there is a also a Shi'i minority in the extreme southern reaches of Iraqi Kurdistan, in addition to groups of Shi'is around Kirkuk and west of Arbil.

Sufi Orders among Iraqi Kurds

The Sufi Orders among Iraq's Kurds are especially influential. According to al-Azzawi,[7] the Kurds adhere more strongly to the Sufi order than other ethnic groups. Two well-known Sufi orders predominate. These are the Qadiri and the Naqshabandi Orders, which have powerful and numerous centres among Iraqi Kurds. Indeed, it may be argued that the Kurdish support for these two orders in past centuries has strengthened them and helped them to flourish. It is commonplace to find adherents to these two orders from outside Iraq, such as in India, Pakistan, the Arab countries and Malaysia, converging on the orders in Kurdistan. Furthermore, the Sahrawardi Order is also said to have had a base in the Kurdish areas. According to Azzawi this was because Shaykh Shihab al-Din al-Sahrawardi originated from adjacent areas. Azzawi states that the Qadiri and Rifa'i Orders came to predominate at a later date.[8]

An Iranian author, Muhammad Ra'uf Tokali, who has written on the history of Sufism in Kurdistan, says that it was initially the Nurbakhshi Order which arrived and spread through al-Sayyid Muhammad Nurbakhsh, brother of Shaykh 'Isa. One might speculate that the strength and extensive spread of Sufism among the people of Kurdistan may have a basis in the ancient Indo-Iranian religious roots of the Kurd, in such religions as Zoroastrianism.

The Qadiri Order

This order is named after its founder, the great Sufi 'Abd al-Qadir al-Gailani (470–561 AH or 1077–1177 AD) whose *kunya* ('*agnomen*') is Muhi al-Din Abu Muhammad. Baghdad was the first centre where the order spread: it is not known exactly when and how the order came to Kurdistan. Some Kurdish Qadiri adherents believe that Shaykh Abd al-'Aziz al-Gailani (532–602 AH or 1140–1211 AD), son of Shaykh 'Abd al-Qadir, introduced it to the region of 'Aqrah in Iraqi Kurdistan.

Kurdish Qadiri mythology also has it that Shaykh Abd al-Qadir al-Gailani himself passed through the Kurdish village of Nirkezjar in the region of Hawraman and stayed there, it is said, at the residence of Shaykh Mustafa at Nirkezjari, while on his way from his home in the Persian district of Gilan in order to continue his religious studies.[9] Other accounts say that the Nurbakhshi Order had a following among the Barazinjis until the time of Shaykh Bab Rassul (d. 1054 H). After that time the 'Alawiyya Order is said to have increased its following among the population in Kurdistan. The latter was a branch of the Khalwatya Order, and it is believed to have maintained a strong following among Kurds until the time of Sayyid Muhammad al-Nodahi, who died in 1126 H,[10] and who was known as the 'red mutch'.[11] It is also said that around that time, Sayyid Ismail Qazanqaya, son of Sayyid Muhammad al-Nodahi, left for Baghdad, where he met Shaykh Ahmad al-Ahsa'i who introduced him to the Qadiri Order, which he then brought to Qazanqaya[12] in the Qara Dagh district of Kurdistan.

According to Zaki, it was Shaykh Ma'roof al-Nodahi (1166–1258 H) who was taken into the order by Shaykh Ali Dolah Pamu, who in turn had been admitted by Shaykh Ismail Qazanqaya.[13] Zaki, however, says that it is not known who brought the latter into the order.

Adherence to the Qadiri spread rapidly among the Kurds during the seventeenth and eighteenth centuries AD, especially after the rise of the Kurdish principality of Baban.[14] It appears that both the Ottoman and the Baban rulers were deeply aware of the social importance of the clergy in Kurdish society, rewarding them with offerings ranging from large landed estates and substantial endowments of *Awqaf* for the benefit of the *takaya*, to food. To illustrate this, one may cite an example from the time of the Ottoman-Russian war of 1292–1293 H, when the Ottoman Sultan granted Kaka Ahmad al-Shaykh (1207–1305 H), a Qadiri Shaykh from the Barzinji family, five villages in return for the use of a Kurdish army sent by the Shaykh under the command of his grandson, Shaykh Sa'eed, to aid the Ottomans against the Russians.[15]

One of the most prominent Qadiri personalities among the Kurds is Shaykh Mahmud al-Hafeed, who acquired his status by his leadership of the Kurdish political nationalist movement during the first half of the twentieth century. He was the son of Shaykh Sa'eed, son of Muhammad, son of Shaykh Kaka Ahmad al-Shaykh.

After the defeat of the Ottoman Empire, Shaykh Mahmud concentrated his efforts into politics and the leadership of the Kurdish movement. During the first half of the century, the Qadiri centres throughout Iraqi Kurdistan had played an important role in the religious life of the Kurds. One such centre was established in the Kirkuk area by Shaykh Abd al-Karim Kasnazan (died 1317 AH), which is presided over at present by his grandson (Shaykh Muhammad bin Shaykh Abdul Karim K. bin Shaykh Abdul Qadir bin Shaykh Abdul Karim Kasnazan.)[16] Other Qadiri centres (*takaya*) are those of Shaykh Mustafa bin Shaykh Abdul Karim dara Karma, known as Shaykh Kaka, in Arbil and Shaykh Ibrahim Chuesa in Qadir Karam near Kirkuk.

The Talabanis have close links with the Qadiri order. They claim that they joined the Qadiri Order in the first half of the eighteenth century[17] and according to Tawakuli, Abdul Rahman Talbani hadmore than 50,000 Kurdish followers in the first half of the nineteenth century.[18]

From 1920–1940 the Qadiri centres did not offer much support to the rebellions of Shaykh Mahmud, himself a Qadiri Shaykh. Generally it could be said that the Qadiri Centres, at that stage, were immersed in the quiet practice of their Sufi rituals, to the extent that even the Iraqi government treated them sympathetically. In 1958, in the wake of the Iraqi republic, Shaykh Abd al-Karim Kirpchna had to leave the country for Iran. However, he returned after only a few months, and rebuilt his *takya* in Kirkuk. He died in the late 1970s.

The Naqshabandi

It was during the days of the leadership of the great Qadiri Shaykh, Ma'rouf al-Nodahi, chief of the family of the Barzinji Shaykhs, that the great Kurdish Sufi, Mawlana Dhia' al-Din Khalid Bin Ahmad Bin Husayn, better known as Shaykh Khalid Naqshabandi, came to prominence. The Naqshabandi Shaykh was born in the Qara Dagh area, part of Sulaymaniyya province, in 1776 AD (1190) and he died of the plague in Damascus in 1827 AD (1242). He was a descendant of the Mika'ily clan of the Jaf tribe, and he is famed for having introduced the Naqshabandi Order from India to Kurdistan, having spent years studying this order in India. However, some surmise that the Naqshabandi Order had spread among the Kurds before the emergence of Mawlana Khalid, but that he had reintroduced it after a period of inactivity.[19]

Shaykh Khalid, it is suggested,[20] was not content to see his order expand in the Sulaymaniyya region alone: he rapidly extended its influence and was joined by the religious Shaykhs of several Kurdish districts, including those of Barzan and Nahri and Shamzini[21] districts of Northern Kurdistan (Turkey) and the Shaykhs of the Hawraman region (Byara and Tawila).[22] The new order also gained adherents among some of the Qadiri Shaykhs, such as Yihya al-Mazuri.[23] Following the death of Mawlana Khalid, the Naqshabandi has, unlike the Qadiri, developed and maintained theological links with some of the Batini sects, such as the Haqqah, which have a following among the Kurds. The tension between the Naqshabandi and Qadiri orders eventually prompted the Naqshabandi Shaykh Khalid to leave Sulaymaniyya twice, once for Baghdad and later for Damascus, where he died. The true causes of the conflict between the two orders are not entirely clear, but it is probably true to say that the Qadiriyya have generally been closer to the ruling authorities, both the Ottomans and the Babani princes. Moreover, the Qadiriyya seems to have relied upon a wide network of feudal Shaykhs and Aghas: the latter were at odds with the majority of the more enlightened townspeople and those engaged in more modern economic activities which were evolving in Kurdish society. The Naqshabandi gained adherents among the latter social groups. Therefore it seems that religious conflicts were impregnated with social content.[24]

The conflict between the Qadiri and the Naqshabandi first arose after the return of Shaykh Khalid to the town of Sulaymaniyya from New Delhi. Shaykh Khalid had stayed with the Indian Master Abdullah al-Dahlawi, and the Princes of Baban accorded him the religious title of head of the 'ulama.[25] It appears, however, that the Babani Princes eventually backed the Qadiri Shaykhs and removed Shaykh Khalid from the leadership of the 'ulama, offering that position to Shaykh Ma'rouf al-Nodahi. Conditions deteriorated to a dangerous extent, forcing Shaykh Khalid to flee from Sulaymaniyya for Baghdad.[26]

The Shaykh's exile did not end the dispute between the two Shaykhs and the two orders. No sooner had Shaykh al-Nodahi died, than the Babani governor called upon Shaykh Khalid to return to Sulaymaniyya, and the conflict erupted again during Kaka Ahmad al-Shaykh's leadership of the Qadiris.[27]

It seems that this time, Shaykh Khalid preferred to emigrate voluntarily: shortly afterwards, he settled in Damascus for the rest of his time. Hawar[28] states that the conflict between the two Orders did not end with the deaths of Shaykh Khalid, Shaykh Ma'rouf and Kaka Ahmad al-Shaykh, but that it continued through the periods of the Qadiri Shaykh Mahmud al-Hafeed (1884–1956). This is reflected in the conflicting positions taken at different junctures. For example, Hawar[29] points out that the Qadiri Shaykh Mahmud's relationship with the Naqshabandi Shaykhs of Byara and Tawila was tense during the time of Mahmud's rule. The adversaries of Shaykh Mahmud did not participate in his rebellions against the British.[30] Furthermore, Shaykh Mahmud was not on friendly terms with the Shaykhs of Nahri and Shamzini. The later Shaykhs are said to have given no assistance whatsoever to Shaykh Mahmud or to his family when he was exiled to India in the early 1920s; nor did they help him after his second period of governorship when he took refuge in the border area.[31]

Hawar considers it possible that the cause of the cool relationships between Shaykh Mahmud and Sayyid Ahmad Khanqah can be attributed to their respective adherence to opposite sides of the Qadiri-Naqshabandi divide.[32]

The religious situation was given considerable attention by the Ba'th Party after it seized political power in Iraq in 1968. In its regional policy in Iraqi Kurdistan, it appears to have made strenuous efforts to win the Kurdish Sufi centres over to its side, or at least to drive a wedge between those centres and the Kurdish political movement which demands national rights for the Kurdish people. The growth in strength of the armed Kurdish movement and the intensification of the conflict between Iraq and Shi'ite Iran at the political level up until 1975, and again during the Iran-Iraq war between 1980 and 1988, have played a role in this Ba'thist effort to win over the Kurdish Sufi orders. The Iraqi government is aware that with backing from the Kurdish Sufi *takya*, it could deprive the armed Kurdish movement of considerable popular support.

Government interest in the Kurdish Sufi centres and *takaya* was evident from repeated official prompts to the local administration to be attentive to the needs of the *takaya*, and to accede to the requests of the Shaykhs of the orders. The government also tends to allocate substantial funds to meet the expenditure of the *takaya* and their Shaykhs. The other side of this policy is that the sons and other relatives of Shaykhs and heads of *takaya* have often been required to form armed detachments to defend government authority and fight the Kurdish peshmarga. These detachments were to be composed of their followers,[33] and of those laymen who tend to congregate around the *takaya* and to accept the authority of the Shaykhs and their sons.

The government has given priority to the establishment of friendly relationships with the Qadiri *takya*, because this order has a wide following among the Kurds of Iran and good relations with them could have yielded useful support for Iraq in its war (1980–1988) against Iran.

There may be other reasons for this policy emphasis, not least that the Qadiri order retains many followers in the Arab areas of Baiji, Takrit, Heet, and Dur, all of which lie to the west or southeast of Kirkuk. Kirkuk is of vital strategic importance to the Iraqi government. The city's ethnic and religious mix weakens the government's claim to Kirkuk as an Arab city separate from the Kurdish heartland. Indeed, Izzat al-Duri, the Iraqi Vice-President, is known to be an adherent of the Qadiri Order and a follower of the *takya* of Shaykh Ibrahim Jawisa in Qadir Karam near Kirkuk.

Religious Sects among Iraq's Kurds

There are many religious sects among Sunni and Shi'i Kurds. In general, we can classify them as follows:

The Haqqah Sect
General observation of the two main Sufi orders among the Kurds reveals that the Qadiri Order has maintained its unity despite having numerous Sufi Centres, while the Naqshabandi Order has generated several separate Sufi orders. One of these is the Haqqah sect which was founded in 1920 by the Naqshabandi Shaykh 'Abd al-Karim bin al-Haj al-Shaykh Mustafa bin al-Haj al-Shaykh Ridha al-'Askari, better known among the Kurds as Shaykh Abd al-Karim Shadala, after the name of his village.

According to one Kurdish source the Shaykh was born in 1310 H (1892–3) and died in his village in 1942.[34] A. al-'Askari,[35] from a Haqqah family, who lives in London informs me that the name Haqqah is derived from the frequently recurrent Sufi concept of *Haq.* (truth), and is used to mean God. He adds that the Haqqah were initially called the '*Haq Shnasan*' sect, i.e. those who know 'Haq'. The Sufi teachings of the Haqqah are not laid down in writing because it is said that members of the sect have felt compelled by Muslim theological pressure to conceal its fundamental teachings. These are said to be based on social equality, truthfulness, effort, distance from base acts, and indifference towards the Islamic obligations of the fast and prayer. Opinions about the Haqqah differ widely: some consider it a new religion 'based on reincarnation and metempsychosis and promiscuity'.[36] This opinion reflects a common trend in Muslim lands to make bizarre allegations about such heterodox sects. Others[37] consider it a purely Sufi movement. A third group of scholars maintains that it is essentially a movement which expressed the interests of peasants in the Dokan area against social injustice, for social and economic equality, and for fraternity among its numbers.[38] Dr Rasul[39] adds that the Haqqah is a peasant movement which has absorbed old and modern theological and socioeconomic ideas and rituals.

It is worth noting here that the area of Sargalu (near Shadala), the home of Shaykh 'Abd al-Karim Shadala's ancestors, was a lively Naqshabandi centre and remained so after the founding of the sect, attracting some Sufis and Batinis[40] to its vicinity. It is said that Mirza Hussain 'Ali al-Mazendarani, the founder of the Babi faith in Iran had to stay in a cave near Sargalu, where he used to attend Sufi assemblies in the lodges, Khanqas of the Naqshabandis.[41] The origin of the Haqqah movement in this particular area may not be unconnected to the stay of Mirza Hussain, or to the short stay of Shaykh Khalid al-Naqshabandi in the area.

The Haqqah movement, which initially began in the villages of Shadala, has spread to many other villages in the provinces of Sulaymaniyya and Kirkuk such as Sargalu, Jalawla, Haladen, Qarank, Yakhsamar, Molan, Tobzawah, Omarqom, Saydara, Kalka, Sumaq, Joblagh, Khorkhora Mulla Safi and Kani Tu in northwest Sulaymaniyya, and Kanibi, Qazlow, Bogurd, Kalisa, Illela and Bulqamish, all around Kuwaisanjaq, and Aghler Dalawa, Klawqut and 'Askar, Goptapa in the area of Garmian near Kirkuk.

Although the areas populated by the Haqqah are known, there are no accurate data on the actual numbers of adherents. The Haqqah themselves, including Ahmad 'Askari, would put their own numbers at 15–20,000.[42] Shakir Fattah,[43] a former chief Administrator of the Nahiyah (Sub-district) of Chem Chemal, says that members of the Haqqah were living in more than 35 villages in the district.

The Haqqah have had somewhat problematical relationships with the Kurdish large landowners (*Aghas*) in the area of Pjdar, who have tended to be either orthodox Muslims opposed to Sufism, or even members of the Qadiri Order. However, the Haqqah people themselves do not appear to have been the cause of any serious problems among the Kurds. Jamal Baban,[44] another former chief administrator of ChemChemal around the middle of the twentieth century, says: 'During my administration of the area, I never, ever once, heard of the Haqqah initiating any fighting or disturbance in the area, and I never heard of them burning a field or house or kidnapping a woman, although such incidents were numerous and not unusual. Indeed, I never saw any member of the Haqqah in a police station. They never complained about anybody and nobody ever complained about them'.

According to local Naqshabandi tradition, Shaykh 'Abd al-Karim was the last Naqshabandi Murshid (guide) in his area. Therefore, on his death in 1942, the Shaykh did not name a successor, and a three-sided disagreement emerged among the Haqqah.[45] First there were the followers of Mam Reza, brother of the late Shaykh 'Abd al-Karim, who claimed the position of guardian of the sect. This claim was met with hostility by some members of the sect, and particularly by Mam Reza's own relations, so he was forced to leave Shadala and to settle in the village of Kalkasumaq about 10km to the northwest of Shadala. In fact, the majority of the Haqqah people followed him. Other groups of Haqqah people followed Hama Sur, who had served in Shaykh 'Abd al-Karim's mosque and claimed the guardianship of the sect. The followers of Hama Sur also left Shadala and settled in the village of Klawqut in the Kirkuk region. When they left Shadala, according to al-'Askari, there were around 200 of them.[46] As for the third group of the Haqqah, they were those Sufis, especially the relatives of the Shaykh, who preferred to follow the teachings of their grand Shaykh without accepting a new guardian for the sect. This group became known as the 'Shaykh's adherents', and were led by Shaykh 'Abdullah bin Shaykh Mustafa al-'Askari. They stayed in Shadala, by the tomb of Shaykh 'Abd al-Karim Shadala.

Mam Riza

The split between the three groups lasted only a few years. All three eventually recognized the right of Mam Reza to accede to the leadership, but each continued to live in its own village and maintained its independent pattern of social, religious and economic life. Thus, some time after the death of Shaykh 'Abd al-Karim, a majority of members of the Haqqah sect agreed that Mam Reza (1905–1961) should administer the religious affairs of the sect. Mam Reza followed his brother, the Shaykh, in preserving the sect and its Sufi teachings.

However, under Mam Reza, the sect underwent a deep social transformation. Mustafa al-'Askari,[47] who is the son of a Haqqah Shaykh, says that 'Mam Reza had become convinced that the Haqqah sect had to be organised on a different basis which would include a social struggle and which would take the sect outside the narrow confines of sufism'. With this interpretation of the Haqqah faith, Mam Reza was very close to the Kurdish peasant movement which was then spearheaded by the Iraqi Communist Party. Mam Reza gave his movement socialist principles which were spreading during the period of the Second World War. Edmonds states that in 1944 'the Mutasarrif of Arbil suddenly arrested Mam Reza who lived in Kalkasumaq on the Arbil side of the river opposite Dokan'.[48] According to A. 'Askari, Mam Reza could not remain in the village of Shadala for two reasons. Firstly, because the sect had begun to split from within after the death of Shaykh 'Abd al-Karim, and Mam Mirza had become tired of the stresses within the sect. Secondly, the original population of the village of Shadala, i.e. those who were Muslims unconnected with the sect, began to resent the presence of the headquarters of the movement in their village. In fact, the Qadiri Shaykhs and large landowners from nearby Bashdar began inciting them to expel the Haqqah from the village. Mam Reza then moved away from Shadala with a majority of the Haqqah and settled in Kalkasumaq, a village adjacent to the western side of Lake Dokan, where he built a Khanqah.

The Haqqah sect began to face persistent accusations from people in Kurdistan: it was alleged that they were promiscuous and participated in annual sexual orgies. These emerged after Mam Reza and his group's settlement in Kalkasumaq and his announcement of a social programme which encountered opposition among landowners and religious Muslims from outside the sect.

The programme which indicates the basic outlines of Mam Reza's thought may be summarized as follows: fraternity, support for what is right, truthfulness, a sense of commitment, financial contribution (with every member required to pay a monthly due to cover the expenses of the *Khanqahs* and *takaya*, mutual consultation, freedom for women, honesty, cleanliness and orderliness.[49]

Hama Sur

Although Hama Sur died as recently as 1987, little is known about his background and ancestry. The Kurdish author, Muhammad al-Mulla 'Abd al-Karim, in a note he wrote for Mustafa 'Askari's book, refers to 'Mulla Salam Tarikkhor' and says: 'his [Hama Sur's] ancestry is not known, but it is said that he is from the "Alan" and "Siuail" area',[50] which is east of Sulaimaniyya close to the Iranian border. However, Rasheed Muhammad 'Ali, writing in an article in the Journal *'Karwan'*[51] states that Hama Sur had himself asserted that he originated from the Mawat area. Apart from these accounts, there are some strange rumours about the origins of this Kurdish Sufi. Such rumours usually originate with intolerant Muslim writers. According to Shaykh Hussain Khanqah, Hama Sur was one of three followers of the Haqqah who had been known to enquire into the question of God's existence. These were usually solitary figures who were not concerned that ordinary believers should know anything of their affairs. Living in isolation, they did not pray and considered prayer as a form of surrender to worldly commitments. Such devotees also waited for the Mahdi to return and let justice predominate in the world.[52]

At Klawqut, Hama Sur established one of the strangest religious beliefs. On the one hand, he glorified his community, emphasising its fraternity, social equality, joint effort, communal ownership of land, tools and items of everyday life, and the abolition of the use of money in transactions among members of the sect. What was astonishing, however, was the evident non-fertility of the women of the Hama Suri sect. Procreation of members of the sect ceased when the Hama Suris arrived in Klawqut in the first half of the 1940s. Whether the Hama Suris use a method of contraception or are celibate is not known to outsiders. Neither Hama Sur himself, nor his followers, have provided a rational explanation for this phenomenon. They remain secretive about the motive for their actions. Rasheed Muhammad 'Ali asked Hama Sur about the wisdom of non-fertility. His reply came in the form of a recitation of a Qur'anic verse which says: 'Thou should learn that thy wealth and thy sons are cause for sedition'.[53] However, the real reason for this phenomenon may be different. It might not be far-fetched to relate it to the Mancheasim religion which existed in western Iran in the third century BC. Mani held that the best course for the individual was to renounce fertility as fully as possible, and to lead a gentle, ascetic life, dying celibate, so that his own soul might go to heaven, and he would have had no part in perpetuating the misery of human existence on earth.[54] Hama Sur also says: 'By God, he who does not close the eye that sees the world, cannot open his other eye to be able to see God'.[55]

The second difference between Hama Surism and Mam Rizaism is reflected in the form of socioeconomic organization practised by the Hama Suris in their daily life.

Narrowing the social divide between rich and poor was one of the basic principles of the teachings of Shaykh 'Abd al-Karim Shadala. His brother, Mam Reza, also adhered to this principle, but Hama Sur gave it a much wider dimension. For instance, members of the sect in Klawqut used to divide the day's work communally among themselves on the previous evening. Early next morning, they gathered outside Hama Sur's house to specify the duties of each of them. All members contribute their earnings to the joint fund. They spend from that fund under the supervision of the responsible member. The sect owned agricultural implements communally and members ate the same diet. The sect maintained this social and economic organisation until most of its members aged or died, and in the absence of reproduction, it could not survive as a community any longer. Hama Sur himself was one of the longest survivors of his sect when he died in 1987. Affairs of the sect are now administered by Hama Sur's successor, Hasan Zaini, but the surviving adherents number a few dozen, who live among others of the Haqqah and with other Muslims in the villages of Klawqut, Babilan, Haji Bikhan and Hasar, near Kirkuk. A number of other Hama Sur families are to be found in the villages of Qarnigew and Haladn to the east of Mont Pira Magrun.

The Barzanis

The name Barzan is used with reference to a small village on the slopes of Mount Shireen near the Iraqi-Turkish border, but it is simultaneously employed to refer to the large tribe which lives in that and in adjacent villages. The same name is occasionally also used with reference to that tribal confederation which includes the Zibari and Shirwani tribes among its numbers.

The Kurdish author Pirash[56] says that the term 'Barzani tribe' was not known during the nineteenth century. It is a new name which came into use after the Zibari tribe split in a bloody conflict which pitched the Aghas on one side and the religious Shaykhs on the other. As the feud inside the tribe intensified and turned bloody, the Zibaris split into two sections, one remaining supportive and subject to the Aghas, and the other going to the side of the Shaykh of the village of Barzan. Since then, the Shaykh came to be known as Barzani, with reference to the village, and his followers as the Barzanis.[57]

At the time of Shaykh Ahmad Barzani, the Barzanis used to be a distinct Sufi sect originating in the Naqshabandi Order. Pirash states that Mulla 'Abdulrahman bin Mulla 'Abdullah bin Mulla Muhammad was the first recognised Naqshabandi Shaykh to emerge and preach in Barzan in the 1830s.[58] Many followers flocked to his congregation, and he was succeeded by his brother, Shaykh 'Abd al-Salam al-Barzani, who started the line of descent of the Barzani religious leadership.

The most remarkable development in the Barzani Naqshabandi centre was initiated by Shaykh Ahmad, the elder brother of the more famous Kurdish political leader, Mustafa al-Barzani, together with the eminent Barzani theologian, Mulla Juje in 1927. It is not easy to discern the new elements and beliefs introduced by Shaykh Ahmad and Mulla Juje. The Barzanis quickly became secretive, probably because of the growth of their leadership role in the Kurdish political movement. They needed to minimise the differences and to reduce distinctions between themselves and the rest of the Kurds. Moreover, hostile governmental and tribal propaganda was utilised to slur the Barzani's reputation. This served to obscure Shaykh Ahmad's ideas.

Close attention to some of the Barzani religious rituals may suggest that this sect has revived some of the influences of the Indo-Iranian religions, and combined them with some Christian practices. For example, the veneration of the black adder, the repudiation of actions that hurt it, the prohibition of bird hunting, the expansion of the Shaykh's role in the sect's life, probably as a reflection of divine presence (Khodan – God or owner) on earth, their veneration of water sources, especially the spring in their village mosque around which myths have been developed. These are all the indications of ancient influences. The Barzani's sanction of the consumption of pig meat in the late 1920s[59] and their tendency to adopt agnostic ideas in the practice of Sufism reflects the Christian influence in Shaykh Ahmad Barzani's and Mullah Juje's message.

It is noteworthy that the district of Barzan contains numerous Christian remains, such as the relics of ancient monasteries. Christian and Jews were the early settlers of the village, and at times formed the majority of its population.[60] Thus, it is not surprising that there are Christian influences.

After the death of Shaykh Ahmad, the religious leadership passed to his son, Shaykh 'Osman. However, a mysterious schism appeared between the Barzani spiritual leadership of Shaykh 'Osman and the political leadership of Mulla Mustafa al-Barzani. Mulla Mustafa was not enthusiastic in his backing for the religious succession of Shaykh 'Osman. He apparently preferred the succession to go to Shaykh Ahmad's second son, Shaykh Muhammad Khalid. This split weakened the Barzani religious authority, and may have contributed to the emergence of Khorshid, a Barzani Shaykh who claimed his right to the religious leadership.

It appears that the long-standing quarrel between the Aghas and the religious Shaykhs which had earlier caused the Shaykhs to split from the Zibari Aghas and from what is known as the Barzani tribe, had begun to revive once more, this time in the form of a dispute between the Barzani shaykhs and the political leadership of the tribe. This conflict intensified and eventually, in early 1974, resulted in the exodus of Shaykh 'Osman and Shaykh Khorshid, together with their followers from areas then controlled by the Kurdish revolution led by Mustafa Barzani. The Shaykhs came to an understanding with the Iraqi government and agreed to live peacefully and in cooperation with its authority. The government housed the exiles in two separate complexes, one for the Khorshidis, or the followers of Shaykh Khorshid, in Qoshtapa, 15km south of Arbil, and the other at Kani Qarzala, for the followers of Shaykh 'Osman. However, in 1983, the Iraqi government arrested the males of those complexes, numbering some 8000, and then secretly executed Shaykhs 'Osman and Khorshid, together with other Barzani detainees.

Important sections of the Barzani tribe had not joined Shaykhs 'Osman and Khorshid, bur remained with their own political leadership under Mulla Mustafa al-Barzani, with the spiritual leadership of Shaykh Muhammad Khalid. Both of these took refuge in Iran after the setback of the Kurdish revolution of 1975, and the arrival of Iraqi forces in the village of Barzan in the same year.

The Barzanis therefore lost effective political leadership and Mulla Mustafa died in 1979. After that, the position of Muhammad Khalid, the Barzani's religious Shaykh, was strengthened and his political role grew. Consequently, in the first half of the 1980s, the Shaykh, with direct backing from Islamic Iran, established an Islamic Political Party named Hizbullah.

Shi'i Kurds

There are neither official statistics nor accurate estimates of the number of Shi'i Kurds in Iraq. However, their presence in the towns and villages at the southern edges of Iraqi Kurdistan such as Mandali, Khanaqin and Badra, and the existence of some Shi'i sects in the vicinity of Mosul, together with figures obtained inside Iran of the extent of deportation of 'Fayli' Kurds from Iraq to Iran after 1972, would all point to an estimate of approximately a quarter of a million.

It should be remembered at this stage that, until recently, some Kurdish tribes used to adhere to Shi'i teachings. However, those tribes emigrated from their original areas, particularly Hawraman, which then attracted Sunni settlers. Examples of tribes affected by migration of at least some of their members are the Lak and Kalhori, who settled in the Arbil plain.

Shi'i Kurds, most notably the Faylis and the Kurds of the towns and villages adjacent to the Iranian border, tend to follow the *'Ithna Ashari'* twelver branch of Shi'ism which is dominant in Iran. There are also other sects in various parts of Iraqi Kurdistan, which may be described as Shi'i due to their extreme reverence of 'Ali and the Shi'i Imams. Examples there are the Kaka'is (righteous people) around Kirkuk and in the Hawraman region, the Shabak between Arbil and

Mosul, the Qalam Haji in Mandali, and also the Bajwanis and Sarlus in the Kurdish edges of Mosul city. The Shi'ism of these sects contain strong elements that are typical of ancient eastern and Iranian religions. Thus, it may be appropriate to consider these sects as possessing the characteristics of religions with ancient roots that are independent of Islam. It would be useful to shed some light on these sects which play an important role in Kurdish spiritual life.

Kaka'i, Ahl al-Haq

Most students tend to accept that the name *Kaka'i*, used with reference to the Ahl al-Haq sect in Iraq, is derived from the Kurdish word *Kaka*, which in general usage is a form of address to an elder brother implying respect. It is also a more general polite and respectful form of address, or it can be a person's name.

In an MA dissertation entitled 'Kaka'ism, its Origins and Principles', Karim Najim al-Shwani states: 'Kaka'is also use the work Kaka to refer to father and use it to mean a brother in religion and thus implying that membership of the sect is a fraternity'.[61]

There is controversy about the origins of Kaka'i. Some say that Kaka'is, be they from the areas of Daquq, Mandali, Khanaqin, or from Karnad, Hamdan, Azerbaijan, or from the Caspian or Damawand or other areas, are all followers of the ancient Kurdish religions, a religious origin they may share with the Yazidis and other Indo-Iranian peoples.[62] Father Anastas al-Karmali says: 'Kaka'ism is a secret society and is not the name of a tribe, a nation or country'.[63]

The main concentration of the Kaka'i sect in Iraqi Kurdistan are villages of the Nahiya (sub-administrative centre) of Daquq in Kirkuk province, 40km south of the city of Kirkuk. These villages are: Ali Saray, Zanqur, Albu Muhammad, Alwat Pasha, Arab Koy, Tobzawa and Khoras. According to al-Shwami, Kaka'is also lived in other villages in the area delimited by Barandagh and nearby hills to the north, the plain along the northern side of Mount Hamrin and Qara Alidagh to the south, the main Baghdad-Kirkuk highway between Taza and Tuzkhormato to the east, and the Hawija area to the west.[64] According to 'Abbas al-'Azzawi, a number of Kaka'i families settled in the villages of Albogassa, Idris and Alboka'uba which belong to the Hawija district administration (*Qadha'*); in time, those families moved to the Qadha centre.[65]

In the province of Sulaymaniyya, many Kaka'is settled in the village of Hawar in the Hawraman area. Most of the population of this village were moved to the compulsory residence complex of 'Anab' in Halabje centre.

After the Iraq chemical attack on Halabje in 1988, survivors were forced to move again to Bayinjan, from where most moved on, this time to 'Ain Kawa in the city of Arbil.

In Arbil, some Kaka'is live in the villages of Safia and Mitrad on the left bank of the Greater Zab river near the confluence of another river, the Khazer.

There are also many Kaka'i families in villages in Nineva Province. Among these settlements are: the village of Wardak on the right bank of the Khazer river 45km from Mosul; the village of Kazakan, also on the same bank near Wardak; Tolaban on the left bank opposite Kazakan; and the villages of Qaraqasha, Qafriyya, Kabarli and Zangal. The Iraqi government has expelled the residents of these villages and rehoused them in the Bayinjan complex and in Kwair Nahiya. Some of the population of these Kaka'i villages have migrated to the city of Mosul and elsewhere. For instance, in the Qadha centre of Tal'afar, 40 miles west of Mosul, a growing family of Kaka'i Shaykhs settled. They are known as the Wahab Agha sect.

In Diyala Province, the Kaka'is live in Khanaqin and around it, and in the villages around Mandali, Qorato. A number of other families live in the village of al-Zawiya in Sa'diyya area, and a few others in Badra, Zarbatya and Mansouriyyat al-Jabal. More Kaka'i families reside in a village called Dali Abas, between Ba'quba and Khalis.

The Shabak

The Iraqi Shabak Kurds are described in the Islamic Encyclopaedia as a sect of 'extremist Shi'ites'.[66] There is controversy also over their religion and ethnic origins. Al-Sarraf maintains that they are 'Turkic communities'.[67] However, Minorsky considers them to be Kurds,[68] while others believe them to be of Persian origin.[69] The Shabak indeed use some Turkish vocabulary in their speech and they recite some Baktashi Sufi verses in Turkish: this could be the reason for confusing them with Turks. They also have some Persian pronunciations which may have led others to believe that they had migrated from Iran to the vicinity of Mosul. In any case, whatever their linguistic or religious origins, the Shabak consider themselves Kurds.

The Shabak live in about twelve villages east of Mosul and around Sinjar. They are to be found in close proximity to the Sarlo and to the Yazidis around Mosul. Like most Shi'i sects, the Shabak were heavily prosecuted by the Ottoman state.[70] The newly established Iraqi state was not mindful of their religious distinctiveness. Until recently, Muslims used to refer to them as 'Ouj', plural of 'Awaj, or crooked. Muslim and Christian circles used to accuse them of promiscuity.

The Shabak reserve a special reverence for the three religious texts, the Old Testament, the New Testament and the Qur'an. They also have their own religious text which is called 'Boryoroq' or 'Almanaqib'. It is possible to discern rituals and rites from the three religions of Judaism, Christianity and Islam among the Shabak. The Christian New Year is one of their main religious festivals. As is the case with the Kaka'is, Shabak men do not trim their moustaches, and the Shabak are not too concerned with the traditional Muslim religious observances. They recite their Muslim prayer once instead of five times daily and they do not fast in Ramadhan.[71]

The Shabak have two shrines. The first is in the village of 'Alirash and is purported by them to belong to Imam Husayn bin 'Ali. They ascribe the second in the village of 'Abbasiyya, to al-'Abbas bin 'Ali bin Abi Talib, the first Shi'i Imam. The Shabak have a religious carnival in which they raise the palm of a hand made of bronze and tour their villages.

There are other minor Shi'i sects known as Bajwan, Ibrahimi and Mawli. Most of their members live in the town of Tal'afar, northwest of Mosul, and some adjacent villages. They practise dissimulation (concealment of faith) for fear of persecution by the state.[72] Their faith differs little from that of the Shabak[73] and some scholars seem to consider them as part of the Shabak order.[74]

The Sarlu

The Sarlu are a small sect found in the villages of Qarqasha, Kazkan, Wardak and Tal al-Laban on the Khizer river between Arbil and Mosul. Some reside in Talla'far. Adherents of this sect avoid speaking ill of the devil, and they revere the sun. They are highly secretive about their rituals and religious rites. This led scholars to believe they are part of the Kaka'i order, and the Kaka'is themselves claim the Sarlu and others are members of their sect. Historians argue that the Sarlu were Yazidis from the Danaya tribe, who had converted to Islam long ago.[75] Nevertheless, they acquired some of their beliefs from their Kaka'i neighbours in Kirkuk, and many of their Yazidi beliefs remained.[76]

The association between the Sarlu and the Yazidis goes back to the centuries which preceded the attacks of the Surani Mir Muhammad Beg al-Rawandoozi against Yazidis in the early 1830s. During those times, the Yazidi faith was dispersed among the population of the area between the Greater Zab and the Tigress, and the Sarlu lived among the Yazidis in the Khazer river area. It is likely that a religious association existed between the two sects.

It is notable that the Sarlu of either sex do not marry outside their sect except for partners from among the Shabak. Evidently this is due to their perceived affinity of beliefs with those of the Shabak. Nevertheless, a woman who marries into the Sarlu is instantly required to enter into the faith and is forbidden from divulging any of its secrets, even in the case of her return to her parental family. It is said that should she divulge any of these secrets, she would be pursued and killed.[77]

The Yazidi Religion

The Yazidi faith, with its beliefs and rituals is probably subject to the most controversy. Early Islamic historians paid little attention to this religion. Moreover, contemporary Arab and Islamic scholars have not gone beyond generalities in their reference to the religious aspects of the Yazidi sect. These usually state that the Yazidis are a Sunni Islamic sect which adheres to the Umayyad Caliph Yazid bin Mu'awiya bin Abi Sufian[78] and that they have faith in the senior Sunni Sufi Shaykh 'Adi bin Musafirn al-Umawi, who had emigrated from his birthplace in Ba'albek into a solitary existence in the Hakkari mountains in the sixth century.[79] According to these scholars, the followers of Yazid also came under ancient Zoroastrian influence at the time of Shaykh Hasan Shamsuldin.[80]

Kurdish scholars, notably Mas'oud Muhammad, tend to argue that Yazidis are among the area's oldest population, that their religious beliefs precede those noted in Zoroastrian's book (Avesta) and that it is possible to trace their historical origins back to the Indian 'Veda' period or even earlier.[81] The area of the Yazidis had been populated by the Iranian branch of Indo-Iranian tribes. A Yazidi scholar, Khadri Sulaiman,[82] considers the history of Yazidi religious beliefs to resemble a long chain, most of the links of which are broken: an analysis of the rituals and religious texts of this sect would reveal that their beliefs originate among those of ancient Iraqis such as the Babylonians and Assyrians. Moreover, those beliefs were influenced by many of the Zoroastrian and sun-worshipping rituals which had been prevalent in Hatra.[83]

Whatever the origin of the Yazidi faith, it is evident that most European and Kurdish scholars argue that the name Yazidi is derived from the Indo-Iranian word *Yazd*, which means 'God' and that the faith's beliefs and rituals are related to those of ancient Iranian and eastern religions which prevailed in Iran and Kurdistan in pre-Islamic times.

There are Yazidi communities in all parts of Kurdistan, but the largest and most important of these is in Iraqi Kurdistan, where Shaykh 'Adi's tomb at Lalish and the other sacred shrines are to be found. The Yazidis' main concentrations are to be found in the western part of Iraqi Kurdistan, particularly in Mount Sinjar and in Shaykhan.

The Yazidis of Mount Sinjar are divided into sections, the Khorkan and the Jawana. They are instantly recognisable from their appearances. The Jawana, old and young, plait their hair and let it rest on their shoulders, and they very often wear long hats. They adhere to Shaykh Sharaf al-Din and they pay their alms and their offerings to the guardians of his tomb, unlike the Khorkan. They refrain from marriage with Khorkanis unless the latter make their offerings to Shaykh Sharaf al-Din and convert to the Jawana. The Jawana claim superiority over the Khorkanis, saying that they had been the earlier settlers of Mount Sinjar since the time of Shaykh Sharaf al-Din, and that it was they who had spread the Yazidi faith.[84]

The Jawana are subdivided into numerous tribes and lineages:

1. The Hababat tribe which is reputed to be one of the strongest of Sinjar's tribes. It has four lineages: the Mala Ato, Mahmi, Mala Sati and Mala Amrouk.

2. The Mahrakan tribe, which is composed of a number of other tribes: the 'Ali Fara, Asna, Kolkan and Hask Ayi.

3. The Malakhalata, also known as Masqura; their origin is said to be from the Danbaly tribe. [85]

4. The Khisak, which is a small tribe not exceeding a few hundred people living in the village of Tarbakah.

The second Yazidi section, the Khorkan, is composed of the following tribes: Qiran, Samouqa, Haskan, al-Dakhi, Jelkan, Fuqara, Musana, Jafriyya, Haliqiyya, Hawiriyya, Korkorka, Mandakan, Rashkan and Sharqiyan.

Apart from these, there are Kurdish Muslim tribes who live within Yazidi society whose origins may either be Yazidi or from Batini religious beliefs which are akin to the Yazidi faith. Within the Yazidi Mandakan tribe, there are three Muslim lineages in addition to three Yazidi ones. The same case is to be found within the Shaikhara tribe which inhabits the Yazidi village of Qaboosiyya. The Kisks'i Babawat tribe has strong links with the Yazidis and it has engaged in numerous feuds with Muslim tribes in defence of the Yazidis. The Babawat also join them in pilgrimage to Malik Tawoos, while the Yazidis defend the Babawat, join them in pilgrimage to Bier Zakar, and they celebrate together the annual Yazidi carnival in his honour.[86] It is also difficult to distinguish between the Babawat and the Yazidis whether by dress, by speech or by customs.[87] A Kaka'i friend has informed me that Kaka'i religious codes permit religious fraternisation with Yazidis and attention to the sermons of their Shaykhs. Similarly, Yazidis can also accept a Kaka'i as a *Krif*, meaning a brother in religion.[88]

The village of Shaykhan about 50km to the northeast of the city of Mosul is considered the centre of the Yazidis' spiritual shaykhs. The population of the village is divided into two parts: the Rohaniyoon (spiritualist) which are composed of Mir, Pasmir, al-Sheik and Bier, and the Maridoon who are the commoners, who form many tribes such as the Basktky, Balasini, Bidatyi, Turk, Hakkari, Khiskami, Doski, Dana, Robneshti, Tazi, Qa'idi, Karni, Mamoosi and Haraqi.

Al-Damlouji says that the Yazidi areas used to extend from the Greater Zab river to Khabur al-Hasaniyya river and included an extensive area of the Nahiyas of Sorjiyya river and Asha'ir al-Saba'a and the Nahiya of Shaykhan and Jabal Maqloub and Sulaifaniyya Nahiya, all the way to the Tigress river. The town of Dohuk itself used to be populated by Yazidis.

It appears that the raids on and the battles with the Kurdish emirates and with the states, particularly the Ottoman Empire, which prevailed over Kurdistan, have all greatly reduced the number of Yazidis. An example of these raids is the attack of the Emir Muhammad Beg al-Rawandoozi, known as the Emir of Soran, in 1833. Indeed such pressure may have been instrumental in the conversion of many Yazidi tribes to Islam. For instance, there is the large Shaykhan tribe, which has kinship relationships with the Yazidi shaykhs. Sections of it, such as the Mamousa and Klaosoori, are still Yazidis and live among them. The Sorani Mir also followed the Yazidi faith. Today, this tribe is found around the Arbil plain and it adheres to Islam and its Sunni sect. Visits continue to be exchanged between this tribe and the Yazidis and both sides consider themselves as belonging to one tribe.[90]

There are no accurate figures for the Yazidi population, which has given rise to controversy. Al-Damlouji says that the Yazidi population in the eleventh and twelfth centuries H (seventeenth and eighteenth centuries) was around one million,[91] but that at the time of his writing (1949), he estimated them to have totalled 100,000 including 30–35,000 in the Shaykhan, Dohuk and Sinjar areas of Iraqi Kurdistan.[92]

The policy of national and religious assimilation practised against the Yazidis in various historical epochs continues to be sternly applied by the Iraqi state. This has made it difficult to estimate their numbers at present. However, taking the figure in the 1957 census and allowing for natural population growth, we would arrive at an estimate for the present Yazidi population of approximately 150,000 in Iraq alone.

Christianity Among Iraq's Kurds

It appears that the Christian religion gained widespread adherence in the northern and western regions of the Kurdish lands, particularly in the centuries preceding the rise of Islam. Not only are these areas adjacent to Syria and in close proximity to Palestine, but they also came under Christian Byzantine control for a time.

Al-Qassab[93] says that, according to Mesopotamian church beliefs, Mar Toma, Christ's disciple, had passed through the land. Furthermore, Mar Mari of the Church of Urfa recorded his own missionary work around present day Kirkuk, in the third century. Muhammad Ahmad, a Kurdish scholar, points to evidence that the Christians founded a synod in Bet 'Athra in Kurdistan. Christian monasteries, both Nestorians and Chaldean, became widespread, and they produced great theologians, some of whom had previously been Zoroastrians. There were also many other churches, one of which is the church of Daquq (a Kurdish town 5km to the south-east of Kirkuk on the Kirkuk-Baghdad highway), where one of Christ's disciples is said to have died.[94] Another is the Church of Shaqlawa, which had gained much fame in the early Christian centuries. One of the many monasteries is that of Rabnaboya, the ruins of which can still be seen at the Kard Hasar pass in Mount Safi. There is also the Mar Ya'qoub monastery a few kilometres from Shaqlawa, and in proximity to two villages which, in times past, used to be entirely populated by Chaldean Christians, but which are now inhabited by Muslims. The villages are known by the same name as the monastery, but with the Kurdish pronunciation 'Aquban'.

For Christians, living conditions and religious survival in the Middle East region has undoubtedly not been easy, particularly under the Ottoman Empire. It is not necessary to elaborate on these: suffice it to say that those difficulties, particularly the massacres of the Armenians and Assyrians at the end of the nineteenth and the beginning of the twentieth centuries have had a considerable effect on the Christian presence in the Kurdish area, on Muslim-Christian relations and on the living patterns of these communities in Kurdish society.

Prior to the flight of the Armenians and Assyrians (Nestorians) from Armenia and the Hakkari mountains respectively, it was said by, among others, Major Kenneth Mason, that those communities used to live happily in Kurdistan. However, the massacres which took place (including the killing of the Patriarch Mar Sham'oun in the first quarter of the twentieth century by the Kurdish insurgent Semko Shakkak, and the flights of the Armenians and Assyrians, brought large numbers of people of these communities from the Hakkari and Van areas into Iraqi Kurdistan. There, they were recruited into the Levies' forces which had been formed to fight the Kurds, thereby generating political tension between the Assyrians and the Kurds. Nevertheless, age-old relations of friendship continue to bind the Kurdish Muslims together with the Chaldean Christian inhabitants of Kurdistan.

Most Christians in Kurdistan are Chaldean Catholics, but there are also Assyrians (Nestorians) and smaller numbers of Armenians. The sizes of these communities are not accurately known. As in the case of other communities, official statistics cannot be relied upon. However, it is evident that most Kurdish cities and towns contain Christian communities. Moreover, there are dozens of Christian towns and villages such as 'Ainkawa, Talkaif, Ba'ashiqa and Bahzani. These are to be found in various parts of the Kurdish land, and some also live in the city of Mosul and outside Iraq. Thousands of Christian founders lived in the town of Shaqlawa, in Harir, 20 km to the north and in rural surroundings: locals say these people had been rooted in the area. However, factors such as lack of government care, prevalence of hostilities for the last thirty years and economic pull factors from outside the Kurdish areas have combined to drive most of this community to emigrate, leaving little more than three hundred Chaldean families in this area, mostly concentrated inside the town of Shaqlawa.

Following Iraq's attainment of political independence in 1932, the state did not meet its commitments to protect the rights of national and religious minorities in the country. The Kurds and the Christians appear to have been among the first to suffer from the policy which was pursued. Hence, in 1933 there was a failed joint attempt to establish a combined Kurdish-Assyrian state. That effort laid a solid basis for Christian participation in Kurdish political life, particularly in the September 1961 revolution. The French journalist, Rene Mauries, spoke admirably of the deep understanding which prevailed among the Kurds of the two religions. In a book he wrote after a tour of Kurdistan in 1966, Maurice declared that he would stand witness to say that there is no Christian problem in Kurdistan.[95]

Baghdad has on several occasions tried to use religion to divide Assyrians and Kurds.[96] More particularly, the present regime in Baghdad tried to force Chaldeans and Assyrians to register themselves in census bureaux as Christian Arabs.[97] In an official decree promulgated in 1973, the Iraqi government granted some cultural rights for the Chaldeans and Assyrians, but these have not been implemented.

It can generally be said that Christians form one of the most important religious groups among Iraq's Kurds. The Christians lived over the ages in the land of the Kurds in harmony with the mainly Muslim Kurds. After the First World War and particularly in the wake of the massacres committed by the Ottomans and by Semko Agha Shakkak, tension marred the relationship between these two religious communities. As this subsided, they returned to their historical harmony. The religious distinction between Christians and Muslims in Kurdish society did not generate lasting problems and tensions between the two sides, despite efforts by governments in that direction. On the contrary, the two communities merged together to such an extent that it became difficult to distinguish Christians or adherents of other religions and sects, in their customs and social and economic patterns, from Kurdish Sunni Muslims. In addition, the apparent attraction of the Kurdish character to the Sufi spirit, which stems from the Kurds' ancient Iranian religions and their beliefs correspond to some basic elements of Christianity, and of the Yazidi and other religious sects. The attraction of Sufism may also be related to the harsh ruggedness of the Kurdish land and natural environment and to the difficult historical and political conditions in Iraq and Iraqi Kurdistan. It appears that these factors have encouraged a measure of solidarity, human understanding and religious tolerance and coexistence in Kurdish society.

Judaism

Between 1949 and 1952, many thousands of Jews who were either Kurdish or who had lived among Kurds in Iraqi Kurdistan, left for Israel. Before their departure, they lived either in their exclusive villages in proximity to Kurdish Muslim villages, or in their own neighbourhoods within Muslim villages and towns. An example of the first pattern is the Jewish village of Shlaimuk near the village of Balisan. The second pattern could be found in Jewish neighbourhoods of the villages of Batas and Harir and of the towns of Zakho and Makhmour.

There is evidence of an ancient Jewish presence in Kurdistan. According to Yona Sabar,[98] the 'Kurdistani Jews are descendants of the Jews exiled from Israel and Judea by the Assyrian king' and referred to by the Prophet Isaiah as lost in the land of Assyria (Isa. 27:13).

The arrival of Islam did not end the Jewish presence among the Kurds. On the contrary, the Jewish community remained large even after a majority of Kurds adopted the Islamic religion. According to Sheikh Mous, there are approximately 150,000 Jews living in Israel who originated from the Kurdish region.[99]

Nowadays, there is no concentration of Jews living among the Kurds, but a number of Jewish families who had earlier converted to Islam continue to live there: these are referred to as '*bin Ju*' or of Jewish origin.

Conclusion

This review of the contemporary state of affairs of religion among Iraq's Kurds may be summed up as follows. It can generally be stated that Kurdish society in Iraq is, in terms of religion, very complex. This complexity stems from the depth of Kurdish irreligious history which the Kurds share with the other peoples who inhabit the slopes of the Zagros mountains. This complexity also stems from the geography, topography and strategic location of the Kurdish homeland which has made it into a conduit for religious ideas.

Those geographical factors did not only establish Kurdistan as a conduit for religious ideas and a trade route, but they also created favourable historical circumstances for the coexistence of religions, sects and beliefs among each other.

Moreover, the rugged mountainous topography and the impregnable valleys of that land have enabled those religions and religious beliefs to survive over the ages.

It may also be said that ideas rooted in the ancient religious beliefs of the Kurds' ancestors dating back to the pre-Islamic ages continue to exist in contemporary Kurdish society. Indeed, those beliefs are frequently found among the Muslim section of the Kurdish population as well. Apart from the Yazidi faith which can be considered a separate religion, there are the Kaka'i and Shabak sects which proclaim an adherence to the Islamic religion, but which retain rituals, religious beliefs and even theories of creation which reflect a persistence of ancient Iranian, Indian and Zoroastrian beliefs. Furthermore, aspects of the Naqshabandi Order and of the sects that evolved out of the Naqshabandi Sufi tradition, such as the Haqqah and its offshoots, all indicate an active presence of an ancient religious inheritance in contemporary Kurdish life. Much of the mythology of Sunni Muslim Kurds may be taken to reflect a similar influence.

Finally, it appears that the Islamic fundamentalist movement among Iraq's Kurds is not very influential as a political movement, but that in its religious orientating, there is a notable mix of religion and nationalism. In this respect, it can be said that Kurdish fundamentalists, whether explicitly or not, tend to consider a 'good' Kurdish Muslim as a person who serves or struggles effectively for the freedom of his people.

On the basis of what has been said, it can be further concluded that Kurdish society is marked by its receptiveness to religious pluralism. Furthermore, religions and religious sects can have no difficulty in coexisting within it. This pluralism would not represent a source of danger for that society's essentially homogenous national composition.

Notes

1. Encyclopedia of Islam, 'Kurds': 1151.
2. Zaki, Muhammad Amin, *Tarikhi Sulaymani wa Wilati* (History of Sulaymaniyya and its region), Baghdad, 1939: 288.
3. Dr. Kreyenbroek:, *A Lecture about the Ancient Religions of the Kurds*, Kurdistan Hallm, Kurdish Cultural Centre, no. 20, 1992.
4. Zaki, Muhammad Amin, op. cit.: 122.
5. Ibid.: 125.
6. Ibid.: 128.
7. Al-'Azzawi, 'Abbas, *Khulafa' Mawlana Khalid*, Bulletin of the Kurdish Academy

Council, vol. 2, issue 2, Baghdad, 1975: 198.

8. Ibid.: 198.

9. Al-Mudarris, Mulla Abdul-Karim, *Bnamalai Zaniaran*, edited by Muhammad 'Ali Karadaghi, 1st edn, Baghdad, 1984: 31.

10. Nodah is a village about 6km from Sulaymaniyya.

11. Tawakkuli, Muhammad Ra'uf, *Tarikhe Tasawf dar Kurdistan* (History of Sufism in Kurdistan), Ishraq Publication, Tehran, (n. d.): 133 (Persian text).

12. Zaki, op. cit.: 219.

13. Ibid.: 219.

14. Sanandaji, Mirza Shukrulla, *Tuhfaiy Nasiry dar Tarikhu Jugrafiyai Kurdistan*, edited by Dr. Tabibi Hismatu, Amiri Kabir Publications, Tehran, 1366 H: 219. The Baban principality ruled over the present-day Sulaymaniyya area of Iraqi Kurdistan and also covered the areas of Kolanba, Mawat, Halabje, Shahrazur, Shahrabazir, Qaradagh and Penjwin. At times, however, it extended its control to Zangabad, Mandali, Badra and Jassan in one direction, and in another direction to Altun Kupri, Koya, Harir and sometimes also Kirkuk and Iranian Sanandaj.

15. Hawar, Muhammad Rasul, *Shaykh Mahmudi Karaman u Dawlatakai Khwarui Kurdistan* (The Brave Shaykh Mahmud and Southern Kurdistan), vol. 1, London, 1990: 36.

16. This centre has numerous Arab and Turkoman adherents as well as thousands of Kurds.

17. In an interview with Dr. Peshawa Talbani (London, 30 July 1992), he said: A Shaykh of Qadiri order, named Shaykh Ahma had come to their area from Lahore and was able to inspire the Talbani's great grandfather, Mulla Mahmud, to enter the Qadiri order (the village of Talbani lies 35km to the east of Kirkuk).

18. Tawakuli, op. cit.: 165.

19. Sanandaji, op. cit.: 65. See also al-Mulla Karim, Muhammad, *Chmkeki Majui Hawraman u Mariwan*, Baghdad, 1970: 26.

20. Hawar, op. cit.: 78.

21. Two Shaykhs from Samzin and Nahri joined Shaykh Khalid's sufi order, Shaykh 'Abdul Qadir Shamzini in 1814 and Sayyid Taha Nahri in 1817 – see Tawakuli: 210.

22. Shaykh Osman Tawila was the most important religious Shaykh who joined Shaykh Khalid. He succeeded Shaykh Khalid after his death, and his descendants continue to lead the Naqshabandi Order in Kurdistan.

23. Yihya, Abdul Ghani Ali, '*al-Mulla Yahya Almazuri wa suqut Amarat Badinan*', *Karwan*, no. 41: 148.

24. Also see Hakim, *Dirasat Kurdiyya*, no. 1, The Kurdish Institute, Paris, January 1984: 61.

25. Hawar, op. cit.: 77.

26. Ibid.: 121.

27. Ibid.: 77.

28. Ibid.: 78.

29. Ibid.

30. Ibid.: 78.
31. Ibid.
32. Ibid.: 79.
33. The followers of Naqshabandi are called *Sufis*, while the followers of Qadiri are called *Darwishs*.
34. 'Askari, Mustafa, *Aurdanawaik la bzutnaway Haqqa*, Baghdad, 1983: 15.
35. An interview with Ahmad al-'Askari, 28 June 1992.
36. Abdul Hamid, Muhsin, *Haqiqat al-Babiyya wa al-Baha'iyya*, Baghdad, 3rd edn, 1977: 56.
37. Askari, Mustafa, op. cit.: 14.
38. Abdulla, Hamza, Appendix no. 1, in al-'Askari, op. cit.: 65.
39. Rassul, Izzadin, Appendix no. 2, *Aurdanawaik la bzutnaway Haqqa*: 73
40. *Batinis* are a sufi sect who revere Ali and adhere to cabbalistic and mystical practices.
41. Abdul Hamid, Muhsin, op. cit.: 168.
42. An interview with Ahmad 'Askari, 28 June 1992.
43. Zuhdi, Ra'uf, *Bo la Haqqa Kawtna Taqa?* Baghdad, 1985: 96.
44. An article about Haqqa, in *'Iraq'* newspaper, no. 2334, 5 October 1983.
45. An interview with Ahmad 'Askari, 28 June 1992.
46. Ibid.
47. 'Askari, Mustafa, op. cit.
48. Edmonds, J., *Kurds, Turks and Arabs, Travel and Research in North Eastern Iraq, 1919–1925*, Persian translation by Ibrahim Yunisi, Tehran, 1367 H: 206.
49. For more details, see Mustafa 'Askari, op. cit.: 38–44.
50. Mulla Karim, Muhammad, Reference no. 31, in al-'Askari, Mustafa, op. cit.: 31.
51. 'Ali, Rasheed Muhammad, *Karwan*, no. 15: 37.
52. Al-Mulla Karim, Muhammad, Reference no. 61, ibid.: 53.
53. Ali, Rasheed Muhammad, *Karwan*, no. 15: 37.
54. Boyce, Mary, *Zoroastrians, Their Religious Beliefs and Practices*, London, 1987: 112–113.
55. Hama Sur, recital recorded on videotape. Copy in our possession.
56. Pirash, *Barzan wa harakat al-wa'i al-qawmi al-kurdi, 1826–1914*, London, 1980: 24.
57. Ibid.: 26.
58. Ibid.: 25.
59. 'Arfa, Hassan, *The Kurds, An Historical and Political Study*, Oxford University Press, London, 1966: 118.
60. Pirash, op. cit.: 41.
61. Al-Shuwani, Karim Najm, *al-Kaka'ia, Usuluha wa 'itigaduha*, MA Dissertation, Baghdad University, 1989: 10.
62. Al-Rojbayani, Jamil Bandi, *Bandajin (Mandali) fi al-Tarikh Qadiman wa Hadithan*, (n. d.): 428.
63. Al-Karmali, Father Anastas, *al-Kaka'ia*, the Journal *Lisan al-Arab*, 1928, vol. 4: 68.

64. Al-Shwani, op. cit.: 31.

65. Ibid.: 31.

66. Minorsky, V., Encyclopaedia of Islam.

67. Al-Sarraf, op. cit.: 139.

68. Minorsky, V., op. cit.

69. Al-Karmali, Father Anastas, an Article in the Journal *al-Muqtatif*, no. 5, 1909: 577–582.

70. An Article signed by 'Amkah' in the Journal *al-Muqtatif*, no. 59, 1921: 230–232.

71. Muslly, Munthir, *Arab wa Akrad*, 2nd edn, Damascus, 1991: 293.

72. Al-Sarraf, Ahmad Hamid, *al-Shabak*, al-Ma'arif Press, Baghdad, 1954: 99.

73. Al-Azzawi, Abbas, *al-Kaka'ia fil tarikh*, Baghdad: 99.

74. Al-Sarraf, op. cit.: 144.

75. Al-Damlouji, Sadiq, *al-Yazidiyya*, Mosul, 1949: 254.

76. Ibid.: 255.

77. Ibid.

78. Taymur, Ahmad, Cairo, 1347 H: 10.

79. Al-Hassani, Abdul Razzaq, *al-Yazidiyun fi Hadhirihim wa Madhihim*, 11th edn, Baghdad, 1987: 21.

80. Ibid.: 27.

81. Muhammad, Mas'ud, *Nusari Kurd*, no. 5, 1978: 15.

82. Sulaiman, Khidr, *Kurt Basak Darbarai Shaikhan w Shaikhanbagi*: 13.

83. Ibid.: 14–15.

84. Al-Damaluji, op. cit.: 224.

85. Ibid.: 238.

86. Ibid.: 239.

87. Ibid.

88. An interview with a Kaka'i friend who does not wish to be named, 16 June 1990.

90. Sulaiman, op. cit.: 51.

91. Al-Damaluji, op. cit.: 288.

92. Ibid.

93. *Karwan*, no. 81, December 1989.

94. Al-Mas'udi, *Muruj al-Dhahab*, Cairo, (n. d.): 344.

95. Mauries, Rene, *Le Kurdistan ou la Mort*, Translated into Arabic by Jawad Mella, Kurdologia Publications, no. 3, London, 1986: 100.

96. Ibid.

97. Stated to the writer by a Chaldean from Shaqlawa City in July 1979.

98. Sabar, Yona, *The Folk Literature of the Kurdistan Jews: An Anthology*: xvi.

99. Sheikhmous, Omar, 'The Kurds in Exile', *The Kurdish Cultural Bulletin*: 16.

CHAPTER EIGHT

The Origins of the Naqshabandiyya Sufi Order

Helkot Hakim

Now much fewer in number and reduced to sporadic appearances, the Kurdish dervishes once used to put on shows which were particularly attractive to the people, who would gather to watch these figures smitten by God, moving their bodies so as to show all miscreants the power the Loved One accorded to those who believed in Him. The power of the dervishes included the ability to be impassive to physical pain at moments of ecstasy, and also not to show any trace of the wounds which they inflicted on themselves with wires, daggers, knives, blades and so on.

These Qadiri dervishes are still seen at some mosques or *takaya*, often on a Friday before the noon prayer. They form one or more circles of the *dhikr*, and the balanced movements of the upper parts of their bodies blend with the rhythmic sounds of the tambourine. The whole spectacle is accompanied by mystical songs, often performed in a high-pitched voice.

However, the gap between Qadiri performers and spectators has been widening in Kurdish circles for some decades, particularly since the First World War. Today's audience are not like they used to be. It is possible to hear reproving comments, and the mocking expressions on people's faces are less discreet; there are always a few blank stares, seemingly a mixture of admiration and bewilderment. The performances convert fewer and fewer people.

The other tariqa order, the Naqshabandis,[1] seems to be in better shape. This is probably because they do not need or do not allow public *dhikr* ceremonies. In fact, the Naqshabandis have only existed in Kurdistan for two centuries in their present form, whereas the Qadiriyya has been part of Kurdish culture for nearly eight hundred years

The Qadiriyya and the Naqshabandiyya are the two most widespread brotherhoods among the Sunni Kurds. Even where there were other brotherhoods, such as the Quizilbashiyya and the Khalwatiyya, they did not constitute any real opposition to the Qadiriyya or the Naqshabandiyya. These two had so much importance in the spiritual, social and political life of the Kurds that their confrontations at the beginning of the twentieth century were marked by violence, and the fall-out from this conflict still affects the relationship between their respective representatives today.

Even though the names of the many past Sufi masters, of both tariqas, are still highly evocative, organised Sufism has lost ground and much of its prestige. Nonetheless, it remains an important element in the modern history of the Kurds. According to Basile Nikitine, a leading authority on the Kurds, any study of the Kurds 'must give a prominent place to the shaykhs, their influence, their likes and dislikes, the number of their followers etc.'[1]

There is not a great deal of information available about the organisation of the Naqshabandiyya, though there is more than on the Qadiriyya.

The Qadiriyya is a brotherhood founded by 'Abd al-Qadir al-Jilani, or Gaylani (1077–1166). Most of his biographers say that he came from the village of Jilan (Gaylan), south of the Caspian Sea in Iran. Among the Kurds, it is believed that he came from the village of Gaylan to the south of Iranian Kurdistan.[2] This second hypothesis has greatly contributed to the popularity and development of the brotherhood among the Kurds. But it is thanks to his son, 'Abd al-Aziz, that it expanded considerably from the thirteenth century. Jilani is considered a great saint among the Kurds and other Sunni peoples. There are many myths and legends surrounding him and his supernatural powers. He spent most of his life in Baghdad, which was then a place of high culture. His mausoleum lies in the Kurdish quarter of the city and is a place of pilgrimage for many devout Muslims.[3] The Qadiriyya was the biggest brotherhood among the Kurds for nearly 700 years. Its dervishes very often came from the underprivileged sections of society. In a text addressed to his son, its founder advises him to remain poor. The Qadiriyya, unlike the Naqshabandiyya, permits *dhikr* in public and the use of musical instruments

The Naqshabandiyya broadened its influence among the Kurds in the nineteenth century, thanks to the efforts of Mawlana Khalid Naqshabandi (1779–1827), who was born in Qaradagh, a village 30 km south of Sulaymaniyya.[4] Like other children of his day, he was educated at various mosques in Kurdistan. At the age of twenty, he was already a schoolteacher in Sulaymaniyya, capital of the Baban principality, which shows his gifts compared to his fellow students. In 1808 he left for India to meet a great Naqshabandi shaykh by the name of 'Ubaidulla Dahlawi, with whom he spent just over one year. The Indian shaykh initiated him in the practices of the Naqshabandiyya and asked him to propagate it in the Ottoman Empire.

On his return from India in 1811, Mawlana Khalid was solemnly welcomed everywhere, and numerous Kurdish, Arab and Turkish personalities joined his tariqa. Before long, his popularity and the number of his disciples had grown so much that the Qadiri Shaykhs, concerned about their own power, declared war on him. The consequences of the conflict frightened the Kurdish leaders of the Baban principality. In 1812 its prince, 'Abdul Rahman Pasha, forced Mawlana Khalid to flee from Sulaymaniyya and take refuge in Baghdad, where the future *wali*, Dawud Pasha, was one of his former 'disciples'.

At the request of the new Prince, Mahmud Pasha, Mawlana Khalid returned to his birthplace in 1813. But things steadily worsened between him and the Qadiri Shaykhs, who won the support of the Pasha in 1820. Mawlana Khalid was once more forced to leave Sulaymaniyya and go again into exile in Baghdad. His welcome was less warm than the first time, even though the *wali* was one of his 'disciples'. His popularity and the conflicts which surrounded him were doubtless seen as a source of instability by the political leaders. In addition, their support had been due to the fact that Mawlana Khalid had involuntarily had a destabilizing influence in the Baban principality. Once that influence had ended, there was no further reason to support him: on the contrary, the presence in Baghdad of such a powerful religious figure, fiercely jealous of his independence, made them anxious. In 1822 Mawlana Khalid was obliged to leave for Damascus, where in 1827 he died from the plague that was then ravaging the city.

The rapid spread of the Naqshabandiyya has struck all researchers of Islam among the Kurds. In the space of a few years, Mawlana Khalid surrounded himself with several thousand followers. According to the representative of the East Indies Company in Baghdad, Claudius James Rich, who spent a few days in Sulaymaniyya in 1820, Mawlana Khalid had 12,000 disciples among the Arabs, Turks and Kurds.[5] 'Abbas al-'Azzawi says that there were 20,000,[6] although he does not indicate his sources for the figure. However, there is no doubt about his great knowledge of Ottoman sources, and it may be noted that the figure can be taken seriously since it referred to a period some years after Rich's visit.

On the basis of these figures, one is forced to take account of a tariqa which had existed for only about ten years. In comparison, attention might be drawn to another *tariqa*, the *Mawlawiyya*, which, after six centuries of activity, had 100,000 followers throughout the whole Muslim world during the First World War.[7]

Mawlana Khalid designated a number of khulafa' who represented him before the peoples of the Muslim world, both near and far, within and beyond the borders of the Ottoman Empire. During his lifetime, there were 34 khulafa' among the Kurds and 33 among other peoples.[8] This was a significant number at the time.[9] He also had 48 Kurdish and 37 non-Kurdish Mansub.[10]

The khulafa' were scattered throughout the Muslim lands and preached on behalf of the Naqshabandiyya and its leader, Mawlana Khalid. They were extremely active, to the point of giving real concern to the provincial governors. Even the Ottoman authorities wondered about the political intentions of this new arrival on the Empire's political and religious scene.[11] The activism of these khulafa' was even mentioned in a firman banning the tariqa, pronounced in 1828. It read: 'Five months ago several of the khulafa of Sheikh Khalid, a religious scholar resident in Damascus, originally from Sulaymaniyya, arrived in Istanbul. They went around the mosques asking people to follow their brotherhood. Many notables and scholars of Istanbul joined them. They are now well-known in the Turkish and Arab countries. Calling themselves khulafa', they are very active in promoting their brotherhood. Apparently, they do not represent any danger. But the Sufis must not become too numerous. We must forbid them from carrying out their activities. It is your Islamic duty to obey this order'.[12]

Disciples of the Naqshabandiyya were better trained than those of the Qadiriyya. Unlike the latter, who preached among the underprivileged, the Naqshabandis generally belonged to middling or well-to-do sections of society. Their *dhikr* was practised discreetly within the four walls of the mosques under the supervision of a Shaykh. This made it easier to train their disciples who, as a rule, did not associate with the followers of another tariqa.

Each candidate who wanted to join the Naqshabandiyya had to be sponsored by one or two long-standing disciples or *khalifa*. According to the letters of Mawlana Khalid, it seems that people could even join the tariqa by correspondence. This was valid for those who lived far away from the homes of the khalifa, though disciples were urged to visit their masters once or twice a year. If there was good reason for this to be impossible, the disciple was to stay in permanent contact with his spiritual guide through correspondence.

A disciple had a relationship with his master which was clearly defined by submission. The latter thus played a dominant role, not just in his disciple's spiritual quest, but also in his life.[13]

It was forbidden for the khalifa of Mawlana Khalid to visit governors and politicians. An infraction of the rules met with a letter of warning. A second offence was also followed by a warning letter. The punishment for the third offence was expulsion from the tariqa. This is what happened to the khalifa from Transoxania, Ismail Shirwani,[14] and the khalifa from Istanbul, Raghib Effendi.[15] After the expulsion of a member of the brotherhood, a note was sometimes sent to all the other members asking them to suspend all manner of contact with him.

The expulsion of another Istanbul khalifa, 'Abd al-Wahab al-Susi, is an example of this kind of practice. In the note to the members of his brotherhood after his dispute with 'Abd al-Wahab, Mawlana Khalid imposed special conditions for each khalifa who wanted to represent him in the Ottoman capital. He was forbidden to frequent the Ottoman leaders, ask for any help from the Sublime Porte or the men in power, marry a woman from Istanbul or even allow women to frequent the *takya*.[16]

The more the tariqa expanded and won followers in distant regions, the more its master closed ranks and imposed his power. From the various places that he lived in, Sulaymaniyya, Baghdad or Damascus, Mawlana Khalid ran the brotherhood with the idea of centralising everything through the intermediary of his khalifa or through sustained correspondence. No Kurdish religious or political figure or man of letters from earlier times has left as many letters as Mawlana Khalid, taking into account only those found and published. No doubt there were many more since he had so many disciples throughout the Muslim lands.

Notes

1. Nikitine, Basile, *Les Kurdes, études sociologiques et historiques*, Paris, Librairie C. Klincksieck, Editions D'Aujourd'hui, 1975: 218. Some people parody the present Kurdish political parties by comparing them with the tariqa of yesteryear.

2. See, for example, Muhammad Ra'uf Tawakuli, *Tarikhe tasawuf dar Kurdistan* (History of Sufism in Kurdistan), Tehran, 1975: 64.

3. For further information about this brotherhood, see M. A. Aini, *Un grand saint de l'Islam, Abd-al-Qadir Guilani, 1077–1166*, Paris, Guethner, 1967; 'Abd al-Qadir al-Djilani' and 'Qadiriyya', *Encyclopédie de l'Islam*; Martin van Bruinessen, *Agha, Shaikh and State: Social and Political Structures of Kurdistan*, 2nd edn, London, Zed Books, 1992; Thierry Zarcone, *'La Qadiriyya'* in Alexandre Popovic and Gilles Veinstein, *Les Voies d'Allah*, Paris, Fayard, 1996: 461–7; Basile Nikitine, *'Une apologie Kurde du Sunnisme'*, Rocznik Orjentalisyczny, tome VIII, 1933: 116–160.

4. There are numerous biographies of Mawlana Khalid. To mention the most detailed: Abbas al-Azzawi, 'Mawlana Khalid al-Naqshbandi', *Govari kori zanyari kure*, vol. 1, 1973:696–727; Ibrahim Fasih al-Baghdadi, *al-Madjd at-Talid fi manaqib al-Shaykh Khalid*, Istanbul, 1872; Halkawt Hakim, *Confrérie de Naqshbandis au Kurdistan au XIXe siècle*, thèse de doctorat, Université de Paris-Sorbonne (Paris IV), 1983; Muhammad Ar'ad Sahib-Zada, *Bughyat al-Wadjid fi maktubat hadrat Mawlana Khalid*, Damascus, 1915; Muhammad al-Khal, *al-Shaykh Ma'ruf al-Nodahi al-Barzindji*, Baghdad, 1964: 33–53.

5. Rich, Claudius James, *Narrative of a Residence in Koordistan and to the Site of Ancient Nineveh*, London, 1836, vol. 1: 140.

6. al-'Azzawi, 'Abbas, 'Mawlana Khalid', op. cit.: 719.

7. Vitray-Meyerovitch, Eva de, *Rumi et le soufisme*, Paris, Seuil, 1977: 2.

8. Mudarris, Mala Abd al-Karim, *Yadi mardan: Mawlana Khalidi Naqishbandi,*u Baghdad, 1979: 83–86.

9. Ibid.: 116–124.

10. In a letter to the *wali* of Baghdad, Dawud Pasha, the Ottoman authorities were getting information on the political objectives of Mawlana Khalid. In his response, dating from the period before Mawlana Khalid had finally left Sulaymaniyya, the *wali* reassured them on this. See Abbas al-Azzawi, *'Khulafa Mawlana Khalid'*, Govari Kori Zanyari Kurd, vol. 2, 1974: 216.

11. Ibid.: 721.

12. For example, the disciple could not pass from one stage of his spiritual journey to the next without being accompanied by his master. In other words, there can be no solitary search for union, whatever the degree of knowledge and ability of the disciple. The place occupied by the Naqshabandi shaykhs in the spiritual and material life of the follower is criticised by other brotherhoods. It is true that submission reached a particularly high level with the Naqshabandis. Muhammad Amin al-Kurdi stresses that the disciple must submit to his master 'financially and physically, for the substance of will and love only appear in this way'. See *Tanwir al-Qulub fi mu'amalat 'Alam al-Ghuyub*, Cairo, 1948: 543.

13. Sahib-Zada, Muhammad Ar'ad, op. cit.: 132.

14. Mudarris, Mala Abd al-Karim, op. cit.: 388.

15. Sahib-Zada, Muhammad Ar'ad, op. cit.: 210–211.

PART III

ISLAMIST SOCIAL MOVEMENTS: GENESIS, DEVELOPMENT, STRATEGIES AND EXILE

CHAPTER NINE

The Daʿwa Islamic Party: Origins, Actors and Ideology

Abdul-Halim al-Ruhaimi

Background and Beginnings

The period from the mid-1940s to the mid-1950s was the formative phase during which the beginnings of the modern Islamic movements in Iraq started to take shape. During those years, various Islamic groups and organizations developed. Some of these were offshoots of mother organizations in Arab countries, and others originated in Iraq. Thus they were triggered both by internal factors and by external influences.

The mid-1940s saw the foundation of the Iraqi branch of the Muslim Brotherhood (MB), which had originated in Egypt in 1928. The first MB cells were organized in 1945 in the Iraqi cities of Baghdad and Mosul.[1] (A leading body was set up, and the movement expanded, particularly in 1948, opening public branches in the towns of Samara, Ramadi and Basrah).[2] In that year the movement launched the Palestine Salvation Association, headed by Shaykh Amjad al-Zahawi. In 1951 a front organization was set up under the name of the Islamic Brotherhood Society: this was also chaired by Shaykh al-Zahawi. In the following year the MB Society published a periodical called the 'Islamic Brotherhood'. The movement made its appearance for the first time on the Baghdad University campuses in 1954. And in the same year the movement gained more momentum, publishing its newspaper, al-Hisab [The Judgement].[3]

Another Islamic movement, Hizb al-Tahrir al-Islami (HT), which had a different ideological thrust from the MB, made its appearance in Jerusalem in 1952, under the leadership of Shaykh Taqi al-Din al-Nabhani. In the same year, Jordanian and Palestinian teachers and students living in Iraq initiated the Iraqi branch of the HT. The party organizations and activities were mainly confined at the beginning to Baghdad, Mosul and Nassiriyya. Shaykh 'Abdul-'Aziz al-Badri, Saleh Sirriyya and 'Abdul-Ghani al-Mallah were among the first prominent party figures. The founders made three applications in 1954 to have the party legalized formally, but the government turned them down because of the party's radical line and manifest opposition to the monarchy.[4]

Both the MB and the HT were characterized by Sunni'ism, and their members were therefore mostly Sunni Muslims from predominantly Sunni areas and towns; however, the HT included in its ranks a number of Shi'i Muslims such as Shaykh 'Arif al-Basri, who was to become a leading figure in the Da'wa Party. Those Shi'i members, however, could not remain in the HT, as it retracted on its pan-Islamic line and revealed a markedly Sunni sectarian leaning.[5]

The early to mid-1950s saw the emergence of the first Shi'i offshoots and outfits which may be seen as distinct to the MB and the HT, whether in objectives, working methods or spheres of activity. They were Shi'i groups operating in predominantly Shi'i areas.[6]

For example, Harakat al-Shabab al-Muslim (Movement of Muslim Youth) was founded in Najaf as early as 1950, broadening its activity to the other holy city of Karbala and, to a lesser degree, to Baghdad and Kazimiyya. It took charge of a review called *al-Thikra* [Memory] financed by the al-Jaza'iri school. The Muslim Youth fizzled out and was disbanded in 1954.[7]

Again in Najaf, a small and ineffective organization made its appearance in 1952, labelling itself the Ja'fari Party. Although devoutly Shi'i, this Ja'fari party, according to one of its co-founders, encountered strong pressure in Najaf and soon withered away.[8]

A new group called Munazamat al-'Aqaidiyeen al-Muslimin (Organization of the Muslim Faithful) was founded in 1957 by one of the leaders of the above mentioned Muslim Youth after he had left his organization. The group extended its clandestine work and influence to Baghdad. In the same year another group of pious Shi'is in Najaf launched a pedagogical Islamic movement focused on educational work, and known as the *Shabab al-'Aqida wal Iman* [Youth of Faith and Conviction]. It also disintegrated after a short while.[9]

These – and possibly other – groups had limited political presence and no clout to speak of. They were soon to make their exit virtually unnoticed. The brief account of their appearance and disappearance in the 1940s and 1950s illustrates that political and social conditions in Iraq at that time were conducive to the development of the contemporary Islamic movement as we know it today. These scattered and fragile groups were the immediate precursors, the beginnings of the real Islamic trend which could not materialize until the 1970s. It was only then that the Islamic movement could assert itself as an effective political force in Iraqi society.

The HT and the MB were virtually the only known organized structures of the Islamic movement before the emergence of Shi'i' Islamic organizations.[10] *Al-Hisab*, the mouthpiece of the MB in 1954, was the sole explicitly Islamic newspaper which had a wider circulation than other Islamic publications.[11]

The Shi'i groups established in that period were weak and ineffective compared to the relative prominence of the MB and the HT. Nevertheless, after the preliminary failures, conditions appeared to improve and to become more favourable for the development of another, better equipped Shi'i Islamic organization. The new, strong offshoot would not only learn from the past failure but would be able to capitalize on the successful experience of the MB and the HT: these latter organizations continued in existence until well after the 14 July 1958 Revolution, before practically disappearing some years later. The emergence of the new Shi'i organization, on the other hand, was a turning point in the history of the contemporary Islamic movement in Iraq. The newcomer was the Da'wa – call – Party.

The Da'wa Party: From Foundation to Transformation (1957–79)

From the outset, the newly formed Da'wa party encountered formidable barriers and pressures which profoundly affected its organizational and leadership structure, as well as its future activity. In consequence there is still disagreement today as to when the party was founded and who its founders were. There are various viewpoints surrounding this issue: three predominate.

The first holds that the Da'wa Party was actually founded a few months after the 14 July 1958 Revolution. According to Talib al-Rifa'i, a co-founder, the three initiators were himself, Sayyid Mahdi al-Hakim and a third individual who remains anonymous.[12]

According to the party's own documents, the Da'wa party was established on 12 Rabi' al-Awal 1377 H, i.e., 12 October 1957. This was also verified by Muhammad Saleh al-Adib, a leading figure in the party.[13]

The third assumption is rather more elaborate. It claims that the constituent meeting of an Islamic organization, still without a name, was initiated by eight clerics and lay figures. The gathering was held at the house of the leading Shi'i authority, Sayyid Muhsin al-Hakim, in the Shi'i holy city of Najaf on 12 October 1957. Months after the 14 July 1958 Revolution, a second meeting was held in the holy city of Karbala: the co-founders of the unnamed Islamic organization mentioned above attended, along with some new members. It was at this second meeting that the organization was named the Islamic Da'wa Party, as proposed by Sayyid Muhammad Baqir al-Sadr, who acted as Chair on that occasion. This was regarded as the first – rather than the constituent – meeting of the Da'wa Party.[14] The Da'wa Party literature, contrary to other claims, states that Sayyid Baqir al-Sadr was the founder of the party and the architect of its ideological and organizational structure.[15]

These three diverging assumptions are not without significance. To claim that the party was founded after the 14 July 1958 Revolution portrays it in an unfavourable light: the implications of this are that it was established as a reaction to the influence and popularity of the Iraqi Communist Party. On the other hand, to stress that the Da'wa party was founded before that date means that it had emerged as an objective response to the existing intellectual, political and social conditions.

On closer examination of these assumptions, it may be concluded that the Islamic Da'wa Party was formally launched under this name after 14 July 1958. The meeting held in October 1957 was a constituent gathering to set up a hitherto undeclared Islamic group. Previous meetings which had taken place since 1956 were preliminaries. The party effectively established its presence after 14 July 1958, and its birth was to a certain extent a reaction to the then powerful Communist Party, as well as to other secular movements.

The ten-month interim period from the constituent meeting in October 1957 to the revolution of 14 July 1958 was virtually bereft of any activity by the new party, save the decision taken by the participants in that meeting to launch a movement.

The party was founded in a highly complex, volatile and sensitive religious and social environment. Most religious quarters, whether in the Madrasa – religious schools – or outside it, were opposed to any political Islamic activism in general, and to any organized partisan activity in particular. Involvement in politics was frowned upon.[16] Party literature makes it clear that Sayyid al-Sadr was aware that his efforts to create an Islamic organization would not be well received within a socially and politically conservative milieu.[17] Popular quarters viewed political activism as a departure from Shi'i Islam and its precepts. Any devout Muslim or clergyman involved in politics would be derided, excommunicated and viewed with suspicion.[18]

This hostile attitude was a reflection of the conservative intellectual, political and social conditions, particularly in the city of Najaf, and in the Shi'i traditional, religious hierarchy. That is why the Da'wa Party and Sayyid al-Sadr were extremely concerned that convincing reasons should be offered for establishing an Islamic party. It also explains the character and social background of the elite that made up the party leadership. About half of the members of the leading body were clerics. The other half consisted of an urban elite, including university and religious school graduates. The membership was predominantly made up of students, and middle class professionals.[19]

The founding members anticipated criticism and objections against their organization. They countered this by claiming that Sayyid Mohsen al-Hakim, an influential Shi'i authority, was present at the constituent meeting, as well as emphasizing the presence of the overwhelming majority of prominent clergymen and public figures in the party leadership.[20]

Nevertheless, some religious circles opposed to involving the Shi'i institution in politics continued their negative criticism. The party was anxious to dispel their apprehensions and win them over. This prompted Sayyid al-Sadr to take issue with them by way of a treatise affirming the legitimacy of Islamic party action, and refuting arguments to the contrary. Educational work in this spirit was also stepped up among party members. The treatise was published in 1961 by the party central organ, *Sawt al-Da'wa* – Voice of the Call – under the title 'On the Name and Organizational Form'. In it Sayyid al-Sadr argued that, 'The name 'al-Da'wa al-Islamiyya' – the Islamic call – is the natural name of our work and the legitimate expression of our duty to call upon people to espouse Islam. There is nothing against expressing ourselves as a party, a movement, an organization. As the Islamic *Shari'a* (law) ordains no specific method of proselytizing and change, we may lawfully pursue any beneficial way to propagate the concepts and tenets of Islam'.

Sadr then concluded: 'Had he [Muhammad] lived in our time, he would, by virtue of his wisdom, have readily used modern and suitable methods of information and "tabligh" [admonition]'.[21]

The Da'wa Party set out its general and final objectives in the party documents. The major aims are to: 'restore Islam to the life of Muslims, government by the tolerant *Shari'a* and establishment of the rule of God on Earth as a final goal'.

To attain these goals, the party adopted a policy of transitional, gradual action as 'a universal norm and Islamic code derived from the prophet's tradition in his first call'.[22]

On this basis it defined four phases of action or struggle:

Stage One: *the transformative phase*, which is 'inspired by the form of struggle waged to change the community'.

Stage Two: *the political phase*, which implies 'political struggle against the enemies of Islam'.

Stage Three: *the seizure of power*, or in the words of the party, 'struggle to lead the community'.

Stage Four: *the final phase*, during which the party 'struggles to apply Islam in part of the community and eventually in the entire community'.[23]

Explaining what the first, transformative phase entails, Sayyid al-Sadr wrote in 1961:

> The general character of the Da'wa struggle at this stage is intellectual trans-formation. It is marked by emphasis on promoting transformative conscious-ness within the community as well as shaping up and educating the transforming mass of militants. At the transformative phase the focus is es-sentially on intellectual struggle and only in a secondary way on political struggle. Our call remains so until we enter the second phase where the char-acter of the call will be a different matter.[24]

The Da'wa Party was active underground throughout the first, transformative phase which started in 1957 and lasted 22 years. It moved forward to the second, political phase by coming out into the open in June 1979, five months after the Islamic revolution in Iran.

Over this prolonged period the path traversed by the Da'wa Party was tortu-ous, uneven and changing due to the political developments in Iraq.

During this first, relatively long period, party activity was mainly carried out in the sphere of education. But the phase of building up the 'transforming mass' did not preclude political actions by the party and violent, protective clashes against the government. Because the party had not yet declared its name, these skirmishes were fought within Islamic religious institutions in general, and the lay, popular extensions, in particular. Religious ceremonies and the accompany-ing rites were often the occasions for political encounters. There were therefore no clear-cut dividing lines between the educational work and political action against the regime. This raises the question of the party's judgment on the gains to be made from taking on the regime in a violent confrontation without intro-ducing itself, its aims and platform, to society at large, especially to the strata whose support it was seeking and whose interests it was supposed to express.

Months after the July 1958 revolution the party held its first meeting in the second Shi'i holy city of Karbala. On the initiative of Sayyid al-Sadr, the party's jurisprudent and leader, together with Sayyid Mahdi al-Hakim, the *Jama'at al-'ulama* fil Najaf al-Ashraf (Society of *'ulama* in Holy Najaf) was launched in 1958: it was formally founded in 1959, having been officially legalized by the govern-ment and supported by Sayyid Mohsen al-Hakim, the prominent Shi'i author-ity.[25] The group had various aims, such as combating communism in terms of movement and ideas, and it started a monthly review called *'al-Adhwa'* – The Light – and then a magazine entitled *'al-Risala'* – The Message. Both became mouthpieces of the Da'wa Party, with Sayyid al-Sadr writing their leader com-mentaries.[26]

The Da'wa Party gained in strength and became more active in the period following the 1958 revolution. The downfall of the first Ba'th regime in late 1963, however, was marked by political turmoil and civil strife.

1964–1968 were the 'golden years' of the entire Islamic movement, with the Da'wa party enjoying particular influence. It played a major role in leading the annual 'student processions' which began in 1965;[27] it expanded its organizational network in a number of Iraqi regions and cities; and its illegal newspaper, *Sawt al-Da'wa*, was widely distributed on the campuses of Baghdad University.[28]

Following the coup of 17 July 1968, the Da'wa Party, like most other political movements, was the target of brutal repression by the regime. According to the party chronicles, an 'all-out offensive to liquidate the party' was launched by the government on 28 September 1971.[29] This began with the arrest of Sayyid al-Sadr, who was later released. More arrests followed in 1971 and 1972. In 1973 'Abdul-Sahib al-Dakhil, a leading party figure, was executed.[30] In 1974 Shaykh 'Arif al-Basri and four of his associates were arrested and later executed.[31]

From 1975 onwards, the Da'wa Party played a leading role in organizing processions marking the anniversary of *Marad al-Ras*, known also as the Arba'in Visitation, an annual pilgrimage to Karbala to commemorate the martyrdom of Imam Hussayn. On this emotive and dignified occasion huge crowds of pilgrims would proceed from Najaf to Karbala, mostly on foot. The processions were banned from 1975–1977. Tension caused by repeated bans culminated in a bloody confrontation in February 1977 between protesting pilgrims and government forces. Participants in the processions were savagely assaulted and dispersed at Khan al-Musalla, also known as al-Nus, near Karbala. More than 30, 000 people were arrested and a dozen executed.[32] This episode is described in the literature of the Da'wa Party and the Iraqi Islamic movement in general as the 'Sufar 1977 Uprising'. It was a turning point for both the Da'wa and the government. The aftermath of the confrontation, together with the effects of the Iranian revolution in February 1979, would prompt the Da'wa Party to move swiftly on to the second, political phase.

The Islamic Revolution and the Iran-Iraq War: 1979–1988

Following the one-day detention of Sayyid Baqir al-Sadr on 13 June 1979 (17 Rajab 1399 H), and the Rajab Uprising in protest, the Da'wa Party leadership, after lengthy deliberations, decided to come out into the open and ushered in the second, political phase of its plan of action. This decision was explained in a statement: 'It is time the movement proclaimed itself as a political entity with its own name ending the "clandestine" stage in its militant existence'.[33]

The party subsequently set about arming itself and carrying out military operations against government officials and organs of repression.[34] It was at this point that Sayyid al-Sadr began to issue his famous political appeals confirming the need to take up arms against the regime and calling for its overthrow.[35]

The political developments ensuing from this decision marked a historical turning point for the whole Islamic movement. The Islamic revolution in Iran was an epoch-making event in the history of the region: it had a direct impact on the situation in Iraq. It was, however, an external factor that would have had limited influence on the course of events in Iraq had it not been backed up by internal forces acting in unison with it. The Islamic opposition was so inspired by the revolutionary experience in neighbouring Iran that it was determined to step up its struggle against the Baghdad government.

In retaliation, the Revolution Command Council (RCC) declared Act No.461 on 30 March 1980, which made membership of the Da'wa party punishable by death. Sayyid Muhammad Baqir al-Sadr and his sister Amina – alias Bint al-Huda – were both executed on 8 April 1980, and the war against Iran was unleashed on 22 September in the same year: it was to continue for eight years (a cease-fire was declared on 8 August 1988). The immediate outcome of these events was a serious escalation in the violent confrontations between the ruling regime and the Islamic movement, particularly the Da'wa party. The government was mercilessly brutal in its repression of the party, decimating its ranks in horrifying massacres. In consequence, and especially after the outbreak of the Iran-Iraq war, the bulk of the party's remaining activists and members had to flee from Iraq, mostly to Iran where the party leadership took up residence.

With a war raging between the two countries, the party's positions and actions were greatly influenced by the Iranian policy. The party was identified with Iran, costing it dearly in terms of popularity, triggering internal controversy over the issue, and leading to dire consequences. Unity of the party was undermined by the formation of factions: each of these took away a chunk of the party's supporters and followers.

The same conclusion applies to most other groups of the Islamic movement which, like the Da'wa Party, identified themselves with Iran in the war. The majority of these groups entered into the hostilities on the side of Iran, mobilizing their forces and potential, whether in the Iraqi army or in exile.[36]

Besides involvement in Iran's war effort, the party waged a destabilizing campaign aimed at toppling the Baghdad government from within Iraq. There were coup attempts as well as efforts on the life of the Iraqi President. Apart from bombing operations against government positions and security forces, a total of 15 such attempts were made. The most notable among these were the coup attempts in the air force on 6 January 1980, and the challenge made in the area known as Jizan al-Choul, where the party was heavily counting on engaging most of its cells in the army. There were also the two assassination attempts on the life of the President in Dujail and al-Khalis.[37]

Despite the fact that the Da'wa Party position was unquestionably identified with that of Iran, a faction began to voice its misgivings and strive towards a measure of independence. The establishment of the Supreme Assembly of the Islamic Revolution in Iraq – SAIRI – proclaimed by Sayyid Baqir al-Hakim in Tehran on 17 November 1982, led to this faction regarding SAIRI as an 'Iranian creation' which, apart from being an Iraqi tool in the hands of Iran against the Iraqi regime, has the aim of containing the Da'wa Party and controlling its decision-making. That is why the Da'wa Party has maintained only formal relationships with SAIRI, although it has kept representatives on the Central *Shura* (consultative) Bureau, SAIRI's highest leading body.

Due to the war and the fact that the bulk of the party organization, as well as its material and media resources, were in Iran, the 'independent-minded Iraqi faction' could not assert its presence in the face of domination by the factions favouring total identification with Iran. The majority of the party activists and members were ambivalently reluctant to side decisively with this faction.

Once the Iran-Iraq war ended on 8 August 1988, the party apparatus and activists began to leave Iran for other capitals all over the world; the pro-independence faction steadily grew in strength with its emphasis on the national Iraqi identity of the party. In the wake of Iraq's invasion of Kuwait and its aftermath it was easier for Iraqis to seek refuge in the west. The Da'wa Party moved out of Iran in large numbers to rebuild its organizations and media resources in western countries, where it has been able to draw up its policies and determine its position without the paralysing pressures surrounding Iranian involvement.

Under the impact of the party's experience from its heavy presence in Iran in the 1980s and its experience in western countries thereafter, the party assimilated the lessons drawn from the turns and twists in Iran, or in other countries of the region, or worldwide developments. As a result, significant political, ideological and organizational changes took place within the Da'wa Party, presumably to better enable it to cope with the new realities in Iraq, the region, and across the globe.

Political, Ideological and Organizational Changes in the Da'wa

Since the shift from the first to the second, political stage, the Da'wa Party has experienced significant political, ideological and organizational changes. These changes have been brought about both by the party's own dynamics and the impact of political developments in Iraq and beyond.

On the ideological and political level, the party has virtually re-examined its stand on the question of Islamic government and the nature of its power structures and jurisdiction. When the party was founded, Sayyid al-Sadr was of the view that the basis of Islamic government at present is the *Shura* [consultation]. He expounded this view in *al-Usus al-Islamiyya*, the Islamic fundamentalist bulletin published in 1960. But in 1979, following the Islamic revolution in Iran, he displaced the *Shura* principle with *wilayat al-faqih* [governance of the jurisprudent]. Later, in a treatise entitled 'Islam Rectifies Life', he argued in favour of a combination of old and new principles, reconciling thereby the *Shura* concept with the *wilayat al-faqih* dogma.[38] In 1981, however, the Da'wa Party reverted, unequivocally this time, to 'the governance of the jurisprudent'. Later on, it gradually retracted on this notion.

In one of its bulletins the party explains how its position evolved and mutated in relation to the concept of *wilayat al-faqih*: 'At the transformative [first] stage, which has a spontaneous character, "governance of the jurisprudent" implies perfecting the element of required obedience in party actions. This, however, does not urgently necessitate intervention by the jurisprudent, effective as it may be to a certain extent. Upon entering the second phase the need for such governance grows stronger'.[39]

The party asserts that: 'Delegating decision-making to the jurisprudent does not mean monopolizing it without consulting qualified people and experts. Attention should therefore be drawn to the important point that devolving governance to the jurisprudent in no way means that he will be the actual ruler or president of the republic, for instance. He may assign execution to whoever is elected by the community while assuming the role of supervisor and guide. Thus practical convergence is achieved between the two notions of Shura and governance of the jurisprudent'.[40]

In programmatic terms, this development found its expression in the 'Statement of Understanding' issued in mid-1980. This was more like a political manifesto. In the introduction the party described the programme as 'an interim vision which, in our view, serves as a basis for mutual understanding between all movements, parties and masses of the nation'.[41]

The statement was well received by Iraqi political parties and in intellectual quarters as an important political document demonstrating the party's opening to other political forces and trends. Promising prospects were in the horizon for dialogue and agreement on joint actions between the various groups. The past ten years bear witness to this.

Driven by rapid developments and concerted actions with several Iraqi opposition groups, the Da'wa Party felt the need to elaborate its conception of the political system in post-Saddam Iraq further. In 1992 it published its politico-economic programme, entitled *Barnamajuna*, outlining Iraq's future as envisaged by the party.[42]

In terms of organization, the party has adopted a structure similar to that of present-day organizations. According to Sayyid al-Sadr, the organizational structure of the Da'wa Party has developed 'as improvement on the form common in contemporary organizations taking into consideration the specific interests of the call to Islam'.[43] Accordingly, the Da'wa organizational structure is a hierarchy based on the cell, which is the basic unit consisting of 4–5 members. Next in line are the vertical committees which are progressively divided into local, district and regional committees up to the general leadership. There are also horizontal committees which are in charge of coordination and external relations.

The Da'wa Party has experienced significant transformations, notably after 1980 when the bulk of its activists and leading figures had to move to Iran. Internal party rules were drawn up for the first time to guide inner party life, regulate relations between its various bodies and define the operation and jurisdiction of each body. In addition, for the first time since the first meeting in Karbala in 1959, a party congress was convened in 1981. It was regarded as the 'first congress' of the open, political phase since the 'constituent congress' in 1957. It was attended by delegates from all regions where the party was active both inside Iraq and abroad. The leading bodies were elected at this conference. Under the new statutes, the party was to hold its conference biennially.

Following the introduction of party statutes and the first conference, the party faced serious organizational problems. A faction dissatisfied with the outcome of the conference split away under the name of the 'Abu Yasin Group', and joined the Supreme Assembly of the Islamic Revolution in Iraq – SAIRI – led by Sayyid al-Hakim. After the occupation of Kuwait in 1990 the group renamed itself as 'The Islamic Da'wa'.

In 1987 a prolonged debate between the Da'wa leadership and the then jurisprudent of the party, Sayyid Kazim al-Ha'iri, on the jurisprudent's relationship to the party and his powers, culminated in Sayyid al-Ha'iri standing down and leaving the party with a few of his supporters. A pamphlet entitled 'The Omission Statement' was published in the name of the 'Jurisprudence Council' headed by the dissident clergyman. But this faction soon died out. Other small, ineffective groups have also defected assuming other names than the Da'wa.

Since its foundation up to the first conference in 1982 the party covered a number of regions, including Lebanon and Gulf countries. After that conference, however, it became a purely Iraqi party in terms of membership and leading bodies. It has been striving to demonstrate its 'Iraqi national identity' and clear up the limits of its relationship with Iran as well as with the other Islamic movements. These concerns have found their expression in a number of writings and actions. But the issue is yet to be conclusively settled due to the existence of a faction which, though small, still favours continued identification with Iran, basing itself on a peculiar religious and political outlook to substantiate its stance.

Notes

1. Al-Mu'min, 'Ali, *Sanawat al-Jamr* (Years of Ember: The Islamic Movement in Iraq, 1957–1986), Dar al-Masira, London, 1993: 23.

2. Shubbar, Hassan, *al-'Amal al-Hizbi fil 'Iraq* (Party Politics in Iraq 1908–1958), Dar al-Turath al-Arabi, Beirut, 1989: 252.

3. Ibid.: 252, and al-Mu'min, op. cit.: 24.

4. Ibid.: 252.

5. Al-Mu'min, op. cit.: 24–25.

6. Ibid.: 25.

7. Ibid.: 254 and al-Mu'min, op. cit.: 25.

8. Ibid.: 255.

9. Al-Mu'min, op. cit.: 26.

10. Ibid.: 24.

11. Shubbar, op. cit.: 252.

12. Muhammad Ja'far, Mullah Asghar 'Ali, 'al-Hayat al-Siyasiyya lil Imam al-Sadr' (The Political Career of Imam al-Sadr), in *Muhammad Baqir al-Sadr*, by a group of researchers, Dar al-Islam, London, 1996: 511.

13. Ibid.: 511, al-Mu'min, op. cit.: 230 and Shubbar, op. cit.: 256.

14. Al-'Askari, Sami, 'al-Imam al-Sadr wa Dawruhu fil Sira' al-Siyasi fil 'Iraq' (Imam al-Sadr and his Role in the Political Struggle in Iraq), in *Muhammad Baqir al-Sadr*, op. cit.: 525.

15. The Islamic Da'wa Party: *Istishhad al-sayyid al-Sadr min Manzur Hadhari* (Martyrdom of Imam al-Sadr from a Civilizational Perspective) Lebanon Information Bureau, 1981: 32–34 and al-'Askari, op. cit.: 525.

16. Al-Mu'min, op. cit.: 34.

17. Ibid.: 24.

18. Al-'Askari, op. cit.: 526–27.

19. Muhammad Ja'far, op. cit.: 483.

20. Co-founders of the Da'wa Party who were associates of Sayyid al-Sadr: Sayyid Mahdi al-Hakim, al-Shaykh al-Fadhli, Saleh al-Adib, Sayyid Murtadha al-'Askari, Abdul-Sahib Dakhil, Sayyid Talib al-Rifa'i, Hassan Shubbar, Shaykh Mahdi al-Samawi,

Shaykh Muhammad Mahdi Shamsuldin, Sayyid Muhammad Hussain Fadh Al-lah, Sayyid Muhammad Baqir al-Hakim, Shaykh 'Arif al-Basri and Sayyid Muhammad Baqir al-Hakim himself. Note that half the eight co-founders are cler-gymen and that some of them are from other Arab countries. Al-Mu'min, op. cit.: 33.

21. Al-Da'wa Bulletin, no. 13, *al-Shahid al-Rabi', al-Imam al-Sadr* (Imam al-Sadr, the Fourth Martyr): 9–10.

22. Al-Mu'min, op. cit.: 36.

23. The Islamic Da'wa Party, *al-Marhaliyya fi Nidhal al-Da'wa* (Stages of the Da'wa Struggle): 17.

24. Istishhad, op. cit.: 64–65.

25. *Min Muthakarat Mahdi al-Hakim* (From the memoirs of Mahdi al-Hakim: Islamic Action in Iraq, (n. p.; n. d.): 19.

26. Ja'far, op. cit.: 511, footnote 14.

27. Student processions and assemblies organized by the Da'wa Party to mark the anniversary of the battle in which Imam Hussain was killed in the sixth century. Political slogans were raised in these events.

28. Ja'far, op. cit.: 476.

29. Al-Mu'min, op. cit.: 113–14.

30. Ibid.: 482.

31. Ibid.: 119.

32. Ibid.: 32.

33. Ibid.: 173.

34. Al-'Askari, op. cit.: 541.

35. Al-Mu'min, op. cit.: 175.

36. Ibid.: 231.

37. Ibid.: 103.

38. Al-Ha'iri, Sayyid Kazim, *Dirasat fil Usul* (Treatises in Methodology), Tehran, 1988: 103.

39. Da'wa Party, *Shakl al-Hukuma al-Islamiyya wa Wilayat al-Faqih* (The form of Is-lamic Government and the Governance of the Jurisconsult Doctrine), 1981: 18.

40. Ibid.: 9.

41. Da'wa Party, *Bayan al-Tafahum*, (Statement of Understanding from the Islamic Da'wa Party to the Nation in Iraq), (n. p.), 1980: 28.

42. Da'wa Party, *Barnamajuna* (Our Programme, Manifesto and Political Platform of the Islamic Da'wa Party), (n. p.), 1992.

43. *Al-Shahid al-Rabi'*, op. cit.

CHAPTER TEN

The Muslim Brotherhood: Genesis and Development

Basim al-'Azami

The Islamic trend in Iraq remained weak and marginal during most of the first half of the twentieth century. It began to crystallize in 1945 under the impact of a multitude of internal and external factors. The formative phase of this trend, as represented by the Muslim Brothers, will be examined in this chapter, focusing on the conceptions of the actors involved and the macro setting which framed their activity.

Beginnings

The Islamist response seems to have its origins in the nature of secularism that has been spreading through the media, the state-controlled educational system or the western ideologies by means of radical social movements, threatening Islam as a value system and a way of life.

After the modern nation-state of Iraq was founded in 1921 official education was geared and designed to promote secularism. The general directorate of education at the time was headed by Sati' al-Husri, a staunch centralizing and secularizing figure. Up until the 1950s, successive governments displayed similar leanings.

However, it may be noted that there was a relatively wide scope for freedom to introduce new ideas in the political and social spheres, as well as in literature and art. Within the official realm, or among discontented social groups and strata, different strands of liberalism, radical nationalism, socialism and Marxism took root and spread widely.

Under the monarchy, Iraq was ruled by a pro-western government allied with Britain under the 1930 Treaty. The country's strong man was Nouri Said. Opposition to the political and social system was fierce and led by those with nationalist, social democratic and Communist leanings. Marxism had then been present since 1924, when the first Marxist circle was created in Baghdad under Hussain al-Rahhal.

In the 1930s the nationalist trend was represented by the al-Muthanna Club. It grew steadily in strength until 1941, when Rasheed 'Ali al-Gailani led an aborted coup against British influence in Iraq. In the aftermath, nationalists suffered a setback: the leaders were imprisoned and expelled from their jobs. The nationalist trend, however, was to re-emerge in 1946 when the government legalized political parties. A group of nationalists approached the Tawfiq al-Siwidi government for permission to establish what they called the Istiqlal (independence) Party, which once boasted a membership of 28,000.

The social democrats founded a movement known as the al-Ahali Group in 1930, which was involved in the 1936 coup led by Bakr Sidqi. The coup failed and its leader was eliminated, resulting in a weakening of the movement. The Ahali group was revived in 1946 when the National Democratic Party, led by Kamil al-Chadarchi, was legalized.

The Communists were represented, as noted earlier, by a group of Marxists. In 1934 the *'Usbat Mukafahat al-Isti'mar wal Istithmar* (Anti-Colonialism and Anti-exploitation League) was launched. The name was later changed to the Iraqi Communist Party. The party was illegal and had to go underground. Socialist ideas had become remarkably popular following the aborted coup of 1941. Marxist intellectuals were able to circulate their new ideas and win over intellectuals and professional people. When the government permitted the organization of political parties, groups of individuals known for their Marxist tendencies applied to have their parties legalized. These were the People's Party, led by 'Aziz Sharif, 'Abdul-Rahim Sharif and Tawfiq Munir; the National Union, represented by 'Abdul-Fattah Ibrahim, Muhammad Mahdi al-Jawahiri and Musa al-Sheikh Radhi; a third group, led by Salim 'Obeid al-Nu'man, had its application turned down by the government on suspicion that it was a front organization for the Iraqi Communist Party. The then interior minister went out of his way to facilitate legalization of the first two groups to ward off accusations that only right-wing, conservative pro-government parties were franchised. The British also wanted to reward the Communists for turning against Hitler, following the Soviet Union's example in siding with the Allies.

In these conditions, the Islamist trend was still embryonic. It was only present in the form of small philanthropic and educational societies such as the Muslim Youth Association and the Islamic Guidance Association (Jam'iyyat al-Shabab al-Muslim and Jam'iyyat al-Hidaya al-Islamiyya). Their activity was essentially confined to marking such anniversaries as Prophet Muhammad's birthday: while these continued the celebration of a traditionally cherished occasion, they had no substantial social or political agendas. The only political action in this period was motivated by the struggle in Palestine between Arabs and Jews. Islamists raised funds and issued edicts prohibiting the sale of Palestinian land to foreigners.

The amorphous Islamic trend remained weak and marginal from 1921 to 1945. In this period, it was represented by groups, clerics and Islamic-oriented public figures, but it lacked any definitive structure. It continued to lag behind the four main trends: the pro-Western, secular liberal trend, the social democrats, represented by al-Ahali Group, the Pan-Arabists and the Communists.

The Egyptian Factor

The Islamists fed on literature imported from other Arab countries, especially Egypt. Books and other publications acquainted Iraqi readers with the Egyptian Muslim Brotherhood (MB) and their contribution to the national movement. Having asserted their presence throughout Egypt, the MB began to look beyond the Nile. Militant activists and organizers were sent from Egypt to spread the word and help establish branches in the Arab region. As a result of this recruitment drive, a division of the MB was opened in Djibouti in 1933. Jordan, Syria and Palestine followed in 1946. Among those who came to Iraq in the early 1940s were Dr Hussain Kamal al-Din, a lecturer at the College of Engineering in Baghdad, and Muhammad Abdul-Hameed Ahmad, who worked in Basrah. Thus the Muslim Brotherhood's call was introduced to the people of Iraq through publications supplied from Egypt and through Egyptian activists sent by the movement. Young people were recruited and cells under the MB name were organized in Baghdad, Mosul and Basrah. The first cell was set up in the Baghdad district of ʿAdhamiyya. Its members were Nizam Abdul-Hameed, a Kurdish student at the Institute of Theology – later the College of *Shariʿa* – Ihsan Shirzad, another Kurdish student at the College of Engineering, Sulaiman al-Qabili, a Turkoman student at the law school from the northern city of Kirkuk, Abdul-Rahman Khidr, a lawyer, Mulla Mahmud al-ʿAzami, a cleric, Nizar Khalil, Hussain Ahmad Saleh, Hassan Ahmad Saleh, ʿAbdul-Sattar al-Jiwari, ʿAdnan Rania and Muhaisin ʿAbdul-Qadir, an engineering student. It is interesting to note the ethnic mix of the first cell, which is representative of Iraqi society: Arabs, Kurds and Turkoman.

This activity gained momentum with Shaykh Muhammad Mahmud al-Sawaf's, a doctor of religion, return from Egypt. He was profoundly influenced by Shaykh Hasan al-Bana and joined his movement there. His arrival was preceded by that of the Muslim Brotherhood's Egyptian journal, which printed his picture, depicting him as 'the general guide (*al-murshid al-ʿamm*) of the Muslim Brothers in Iraq'. Al-Sawaf was active, giving lectures in mosques, opening bookshops and promoting Islamic literature supplied from Egypt. As a general guide he was able to bring together and link all the scattered circles in one organization.

First Organization

In 1948 members of the 'Muslim Brothers' formally established themselves through the Society for the Salvation of Palestine (*Jam'iyyat Inqath Falastin*), founded under the chairmanship of the highest-ranking Iraqi cleric, Shaykh Amjad al-Zahawi. Through this society, work focused on religious education and public mobilization around the extremely important issue of Palestine. Three brigades of Iraqi volunteers were dispatched by the society to fight in Palestine.

Also in 1948, the Muslim Brotherhood (MB) were involved in popular protests against the Portsmouth Treaty, signed by the Iraqi government with Britain. Clergymen and religious students in their traditional robes took to the streets with other protesters. Six Muslim Brothers were expelled from the College of Islamic Law in Baghdad for their involvement in the action.

Of paramount importance within the MB were the struggles to combat and reverse the perceived deviations from Islamic values and morals: these were the root causes of all other ills and evils in society, and the reason for its backwardness and weakness. Therefore, the MB saw their incumbent task as restoring the values and meanings of Islam, opening the eyes of the people to its tenets, and relating it to contemporary issues. Emphasis was laid on driving home the message that the causes of the situation provoking such discontent within society is to be sought in the departure from true Islam. The MB set about preaching and propagating their ideas through lectures and sermons usually delivered at mosques. They carried the same message to the rural areas: 'The cause of corruption throughout the land of Islam is deviation from its fundamental teachings and rules. This corruption can be eliminated by creating a virtuous Islamic situation as the only means of doing away with oppression and corruption and safeguarding people's rights'.

The MB viewed the Communists as apostates to be relentlessly opposed, fought and shunned. MB members were prohibited from contact or debate with the Communists, 'not even in the hope of winning them over'. It is not known whether this uncompromising position was a result of a lack of confidence in the MB's ability to argue effectively against the Communists, or in order to avert sideline skirmishes at the inception of their proselytizing work.

In 1951 the Islamic Brotherhood Society was founded with Shaykh Amjad al-Zahawi as president. In 1952 the society published a journal by the same name. Among its non-Iraqi contributors were such Islamic scholars and writers as Sayyid Qutb (Egypt), 'Abdul-Wahab 'Azzam, Muhammad al-Bashir al-Ibrahimi (Algeria), Muhammad Bahjat al-'Attar and Muhammad Taqi al-Din al-Hilali. As the society grew stronger, harassment became more frequent, culminating in 1954 in the banning of the society: its branches were closed down and its property, including many bookshops and libraries, was seized. The journal's licence was terminated. This ban continued until the revolution of July 14, 1958. During that period MB activity was characterized by:

- openness, in contrast to clandestine cells. Meetings and other events were public, and held in branches or headquarters;
- work focused on education and promotion of Islamic precepts and values on both individual and societal levels;
- emphatic rejection of any form of sectarianism. The Islam preached by the MB was idealized as the pure form of pristine Islam, as known by 'pious ancestors';
- the advocates of westernization, secularism, nationalism and Marxism were uncompromisingly denounced, as were the ruling elite, its parties and supporters of their perceived deviation from Islam;
- the Muslim Brothers did not consider themselves a political party but a genuine and new trend. They saw their mission as bigger than that of a political party and their role equally involving political, social and intellectual endeavours;
- the unequivocal support for Islamic causes, as in Palestine and Algeria.

In 1954 the Muslim Brothers defended their counterparts in Egypt against persecution by the Nasser regime. However, during the Suez crisis in 1956 the MB throughout the Arab region sided with Egypt against the tripartite invasion by Britain, France and Israel.

Under the Post-Monarchy Regimes

Following the July 1958 revolution in Iraq, the MB offered their support and allegiance to the new republican regime. But the instigators of the revolution were soon to split into two factions: the pan-Arabists rallied around Abdul-Salam 'Arif, and the Iraqi nationalist and Communist backed General Abdul-Karim Qassim. Ironically, both camps were opposed to the MB for different reasons. At the peak of conflict between the nationalists and Communists, the MB felt they should have their own platform to espouse their party line. They applied for a licence to publish a weekly called 'Banner of the Islamic Brotherhood' (*Liwa' al-Ukhuwa al-Islamiyya*). The revolutionary government obliged and the first issue appeared on 22 January 1959. But after only seven issues the new publication was stopped.

The MB viewed the growing influence of the communist movement with its ideas and working methods as an immediate threat, and was determined to fight the communist menace by every intellectual and propaganda means at their disposal. Religious anniversaries were the most effective way to mobilize men of religion and poets in popular demonstrations against communism.

Following the aborted revolt by al-Shawaf in Mosul 1959, the communist clout was enhanced and they reacted against the MB. As a result, MB activists became targets. Leading figures fled Iraq and a new leadership was set up which went underground and adopted a hierarchical party organization where educational work would be carried out in cells. When General Qassim promulgated the new law on political parties and associations in 1960, the MB saw a second chance for public activity. They applied for licence under the name of the Islamic Party. The founding group included twelve leaders (see table).

Wishing to have the two major Muslim sects, Sunnis and Shi'is, represented in the new party, the MB approached the highest Shi'i authority, Sayyid Mohsen al-Hakim. Not only was he uncooperative but he also banned two Shi'i clergymen, Sayyid Abdul-Zahra al-Saghir and Shaykh Kazim al-Sa'idi, from joining the party. However, a *fatwa* was obtained, declaring the Communists as blasphemous, and published in the Fayha' newspaper on 13 February 1960.

Table of the leading body of the Islamic Party 1962

Name	Sect	Profession	City
Sheikh Abdul-Jalil Ibrahim	Sunni cleric	mosque preacher	Ramadi
Ibrahim Abdullah Shihab	Sunni	businessman	Mosul
Yousif Taha al-Haj Yasin	Sunni	lawyer	Ramadi
Haj Mahmud Allafi	Sunni cleric	merchant	Ramadi
Ibrahim Munir al-Mudarris	Sunni cleric	teacher	Baghdad
Jassim al-'Ani	Sunni	physician	Ramadi
Fadhil Dolan	Sunni	lawyer	Ramadi
Walid Abdul-Karim al-'Adhami	Sunni	poet and calligrapher	Baghdad/ Azamiyya district
Hameed Haj Hamad Thahabiyya	Sunni	merchant	Ramadi

Name	Sect	Profession	City
Nu'man al-Samara'i	Sunni	teacher	Samara
Filayih al-Samara'i	Sunni	agronomist	Samara
Sabri Mahmud al-Leila	Sunni	businessman	Mosul

Strategy and Methods of Struggle

The Muslim Brothers opted for a political Islamic party on the grounds that political action was both a religious and national duty, that the nature of Islam demanded organized action, that leaving 'un-Islamic' parties unchallenged in the political arena was a fatal mistake, and that Islam as a faith required propagation and promotion through organized action.

From the foundation of the Muslim Brotherhood movement in 1954 until the July 1958 revolution, it had no specific programme. Its main concern was educational work through sermons and lectures at mosques. In addition, it may be argued that the movement perceived itself to be a trend within society, rather than a political party. When the opportunity presented itself under the 1960 associations law, the movement drafted a specific programme entitled 'Manifesto of the Iraqi Islamic Party'. The manifesto states that the party seeks to apply fully the rules of Islam in all spheres of life and affairs of both the individual and the state. This leaves no doubt as to the final goal of the party: the establishment of an Islamic state in Iraq. The means by which to attain this objective, as described in the manifesto, are a combination of pedagogical indoctrination and institutional politics, namely educating people in the Islamic culture, and participation in elections when the party is ready to accept responsibility to assume power. The implication is that the party adopted peaceful, institutional means in its campaign to establish an Islamic state.

Although Islamic in nature, the manifesto (Article 6) states that non-Muslims enjoy the same political, public and individual rights as Muslims, except in matters of religion. As an institution of governance, the state is duty-bound to guarantee all these rights. The manifesto also envisages that citizens would have equal opportunities in employment unless otherwise specified. This restriction applies to posts which by their very nature must be occupied by Muslims, such as the head of state and responsibility for *jihad*. The head of state is guardian of the faith and the Islamic state and only Muslims have the duty to go to *jihad*. Needless to say, Islamic religious rites shall be conducted by Muslim doctors of religion and clerics, such as prayer leaders and preachers, just as rites of other religions shall be administered by their respective clerics.

In public life, non-Muslims have the right to vote, elect their own representatives and to be elected to the national assembly. Since the assembly serves as an arena for airing views, counselling the government, discussing problems of the electorate etc., non-Muslims may be fully involved in such activities. They are also entitled to vote in the presidential election, because the office of the head of state has assumed a mundane function, although retaining some of the meanings of the caliphate in the traditional sense.

The manifesto also stipulates that non-Muslims shall not in any way be coerced into Islam, but they may be called upon to espouse it.

In Chapter Two, the manifesto deals with the judiciary of the envisaged Islamic state. It points out that a judiciary is to be established to safeguard the rights of both individuals and communities, and to see that justice is carried out. But it does not specify whether Islamic or positivist laws will be observed by the courts. Apparently, the party saw no need for further elaboration on the issue, as it has stated in the introductory Articles of the manifesto that society shall be ruled according to the Islamic *Shari'a* – law – which draws on the Qur'an, tradition – Prophet Muhammad's sayings and deeds – and 'other' sources. It is these 'other' sources which are a point of contention. In Sunni Islam these include precedent and consensus. In contrast, Shi'i Islam does not recognize precedent as a source of legislation; instead reason supplements the other acknowledged sources. The Islamic Party leaves the question of accommodation between the two schools, the Shi'i and the Sunni, open.

In the social sphere, the Islamic Party holds that the family is society's building block, and that men and women are the pillars of the family, shouldering its burdens. Relations between them are based on equality in rights and duties unless otherwise stipulated by the *Shari'a*. The *Shari'a* states that the woman is the responsibility of the man.

Recognizing the importance of the issue of women, the MB founded the Muslim Sisters Society, headed by Nahla al-Zahawi, Shaykh Amjad al-Zahawi's daughter. The society initiated its activity from the Shaykh's residence until the MB purchased a plot of land for premises in which to house it.

The Islamic Party recognized the right of women to work, but set some conditions based on traditionally held physical and biological limitations. Other reservations were related to what the party termed the 'moral hazards' of certain jobs to women, as well as the risk of neglecting their original duties, which are domestic management and raising children.

The party was of the view that the state should provide for disadvantaged groups by adequate benefits, irrespective of religion or sect; in addition, the state was to shoulder the task of preparing and training people for meaningful employment, generalizing basic education and eliminating illiteracy. In its manifesto, the party pledged to remove secularism.

The envisaged social system was described in the party manifesto as being neither capitalist nor socialist, but an Islamic system in its own right. This third or middle option was characterized by safeguarding private property in general; however, any activity by private enterprise which is either detrimental to society or based on usury or monopoly is prohibited.

Land, however, was to be distributed to the peasants, who will receive interest-free loans to help them set up their own farms. It is not clear whether or not the distributed land is to be state-owned or expropriated from the big landed classes.

The workers were to be organized in non-partisan trade unions to ensure their independence. Without further elaboration on workers' rights, the Islamic Party held that the state was bound to provide employment for the workers who should enjoy a decent life free from exploitation by employers.

The party underlined the need for the state to explore and tap the country's natural resources in the interests of the people as a whole. However, it did not specify how; nor did it mention Iraq's greatest asset, the oil sector, which at that time was exploited by foreign companies.

The party laid emphasis on developing the Iraqi economy in general terms. The driving force of the Islamic economy, be it the state, private enterprise, individual initiative or foreign investment, was ambiguous.

On the home front, the Islamic Party upheld national unity on the basis of Iraqi citizenship irrespective of religion, ethnicity or sect. This was to serve as a nucleus of Pan-Arab unity, which would in turn be the nucleus of Islamic unity as advocated by the party. Unity should be achieved gradually, beginning with unity of Iraq, then unity of the Arab nation and at some point in the future unity of the Islamic community. The party, however, did not specify the means by which to attain Arab unity.

The party came out against colonialism for the independence of Iraq without a definitive plan of action to realize this goal.

The party programme asserted that the Palestinian problem could only be solved by force. The MB viewed the Arab-Israeli conflict as the central issue concerning the entire Islamic community. The Society for the Salvation of Palestine founded by the MB had dispatched volunteers to fight in the 1948 war in Palestine. The manifesto called for the Palestinians to mobilize and prepare to fight the next war.

Accordingly, it may be understood why the Islamic Party reacted angrily to Iran's recognition of Israel, branding the Shah's move as a crime against Islam. It sided with President Nasser's decision to sever diplomatic relations with Tehran.

In its global outlook, the party conceived the people of all nations as integral parts of a united whole – humanity – irrespective of ethnic origin or religion. This pan-human fraternity is consistently applied to non-Muslims within or beyond the national community.

The party's programme gave no mention of the Iraqi army and its role in politics. This may be explained by the fact that the 1960 Law of Associations banned members of the armed forces from joining political parties.

Legal Confrontation

In the spring of 1960, the founding group applied for a licence to launch the new party; this, however, was turned down by the Interior Ministry under various pretexts, including the claim that sections of the party's programme were neither compatible with the spirit of the age nor with the tolerant *Shari'a*, and that some of the founders and supporters had connections with foreign groups and figures. On 9 April 1960 the constituent body of the Islamic party appealed against the decision, and on 26 April the court of appeal overruled the ministry's verdict, legalizing the party as an organization with a manifesto in line with the country's provisional constitution.

The Islamic Party was thus legalized by the court of appeal, not by the Interior Ministry. The Iraqi judiciary was independent of the executive at the time. The only action taken against the members of the court was to deprive them of the new building which was to house their court. (It was demolished on the order of General Qassim.)

Having been legalized by the court of appeal as from 26 April 1960, the Islamic party decided that it was time to establish its own newspaper which would be used for the expression of its views in accordance with the law. The Ministry of Information and Guidance denied the party this right: the planned newspaper's editor, Fadhil Dolan, a lawyer, was objected to and a replacement was demanded. The party did not comply, and pointed out that the appointed editor was a co-founder of the party and already editor of the party's publication, *al-Hiyad*.

Political Clash with Qassim and Beyond

Al-Hiyad waged two major battles. One was a petition demanding the formation of a committee of experts in Islamic law to review all existing laws and keep only those in harmony with the *Shari'a*. Another was a plan on the ways and means by which to combat communism. In this atmosphere, the Ministry of Guidance eventually gave the party permission to have its own newspaper, *al-jihad*, of which about 20 issues appeared before it was closed down by the authorities. On 15 November 1960 the party addressed a memorandum critical of the Prime-Minister, General Abdul-Karim Qassim. As a result, the party was suspended and its leaders rounded up. They were freed after five months in detention and received by General Qassim. During a meeting that lasted several hours, he asked them to change the party into a public association. They refused and the party remained suspended.

The years following the downfall of General Qassim in 1963 and the rise of General Abdul-Salam ʿArif, the Baʿth Party and pan-Arabism as a whole, were marked by severe restrictions in political life. In those years the MB focused on re-grouping and recruitment. Since public political activity was inhibited, political parties shifted their spheres of action to the professional and labour unions. The MB had strong influence in the teachers' and students' unions.

It was the MB who had launched the Islamic Teachers' Association in 1960 to promote their ideas in the field of education and counter communist influence. At its first conference, held on 2 August 1961, the association adopted its statutes and decided to fight the teachers' union elections in alliance with Baʿthists and nationalists against the communists. The MB justified this tactic on the grounds that the professional and labour unions were more concerned with social issues than politics. Besides, in the face of communism, the Baʿthists and nationalists were viewed as the lesser of two evils.

In 1966 the MB decided to fight the teachers' union election on an independent slate. The rival, disunited nationalist groups patched up their differences and thwarted what would have been a spectacular breakthrough by the Islamists. Another reason for the defeat was the insufficient attention paid by the MB to female teachers, who accounted for a considerable proportion of the membership of the teaching profession and turned out in force to cast their votes in the union election.

In mid-1967 the MB leadership in Iraq had become aware that the Islamic education of its members was suffering due to its preoccupation with political action and trade union elections. A decision was taken to prioritize party education, organization and recruitment, and to shelve political action for the time being.

On 17 July 1968 the Baʿth Party came to power by a coup d'etat. When the first government, headed by Abdul-Razzak al-Nayif, was formed, Dr Abdul-Kareem Zaidan, a Muslim Brother, was nominated Minister for Religious Affairs. In fact, Dr Zaidan had not been approached about this appointment: his name was proposed by Ibrahim al-Dawood, one of the army officers who were in league with the Baʿthist putschists. Dr Zaidan was not aware of his new position until a friend called to offer his congratulations.

Army officers who collaborated with the Baʿth Party in staging the coup had recommended Dr Zaidan, probably because they recognized their lack of a power base. They felt the need for a constituency drawn from established groups to lean on in what they perceived as an inevitable showdown with the Baʿth Party. The latter, however, pre-empted their move on 30 July 1968 by dismissing those army officers who had helped the Baʿth Party to carry out its coup against President ʿAbdul-Rahman ʿArif.

Islamic groups were unanimous in their opposition to the new Baʿth secular regime. The expected conflict was not long in coming. Tension was rising by the day, as arrests of Islamic activists by the regime increased. A number of detained Islamists were tortured to death in the Ba'th dungeons: the most prominent among these was Shaykh 'Abdul-'Aziz al-Badri, who died in 1969. On 1 April 1971 the entire leadership of the Muslim Brotherhood, as well as high-profile activists, were rounded up. Others fled Iraq and sought refuge in a neighbouring country. Reassessing the situation in the wake of these developments, the MB concluded that:

- the Ba'th Party had seized power with foreign backing;
- the opposition forces were too divided to put up an effective resistance;
- the profound and rapid changes put into place in the armed forces by the Ba'th Party had made it almost impossible to count on the army for counter-action;
- the Muslim Brotherhood was out-matched by the Ba'th Party;
- Ba'th in-fighting could undermine the ruling party and bring down the regime.

In the light of this assessment, the MB opted for retreat rather than confrontation with the Ba'th Party. The immediate task was to absorb the blows dealt to the movement and to overcome the aftermath of the regime's crackdown. The MB decided that the next phase should focus on ideological struggle between Islam and the Ba'th Party. To succeed in this, the MB thought it was vital not to provoke the Ba'th into wiping out Islam under the pretext of combating their enemies. The movement was also convinced that the period 1959–1968 had so forged its members as to render them ideologically immune and discretely capable of action under almost all circumstances.

This policy imposed self-marginalization. The movement was stunted in Iraq for years to come, although it had active members in the community. Yet they were the target of harsh persecution, arrests and execution. Many had to flee the country. Those who remained were able to replenish the movement with new recruits, preserve its existence and maintain what popularity it enjoyed in Iraq.

After the Second Gulf War

In 1991, following the dramatic events triggered in Iraq by its invasion of Kuwait and the ensuing military campaign launched by the international coalition forces, intensive talks were held between former members of the Islamic Party and activists of the MB, especially those in exile. The talks, spanning the entire first half of 1991, resulted in an agreement to revive the Islamic Party on the basis of its original principles and guidelines. Britain was chosen as the seat of the resurrected party's declared leadership and press organs. Among the leading names made known to the public were Usama al-Tikriti, physician, Ayad al-Samarra'i, engineer, Farouk al-'Ani, engineer, and Basim al-'Adhami, lawyer – all middle-class Sunni Arabs.

The first issue of the party's central organ, *Dar al-Salaam,* appeared on 1 November 1991. Reintroducing itself in a leader entitled, 'Who we are and what we want', the party stated its aim to be the salvation of Iraq against a US-led western conspiracy which was plotting to destroy it in the interests of Israel and ensuring oil supplies to the western world.

When opposition groups mushroomed in the wake of the Gulf War, with many counting on US efforts to overthrow the Baghdad regime, the Islamic Party reacted against this line which was depicted as feeding on 'illusion'. It declared that: 'After all, it was America which had installed a dictatorship in Iraq. We do not want to replace a party by another or a tyranny by another . . . Islamic Party believes that all parties are free to put forward their ideas in a peaceful way because the dire state Iraq has been reduced to is due to denying freedom to the others'.

In a pamphlet entitled *'The Iraqi Islamic Party, Guidelines and Concepts'* the party set forth its views on the situation in the country and its proposed remedies: these include the plight of the Iraqi people as a result of international sanctions imposed after the invasion of Kuwait. The pamphlet may be considered as a party programme.

In this pamphlet, the party calls for the establishment of an Islamic state in Iraq, viewing this as a way out of the country's isolation: the reasoning behind this is that all Muslim countries will then rally around the Iraqi people and support them in the massive task of reconstruction. Islam will also accommodate pan-Arab and other nationalist sentiments by virtue of its being the only common denominator uniting Arabs, Kurds, Turkomans and other ethnic groups, including Sunnis and Shi'is.

The pamphlet stressed that the Islamic Party recognized that Islam could only be applied in gradual steps after such a long period of 'deviation'. Distancing itself from any particular Islamic school of law, the party declared that all jurisprudential judgments – *ijtihad* – of all confessions serve as sources of legislation.

The Islamic Party holds that pluralism goes beyond that of parties to plurality of thought, approach and view, which is acceptable in politics. But the party qualifies this by stipulating respect of the Islamic faith and its precepts. It argues that there is no system without clearly defined boundaries. However, persuasion through dialogue rather than coercion is the way to change.

The Iraqi Islamic Party views democracy as a term that originated in the west and led to a variety of political theories and notions that have branched out of the fundamental concept. The existing consensus is that democracy means pluralism, freedom and universal suffrage. But the Islamic Party is in favour of the Islamic political theory, which it conceives to be more original than western-style democracy. Islam, according to the party, believes in freedom, tolerates differences of opinion and refers to consultation – *shura* – in decision-making. It is thus in agreement with the basic principles of democracy but discards the flaws which may turn freedom into anarchy, plurality into a sell-out of the nation's interests, and the ballot box into an instrument to legalize what is forbidden, which is religiously impermissible. In short, Islam would provide for a higher form of government that would better safeguard the rights and interests of both individuals and community than western democracy.

The Islamic Party holds that it is in the interests of Iraq for all political parties to promote peaceful, electoral practices, as opposed to political violence.

Accordingly, the Iraqi Islamic Party propounds its ideas by means of educational work, the media and all other forms of peaceful action, provided that people's freedom and political rights are respected.

Notes

1. Ghafouri, Khalil 'Adil, *Ahzab al-Mu'aradha al-'Alaniyya fil 'Iraq* (Parties of Legal Opposition in Iraq), *1946–1954*, Baghdad, 1984: 32.
2. Al-'Akkam, Abdul-Amir Hadi, *Tarikh Hizb al-Istiqlal al-'Iraqi* (History of the Iraqi Independence Party), *1946–1958*, Baghdad, 1980: 12–15.
3. Batatu, Hanna, *The Old Social Classes and the Revolutionary Movements of Iraq*, Princeton, Princeton University Press, 1978: 389–408.
4. Khalil, op. cit.: 82.
5. Ibid.: 131.
6. Al-Hasani, 'Abdul-Razzak, *Tarikh al-Wizarat al-'Iraqiyya* (The History of Iraqi Cabinets), Baghdad, 1988: 44.
7. Al-Sudani, Sadiq Hassan, *al-Nashat al-Sahyuni fil 'Iraq* (Zionist Activity in Iraq), *1914–1952*, Baghdad, 1986: 130–146.
8. *Al-Mujtama'* Journal, no. 127, Kuwait, 21 July 1997.
9. Al-Gaylani, Musa Zaid, *al-Harakat al-Islamiyya fil Urdun* (The Islamic Movements in Jordan), Amman, 1990: 8, 27.
10. Al-Aloosi, Muhammad, *interview,* London, 25 November 1997.
11. Al-Sawaf, Muhammad Mahmud, *Min Dafatir Thikrayati* (Notes from my Memoirs), Cairo, 1987: 178.
12. *Al-Thakafa al-Jadida*, monthly review published by the Iraqi Communist Party, no. 103.
13. Conversation in Baghdad with Shaykh Ibrahim Munir al-Mudarris, one of those expelled.
14. *Risalat al-Siyasa* (Messages of Politics), unpublished party literature, Muslim Brothers: 42.
15. Ibid.
16. *Nashrat Jam'iyyat al-Ikhwan al-Muslimin* (Bulletin of the Islamic Brotherhood), general headquarters, (n. d.) (n. p.): 2.
17. *Al-Fayha'* newspaper, (Arabic), no. 87, Baghdad, 16 April 1960.
18. Ibid.

19. *Al-Fayha'* newspaper, (Arabic), no. 26, Baghdad, 30 April 1960.
20. Conversation with Nizamuddin Abdul-Hameed, member of the executive of the Islamic Party in 1960, conducted in Leeds, 7 February 1998.
21. *Al-Hiyad* newspaper, no. 85, 27 July 1960.
22. *Al-Hiyad* newspaper, no. 45, 31 May 1960.
23. Ibid.
24. *Al-Hiyad* newspaper, no. 81, 24 July 1960.
25. Conversation with Nizamuddin Abdul-Hameed, 7 February 1998.
26. *Risalat al-Siyasa*, op. cit.: 32.

CHAPTER ELEVEN

Islamist Fundamentalist Movements Among the Kurds

Sami Shourush

The 1980s and 1990s witnessed a strong fundamentalist resurgence among Iraq's Kurds, greatly spurred on by the intensification of national oppression against them. However, the origins of Kurdish Islamic fundamentalism go back to the nineteenth century, when the Kurdish political nationalist movement came to be led by Kurdish Shaykhs and clergymen such as the Naqshabandi Shaykh, 'Obaidullah al-Nahri, who led an extensive armed movement against both the Iranians and Ottoman authorities in 1820. Thus, in particular circumstances of the nineteenth century, the Kurdish liberation movement acquired an Islamic veneer.

Within Iraqi Kurdistan, there are at present a number of relatively weak and organisationally disparate Islamic organisations. However, when combined, these organisations form the basis of the Islamic fundamentalist movement among the Kurds, and they are in themselves a noteworthy political and religious phenomenon.

The Islamic Movement in Iraqi Kurdistan

The political, or more precisely, the organisational form of the Kurdish Islamic fundamentalist movement began in 1952 with the spread to Kurdistan of the fundamentalist Egyptian-based movement of Imam Hasan al-Banna of Egypt. The man who initiated contact with that movement is said to have been Mulla 'Osman 'Abdul-'Aziz, who is currently the main Spiritual Guide of the Islamic movement in Kurdistan. The Muslim Brother (MB) movement in Iraq gained strength during the years 1961–63; it was joined by Kurdish clergymen, including Mulla 'Ali 'Abdul-'Aziz, the current Deputy Spiritual Guide, Mulla 'Omar 'Abdul-'Aziz, their cousin, Shaykh Salih 'Abdul-Karim[1] and Mulla Muhammad al-Shahrazoori, who died in the mid-1980s. After the intensification of the Ba'thist onslaught against the Kurds, those Kurdish members identified two main failings within the MB: that it had not taken note of Kurdish national particularities, and that it had not called for armed struggle against the Ba'th Party. In the words of those Kurdish Muslims, the Ba'th Party 'ruled Iraq with an infidel ideology based on a heathen nationalism and racism on the one side, and a communist socialism on the other'.[2] Those Kurdish members also objected to the MB's primarily peaceful and pious methods of advancing its political aims. Consequently, they developed the idea of establishing a Kurdish Islamic organisation as the basis for its political and armed activity.

The Kurdish Islamic publication, al-Nafeer, has taken a critical stand regarding the positions adopted by the various organisations of the Islamic movement in Iraq towards the Kurdish people. In an article commemorating the anniversary of the September Kurdish revolution of 1961, the paper charges that these organisations neglect the Kurdish question, and says that such an attitude has caused Kurdish Islamists to distance themselves from those movements. It also notes that those organizations have not issued a statement of their views of an Islamic position towards the Kurdish popular movement, and that they have attempted to educate Kurds away from armed confrontation and to discourage even the thought of a reliance on arms (for example, by preaching that 'people have to hold back and take to prayer').[3] Al-Nafeer elaborates on its criticism of the Islamic movement in Iraq by recalling that after the inception of the September 1961 revolution, Kurdish cadres in the Islamic movement raised the issue of revolution with Dr 'Abdul-Karim Zaidan, who was acting as general 'supervisor' of the MB movement in Iraq at the time. They also requested the deployment of advanced cadres capable of occupying what the Kurdish Muslim militants believed was their natural position of leadership and guidance of the Kurdish movement, but Zaidan rejected their request.[4]

The Kurdish Muslim cadres were strengthened in their determination to form their own organisation and declare armed struggle against the regime of Saddam Hussayn after the intensification of Iraqi policies against the Kurds, such as the destruction of Kurdish villages, deportation of their inhabitants and the use of chemical weapons against Kurdish civilians, especially against the town of Halabje, which had itself been an important centre of those Islamic cadres. These conditions led to the creation of the Islamic movement in Iraqi Kurdistan and the decision to focus on armed struggle. It began that struggle (jihad) in the Kurdistan mountains, through an armed organisation composed mainly of Islamic Kurdish fighters. The basic objective of that organisation is to rid Iraq and Kurdistan of 'Saddam's infidel regime'.[5]

In the first half of the 1980s and during the years of the Iran-Iraq war, the Iraqi government had in various ways encouraged the emergence of a Sunni religious movement in order to act, as that government had hoped, as a barrier against the penetration into Kurdistan of the religious and political influence of Iran and its Shi'i forces. The government had viewed the Islamic movement as a useful counterweight to its adversary, the armed Kurdish movement, which it accused of cooperating with Iran. However, things did not work out as planned for the Iraqi government. The Islamists soon turned to violence in their struggle against the 'infidel regime'.

The Islamists' proclamation of violence against the Iraqi government has in fact been a blow to Iraq's sectarianism. It is evident the Iraq's sectarian balance depends on the proportion of Sunni Kurds (18.4 percent of the population according to Batatu).[6] Thus, the emergence among Iraq's Kurds of a Sunni Islamic organisation which calls for *jihad* against the Sunni government, is of significance – whether direct or indirect – for the sectarian foundations of government. It is for that reason that the Iraqi government reacted strongly to the proclamation of *jihad* by the Islamic movement in Iraqi Kurdistan.

It appears that the government had been aware of the inclinations of this organisation, particularly in the latter's stronghold of Halabje, since 1986. In April of that year, the Ba'th Party in the Halabje area circulated to its organs and branches a study of the religious phenomenon in that area, referenced 12/275 and dated 2.4.1986. That was then followed with directives to those branches to monitor clergymen, to keep watch on Muslim students and to maintain a continuous, close and vigilant surveillance of the phenomenon of religious adherence and of its trappings.[7]

The Islamic movement has been a newcomer to political organisation in Iraqi Kurdistan, and it has had to contend with a deep-rooted nationalist movement which deprived it of possibilities of rapid growth and expansion in the area. Nevertheless, the organised Islamic movement was able to achieve perceptible advances, as in the recent elections in Iraqi Kurdistan where it polled 47,000 votes and ranked in third position, albeit a long way behind the large Kurdish parties, the Kurdistan Democratic Party and the Patriotic Union of Kurdistan.

As the Islamists themselves believe, it is possible to consider the phenomenon of the formation of armed Kurdish Islamic organisations as a clear reflection of a number of factors: firstly, the destruction of Kurdish towns and villages by the Ba'th Party in Iraq; secondly, the proclamation by the Islamic Republic of Iran of its willingness to support the 'oppressed' of the world, especially Muslim fighters. Both factors have encouraged the Kurdish Islamic movement to organise in armed national organisations.

The Islamic Movement of Iraqi Kurdistan is among the largest Islamic organisations in Iraqi Kurdistan. This movement has succeeded in entering the Kurdistan Front, formed by the Kurdish parties in 1988, and it has been able to establish alliances with both Saudi Arabia and Iran, despite the political tension between the two states during the Iran-Iraq war. In addition, the movement maintained close links with Arab Islamists and a friendly relationship with the Christian west. 'Jihad' for this Kurdish Islamic organization differs to some extent from the meaning the concept has for the Shi'i Islamic parties. For this movement, it does not imply action against western interests, but action to overthrow the regime of Saddam Hussayn. This is why it was successful in building alliances outside the confines of the Islamic religion.

In addition to this organization, there are other Kurdish fundamentalist Islamic groups both inside and outside Iraqi Kurdistan. These other organizations do not enjoy the same degree of mass support. Together, however, they represent a noteworthy fundamentalist phenomenon.

The Kurdish Islamic Association

This organization is headed by Shaykh 'Ali al-Qaradaghi, a professor at Riyadh University in Saudi Arabia, and it forms a Kurdish arm of the Iraq organisation of the Muslim Brotherhood. It calls for the rejection of nationalist ideas in favour of the Islamic religion and the Islamic caliphate, as the answer to national questions in the Islamic world.[8]

The Association publishes the journal *Banki Haq* in both Arabic and Kurdish, and it has a limited perceptible presence in Kurdish cities. Its main activities tend to be concentrated outside Kurdistan and outside Iraq, particularly in Pakistan, Jordan and the Gulf countries. Shaykh 'Ali's initiative to reorganise the Kurdistan regional organization of the Iraq Muslim Brotherhood has not borne fruit, although the Association has become more inclined towards dealing with the particularities of the Kurdish question.

The Kurdistan Hizbullah (Party of God)

This organisation is composed primarily of the Barzanis, who took refuge in Iran after the collapse of the armed Kurdish movement in 1975. It is led by Shaykh Muhammad Khalid al-Barzani, the spiritual guide of the Naqshabandi order among the Barzanis. The Party was formed after the beginning of the Iran-Iraq war, and it is supported by Iran. It appears to have taken this name for itself in order to be identified with the similarly-named Iranian-backed Shi'i parties. However, the movement has distinguished itself from other pro-Iranian Hizbullah by avoiding the practices associated with those parties, except for its armed struggle against the Iraqi government.

There is no reliable information on the Kurdistan Hizbullah, but the party's influence among the Kurds appears to be very limited. Moreover, it seems unable to expand its membership outside the circle of Barzani supporters of Shaykh Muhammad Khalid. A notable development in this party is the sudden split which took place a few years ago when Shaykh Adham al-Barzani broke away from the party of his uncle Shaykh Muhammad Khalid, and established a separate Islamic party known as the Islamic Revolutionary Party.

The Association of Muslim Students in Kurdistan

The members of this association rally around the journal *Alai Islam* published by the Association in America in both Arabic and Kurdish. The first issue, published in July 1986, was edited by Azad Karmiyani and Kolala Asinker. Later, the editorship passed to Dr Kawah 'Abdullah. The success of the Association in mobilising some Kurdish youth in Europe and in establishing a web of relationships among Iranian, Turkish, Kurdish and Arab Islamic tendencies, provided this Association and its monthly journal with a good opportunity to expand outside Kurdistan. One of its most prominent achievements was the prime role played by its cadres in organising the Köln meeting in Germany during 19–21 January 1990.

This Association had been founded in a conference in Canada in early 1988. It declared itself a professional non-party association of Muslims in Kurdistan. Simultaneously, its aims were defined as: the Islamisation of the Kurdish issue through the establishment of an Islamic alternative for the Kurdish people's struggle to win its just rights; training of Islamic cadres to operate in Kurdistan; cooperation with other Islamic organisations in order to combine their efforts for the establishment of an Islamic state.[9]

With its activity concentrated outside Kurdistan, the Association lacks an effective presence among the Kurds. However, it plays an essential role in enhancing mutual understanding among Kurdish Islamic organisations. It also tries to develop common action with the Islamic movements of the Arab countries, Turkey and Iran, and it increases awareness among these movements of the justice of the national cause of the Kurdish people.

The Association of Fayli Kurdish Muslims

This is a small organisation which lacks clear objectives. It is essentially composed of some Shi'i Kurds who were exiled by the Iraqi government to Iran during 1971–1975. They are mostly concentrated in the Iranian town of Islamabad, and they aim to establish an organised Kurdish Fayli Islamic Party, which would both cooperate with Iran, and distinguish itself from the Supreme Islamic Council which is led by Sayyid Muhammad Baqir al-Hakim.

This organisation has been unable to extend itself into Iraq, because of the oppression directed at the Fayli Kurds in Baghdad and other Iraqi cities, and also because few Fayli Kurds remained in Iraq after recurrent campaigns of expulsion to Iran. Indeed, this organisation has not even gained wide support among the Shi'i Iraqi Faylis, a majority of whom support either the Supreme Iraqi Islamic Council which has Kurdish Shi'i representatives inside Iraq, or they support the Iraqi opposition Kurdish nationalist parties.

These are some general features of the fundamentalist Islamic Kurdish movement in Iraq, which can be described as organisationally weak on the one hand, and committed to the Kurdish national spirit on the other.

Notes

1. *Al-Nafeer* Newspaper, no. 3, 1989.
2. Ibid., no. 1, 1988.
3. Ibid.: 7.
4. Ibid.
5. Ibid.: 3.
6. Batatu, Hanna, *The Old Social Classes and the Revolutionary Movements of Iraq*, Princeton, Princeton University Press, 1987: 60.
7. *Al-Nafeer*, Issue 3: 3.
8. Al-Karadaghi, Ali Muhiaddin, *The Kurdish Question, The Problem and the Islamic Solution*, (n. d.) (n. p.): 16–18.
9. *Alay Islam*, the Central Journal for AMSK, Issue 14.

CHAPTER TWELVE

The Deportation of Shi'is During the Iran–Iraq War: Causes and Consequences

Ali Babakhan

Introduction

Take your belongings and leave. You have come to us bare-foot, and now that the country had educated you into a civilized human being, you are seeking [to rejoin] your paternal uncles [the Iranians]. Go back to them then.

That is what we have done in Iraq . . . There are some Iraqis who had come 50 years ago or their seventh grandfather was non-Iraqi. But once they misbehave, they will remind us of their past affiliation. Then we will tell them

You have remembered your background, Leave in a hurry. This is our policy in Iraq.[1] The basic criterion for those of Iranian origin whom we will grant permit to remain or not, even when they have been naturalized, is whether or not they behave in accordance with the country's security and national interest; when they misbehave they remind us of their past affiliation and hence we tell them: the Iraqi citizenship no longer applies to you, this is our course of action.[2]

These statements by Iraq's President, Saddam Hussein, refer to Iraqi Shi'i citizens deported to Iran. They are but one example of the hostility harboured against the Shi'is of Iraq not only within the ruling Ba'th Party and by state officials, but at the highest decision-making level. It has resulted in the deportation of hundreds of thousands of Iraqis under the pretext that they have no Iraqi citizenship or are of Iranian origin, or are unfaithful to the 'Ba'th revolution'. Many have been deported on mere suspicion regarding their political allegiance.

The methods employed in carrying out the deportations were characteristically brutal and involved midnight raids, rounding up those targeted for expulsion, cramming them into buses without a chance to take any belongings, seizing what papers they had, holding them in concentration camps, transporting them to the Iranian border, dumping them in the wilderness and then forcing them at gun-point to walk into Iranian territory in treacherous climatic conditions and across a mined terrain. Hundreds of children, pregnant women and old people perished as a result. The Iraqi government systematically confiscated the property and life-savings of the deportees. It has since been holding males between the ages of 18 and 28 – who are considered fit and eligible to take up arms – in special camps.

Those familiar with Iraq's modern history will readily recognize that there had been cases of deportation, exile or denial of citizenship rights in the past: never, however, on such a massive scale or coupled with such savagery. Even the most anecdotal of evidence testifies to the fragile nature of citizenship rights in Iraq. Take the following examples:

Muhammad Mahdi al-Khalisi, his sons and Muhammad al-Sadr were deported to Iran in 1923 on the grounds that they were of Iranian origin, although they were Iraqis of unquestionable Arab background.[3] In 1934 Raisan al-Gassid, Farhud al-Findi and Mizhir al-Gassid, chieftains of insurgent tribes in the region of Suk al-Shiukh in the south of Iraq, were exiled to Ramadi, west of Baghdad. After a short while they were allowed back to their homes. Following his revolt Shaykh Sha'lan al-'Attiyya was exiled to Ramadi and from there to 'Aana. Thiban al-Ghabban and Muhammad al-Cherchafchi, both lawyers, were exiled to Kirkuk in the North where they remained for six months.[4] In 1935 Ahmed Asadallah, a cleric, was stripped of his Iraqi citizenship for allegedly inciting disobedience to the central government among tribes in Rumaitha. On 4 August 1936 'Abdul-Qadir Isma'il and his brother Yousif Isma'il were stripped of their Iraqi citizenship and later, on 2 August 1937, were sent into exile abroad.

Accused of being communists in 1954, Kamil Qazanchi and Tawfiq Munir were exiled to Turkey, having been stripped of their Iraqi citizenship.[5] In 1956 Saddiq Shanshal and Fa'iq al-Samara'i, both pan-Arabists, were to have been exiled to Qala'at Diza and Halabje in northern Iraq respectively, but were allowed to remain in Baghdad having presented the required bond. During the same period the then dean of the law school, 'Abdul-Rahman al-Bazzaz, later Prime-Minister under President 'Abdul-Rahman 'Arif, and other university lecturers were exiled to the Kurdish town of Penjawin. They were then ordered by the government to be moved to the Arab town of Takrit. They were exiled for supporting Egypt against the tripartite invasion by Britain, France and Israel during the Suez crisis in 1956,[6]

The Assyrians, one of Iraq's ethnic groups, have also had their share of deportation and exile. On 15 August 1933 their spiritual leader, Mar Sham'oun, and followers were sent into exile abroad having been stripped of their Iraqi citizenship,[7]

On 2 March 1950 Iraqi Jews were stripped of their Iraqi citizenship.[8]

Among the Kurds, Shaykh Mahmud al-Hafeed was exiled to Nassiriyya in 1931 and later to 'Aana. Eventually he was put under house arrest in Baghdad until 1941, after which he returned to the Kurdish town of Sulaymaniyya, where he died in 1956.[9] His son, Shaykh Latif Mahmud al-Hafeed, was exiled to Nassiriyya in 1941.[10]

In 1932 the Iraqi authorities exiled Shaykh Ahmed al-Barzani, chieftain of the Barzani tribe, his brother, the legendary Kurdish leader Mullah Mustafa al-Barzani, and followers to Nassiriyya, Hilla and then to Diwaniyya. They were later sent back to the northern town of Sulaymaniyya, where they were kept under house arrest until Mullah Mustafa al-Barzani staged his revolt in 1943.[11]

These are the cases compiled between the time of the foundation of the Iraqi state and the assumption of power by the Ba'th Party in 1968. A few years later the phenomenon of mass deportation had set in.

There have been recurrent disputes between Iraq and Iran: the Shatt al-Arab waterway; the 1979 Iranian revolution and Saddam Hussein's ambition to act as the region's policeman filling the strategic vacuum caused by the Shah's downfall, as well as forestalling a spill-over from the Islamic revolution into Iraq, which has a Shi'i majority, or into the Gulf states. Yet the practice of mass expulsions seen in the 1980s cannot be understood exclusively in this context alone. There are underlying causes linked to the historical and social development of the Iraqi state since its foundation. These were merely exacerbated by the Iran-Iraq war.

The objective of this study is to shed light on some of the political, historical and social aspects related to deportation, and its consequences.

Historical Background

The provinces of Basra, Baghdad and Mosul were the scenes of long-standing rivalry between Shi'i, Safavid Persia and the Sunni, Ottoman Empire for control of these regions by military force. War would often break out over the coveted territories.

Civilians from either sect – Shi'i or Sunni – were invariably victimized on grounds of communal affiliation. When the Safavids captured Baghdad in 1508, for example, Shah Isma'il destroyed the tombs of Sunni saints and slaughtered Sunni clergymen.[12] In 1512 the Ottoman Sultan Saleem did the same to the Shi'is, eliminating some 70,000 of them.[13] This was the norm whenever the three regions changed hands between Safavid and Ottoman rulers.[14] There was, therefore, deep-seated resentment, not only on the part of Shi'is against the Ottomans or the Sunnis against Safavids, but also between the two sects. The conflicts did not end when the three regions finally came under the firm control of the Ottomans. It simply acquired another form, this time between the Ottoman Empire and the predominantly Shi'i population of the three provinces. Britain replaced the Ottomans when it occupied the three regions on 7 November 1918.[15] Following in the footsteps of the Ottoman Empire, the British authorities in Iraq pursued a policy that precipitated a series of Shi'i revolts against them, culminating in the 1920 revolt.[16] Britain also institutionalized anti-Shi'ism when building up the nascent Iraqi state by installing a Sunni monarch with a government and bureaucracy that were virtually a Sunni preserve.

Causes of Deportation: Communalization and Arabization of the Iraqi State
'Beware. Beware of the Shi'is.'[17] 'Three I hate more than the devil: the Jew, the Shi'i and the French.'[18] That is how Abdul-Rahman al-Naqib, head of the first Iraqi government formed by the British to run the country on 23 October 1920, expressed his feelings towards the Shi'is. Shaykh Khaz'al of the Muhammara, a contender for the Iraqi throne, said:

> It seems HM Government is looking for a prince to rule Iraq. No suitable candidate has come forward. Since nine-tenths of the population in Iraq are Shi'is, the prince too should be a Shi'i. I am from Iraq. I was born and grew up in the Shatt al-Arab area, I have demonstrated my loyalty [to Britain] and as a prince I shall be the required formal head of the envisaged Arab state. In all matters I will act in accordance with the wishes of the High Commissioner.[19]

According to the British High Commissioner, Sir Percy Cox, Shaykh Khaz'al was dismissed as a candidate for the Iraqi throne because the installation of a Shi'i king would not have been well received by the more powerful Sunnis. Prince Faisal Ibn Hussein was crowned King of Iraq on 23 August 1921 because, although non-Iraqi, he was as a Sunni Arab more eligible to rule Iraq, and because 'he would seek British help, even against his own people sometimes, in running the country'.[20]

Thus Britain had created an Arab state, an Arab government, an Arab King and an Arab army.[21] Southern Kurdistan, which made up the greater part of the province of Mosul, was incorporated into the new Iraqi state against the wishes and aspirations of the Kurdish people.[22] Shi'is, the Kurds and other minorities were excluded from state institutions and decision-making processes. Anti-Shi'ism persisted despite the successive change of government. It climaxed, however, under the present Ba'th regime, when Shi'is have come to be called Persians instead of Shi'is. In the 1980s, 59 years after the foundation of the modern Iraqi state, Khayrallah Tilfah, Saddam Hussein's maternal uncle, was to reiterate what the first Iraqi Prime-Minister said in the 1920s: 'Three God should not have created, the Persians, the Jews and flies'.[23] Is this a mere coincidence, or is it a consistent state policy?

Minority Rule

Taxes are paid by the Shi'i. Death is the lot of the Shi'i, but government posts go for the Sunni. What belongs to the Shi'i? Even his religious rituals are disregarded. Iraq is a kingdom ruled by a Sunni Arab government. A government made of impulsive young men, mostly Sunnis or Arabs.

Iraq is a country which lacks the most essential component of social life, namely intellectual, national and religious unity.

They [the Shi'is] have suffered persecution under the Turkish rule which had denied them a share of power.[24]

These are quotations from statements made by King Faisal Ibn Hussein of Iraq in his later years. They graphically describe the Shi'is' status under his rule as well as during the Ottoman period when 'they were deprived of the possibility for advancement in any sphere of public life. A striking example is that a Shi'i is seldom accepted in the military college or for state employment'.[25]

In a nutshell, the British maintained the Shi'is' lowly status, and the ruling Sunni Arab minority continued the policy pursued by the British against the very constitution they had drafted for Iraq. Article 6 of that first Iraqi basic law states that: 'Iraqis have equal rights before the law irrespective of their ethnicity, religion or language'.[26]

When modern Iraq was created, Shi'is accounted for 53.1 percent of the population, while the Sunni Arab minority was less than 25 percent of the population.[27]

The extent of exclusion practised against the Shi'i majority under the monarchy is shown by the following statistics: the Shi'is had never accounted for more than 27.7 percent of ministerial posts. In the 27 years following the foundation of the Iraqi state there was not a single Shi'i Prime-Minister until Saleh Jaber was appointed (1947–48), to be succeeded by Muhammad al-Sadr (1948). A third Shi'i premier, Fadhil al-Jamali, assumed the leadership in 1954 and a fourth, 'Abdul-Wahab Marjan, in 1958. It may be seen, therefore, that only four Shi'is were appointed as heads of government out of 23 Prime-Ministers and 58 cabinets. Their total tenure lasted only 2.5 years out of 38 years of monarchy in Iraq.[28]

In republican Iraq under General Qassim (1958–1963), state policy was marked by non-discrimination against the Shi'is. Qassim's father was a Sunni and his mother a Shi'i. Yet his first republican cabinet was similar in composition to those formed under the monarchy. The state apparatus and decision-making centres remained in the hands of the Sunni Arab minority. In 1958, out of 15 members of the so-called Higher Council of Free Officers there were only two Shi'i officers, and only one Shi'i in the reserve committee set up by the free officers.[29] In the command council appointed by Qassim, there was only one Shi'i out of nine military members. Out of 16 members of the first republican cabinet there were five Shi'is: none held any key portfolios such as foreign affairs, defence or the interior. In Qassim's second cabinet the number of Shi'i members was reduced to 3 out of 14.[30]

Under the 'Arif brothers, Sunni sectarianism became even more pronounced, not only in the composition of government and the army which had already been a Sunni preserve since the Ottoman rule: this time it also extended to the hitherto Shi'i-dominated business community following the exodus of the Jews in the late 1940s and early 1950s.[31] In 1964 President 'Abdul-Salam 'Arif pursued a nationalization policy which subsumed the already feeble private sector, notably in trade and commerce. He appointed a non-Shi'i as head of the Baghdad Chamber of Commerce. In the media all existing newspapers had their licenses withdrawn when 'Arif came to power in 1963, and all the newly licensed ones had Sunni editors. Under his brother, 'Abdul-Rahman 'Arif, a law was passed turning the press into a state-owned establishment publishing all national newspapers and headed by a Sunni intellectual from Mosul.[32]

The presidency was the exclusive domain of Sunni officers from a specific Sunni-populated geographic location represented by Samara, Heet, Haditha, 'Aana and Takrit. All the Iraqi presidents to date (except Qassim) have come from these towns – the 'Arif brothers, Ahmad Hassan al-Bakr and Saddam Hussein. The latter is a civilian, but on 29 August 1979 he became the highest ranking officer in Iraq when the so-called Revolution Command Council (RCC) – headed, of course, by Saddam Hussein himself – conferred the rank of Field Marshal on him.[33]

Legal Factors

The ruling Sunni Arab minority in the nascent state of Iraq had, in legal terms, expressed hostility to the Shi'i majority in the two most important laws in the country: the Iraqi constitution and the Iraqi nationality law.

The first Iraqi constitution was adopted during the tenure of the second government headed by al-Naqib (12 September 1920 to 11 August 1921).[34] The draft text was reviewed by an *ad hoc* committee under al-Naqib's third government (30 September 1922 – 26 November 1924).[35] Many Articles of the constitution were deemed important and worth discussion, but there is one in particular, Article 16 – originally 17 – which received the lion's share of attention from the constituent assembly. This Article divided the citizens of the new state into 'original' and 'non-original' Iraqis: formerly there had been no such entity as Iraq but the *wiylayats*, provinces of Basra, Baghdad and Mosul. This division of citizens was contrary to the spirit and letter of Article 6 of the same constitution which pronounces equality of all Iraqis before the law.[36] The original text of Article 6 reads as follows: 'Iraqis are equal in enjoying their rights and fulfilling their duties. They are employed according to ability and qualification without discrimination'. After amendment, this Article reads:

> Iraqis are equal in enjoying their civil and political rights and fulfilling their civic duties and tasks. *Only original Iraqis* are entrusted with public jobs according to ability and qualification without discrimination, *except for cases specified by law*. [Italics added]

When questions were raised about what was meant by 'original Iraqis' it turned out that they were those people who had been subjects of the Ottoman Empire.[37]

Thus discrimination between citizens of one and the same state has since been institutionalized by the constitution. Accordingly, any Arab citizen is of Iranian origin unless this citizen or the citizen's ancestors were subjects of the Ottoman Empire. This duality of citizens' rights was established and kept in the constitution.

As for the nationality law, the Ottoman Empire is known to have excluded the Shi'is from employment in the bureaucracy and the military out of communal hostility. Ottoman citizenship was required for such employment. The Shi'is were not overtly keen to acquire this citizenship viewing the disadvantages as outweighing the benefits. After all, the Ottoman Empire was constantly at war with one rival or another. Having Ottoman citizenship meant conscription and probably dying at the front. Indeed, there was hardly any awareness of the significance of citizenship under the circumstances. Nor were there rigidly delineated borders between the Ottoman regions and Safavid or Qajar Persia. That is why Shi'is were simply not interested in citizenship until the Iraqi Nationality Law was enacted on 9 October 1924.

This law, like the constitution before it, divided the population of Iraq into two categories. Ottoman subjects, i.e. inhabitants of the three former provinces or others with Ottoman citizenship, who up until 6 August 1924 were residents of the territory of the Iraqi state, were considered by law to be 'original' Iraqis in accordance with Article 3 of the nationality law.[38] They were granted first class Iraqi citizenship. The other category consisted of those inhabitants of the three provinces who did not have Ottoman citizenship, or any other for that matter, and had acquired Iraqi citizenship later. They were mostly Shi'is, and as such were declared Iraqis of formerly Persian 'dependency'. This was the case even when they themselves and their parents had been born in Ottoman provinces. Accordingly, they were granted second class Iraqi citizenship. This lower status would apply to their sons, grandsons and great-grandsons in perpetuity. This dual notion of citizenship, derived as it were from pre-national arrangements and affiliations, and which runs counter to modern concepts of nationhood and human rights, is still in force in Saddam's Iraq.

To illustrate the extent of injustice resulting from this practice, look at the following example. 20-year old Ali had acquired second class Iraqi citizenship in 1925; he married and had a son called Hussein. In 1945 Hussein, aged 20, married and had a son called Ja'far. In 1965 Ja'far (20) married and had a son called Kazim. In 1985, 20–year-old Kazim would be deported on the grounds that he was 'of Iranian origin' although his grandfather, father and he himself were born in Iraq. Such Iraqis are liable to deportation because, according to the then head of security, Fadhil al-Barrak, 'many members of the Iranian community in Iraq were able to acquire Iraqi citizenship by various means'.[39] It might be noted that the services rendered by al-Barrak to Saddam Hussein as the highest security official in the country did not save him from being executed later on charges of spying – typically without trial.

Ideology

Sectarianism and national oppression against the Shi'is, the Kurds and other ethnic minorities have existed since the emergence of the modern Iraqi state: this is essentially identified with the predominant Sunni minority. However, an ideologically-based political rationale to mask the reality of the situation was lacking: it was found in the Iraqi Ba'th Party. The party's motto is 'One Arab nation with an immortal message'. This motto would prove disastrously sinister in the multi-ethnic Iraqi society. Non-Arabs would have to be Arabized and assimilated. The state apparatus and political life as a whole would have to undergo Ba'thization in a country with multiple political trends. The Marxist left, the Kurdish national parties and all non-Ba'thist trends had to be wiped out. The predominantly Muslim identity of the Iraqi society was to be rid of its strong Shi'i element. The Shi'is, not only of Iraq but of the world at large, have their highest religious authority in the holy city of Najaf. This authority was to be reined in and placed under total Ba'th control.

The Ba'th first emerged in the student body of Iraq as a small, politically insignificant party in the early 1950s.[40] It only gained ground in the political arena after Iraqi Shi'is had embraced Ba'th ideology and propagated Ba'th ideas. But even with those inroads it had little political influence and insignificant membership. Following the downfall of the monarchy on 14 July 1958 the Ba'th Party had only 300 activists, 1200 candidate members and about 2000 organized supporters.[41] On 8 February 1963 it took over power in a bloody coup planned with nationalist officers.[42] The reign was short-lived, ending in November of the same year and was marked by a bloodbath against Iraqi Communists and all-out war against the Kurds. In-fighting and factional struggle within the Ba'th paved the way for General Abdul-Salam 'Arif to assume power on 18 November 1963. But the Party staged a comeback in a second coup on 17 July 1968.

The second Ba'th regime sustained a radical change in the nature of the leading elite. A predominantly Shi'i civilian leadership has now been replaced by a Sunni Arab, mostly military, element in the leadership, as a result of the power struggle within the party in 1963 between two leading Shi'i personalities: 'Ali Saleh al-Sa'di, then General Secretary of the Party, and Hazim Jawad. On 11 November 1963 al-Sa'di was exiled to Madrid. Jawad was also exiled, as were most civilians in the party leadership. A crucial role was played in this struggle by the Ba'thist officers, all Sunnis, who were able to settle it in their own favour. In a sense, this development marked a shift towards the 'sunnization' of the Ba'th leadership. It is interesting to note that Shi'is accounted for 60% and 75% of the party regional – Iraqi – leadership in 1953 and 1957 respectively.[43] In 1963 – 1970 they accounted for less than 6%. In the period 1968 – 1977 not a single Shi'i Ba'thist made it to the Revolution Command Council.[44]

1968 was a watershed in Iraq's modern history. In that year the centre of power shifted to the Sunni Arab triangle north of Baghdad; in addition, there was a fusion between the ruling military elite and the Ba'th civilian elite. Both were of the same regional and communal backgrounds. The leading figures in the Ba'th civilian group included Saddam Hussein, Salah 'Omar al-'Ali, 'Adnan Khayrallah Tilfah and Murtadha al-Hadithi, all from Takrit; 'Abdul-Khaliq al-Samara'i and 'Abdullah al-Samara'i, from Samara; 'Izzet Mustafa, from 'Aana, and 'Izzet al-Duri, from Dur. Most of the top brass were from Takrit, including Ahmad Hassan al-Bakr, Hardan al-Tikriti, Hammadi Shihab and others.[45]

The Iran-Iraq War

The Iran-Iraq border dispute which had been a constant source of tension since the foundation of the Iraqi state, was finally settled when the two countries signed a border agreement complete with an annexed protocol on 4 July 1937.[46] The problem, however, surfaced again in republican Iraq, especially under the Ba'th regime. Another deal was struck between the Shah of Iran and Saddam Hussein in the 1975 Algiers agreement. However, tensions resurfaced when Khomeini triumphantly returned to Iran and the Islamic republic was established there. Saddam Hussein tore up the 1975 Algiers agreement, setting the stage for an eight-year war with Iran.[47] The war was started by the Iraqi president to prevent a spill-over from revolutionary Iran into Iraq; he assumed that overrunning a country in turmoil would be a picnic for his army.

It was in this context that the Iraqi government stepped up its drive to uproot and expel unwanted Iraqi Shi'is to Iran.

Saddam's Excuses for Deportation

Saddam Hussein followed the example set by his Sunni predecessors in the excuses he offered for deporting Iraqi Shi'is. There was a striking resemblance in the methods, accusations and idiom used against the targeted population. Both the nationality law and the constitution were invoked to justify the expulsions. The alleged Iranian origin of the deportees, offending the so-called host country by their disloyalty, their anti-Arab and pro-Persian sympathies, were an integral part of the legal arguments put forward by the Iraqi government for its actions.

In monarchic Iraq the charge of Iranian origin was used to deport the prominent cleric al-Khalisi and his sons in 1924. The Assyrians were expelled in 1933 for allegedly offending the country and the nation's unity. Yasin al-Hashimi, head of the Iraqi delegation to the League of Nations in Geneva, declared in reply to questions about the Assyrian problem: 'The Assyrians who have offended the country must be deported from Iraq'.[48] The non-Iraqi Sunni ideologue of pan-Arabism, Sati' al-Husri, accused the Shi'is of Persian loyalties and anti-Arabism. The then acting Shi'i Minister of Education was branded in this connection. According to Husri, Shi'i employees at the Ministry of Education had seriously undermined its work because of 'actions by Persians born in Iraq'. He even refused to employ the great Arab poet, Muhammad Mahdi al-Jawahiri, who in the 1920s was the court's favourite man of letters. Blinded by bigotry, al-Husri interpreted one of al-Jawahiri's poems as praising Iran and vilifying Iraq. Indeed, Husri claimed that the damage caused by those alleged Persians had come about as 'a result of the tolerant and indulgent policy pursued for some time by the government towards those people'.[49] Saddam Hussein and the Ba'th leadership were later to strictly carry out what al-Husri ordered under the monarchy.[50]

An incident that occurred at Mustansiriyya University in Baghdad on 1 April 1980 gave the President all the excuses he needed to get rid of unwanted Shi'is in Iraq. A hand grenade was thrown at a cavalcade of high officials led by Tariq 'Aziz who was on his way to visit the university. 'Aziz was wounded in the attack which was allegedly carried out by a Fayli Kurd called Sameer Ghulam Ali, who was a member of the Islamic Action Organization. Saddam Hussein appeared on TV visiting 'Aziz in hospital. The camera zoomed on a young girl who was cued into saying dramatically: 'Oh, I hate Persians', to which Saddam replied, 'Not a single Persian will remain after today on the land of the party and revolution'.[51]

The Iraqi government used the pretext of Iranian origin to deport Shi'is from all walks of life. Among the hardest hit were Shi'i merchants and businessmen. On 7 April 1980 around 800 Shi'i merchants and businessmen were deported in one go, having been summoned to the premises of the Baghdad Chamber of Commerce, ostensibly to discuss matters related to the import trade. The reason for singling out Shi'i merchants was explained by the then head of security, Fadhil al-Barrak. He said that,

> Control of the wholesale trade by merchants of Iranian origin has put them in control of daily business on the market. This has enabled them to play a prominent role in serving hostile foreign companies, apart from the great potential in organizing illicit operations to smuggle currency abroad using import transactions; being hostile to Iraq and its people, those merchants have one way or another been involved with the Da'wa – call – Party and the Islamic Action Party in their conspiracies and subversive schemes. They have joined the ranks of the two parties and collaborated with them.[52]

These claims were unfounded, for the simple fact that Article 156 of the law passed by the Revolution Command Council on 31 March 1980 provides for the execution of whoever joins the two Islamic parties. Saddam Hussein, who is not known for his benevolence and leniency, was content to deport the merchants in question to Iran. They could never have been involved with either of the two parties.

Undoubtedly, there were some Iraqi Shi'is answering the regime's description as to links with Islamic organizations or even pro-Iranian sympathies. But to hold the entire Shi'i community in Iraq responsible for the actions and affiliations of a few of its members is a violation not only of Iraqi citizenship rights and laws themselves but of the tenets of Islam, all of which forbids collective punishment for individual actions.[53]

Secular and nationalist parties, including the ruling Ba'th party itself are, of course, predominantly Shi'i at the grass-roots level. Shi'is also account for the great majority of conscripts and NCOs in the Iraqi army. If their loyalty had been to Iran it would have hardly been possible for Iraq to sustain its war effort over eight years of conflict with Shi'i Iran.

The Aftermath

In statistical terms, deportation has resulted in large numbers of Iraqi citizens ending up as refugees in a foreign country. Estimates of their volume vary from tens of thousands to hundreds of thousands. Although they were non-Iranian citizens, the Islamic Republic of Iran did receive the deportees, because the Iranian authorities were well aware of the persecution suffered by Shi'is in Iraq under the Ba'th regime. Khomeini himself had a taste of this injustice when he lived as an exile in the holy city of Najaf. Another reason for the Iranians to offer refuge to the deportees is the communality of religious identity and the historical links between the Shi'is of Iraq and Iran, as well as the compassionate attitude of Islam towards the homeless and the needy. Iran's resources were already stretched to the limit by the huge numbers of Afghan refugees on its territory. The fact that Iran was locked in a war with Iraq had created serious economic and security problems.

In terms of ethnicity, the deportees were either Arabs or Fayli Kurds, both belonging to the Shi'i community. Fayli Kurds are part of the Kurdish people in Iraq. Their dialect is the third spoken by Kurds after the Kirmanji and Surani dialects. They live in the Kurdish region divided between Iraq and Iran following the demarcation of international borders between the two countries. In Iran they are known as the Lor, inhabitants of the Kurdish region of Loristan. In Iraq they are called Fayli Kurds, inhabiting the region extending from Khanaqin to Badra and surrounding areas in the South. The majority of Fayli Kurds lived in the Iraqi capital, Baghdad, long before the foundation of the modern Iraqi state.

Through their diligence, honesty and self-reliance, Fayli Kurds have risen to a distinct status in economic and political life since the 1950s. Many of the most successful and influential merchants in the Shorja bazaar, the backbone of the Iraqi business community, were Fayli Kurds, especially in the tea, sugar, steel and timber trade. The Fayli Kurds have traditionally had a higher level of education among Iraqi Kurds.

The Fayli Kurds have also been powerful politically. Many leading figures and activists of the Iraqi Communist Party are Fayli Kurds. They have also held leading positions in the Democratic Party of Kurdistan: this was particularly true in the early 1970s, when the party general secretary, presidents and chairpersons of the Kurdistan students, women and youth unions and associations were all Fayli Kurds.[54] They also formed the majority of the KDP grass-roots activists and supporters in such important Arab cities as Baghdad, Kut and Basra.

The Baʿth party viewed the Fayli Kurds as a prime target for deportation. It should be pointed out that they have always been the victims of dual oppression: they are both Shiʿis and Kurds. In consequence, they accounted for the majority of those deported in the 1970s and part of those expelled in the1980s.

Phased Deportation

Iraqi Shiʿis were deported to Iran in two stages. The first stage took place between 1969 and 1971. The Iraqi government exploited the frequent political disputes with Iran as a pretext to deport Iraqi Shiʿis. The first crisis in Iran-Iraq relations occurred in April 1969 when the Iranian government unilaterally abrogated the 1937 agreement on the Shatt al-Arab waterway on the grounds that it was designed to serve British interests, recalling that Iraq allowed the British navy into the waterway to attack Iran in 1941.

A second crisis followed a foiled coup attempt in Iraq in 1970. Iraq accused Iran of masterminding the plot and diplomatic relations were severed between the two countries.[55] The RCC held a meeting at which the interior minister and RCC member, Saleh Mahdi ʿAmmash, advanced plans to deport Iranian nationals. He is quoted as saying,

> This is the chance of a life-time and we must seize upon it to get rid of the Iranians in one month. This way we will create a big problem for Iran. There are over half a million Iranians living in Iraq. Turned into refugees, this huge number is enough to pressure Iran's resources. It will also save huge funds because we will prevent the deportees from taking any money or belongings with them to Iran, which runs into millions and millions [in Iraqi Dinars].[56]

The RCC eventually decided that the operation should be carried out in three months instead of the one month suggested by ʿAmmash. At the same time there were diplomatic efforts to ease tensions. The RCC had already delegated the Minister of Defence, Hardan al-Tikriti, to meet Ayatollah Mohsen al-Hakim, then the highest religious Shiʿi authority in Iraq, and ask him to mediate between the two countries. Takriti explained that the Iraqis wanted Iran to abandon its claims to the eastern bank of the Shatt al-Arab waterway and reinstall the 1937 agreement; in return Iraq would release all detained Iranians and end the deportations. Mohsen al-Hakim was quoted as replying: 'The Iranians are not simply a community of emigrants. They are genuine Iraqis in both background and lineage. But they have been denied Iraqi citizenship under former governments'.[57]

The deportation of Fayli Kurds to Iran at this stage had also created a serious crisis between the ruling Ba'th Party and their temporary ally in the government, the Kurdistan Democratic Party (KDP). It was in breach of the March 1970 agreement between them and a precursor not only for breaking off the agreement but also for the subsequent war launched against the Kurds few years later.[59]

The second stage of deportation started in April 1980, a few months before the break out of the Iran-Iraq war on 22 September 1980.[60] Internal, regional and international conditions differed from those which had characterized the 1969–1971 expulsions.

At home, political, economic and social spaces had been thoroughly Ba'thized, i.e subsumed under the control of the single party system. The entire military had been restructured along similar lines, creating what Saddam Hussain called the 'doctrinal army', al-Jaysh al-'Aqa'idi.[61] The military was now a formidable machine, both for the protection of the regime and as a tool of repression. The army/party formed the backbone of the new regime.[62]

By that time the ruling Ba'th Party had virtually eliminated the biggest two popular forces in Iraq, using a mixture of trickery, deception, false agreements, broken promises, prosecution and persecution. The first target was the Iraqi Communist Party. Following an alliance between the Ba'th Party and the ICP sealed in 1973 by the so-called Progressive National Front, the Communists turned into promoters of the Ba'th image at the fora of the international Communist movement.[63] Internally they connived at the Ba'th brutal repression, calling Saddam Hussein 'the Castro of Iraq'. The alliance, however, did not last long; its disintegration resulted in the leaders of the Communist Party fleeing Iraq for the countries of the Eastern Bloc 1978 onwards, leaving behind thousands of Iraqi Communists languishing in the Ba'th prisons.

The second powerful force, seriously weakened by the Ba'th regime, was the KDP. In contrast to the Communists, the KDP was an armed political force in control of a specific region in northern Iraq. Four years after the 1970 March agreement with the Ba'th Party and the collapse of the Kurdish revolt which followed the Algiers 1975 agreement between the Shah and Saddam Hussein, the KDP suffered a crushing defeat that turned it in that year into the remnants of a vanquished army.

The whole Islamic movement was similarly decimated by the Ba'th onslaught. Laws were enacted providing for the execution of individuals who joined the Da'wa Party or the Islamic Action Organization. As a result, many activists and supporters were lost in torture chambers and before firing squads. Many more fled to Iran in the wake of the 1979 Iran Islamic Revolution, especially clergymen in the Shi'i holy cities, who left after the execution of Muhammad Baqir al-Sadr, his sister Bint al-Huda and other prominent clerics in April 1980.

In Baghdad, Saddam Hussein was able to realise his ambition to be Iraq's absolute ruler by forcing al-Bakr out of office on 16 July 1979. Addressing a wider audience, he asserted that: 'We want an Iraq that will play a vanguard role in the region and specifically in the Arab world.'[64]

In 1975 Iraq was the third largest oil exporter after Saudi Arabia and Iran. In 1979–1980 it was second only to Saudi Arabia, with Iran relegated to third and in 1980 to fifth place.[65] Iraq's oil revenues rocketed from $575 million in 1972 to $26.5 billion in 1980.[66] The aftermath of the Iranian revolution presented Saddam Hussein with an opportunity to fill the vacuum left by the Shah's departure as the region's gendarme.

These were the prevailing circumstances under which the second stage of deportation was carried out in 1980. It affected huge numbers of Iraqis. *Le Monde* of Paris wrote at the time that 'For a week now more than 2,000 Iraqis of Iranian origin have been deported every day by the Iraqi authorities'.[67]

Deportation in Figures
Estimates vary as to the number of those deported in both the first and second stages of expulsion.

The First Stage (1969–1971)
According to the *al-Shahada* newspaper, 'In 1969 the Iraqi authorities had deported more than 500 Iraqis claimed by the Ba'th to be Iranians. The second batch involved 660 people'.[68]

In a document entitled 'Deportation: Crime of the Age', the number for 1970 is estimated at 100,000.[69] Khafaji puts the number at 50,000 people deported in the late 1970s, allegedly for being of Iranian origin.[70] Ahmad al-Katib estimates that 160,000 people have been deported.[71] Majid 'Abdul-Ridha maintains that 'Tens of thousands of Fayli Kurds have been deported'.[72] Sluglett puts their number at '40,000 Fayli Kurds deported in September 1971'.[73]

'Issmat Sharif Wa'eli claims that 'The Iraqi government has deported 50,000 Iraqis of Iranian origin, including 40,000 Fayli Kurds deported in late September 1971'.[74]

The memorandum presented by the Democratic Party of Kurdistan to the UN on the situation of the Kurdish people in Iraq says that '40,000 Fayli Kurds had been deported between 1971–1972'.[75]

Describing the deportees as Iranian citizens, Khadouri puts their number at 10,000.[76] In his writings on Iraqi politics, Hassan al-'Alawi does not even bother to mention deportations carried out in the seventies.[77] 'Abdul-Majeed Krab Zamzami, on the other hand, estimates that 60,000 people had been deported.[78]

The figures given by the *Liwa al-Sadr* newspaper and Ahmad al-Katib seem to be exaggerated compared with other estimates which range from 40,000 to 50,000. It may also be noted that 90% of the Iraqis deported in the 1980s are Fayli Kurds.

The Second Stage (1980)

1) Figures According to the Iraqi Opposition:

1. In a note to the UN Human Rights Commission, the International Committee of the Red Cross, the UNHCR and the Iranian Red Crescent, the Fayli Kurdish Muslim Movement, based in the Kurdish town of Ilam in Iran, claimed that 150,000 Iraqis had been deported as from 1980, 80% of them Fayli Kurds.[79]

2. Sayyid Muhammad Taqi al-Mudarissi, leader of the Islamic Action Organization, stated that 'The total number of deportees, exiles and [Iraqi] POWs in the Islamic Republic is about 250,000'.[80]

3. The Iraqi Communist Party does not quote any figures but talks about 'mounting persecution of the Shi'i community and wholesale deportation with continued confiscation of property'.[81]

2) According to Foreign Sources:

4. Chabry says that between the years 1975–1980 the Iraqi Ba'th deported 75,000 people in successive waves.[82]

5. U. Zaher puts the number of deportees in the tens of thousands since 1980.[83]

6. Sluglett puts the number of deportees in April 1980 at 40,000, and estimates a total of more than 100,000 Iraqi Shi'i refugees in Iran and Syria.[84]

3) According to Opposition Literature and Activists:

7. Al-Katib says that 100,000 Iraqis have been deported[85]

8. Al-'Alawi maintains that 'Accusing the Shi'is of being non-Arabs or Iranians has facilitated the shift to a higher stage of sectarian discrimination by passing the deportation law under which thousands of Iraqis have been the victims of mass deportation and expulsion'[86]

9. In its book entitled 'The Path to Arrogance', the al-Da'wa Party declares that over 100,000 Iraqi Muslims have been deported under the pretext that they are Iranians[87]

10. Sayyid Abdul-Wahab al-Hakim claims that between 350,000–500,000 Iraqis have been deported since 1980. However, the figure he quotes from an Iranian border province for the period 1980–1982 is only 21,772 deportees.[88]

4) According to Regional and International Human Rights Groups:

11. The World Human Rights Guide bulletin published in London in 1983 puts the number of those stripped of their Iraqi citizenship at 30,000.

12. In its 1987 annual report the Arab Organization for Human Rights states that anywhere between 100,000 and 400,000 Iraqi Shi'is have been deported.[89]

13. The French Committee of the Human Rights International Federation claims that around 400,000 Iraqis have been deported to Iran because the regime suspects them of disloyalty.[90]

Discrepancies notwithstanding, there is no doubt that the number of Iraqis deported to Iran runs in the thousands. Their huge number created considerable difficulties for the Iranian authorities, who had to provide tents, food, security and protection, especially in areas that were sometimes only a stone's throw from the front-line.

Due to a lack of available resources, or perhaps for reasons of their own, the Iranians did not keep complete records of all the Iraqis dumped on them. However, in 1986 the Iranian Minister of the Interior stated that there were 500,000 Iraqi refugees and deportees in Iran.[91] The Shi'i Islamic opposition based in Iran were busy licking their wounds following the severe blows dealt to them by Saddam Hussein. They did not have enough personnel they could assign to the task of keeping records or undertaking studies on such large numbers of people. Moreover, they were confident that Iran would win the war with Saddam and the problem would be resolved without further ado by the deportees' return to Iraq with the Iranian victors. Their hopes and those of the deportees proved to be unfounded.

Deportation Laws

The Revolution Command Council (RCC) is known to be the highest decision-making body in Iraq. It is the legislative, executive and judiciary rolled up in one. Though non-elective, the RCC makes and repeals laws at will. For example, on 16 July 1970 an interim constitution drafted and adopted by the RCC was announced to the country.

It is within this legal – illegal? – context that the deportation laws were passed and enforced. These are laws that run counter to elementary human rights by breaking up families to be deported and holding their younger members in detention.

1) Decree 474, 15 April 1981

This decree reads as follows:

In accordance with Clause (a) of Article 42 of the interim constitution, the RCC meeting on 15 April 1981 decreed that,

(i) Any Iraqi husband married to a woman of Iranian origin is paid ID4,000 if he is in the military and ID2,500 if he is a civilian should he divorce his wife or his wife is transferred abroad.

(ii) A proof of the divorce or the transfer, officially certified by the competent departments, as well as a new marriage contract is required for the sum referred to in (a) to be paid out.[92]

2) Classified
On 10 April 1980 the interior ministry circulated Directive 2884 which provides for the following:

(i) All Iranians in the country, as well as those who do not have Iraqi citizenship and those whose naturalization applications are being processed, shall be deported.

(ii) In cases where some members of the family have Iraqi citizenship and others have not, the principle of 'family reunion beyond the border' shall be applied. Citizenship papers, if any, shall be withdrawn from those who have them and later sent to the ministry with lists of those covered by this decision to have them stripped of their citizenship.

There are, however, exceptions to the rules, such as 'military personnel of various ranks who are to be handed over to the military police in Baghdad' and 'young people between 18–28 who are to be held in detention until further notice.'[93]

Refugees in Iran
In the 1980s, the presence of few hundred thousands of Iraqis on Iranian soil was unprecedented in the history of relations between the two countries. Traditionally, Iraq always had an Iranian community consisting of clergymen, religious students and ordinary Iranians in its holy cities. The reverse had never happened before the mass deportations carried out by the Ba'th regime.

Iraqi exiles arrived in Iran distressed: many of them were in poor health as a result of the horrors they had been through in the course of deportation. They were offered food and tents for accommodation. The sick were taken to hospitals. Shortly afterwards the new guests were moved to various parts of Iran, where they were placed in special camps. The major camps were in Juhrum, Malavi, Lorstan and Khozistan. According to Sayyid Hassan Basheer, head of the Refugees' Bureau at the time, there were 18 other camps located in various provinces.[94]

Overnight, thousands of Iraqis found themselves homeless, deprived of their relatively comfortable life, living as refugees in tents where food is rationed and doled out in limited quantities at specified times. This was to them a mindboggling situation. A more serious problem was the feeling of confinement. Younger refugees with skills who wanted to go out and work in nearby towns were particularly affected. The major concern, however, was leaving the camp altogether for the major cities in the hope of a better life. In order to do so, a guarantor of Iranian citizenship had to be found.

In the event, hundreds of Iraqi exiles found Iranians who would vouch for them, and were able to leave the camps. Many of those deported in the 1980s had relatives in Iran who had been expelled in the 1970s. Some of the latter had become naturalized Iranians and others had Iranian friends who could help their relatives get out of the camps.

Conditions for leaving the camp were later eased. Any Iraqi exile with a green card or official residence permit could act as guarantor of a deported family.[95]

Having finally left the camp, Iraqi exiles in the major cities had a hard time finding accommodation and employment. Iran was facing an acute housing problem, especially in the capital Tehran, due to the exodus of Iranians from towns and villages bombed by the Iraqi air force. Many of the younger Iraqis had volunteered as paid fighters in the armed outfit of the Supreme Assembly of the Islamic Revolution in Iraq – SAIRI. This was a combination of both employment and *jihad*.

Food prices were high so the SAIRI interceded with the Iranian authorities to give Iraqi exiles vouchers to purchase subsidized food at state-run stores opened for the benefit of disadvantaged Iranians.

Recognition of school certificates and other academic qualifications was another serious problem for the exiles. An attempt was made to solve it by exams to determine the educational levels of the Iraqis concerned. However, the exams were in Persian which none of the deportees knew. As a way out, the Martyr al-Sadr Foundation, seated in Tehran since its establishment in 1980, opened schools covering various stages of education for members of the deported Iraqi families.

Although 'green cards' had been issued as IDs, these were of little use in practical terms. The bearer could not find employment, get married or buy property on the basis of this document.

Leading members of various Islamic Iraqi parties met with high-level Iranian officials to discuss ways of alleviating the Iraqi exiles' plight. When Sayyid Muhammad Taqi al-Mudarissi of the Islamic Action Organization was received by the then President Rafsanjani, he laid emphasis on 'paying more attention to the humanitarian aspects in the life of exiles and deportees'.[96]

Sayyid Muhammad Baqir al-Hakim of the SAIRI impressed on Muhtashimi, the then Iranian minister of the interior, 'the need for a speedy solution to the exiles' problems'.[97]

In reply to a question on the subject during a press conference President Rafsanjani said 'I personally wish to see less of these problems and will help as much as I can'.[98]

Many of those problems remained unsolved: they were inseparably linked to Iran's economic and political developments as well as to the relations between leaders of the Iraqi Shi'i parties and Iranian officials and, in a wider context, to Iran-Iraq relations.[99]

Eventually, thousands of Iraqi exiles and deportees managed to leave Iran – by every imaginable means – and found their way to Europe, particularly Scandinavia, where they have been accepted as political refugees.

Political Forces in the Iraqi Community of Refugees
Mass deportations of Iraqi Shi'is to Iran, brutal repression against Shi'i Islamic parties in Iraq, execution of their leaders and other prominent clergymen sympathetic to the Islamic revolution, the presence of many leading Iraqi Shi'i dissidents in Iran, their recognition of Khomeini as leader of the Islamic community and their endorsement of the principle of 'governance of the jurisprudent' – all this had resulted in close cooperation to mobilize the community of Iraqi exiles within an Iraqi Islamic political structure perceived as the core and future lever of power in Iraq following the defeat of Saddam's armies by the armed forces of Islamic Iran. In the meantime, Iraqis in Iran would be recruited to contribute to the war effort by volunteering in the Iranian forces and later as members of an Iraqi Islamic force fighting alongside the Iranian army against Saddam Hussein. It was in this context that the Supreme Assembly of the Islamic Revolution in Iraq – SAIRI – was founded.

In November 1982 Sayyid Muhammad Baqir al-Hakim launched the SAIRI at a press conference held in Tehran. A 'historical' declaration introduced the new organization, SAIRI[100] which claimed to 'represent the various Islamic forces acting in the Iraqi arena through Islamic groups and personalities'.[101] Defining its aims and the forces it represented, the SAIRI set itself the task of overthrowing the regime of Saddam Hussein and establishing an Islamic government in Iraq.[102] Militarily, it would adopt armed struggle, mobilize Iraqi Islamic forces and build an Islamic army. Politically, its platform was based on the underlying thesis that the struggle with the Iraqi regime is not confined to this regime alone but is also waged against the forces of both eastern and western powers supporting and propping up this regime. Political action by the SAIRI would essentially rely on 'the potentials of the oppressed Iraqi masses both in Iraq and abroad.

This struggle is only one link in the struggle between world blasphemy and Islam which has its rule under the blessed Islamic Republic of Iran.'[103]

On 20 September 1983 SAIRI members met the late Khomeini who gave his blessing to their work and instructed them that 'your goal must be the establishment of an Islamic government and enforcing the rules of the Almighty God'.[104] Later Sayyid Muhammad Baqir al-Hakim was promoted from spokesman to chairman of SAIRI.

SAIRI had its own military formation constituted by the Iranian command under the name of the 'Badr Corps'. They fought alongside the Iranian forces against the Iraqi army before the 1988 cease-fire between the two countries. The Badr Corps had grown in strength to the level of an army division. SAIRI has been active with other forces against the Saddam regime and is now one of the biggest Islamic groups in the Iraqi opposition.[105]

SAIRI has come under severe criticism for both its policy of alliances and political platform. It is regarded as having sympathetic leanings towards the Iranian leadership. Its political platform overlooks many vital Iraqi issues such as the rights of Iraqi Christians and other ethnic minorities. SAIRI has no plan for solving the Kurdish problem, which is a burning issue in Iraqi politics. There is no mention of the Kurds' national rights in its manifesto. It has also been criticized for disregarding other major forces such as the Iraqi Communist Party and Arab nationalist parties. There is no mention in its programme of democracy and peaceful transfer of power. Its programme is modelled on Iran's officially-sanctioned version of Islam.

To politically mobilize Fayli Kurds who account for the majority of Iraqi exiles and deportees in Iran, a group of young Fayli Kurds led by Abdul-Jalil al-Fayli founded the Fayli Kurdish Muslim Movement which was formally launched on 21 March 1981, that is, before the SAIRI came into existence. Its foundation was in response to the mass deportations.[106] The movement enjoys support among Fayli Kurds living in various Iranian cities, especially the capital Tehran, Kermanshah, Ahwaz, Arak, Ivan and Islam Abad as well as inside Iraq, some European countries and Canada.[107] Its founder, Abdul-Jalil al-Fayli, was formerly a member of the KDP and one of its activists between 1965 and 1975. Although of a pro-Iran, Shi'i Islamic orientation, the Fayli Kurdish Muslim Movement is distinct for being the first such movement to represent Fayli Kurds in Iraqi modern history and for its position in favour of autonomy for the Kurdish people. In the early 1990s the movement called for a federal Iraq to ensure the national rights of the Kurdish people. In addition to its call for the return and compensation of Iraqi deportees, the movement holds that the autonomy envisaged for the Kurdish people is to include areas inhabited by Fayli Kurds, such as Khanaqin, Badra, Mandili and other Kurdish regions populated by Fayli Kurds.

The movement may have espoused the Shi'i brand of Islam by virtue of its presence on Iranian territory. The Kurdish nationalist dimension of its platform may be explained not only by the fact that its founder is a former activist in the KDP, but also because its leaders are aware that the nationalist feelings of Fayli Kurds are stronger than their identity as Shi'is. The majority of young Fayli Kurds were more or less politicized in Iraq, and were involved one way or another with either the ICP or the KDP.

The movement had its own publications and central organ. Its relations with other Iraqi Shi'i groups in Iran were strained. It was seen as a dangerous rival and efforts were made to block its advance, especially its endeavours to develop good relations with the Iranian leadership and make further gains at the expense of other groups whose bases of support were predominantly made up of Fayli Kurds.

The movement organized public events in Iranian towns inhabited by Fayli Kurds, especially after the chemical bombing of Halabje by Iraqi aircraft killing thousands of Iraqi Kurds. The movement also strengthened links with the Kurdistan Front in Iraq and took part in military encounters with government forces in Iraqi Kurdistan. The movement was opposed to the talks held by representatives of the Kurdistan Front with the Iraqi regime in 1991. It published pamphlets entitled *'Whither the Dialogue with the Saddam Regime?'* and *'Open Letter to our Brethren in the Kurdistan Front on Negotiations with Saddam'*.[108]

Being an active group in the Iraqi opposition, the Fayli Kurdish Muslim Movement attended the plenary meeting held by Iraqi opposition groups in Beirut, 11–13 March 1990.[109] In 1991, following the liberation of Iraqi Kurdistan, the election of a Kurdish parliament and formation of a Kurdish government, disagreements within the movement resulted in its leader Abdul-Jalil Fayli defecting back to the Democratic Party of Kurdistan. The remaining faction has in the meantime allied itself with the Jalal Talbani's Patriotic Union of Kurdistan.

Other Consequences of Deportation

Deportation caused a loss of human resources. A considerable number of deportees were from educated and learned classes. All the deported families had children who were pupils and students at various stages of their education. They were potential future professionals in various fields.

The confiscation of property and assets belonging to hundreds of deported merchants, industrialists and other business classes had a disruptive effect on the Iraqi economy. Virtually an entire class with business expertise was displaced from the economy. This accentuated labour shortages already resulting form the 1970s and aggravated by the war effort in the 1980s. The labour force available in the 1970s was hardly adequate to keep pace with the new development drive marked by a rapid rate of growth. Arab and foreign workers had to be imported to offset the shortage. The deportation of thousands of Iraqis to Iran further aggravated the crisis and more workers had to be brought in from different parts of the world. In 1984 there were an estimated '5 to 7 million foreigners, including 3 million Egyptians, in a country of about 14 millions'.[110]

In political terms, the Iraqi regime created new enemies for itself. Most of the deportees were apolitical and posed no threat to state security. Consequently, by their deportation the regime played in the hands of the Islamic republic and the Iraqi Shi'i opposition, who won their sympathy and recruited them for their own purposes. Having lost their properties, life-savings and businesses, the deportees were only too willing to join in.

Conclusion: Is there a Solution?

There is not much that can be done in practical terms at present to put the exiles and deportees out of their misery. In theory, however, both a partial and a radical solution may be proposed.

The problem can be partially resolved by the return of the exiles to Iraq, compensating them for lost property and releasing their sons who have been imprisoned since the 1980s. Such a solution is inconceivable without strong international pressure on the Iraqi government. Success depends on the international community taking the deportees' cause to heart: the Iraqi government would also have to accept them back. However, it is doubtful that agreement to their return could be won, for the simple reason that all the excuses and accusations put forward by the Iraqi government in order to justify its actions would be shown before the world to be false and groundless. A regime such as Saddam Hussein's will never admit its mistakes, offer an apology to its victims and take a self-critical view of its record. Democratic governments might do so: a brutal dictator like Saddam Hussein will not.

It is also debatable that the deportees and exiles would trust Saddam Hussein again after what they have been through at the hands of his government. At best they would accept compensation and rejoice in the release of and reunion with their imprisoned sons.

The Iraqi government is known to have relocated hundreds of thousands of Kurds. They were resettled in the predominantly Arab South or in special housing complexes. 4,000 Kurdish villages have been razed to the ground in the process. Assyrian villages are also believed to have been destroyed.

The problem can be solved by eliminating its root cause, which has made displacement and deportation a recurrent phenomenon at various stages in the development of the modern Iraqi state. The first step towards a radical solution is the overthrow of the present regime by Iraqi forces with a radically new outlook. This will hold out the promise of democracy, respect for human rights, peaceful change of government by election, de-communilization of the Iraqi state structure, independence of the judiciary, rule of the law, separation of religion and state, recognition of the Kurdish people's right to self-determination within a federated Iraq and granting other ethnic minorities their national rights – which is the second step.

It will be necessary to overhaul the Iraqi constitution and revoke many laws, especially the nationality law, in order to do away with the legal grounds used by former governments to carry out such misdeeds as deportation or denial of citizenship rights.

Notes

1. Excerpts from an interview given by Saddam Hussein to Kuwaiti reporters, 30 April 1984, published in *al-Thawra* daily, Baghdad, 5 May 1984.
2. Excerpts from an interview given by Saddam Hussein to the chief editor of *al-Sharq al-Awsat* daily, no. 3753, London, 8 March 1989.
3. Longrigg, H. S., *Iraq, 1900 – 1950*, Arabic translation by Saleem Taha al-Tikriti, Baghdad, vol. 1: 245.
4. Al-Hasani, 'Abdul-Razzak, *Tarikh al-wizarat al-'Iraqiyya*, 20th edn, Baghdad, 1988, vol. 4: 105, 125 and 180.
5. Ibid. vol. 9: 149.
6. Ibid. vol. 10: 121.
7. Ibid. vol. 3: 302.
8. Ibid. vol. 8: 156.
9. Ibid. vol. 3: 133.
10. Ibid. vol. 3: 192.
11. Ibid. vol. 6: 36.
12. Longrigg, H. S., *Four Centuries of Iraq's Modern History*, translated by Ja'far al-Khayatt, Baghdad, 5th edn, 1942: 43.
13. Al-'Alawi, Hassan, *al-Shi'a wa al-dawla al-qawmiyya fil 'Iraq*, CEDI, France, 1989: 45.
14. The exception is Sulayman, the Law Giver, who conquered Baghdad in 1534 and restored tombs of both Shi'i and Sunni saints. See al-Alawi, Hassan, op. cit.: 46.
15. Al-Akkam, Abdul-Amir Hadi, *al-haraka al-qawmiyya fil 'Iraq*, (The National Movement in Iraq: 1921–1933), al-Aadab Press, Najaf, 1975: 21.
16. Yitzak Nakash, *The Shi'is of Iraq*, Arabic translation, al-Meda Publishing House, Damascus, 1st edn, 1996: 114.

17. Wilson, *Loyalties*, Appendix 111, Annex a, 'Political Views of the Naqib of Baghdad'.

18. F. O. 371/5228/E 8448.

19. Al-'Attiyya, Ghassan, *Iraq 1908–1921, The Emergence of the State*, (Arabic), Lam Publishing House, London, 1988: 472.

20. Al-'Attiyya, ibid.: 475.

21. Reference is made to 'Arab' instead of 'Iraqi' state on p. 52, Arab kingdom: 68, Arab king: 111 and Arab army: 41, 47. See al-Hassani, op. cit., vol. 1. Reference to 'Arab' state is also made in Attiyya, op. cit: 457.

22. Pirash, *al-Iraq, Dawla bi al-'unf: al-muqawama al-kurdiyya dhid 'amaliyyat ilhaq kurdistan al-janubi bil 'iraq 'ala dhaw' arshifat alhukuma al-birataniyya* (A State by Violence : Kurdish Resistance against Incorporation of South Kurdistan into Iraq in Light of British Government Archives), 1918–1937, Kurdologia Publications, London, 1986.

23. Tilfah, Khayrallah, *Thalatha kan 'ala allah anla yakhluqahum, al-furs, wal yahud wal thubab* (Three God should not have Created: The Persians, the Jews and Flies), al-Hurriyya Printing House, Baghdad, 1980: 5, 8.

24. Al-Hasani, op. cit., vol. 3, excerpts from King Faisal's memoirs: 315–21.

25. Al-Chadarchi, Kamil, *Min awraq kamil al-chadirchi* (From Kamil al-Chadarchi's Papers), al-Talia Publishing House, Beirut, 1971: 86.

26. Al-Hasani, op. cit., vol. 1: 239.

27. Batatu, Hanna, *The Old Social Classes and the Revolutionary Movements of Iraq, A Study of Iraq's Old Landed and Commercial Classes and of its Communists, Ba'thists and Free Officers*, Princeton University Press, 1978: 40.

28. Salama, Ghassan, *al-mujtma' wal dawla fil mashriq al-'arabi* (Society and State in the Arab Mashreq), Centre for Arab Unity Studies, Beirut, 1st edn, 1987: 87.

29. Ibid.: 91.

30. Al-'Alawi, op. cit: 197.

31. Longrigg, *Iraq*, op. cit., vol. 2: 624.

32. Al-Alawi, op. cit.: 216.

33. See text in *Decisions that Expose Human Rights Violations in Iraq*, (Arabic) Committee for Defence of Human Rights in Iraq, Damascus, Feb. 1993: 13.

34. Al-Hasani, op. cit., vol. 1: 73.

35. Al-Hasani, op. cit., vol. 1: 130.

36. Al-Hasani, op. cit., vol. 1: 239–40.

37. Al-Khitabi, Raja' Husayn Hasani, *al-'iraq bayn 'awam 1921–1927, dirasa fi tatawur al-'alaqat al-'iraqiyya-al-iraniyya wa ta'thiraha* (Iraq between 1921–1927: Study in Development and Effect of Iran-Iraq Relations), Baghdad University, (n. d.): 165.

38. Al-Hadawi, Hassan, *al-jinsiyya wa markaz al-ajanib wa ahkamaha fil qanun al-'iraqi* (Citizenship, Status of Foreigners and Provisions of Iraqi Law), Baghdad University, 4th edn, (n. d.): 80.

39. Al-Barrak, Fadhil, *al-madaris al-yahudiyya wal iraniyya fil 'Iraq* (Jewish and Iranian Schools in Iraq) al-Rasheed Publishing House, Baghdad, 1984: 218.

40. Al-'Aysami, Shibli, *Hizb al-Ba'th al-'arabi al-ishtiraki, 2, marhlat al-numwo wal tawasu'* (The Socialist Arab Ba'th Party 2, The Stage of Growth and Expansion, 1949–1958), al-Talia Publishing House, Beirut, 2nd edn, 1979: 199.

41. Batatu, op. cit.: 226.

42. Khadouri, Majeed, *al-'Iraq al-jumhuri* (Republican Iraq), al-Muttaheda Publishing House, Beirut, 1st edn, 1974: 262.

43. These are derived from date in al-Alawi, op. cit.: 224–25.

44. Batatu, 'The Old Classes', quoted in Salama, op. cit.: 93.

45. Salama, Ghassan, op. cit.: 226.

46. Al-Hasani, op. cit., vol. 5: 24.

47. Zamzami, Abdul-Majeed, *al-harb al-'iraqiyya-al-iraniyya, al-islam wal qawmiyyat* (The Iran-Iraq War: Islam and Nationalisms), Edition Albatros, Paris, (n.d).

48. Al-Hasani, op. cit., vol. 3: 305.

49. Al-Husri, Abu Khaldoun Sati', *Muthakarati fil 'Iraq, 1920–1927*, (My Memoirs in Iraq), vol. 1, al-Talia Publishing House, Beirut, 1st edn, 1967: 597–98.

50. Hussein, Saddam, *Le conflict Irako-Iranien, les origines et les aspects*, Dar al-Mamun, Baghdad, 1981: 25.

51. *Risalat al-'Iraq*, London-based monthly issued by the ICP, no. 47, November, 1984: 11.

52. Al-Barrak, Fadhil, op. cit.: 152–53.

53. See Qur'an, verse 17 of the Fatir sura.

54. Babakhan, Ali, *Les Kurdes D'Irak, leur histoire et leur deportation par le regime de Saddam Hussein*, Paris, 1994: 54–71.

55. Khadouri, Majeed, op. cit.: 244–45.

56. *Muthakarat Hardan Abdul-Ghaffar al-Tikriti*, published by Iraqi Muslim Students Organization, (n. p.) (n. d.): 32.

57. Khadouri, op. cit.: 99.

58. Memoirs of Hardan, op. cit.: 37.

59. Zamzami, op. cit.: 41.

60. Ibid.

61. A. Abbas, 'The Iraqi Armed Forces: Past and Present', in *Saddam's Iraq, Revolution or Reaction*, CARDRI, 1989.

62. Salama, op. cit.: 153.

63. Sluglett, Marion Farouk and Sluglett Peter, *Iraq since 1958: From Revolution to Dictatorship*, I.B. Tauris, London, 1990: 151.

64. Saddam Hussein, *al-Hasana al-mabda'iyya fi al-'amal al-jabhawi*, a speech by Saddam Hussein at the plenary meeting of committees of the Progressive National Front, 7 April 1975, al-Hurriyya Publishing House, Baghdad, 2nd edn, 1980: 7.

65. Al-Khafaji, Issam, *al-'Iqtisad al-'iraqi ba'd al-harb ma'a Iran* (The Iraqi Economy after the War with Iran) in the periodical *Arab Strategic Thought*, no. 32, April 1990: 8.

66. Whittleton, Celine, 'Oil and the Iraqi Economy', in *Saddam's Iraq*, CARDRI, op. cit.: 54–69.

67. *Le Monde*, 15 April 1980.

68. *Al-Shahada* weekly, 1985.

69. Liwa' al-Sadr, *Deportation: Crime of the Age*: 15.

70. Al-Khafaji, op. cit.: 196.

71. Al-Katib, Ahmed, *Tajribat al-thawra al-islamiyya fil Iraq* (TheExperience of the Islamic Revolution in Iraq), Dar al-Qabas al-Islami, Tehran, 1st edn, 1981: 207.

72. Abdul-Ridha, Majid, *al-Mas'ala al-qawmiyya fil Iraq* (The National Question in Iraq, 1958–1975), al-Haqiqa Press, (n. p.), 1st edn, 1987: 274.

73. Sluglett, Peter, 'The Kurds', in *Saddams Iraq*, CARDRI, op. cit.: 196.

74. See a memorandum by Ismat Sharif Wa'ili, A Statement to the Fighting Kurdish People on our Delegation's Visit to Iraq and Iraqi Kurdistan, (Arabic), August-September, 1975: 19.

75. See the memorandum addressed by the Kurdistan Democratic Party (KDP) to the UN Secretary-General Kurt Waldheim on conditions of the Kurdish people in Iraq, 1974.

76. Khadouri, Majeed, *al-'Iraq al-Ishtiraki*, (Socialist Iraq), al-Dar al-Muttaheda Publishers, Beirut, 1st edn, 1985: 245.

77. Al-'Alawi, Hassan, op. cit.

78. Zamzami, op. cit.: 57.

79. Text of memorandum published in organ of the Islamic Action Organization, *al-'Amal al-Islami*, no. 153, 27 January 1985.

80. Al-Shaykh, Tawfiq, '*An al-'Iraq wal Haraka al-islamiyya* (On Iraq and the Islamic Movement), SAFA, London, 1st edn, 1988: 72.

81. See communique on regular plenary meeting of CC, Iraqi Communist Party, June-July, 1984: 23.

82. Chabry, Laurent and Annie Chabry, *Politiques et Minorité au Proche-Orient: les raisons d'une éxplosion*, Maisonneure et Larose, 1987: 131.

83. U. Zaher, 'The Opposition', in *Saddam's Iraq*, CARDRI: 161.

84. Sluglett, *Iraq Since 1958*, op. cit.: 25.

85. Al-Katib, Ahmad, op. cit.: 207.

86. Al-'Alawi, Hassan, op. cit.: 248.

87. *Kitab al-jihad*, al-*jihad* Press and Publishing House, Tehran, 1st edn, 1983: 153.

88. Al-Ansari, D. Mustafa, '*Amaliyyat al-tahjir fil 'Iraq* (Deportations in Iraq), The Human Rights Documentation Centre in Iraq, Tehran, 1991: 126.

89. The Arab Organization for Human Rights, Report on Human Rights in the Arab World, (Arabic), Cairo, 1987: 75.

90. *Huquq al-Insan fil 'Iraq* (Human Rights in Iraq), periodical bulletin (Arabic), no. 2, February 1989: 3.

91. *Al-Amal al-Islami*, organ of the Islamic Action Organization, no. 218, 21 December 1986.

92. Decisions Exposing Human Rights Violations in Iraq, op. cit.: 23.

93. Ibid.: 26.

94. *Liwa al-Sadr*, no. 335, 17 January 1988.

95. Interview with Iraqi deportee in Tehran, 1986.

96. *Al-Amal al-Islami*, no. 285, 11 December 1988.

97. *Al-Amal al-Islami*, no. 414, 20 August 1989.

98. *Liwa al-Sadr*, no. 424, 29 October 1989.

99. For a more detailed account of conditions of deportees in Iran see Babakhan, *Les Kurdes d'Irak*, op. cit.

100. *Al-'Iraq al-Jarih*, (Wounded Iraq), France, no. 1, November 1982.

101. SAIRI, Executive Bureau, Information Unit, *al-Muntalaqat wa al-ahdaf* (Guidelines and Objectives), Spokesman Office, January 1983: 12–14.

102. Ibid.: 20–22.

103. Ibid.: 30.

104. Ibid.: 61.

105. For more on political activity of SAIRI and its president Muhammad Baqir al-Hakim, see Babakhan, Ali, *L'Irak: 1970–1990, Deportations des Chiites*, Paris, 1994: 146–61.

106. In a letter from Abdul-Jalil Fayli to Ali Babakhan.

107. Ibid.

108. Preparatory Committee of the Fayli Kurdish Muslim Movement, an open letter to the Kurdistan Front.

109. For more on the movement's political activity see Babakhan, *Les Kurdes d'Irak*, op. cit.: 258–67.

110. Zamzami, op. cit.: 61.

CHAPTER THIRTEEN

Iraqi Shi'is in Exile in London

Jens-Uwe Rahe

The question of a latent or open conflict between Sunnis and Shi'is in Iraq is as old as the state of Iraq itself. Since the establishment of the monarchy in 1921, the Shi'ites, though making up more than half of Iraq's population, have never been adequately represented in the country's government and administration. Throughout the history of modern Iraq, the Shi'ites protested against this discrimination. They found different ways and means to articulate their protest: tribal uprisings in the thirties, communism in the fifties, and, most strikingly, the Islamic movement which appeared in the sixties.

The Islamic movement of Iraq, which is composed of various Islamist groups, took shape around the outstanding Shi'i scholar, Sayyid Muhammad Baqir al-Sadr (1931–1980). It was a response of the *'ulama* of Najaf to the success of communism among Iraq's Shi'ites, which threatened the authority of the religious establishment. Today, the Islamic movement is one of the pillars of the Iraqi opposition, besides the Kurds, communists and Arab nationalists.

Sadr himself, the brain behind the movement, was fully aware that the legitimacy and the appeal of an explicitly Shi'i movement in Iraq would be limited, due to the fact that 40% of the population are Sunni Arabs and Kurds. Shortly before his execution on 8 April 1980, he called upon Sunnis and Shi'is to fight the regime in a combined effort.[1] He acknowledged the first two caliphs, Abu Bakr and 'Umar, as defenders of Islam and denounced the Ba'th regime as non-Sunni.

On the other hand, such attempts to unify the political endeavours of Sunnis and Shi'is were undermined by the objective of the Islamic movement to set up a political *marja'iyya* in Iraq. In 1979, upon the request of Lebanese *'ulama*, Sadr wrote a draft constitution for an Islamic state.[2] In this draft, the most learned Shi'i jurist (*al-mujtahid al-mutlaq*) is the supreme institution of the state. He supervises the compatibility of the legislation with Islam and enjoys far-reaching executive responsibilities such as the command of the armed forces. His authority goes beyond the responsibilities of the traditional three powers. In Sadr's proposal, the final say about all relevant matters of the state goes to al-mujtahid al-mutlaq.

Sadr's concept, however, could not attract Sunni believers, who do not accept the Shi'i concept of *marja'iyya*³ which means to emulate a chosen *'alim* in all questions of life. An example of the practical consequences of ideological differences among Iraqi Muslims can be observed in the uprising of March 1991, Intifada Sha'ban. In the wake of the second Gulf War, when military operations came to a halt, the population of Southern Iraq and Iraqi Kurdistan spontaneously revolted against the government. Apparently, the organised opposition had no part in the beginning of the Intifada. Soon, however, mujahidin of the Tehran-based Supreme Assembly of the Islamic Revolution in Iraq (SAIRI) moved in from Iran and began to disseminate slogans and posters of Iran's revolutionary leaders, Khomeini and Khamenei, and the head of SAIRI, Sayyid Muhammad Baqir al-Hakim.

All this, it seems, changed the character of the uprising in the sense that it gave it a more radical and particularist label, which made the non-Islamists, generally Sunnis, refrain from extending their support to the rebellion. In addition, it provided the regime with an opportunity to portray the uprising as a foreign conspiracy and to respond to it with an explicitly anti-Shi'i campaign. Hundreds of *'ulama* were jailed, libraries looted and religious sites destroyed. The Ba'th regime enforced the drying-up of the marshes and in its official media it launched an unprecedented propaganda attack against the Shi'ites, describing them as primitive and 'un-Iraqi'.⁴

Against this background the relationship between confession and opposition (more accurately, between confessional thought and political agenda), emerges as a problem of paramount importance for the Iraqi opposition. This question will be looked at here in the context of Iraqi Shi'i organisations in exile in London.⁵ The British capital accommodates a community of 60.000 to 80.000 Iraqi expatriates and refugees. Compared with other places of exile such as Tehran or Damascus, London offers a liberal climate which allows Iraqis to set up associations of all kinds, to discuss politics in public and to publish. Moreover, due to the factors mentioned, the city became a turntable and centre of the Iraqi opposition after 1991.

Iraqi Shi'i Organisations in London

Firstly, a brief survey of the spectrum of Iraqi Shi'i organisations in London, as discernible in the spring of 1994, will be given. The first religiously oriented groups of Iraqis which appeared in the United Kingdom were Muslim student associations like the Muslim Youth Association (*Rabitat ash-Shabab al-Muslim fi Britaniyya*) in the 1970s. In the mid 1980s, due to a rising number of refugees leaving Iraq during the Iran-Iraq War (1980–1988), the first Islamic centres were established. Offering Islamic education, prayer facilities, libraries and different kinds of social services, they were registered, in accordance with British law, as charitable organisations. In most cases they were – and still are – led by *'ulama* of a prominent family background such as Hakim, Bahr al-'Ulum, al-Kho'i and Sadr, which provides them with religious authority and legitimacy.

At the same time, Iraqi Islamist groups began to work in London. They did not appear as independent groups but as extensions of the Islamic movement of Iraq. Initially, they could not operate openly, because Baghdad was still considered an ally of the west and such groups were looked on as terrorist organisations. It was only after western governments dissociated themselves from Saddam Hussein after Iraq's invasion of Kuwait, that the opposition in exile could step forward and present itself in public.

In 1994, the year of this research, at least five religious institutions of Iraqi Shi'is existed in London: four community centres (Markaz al-Imam al-Kho'i, Markaz Ahl al-Bait, Dar al-Islam, Husainiyyat ar-Rasul al-A'zam) and one educational institute (Ma'had al-Sayyid al-Sadr). In addition, five political groups were active, among them branches of the most important forces of the Islamic movement of Iraq: the Islamic Call Party (*Hizb ad-Da'wa al-Islamiyya*), the Supreme Council of the Islamic Revolution in Iraq (*al-Majlis al-A'la li al-Thawra al-Islamiyya fi l-Iraq*) and the Islamic Action Organisation (*Munazzamat al-'Amal al-Islami*). Further, there was Sayyid Muhammad Bahr al-'Ulum, a non-party scholar, who as a member of the presidential council of the Iraqi National Congress (INC) [until 1996] represented the Shi'i segment of the population in this umbrella organisation of the Iraqi opposition.

The close co-operation between religious institutions and political groups was strking. Four of the five centres were each associated with a political group or leading political figure. The only exception was the al-Kho'i Foundation (*Mu'assasat al-Imam al-Kho'i al-Khairiyya*) which did not serve as a forum of a particular party. Yet the Foundation itself was searching for a political role during the period under examination.

The Da'wa

This section will focus on the confessional thought of Iraqi Shi'i Islamists in

London, i.e. the confessional self-image of the organisations concerned. This will include those aspects of their ideology and political agenda which are exclusively Shi'i.

Based on an extensive analysis of texts by and interviews with Iraqi scholars, political scientists and Islamist activists, two major currents of Islamist groups among Iraqi Shi'is in London, it was possible to discern a moderate camp, defining itself as 'liberal' and 'democratic', and a radical, 'revolutionary', camp. The first tended to support a liberal society with a pluralist political system, whereas the second promoted a revolutionary change of society, aiming at the establishment of an Islamic state, supervised by the *marja'iyya*. Interestingly, this differentiation between moderates and revolutionaries corresponded to significant differences in the confessional thought of these groups.

With respect to the radical groups, a close relationship between their political thought and the ideology of Muhammad Baqir al-Sadr is clear. In spite of internal ideological disputes and differences, these groups represent the main stream of the Islamic movement of Iraq. Its oldest and most experienced organisation is Hizb ad-Da'wa al-Islamiyya, which was founded with Sadr's support in the late fifties in Najaf and is sometimes referred to by Islamic activists as their school.

In its writings, the Da'wa plays down the existence of more than one religious community in Iraq. Instead, the party seeks, at least rhetorically, to gather not only the different Islamic forces but all factions of the Iraqi opposition. In 'Our Programme' *(Barnamajuna)*,[6] the official party programme published in 1992, the Da'wa consequently refers to the Iraqi population as Muslims: *sha'buna al-muslim, al-sha'b al-'iraqi al-muslim, al-kurd al-muslimun*. While strong emphasis is laid on the overall Islamic identity of the Iraqi people, its different confessional identities are neglected.

Yet the Da'wa reveals a more Shi'i profile in its newspaper 'Voice of Iraq' *(Saut al-'Iraq)*. For example, an editorial on the occasion of Muharram, the Shi'i month of mourning, links the resistance against the Ba'th regime with the tradition of Karbala, according to which the third Imam al-Husayn, leader of Shi'at 'Ali, was here defeated and killed by Umayyad troops.[7] Although the article does not identify the conflicting parties as Shi'i and Sunni, the reference to Karbala is by no means a suitable way to close the historical and cultural gap between the two groups. In fact, what happened in Karbala has been called the 'big bang'[8] that pushed forward the development of the so far political Shi'ism as a religious movement, separated from the Sunni majority.

In its political objectives, some of the Da'wa, including members of its political bureau, are flirting with the idea of a political *marja'iyya* as outlined by Sadr in 1979. This has been admitted by Da'wa activists *(du'at)* in London, who represent the moderate wing of the party.[9] Seeing itself as a mass movement, the Da'wa accommodates various schools of thought, the most important of which are the ones located in Tehran and the UK. According to information given by former *du'at*, parts of the Da'wa still hold on to literature promoting Khomeini's doctrine of *wilayat al-faqih*, the rule of the jurist.[10] If this is so, the non-confessional, patriotic approach of the Da'wa remains dubious.

The al-Kho'i Foundation

In comparison with the Da'wa, those Iraqi Shi'i groups which may be considered more liberal show a different, much stronger confessional self-image. This was not particularly surprising in the case of the al-Kho'i Foundation, which defines itself as 'the continuation of the charitable and educational functions historically associated with the office of *marja'iyya*'.[11] However, the strong political involvement of the Foundation during 1991 to 1994 was startling: the Foundation would more usually be expected to follow the submissive line of its founder, Grand Ayatollah Sayyid Abu al-Qasim al-Kho'i. Yet it was making use of its London base to establish contacts with western governments and international organisations such as the United Nations Centre for Human Rights in Geneva. In its publications and through diplomatic channels, the Foundation promoted the idea of a 'safe haven' in Southern Iraq, similar to the one set up in Kurdistan after the Gulf War.[12] It also demanded the monitoring of human rights violations in Iraq, a modification of the economic sanctions against the country[13] and the removal of Saddam Hussein.[14]

This political activism was justified by the Foundation by the precariousness of the *marja'iyya* in Najaf: 'Obviously, the gravity of the situation inside Iraq forced al-Kho'i Foundation to break a long held tradition by the Shi'i clergy in Iraq of not visiting political and international institutions'.[15] In fact, Imam al-Kho'i was under house arrest, dozens of *'ulama* were kept in jail, and many religious institutions had been destroyed or confiscated by the regime. Against this background, the Foundation's excursion onto the political stage may be seen as an attempt to defend the institution of *marja'iyya*.

In the spring of 1993, al-Kho'i Foundation organised four conferences on 'The crisis of the Shi'ites of Iraq' (*Azmat Shi'at al-'Iraq*) at its headquarters in London. More than one hundred *'ulama*, Islamists and secularist thinkers discussed the situation and the state of Iraq's Shi'i population. Dr. Laith Kubba, Head of Public Relations at the Foundation, later summarised the discussions and conclusions reached by the participants in closed sessions.[16] His text gives an insight into what the Foundation had in mind when the concept of the conference was developed: 'The Shi'ites constitute a body, the organs of which are the *marja'iyya*, the parties, the militias, the *hawza*, the tribes and the intellectuals. These organs co-operate with each other to different extents, but they are rarely complete . . . The Shi'ites with all their elements are neither united nor do they have a clearly defined goal. Each of their elements follows its own objectives. And the result is: no objective at all'.[17]

Kubba defined Shi'ism as '. . . not a race and not a class. It is not acquired by birth. Shi'ism is rather a loyalty and an affiliation, and lately, due to the oppression, an everyday feeling (*shu'ur/hiss yaumi*), which the Iraqi Shi'i has, even if he is not religious'.[18]

This was an uncommon and interesting definition of Shi'ism. Instead of referring to the religion itself, to its doctrine or history, a prominent representative of the Foundation chose a socio-political criterion with which to identify Shi'ism: state oppression. Through this definition the Foundation addressed the widest possible scope of Shi'i society. It also, of course, provoked the obvious question: was it exploiting or even stirring up the confessional conflict in Iraq?

The Foundation, fully aware of this charge, argued that confessional sensitivity in Iraq had been a fact of life for a long time, and that open debate was needed. In the words of Sayyid Yusuf al-Kho'i, grand-son of the Grand Ayatollah: 'The open talk about the crisis of Shi'ites of Iraq, as well as confessing one's Shi'i identity, does not mean to disparage the identity of others nor to sow discord. Each individual has the right to be conscious of his ethnic background, family, faith and homeland . . . We do not demand a confessionalist constitution but the protection of the freedoms of the individual and the society's institutions in the framework of the one home country . . .'[19]

By stressing its commitment to national unity, al-Kho'i Foundation intended to refute the charge of deepening the rift between Sunnis and Shi'is. According to the Foundation, confessional sensitivities should be channelled rather than ignored, and confessional conflict should be solved by harmonising the different confessional identities with a national agenda.

Bahr al-'Ulum

Another political protagonist of Iraq's Shi'ites in exile is Dr. Sayyid Muhammad Bahr al-'Ulum (b. 1927), who is running the Islamic centre Markaz Ahl al-Bait in London. At the time of this research he was the principal representative of the Shi'ites in the INC, the umbrella organisation of the Iraqi opposition. Bahr al-'Ulum was among those who considered themselves to be moderate and used the term 'democracy' without hesitation. In common with the al-Kho'i Foundation, he appeared as an advocate exclusively of the Shi'ites. In his writings, he described the Shi'i population of Iraq as *aghlabiyya, ghalibiyya* or *akthariyya,* which all means majority – yet a majority playing the role of an oppressed minority *(aqalliyya mudtahada).*

According to Bahr al-'Ulum, the thinking of Iraqis in confessional and ethnic patterns is a result of Saddam's dictatorship, which profits from the exaggeration of such categories. The scholar turns upside down the common argument that Saddam's iron fist is the last and only guarantee of Iraq's unity as a state. In contrast, Bahr al-'Ulum postulates that the regime itself applies a confessionalist policy *(siyasa ta'ifiyya)* and thereby ruins the national consensus.

Last but not least, the writings of Bahr al-'Ulum highlight a question related to confessional identity which is crucial to Iraqi Shi'i Islamists: their relationship with the Islamic Republic of Iran. Whereas opposition groups based in Tehran are generally loyal to the Islamic Revolution, Bahr al-'Ulum, like the al-Kho'i Foundation and even the London wing of the Da'wa, pleads for cultural and political detachment from the Islamic Republic: 'With the undermining of Najaf as the ultimate guide of world Shi'ism, signs of tension emerged between the Shi'ites and the international community, which ultimately led to the widespread conviction that the Shi'ites are a community of blind fanatics. This conviction was only strengthened by the success and evolution of the Islamic Revolution in Iran, causing many international institutions to identify terrorism with Shi'ism'.[20] Bahr al-'Ulum thus attempts to draw a positive picture of the Iraqi Shi'ites, even at the expense of the Islamic Republic. Like al-Kho'i Foundation, he wants to raise awareness at international level to protect the South of Iraq.

Conclusion

Confessional thought and political agenda are closely interlinked in the political ideology of Iraqi Shi'is in exile. The findings of this study can be summarised in four points:

1) The traditional Islamic movement, as represented by Hizb ad-Da'wa, continues to play down confessional and sectarian differences in Iraq. Nevertheless, it is not ready to give up its vision of a political *marja'iyya*, which means a supervision of the legislation and other state affairs by the Shi'i *'ulama* and thus undermines the party's all-embracing Islamic-nationalist approach.

2) More liberal groups, such as al-Kho'i Foundation, explicitly act as representatives of the Iraqi Shi'ites, speaking up undaunted for the interests of Iraq's

Shi'i population. They do not define Shi'ism as a religious confession, but rather as part of a social and political crisis. This crisis encompasses two disparate aspects: oppression from the outside, by the regime, and a lack of unity within, including towards common goals. The more moderate stream of Iraqi Shi'i Islamism tends to support a liberal society and a pluralist system in order to neutralise and control the strong confessionalist sentiments and aspirations of Iraq's various communities.

3) The developed awareness of confessional differences and the strong commitment to Shi'i affairs, which are important aspects in the ideology of the moderates, may be called Shi'i regionalism. The term seems appropriate as the goals of this part of the Shi'i spectrum are linked with regional interests, foremost of which is the protection of Southern Iraq against repression by the regime (for example by the establishment of a 'safe haven'). Shi'i regionalism is Shi'i in the sense that it serves the interests of Shi'i people. It was triggered off by the Intifada of March 1991 and, more importantly, by the harsh retaliatory measures which the government took with a clear anti-Shi'i direction.

4) The confessional thought if Iraqi Shi'is, as studied among their exile groups, is strongly developed, possibly more than ever before. Yet this is combined with political pragmatism and a flirtation with democracy. The lessons of the Gulf crisis, as well as the experience of exile in the United Kingdom, seem to make a rising number of Iraqi Shi'is realise that a democratic solution in Baghdad may help them to practise their legitimate rights in a future Iraq.

Notes

1. See Baram, Amatzia, 'The Radical Shi'ite Opposition Movements in Iraq', in Emmanuel Sivan and Menachem Friedman (eds.), *Religious Radicalism and Politics in the Middle East*, New York, 1990: 108–109.

2. On Sadr's *Lamha fiqhiyya tamhidiyya 'an mashru' dustur al-Jumhuriyya al-Islamiyya fi Iran*, Beirut, 1979, see Chibli Mallat, *The Renewal of Islamic Law, Muhammad Baqir al-Sadr, Najaf and the Shi'i International*, Cambridge, 1993: 69–78.

3. See Chibli Mallat, 'Religious militancy in contemporary Iraq: Muhammad Baqir al-Sadr and the Sunni-Shi'i paradigm', in *Third World Quarterly*, vol. 10, no. 2, April 1988: 699–729. See also Baram: 112–125.

4. See Makiya, Kanan, *Cruelty and Silence: War, Tyranny, Uprising and the Arab World*, London, 1993: 101–102.

5. The present article is based on Jens-Uwe Rahe, 'Irakische Schiiten im Londoner Exil, Eine Bestandsaufnahme ihrer Organisationen und Untersuchung ihrer Selbstdarstellung, 1991–1994', in Peter Heine (ed), *al-Rafidayn. Jahrbuch zu*

Geschichte und Kultur des modernen Iraq, Band IV (Würzburg, 1996).

6. Hizb ad-Da'wa al-Islamiyya, *Barnamajuna, al-bayan wa-l-barnamaj al-siyasi li Hizb ad-Da'wa al-Islamiyya*, London, 1992.

7. *Saut al-'Iraq*, 'al-Iftitahiyya: Hayhat minna adh-dhilla', no. 132, 15 June 1993: 1.

8. Heinz, Halm, *Der schiitische Islam. Von der Religion zur Revolution*, München, 1994: 19, 28.

9. Interview with Dr. Muwaffaq al-Rubai'i, former spokesman of the Da'wa Party in London, 24 March 1994.

10. Interviews with Muhammad 'Abd al-Jabbar, spokesman of Harakat al-Kawadir al-Islamiyya, a splinter group of the Da'wa, 15 and 29 March 1994.

11. Mu'assasat al-Imam al-Kho'i, The al-Kho'i Foundation, Concepts and Projects, London, 1992: 11.

12. Public Affairs Committee for Shi'i Muslims (a branch of the al-Kho'i Foundation), 'Marsh Arabs Threatened with Annihilation', in *Dialogue*, August 1992: 1.

13. Kubba, Laith (Director of Public Relations at the al-Kho'i Foundation), 'Reviewing the UN Sanctions Against Iraq', in *al-Noor*, no. 34, April 1994: 3.

14. Public Affairs Committee for Shi'i Muslims, 'Towards a New Policy in Iraq', in *Dialogue*, August 1994: 1.

15. Public Affairs Committee for Shi'i Muslims, 'Meeting the UN', in *Dialogue*, November 1991: 1.

16. Kubba, Laith, *Azmat Shi'at al-'Iraq* (The Crisis of Iraqi Shi'ites), London, 1994, a draft booklet which was never published.

17. Ibid.: 37.

18. Ibid.: 9–10.

19. Al-Kho'i, Yusuf, 'Azmat Shi'at al-'Iraq, Akthariyyat al-sha'b al-akthar hirmanan', in *al-Noor*, no. 37, July 1994: 20. Originally a paper presented at the conference on 'Rights of Minorities in the Arab World', Cyprus, 12–14 May 1994.

20. Al-'Ulum, Muhammad Bahr, *Najaf's Leadership Role and the Safe Haven in Southern Iraq*, manuscript, March 1993: 3.

PART IV

SYSTEMS OF THOUGHT

CHAPTER FOURTEEN

Grand Ayatollah Abu al-Qassim al-Kho'i: Political Thought and Positions

Yousif al-Kho'i

In the Shi'i realm, renowned for its pluralism and different trends, the school of Grand Ayatollah Sayyid Abu al-Qassim al-Kho'i stands out in bold contrast. His spiritual work and scholastic research combine with charitable endeavours and moderate political activism to protect both the centres of Shi'i learning and the community of the Shi'ites across the world. This combination of spirituality and moderate activism made the Kho'i school a *sui generis* in its own right. This chapter focuses on a review of al-Kho'i's works and positions which clearly contrast with other schools of thought in the second half of twentieth century Shi'i Islam.

Early years

Sayyid Abu al-Qasim Mussawi al-Kho'i was born into a clerical family from a modest background in the city of Khoy in Iranian Azerbaijan on 19 November 1899. His primary school education was at his local 'Namazi school'. When he was only thirteen, he migrated to the holy city of Najaf – the burial place of Imam Ali and the major centre of learning in Shi'i Islam.

Even at this early age, al-Kho'i took his religious studies very seriously. It is said that when he was in his early twenties he was already acknowledged by some of his peers as an outstanding student and became a lecturer at an advanced level in the *hawza*, religious seminary, of Najaf.

During this period the Middle East region was going through turbulent events – the end of the First World War brought the demise of the Ottoman Empire, the occupation of Iraq by the by British, the blockade of Najaf, and the eruption of the 1920 Iraqi revolt against the British colonial administration. There were also turbulent developments in Iran which, following years of struggles for and against constitutionalism, brought an end to the Qajar dynasty.

Despite the fact that al-Kho'i's teacher and mentor, Grand Ayatollah Sheikh Muhammad Husayn Na'ini, was a strong advocate of constitutionalism in Iran and the Shi'i *ulama* were generally taking a more active role in political events in Persia, there would appear to be no known record of al-Kho'i's active involvement in these events.

After the death of the Grand *Marja'*, Ayatollah Sayyid Abul Hassan al-Isfahani in Najaf in 1945, al-Kho'i began to be recognised in the *hawza* as a *marja'*, having already completed several courses of teaching of advanced studies (Dars al-Kharij). By then he had a number of advanced students under his tutorship. In addition to traditional studies in jurisprudence (Islamic law) and *usul al-fiqh* (methodology and principles of jurisprudence), al-Kho'i also lectured on the Qur'an. His commentary was later published under the title *al-Bayan fi Tafsir al-Qur'an*, which was regarded by the *hawza's* more prominent intellectuals and scholars as a masterpiece of scholarly work.

Rising Marja'

In the early 1950s, al-Kho'i had some limited following in Iraq as well as in Iran, and was developing a reputation within the *hawza*. His lectures were delivered in Arabic which made them popular with Arabic as well as Persian and Turkish-speaking students. He also had good command of both Persian and Turkish and composed poems in all three languages. From the early 1960s, there are records of al-Kho'i's involvement in issuing political *fatwas*, or edicts, including a warning to the Shah of Iran about the increased role of the Baha'i and Zionists in the Iranian Government and administration (*al-Tasreehat al-Khateera lil Nufudhh al-Baha'i wal Sahyuni fi-Iran*). Moreover, his *Resalah al-'Amaliyya* (A Practical Guide for the Faithful) has been one of the few such works which contained a chapter on *jihad*. In addition, and after the death of the Grand *Marja'* Sayyid Husayn Brujerdi in 1963, al-Kho'i joined Grand Ayatollah Sayyid Muhsin Tabataba'i al-Hakim in his famous *fatwas* on communism (1960) and on the illegality of the Iraqi government's actions against the Kurds in northern Iraq (1962). He also issued *fatwas* in support of the Palestinian cause and the Algerian resistance against French colonialism.

Kho'i and Khomeini

In 1963, when Sayyid Ruhallah Mussavi Khomeini was threatened with execution after his public protests against the Shah's rule, al-Kho'i also played a direct political role. He personally lobbied within the *hawza* milieu in Najaf and went to Ayatollah Hakim's residence to discuss plans for intervention to save Khomeini's life. Together with Ayatollah Sayyid Mahmud Husayni Sharoodi, they warned the Shah against the execution of Khomeini. This assisted the endeavours made in Qum by Grand Ayatollah Sayyid Muhammad Qadhim Shariatmadari who released a statement to accord Khomeini with the status of *mujtahid'*. This recognition of Khomeini as a *mujtahid* made his execution an illegal procedure under the Iranian constitution, and did actually deter the Shah from harming him. When Ayatollah Khomeini was exiled to Najaf, al-Kho'i paid him a visit shortly afterwards; this was reciprocated by Khomeini. However, al-Kho'i never subscribed to the revolutionary vision of Islam; in particular, he differed with Khomeini on the concept of *wilayat al-faqih al-mutlaqa* (the absolute rule of the jurist). Al-Kho'i only believed in the *'al-wilaya al-khassa'*, the limited guardianship of the jurist during the age of occultation, i.e in the absence of the Infallible Imam who is awaited by the faithful, no jurist has the right to rule (*wilaya*) except over people who cannot fend for themselves. This may include, for example, minors who have no guardians. Moreover, al-Kho'i did not consider the rule of the jurist on a number of subjects as binding on the faithful. In this regard, al-Kho'i considers the *faqihs* to have limited authority on the affairs of the umma, and the jurists may conduct their political rights as any other member of the Muslim society, i.e., jurists are part of the umma, not above it. Hence, al-Kho'i's political views stem from his belief that sovereignty belongs to the Muslim umma, community, not to the jurists.

Relations between al-Kho'i and Khomeini during the pre-1979 Revolution period can be described as cordial but cool. It was not traditional for a *marja'* to show open disagreement with another *marja'* in public. Al-Kho'i and Khomeini would see each other at public events or during visits to the holy shrines, but there was no other known social interaction between the two. There was, however, some social interaction between family members, including women's circles.

Kho'i versus the Ba'th: Early Tensions

After the Ba'th takeover in 1968, tensions developed between Ayatollah Hakim and the new rulers in Baghdad: these resulted in one of Hakim's sons, Sayyid

Mahdi, being publicly accused of espionage by the Iraqi government. Al-Kho'i stood side-by-side with Hakim during those tough days of confrontation with the Ba'th rulers, and he was the first visitor to offer support and solidarity to Hakim in his house in the city of Kufa after Hakim's self-imposed house arrest. After the death of Hakim in 1971, al-Kho'i reluctantly accepted the position of the Grand *Marja'*, the supreme spiritual authority of the world's Imami, or Twelver (*Ithna' Ashari*) Shi'i Muslims. Like the other Grand Marja's, al-Kho'i neither had a strong infrastructure to lobby for him nor was he motivated by personal ambition: he assumed the position mainly as a result of the strong recommendations of his numerous students in Najaf and beyond and his staff.

Moderation in Politics

Kho'i charted a moderate and cautious political course. This was greatly influenced by the way the Ba'th government had treated, or maltreated, Ayatollah Hakim. Al-Kho'i must have formed the opinion that the religious establishment should not be directly involved, in general terms, in political affairs. Although al-Kho'i was personally keen on following international and regional news on various radio stations at night, and was generally well aware of world events, he nevertheless must have thought that international relations and world politics required a certain amount of expediency and immoral manoeuvering, and that politics was generally manipulated and controlled by certain corrupt élites. He was neither willing nor able to play the rules of the game nor to be directly involved in such affairs. He saw his role mainly as a 'protector of the faith' and thought this would be best fulfilled by supporting and encouraging the projects of his predecessor, as well as building new social, educational and philanthropic institutions to serve the community. His priorities lay in the teaching and training of Islamic scholars. His political role was usually consciously confined to offering opinions when the Islamic religion itself was in real danger or under threat. He also voiced concerns when certain groups or governments tried to use his name for their own political ends, or when they claimed that he supported them, as happened during the Iran-Iraq War. Al-Kho'i also reacted with anger when a Saudi newspaper falsely claimed that he had sanctioned the execution of some Kuwaiti pilgrims on their pilgrimage to Mecca.

Charity Work

Kho'i paid particular attention to the Shi'i Muslim community in the Lebanon, the only Muslim country he visited after becoming Grand *Marja'*. He also took a keen interest in the welfare of the Shi'i Muslim communities in India, Pakistan and the Gulf, and the small minority of the Shi'i Ithna' Ashari Khoja community in East Africa and Zanjibar (Tanzania). With the rise of oil prices in the mid 1970s, the religious contributions from the faithful reached unprecedented levels. But al-Kho'i gave a great deal of autonomy to his representatives and followers in their use of the *khums*, a special tax akin to the *zakat*, which is administered by the *marja'* in the absence of the Twelfth Hidden Imam. These revenues were spent on local projects such as schools, libraries, orphanages, housing and clinics, as well as extending income support to needy members of the community, be they next of kin, friends or colleagues.

In Iraq, al-Kho'i supported existing projects, including many libraries which were set up by al-Hakim, or the private Shi'i schools in Baghdad and Najaf. He set up a primary school for girls in Najaf which was run by Amina Bint al-Huda, the sister of Ayatollah Sayyid Muhammad Baqir al-Sadr, who was later executed along with her brother in 1980.

Resisting Ba'th Pressure

In the early 1970s, pressure from the Ba'th regime in Iraq against the *'ulama* and religious institutions and activities increased dramatically.

Among other things, the government enforced the expulsion of *'ulama* from the country, drafted clerics and seminarians into the military, imposed a ban on all mourning rituals during the much revered commemorations of 'Ashura, the ten day rituals observing the the memory and martyrdom of Imam al-Husayn, pressurised the *marja'* into declaring such practices illegal, and nationalised Shi'i private independent primary and secondary schools. This drive was coupled by constant intervention in the running of the *hawza* and the holy shrines, and culminated in the execution, for the first time, of Shi'i clerics in 1974. The list of victims included Sheikh 'Arif al-Basri and Sayyid 'Izz al-Din Qubanji. The Ba'th government also tried to force certain clerics into attending government-sponsored conferences. Other pressures included the detention and arrest of clerics and younger students, who were accused of being Da'wa Party militants. The Ba'thist regime also, for the first time, dared to issue a court summons to Grand Ayatollah Mahmud Shahroodi, who had a significant following in Kuwait, on the grounds that he had been involved in illegal money transfers overseas (*Tahwil al-Khariji*). Al-Kho'i made strong protests against this accusation: Shahroodi's death soon afterwards brought this episode to an end.

Kho'i and Iran

As far as relations with the Shah are concerned, there was no formal link between al-Kho'i and official Iran. It is a fact, though, that the Shah sent a telegram of condolences to al-Kho'i after Hakim's death, a signal of recognition of his religious authority. Al-Kho'i, however, declined to meet Abbas Howeida, the Shah's Prime-Minister, during the latter's visit to Najaf in 1975 after the Iran-Iraq Algiers Agreement was signed. When the mass upheaval started in Iran in 1978 and 1979, Empress Farah, the Shah's wife, visited Najaf to seek support from al-Kho'i. Though he received her, he refused to intervene on behalf of her husband. After the success of the Islamic Revolution in Iran, al-Kho'i sent a telegram of congratulations to the new Government in Tehran but deliberately kept his distance from Iranian politics. He was disliked, sometimes vehemently, by some of the more hard-core revolutionaries in both Iran and the Lebanon. His broad advice to his representatives was to refrain from any confrontational attitude against his antagonists or adversaries. Many of his grand projects in Iran were temporarily halted for two to three years. His main bank account in Iran was frozen for some time and was only released on the direct instructions of Ayatollah Khomeini after the intervention of Ayatollah Ashtiani.

During the Iran-Iraq War, al-Kho'i again refused to be drawn into the conflict; and when the Iraqi Government claimed in the media that he had prayed for the Shuhada' or martyrs of Saddam's Qadissiyya, he denied this through his representatives abroad. As a result of his position towards the Iran-Iraq war, his senior assistants were arrested and one of his closest advisers, Ayatollah Sayyid Muhammad Taqi al-Jalali, was executed. Jalali's mutilated body was unceremoniously handed over to al-Kho'i in 1981. Eight other members of his staff, including Ayatollah Sheikh Muhammad Taqi Jawahiri and Shaykh Hashimiyan, have remained unaccounted for since the early 1980s, and may have perished in the security service dungeons.

During the Iran-Iraq War, al-Kho'i allocated funds and sanctioned the payment of *khums* money to refugees on both sides of the border. He treated Afghani Shi'i Muslim refugees during the war with the Soviet Union in a similar fashion. During the 1990–1 Gulf War, he showed similar concern over the fate of the Kuwaiti refugees called the Bedoon, those who were not recognized by the Kuwaiti authorities as being of authentic Kuwaiti origin, yet were given leave to remain in the country. Al-Kho'i instructed his representatives in the Gulf to help the displaced people.. In addition, he issued a well-known *fatwa* forbidding any dealings with any item or property looted from Kuwait, a daring stand defying the Ba'th government who had annexed Kuwait as the nineteenth Iraqi province. As a result of this *fatwa*, a great number of people actually refused to deal publicly with the Kuwaiti goods which were flooding into Iraqi markets.

fatwas on the 1991 Uprising

In the aftermath of the Gulf War in 1991, al-Kho'i responded to public pressure to intervene in the uprising which started in Najaf on the 3 March 1991. On the second and third day of the uprising in Najaf, tribal, military and community leaders came to see him and plead for his intervention. He issued two statements, the first on 6 March, urging the people to maintain order and respect public and private property. He also instructed that all the corpses littering the streets should be buried. In the second *fatwa*, issued shortly afterwards, he appointed a committee comprising 9 clerics to supervise the affairs of the community during those turbulent days.

True Legacy

Kho'i's real legacy has been, and will remain, his academic work and charity institutions. In addition to establishing the al-Kho'i Foundation (offices and schools) in London, New York, Islamabad, Bombay, Thailand and elsewhere, al-Kho'i has many projects to his name in Iran, including major centres of religious studies in the holy cities of Qum and Mashhad. Within the realm of Shi'i Islam it is difficult to find any charitable projects without some form of contribution either direct or indirect from al-Kho'i. His other legacy is the great number of prominent *mujtahids* who graduated under his tutorship. Many of today's marja's and key Shi'i personalities were his students, including Ayatollahs Sayyid Ali Husayni Seestani, Sayyid 'Ali Beheshti, Sheikh Mirza 'Ali Gharawi, Sayyid Muhammad Taqi al-Hakim (Iraq), Sheikh Mirza Jawad Tabrizi, Shaykh al-Waheed al-Khurasani, Shaykh 'Ali Falsafi, Sayyid 'Abdul Kareem Mousavi Ardabili (Iran), Sayyid Muhammad Hussain Fadhl Allah, Sheikh Muhammad Mahdi Shams al-Din (Lebanon), Sayyid 'Ali Makki (Syria), Shaykh Muhammad Ishaq Fayaz (Pakistan), Shaykh Muhammad Asif Mohsini (Afghanistan), Shaykh 'Abdul Hadi al-Fadhli, Sayyid 'Ali Nassir, Shaykh 'Abdullah Khunayzi (Saudi Arabia), Sayyid Jawad Shahroodi (Kuwait) and the late Ayatollahs Muhammad Rouhani (Iran), Sayyid Muhammad Baqir al-Sadr, Sayyid Sahib al-Hakim (Iraq) and Sayyid Mohyi al-Din al-Ghorayfi (Bahrain).

Many of his prominent students, together with his son and son-in-law, have remained in Iraqi jails since March 1991. The list includes Ayatollahs Sayyid Murtadha al-Musawi al-Khalkhali, Shaykh 'Ali Ahmadi, Sayyid 'Ala' al-Din Bahr al-'Ulum, Sayyid Muhammad Redha Mousavi Khalkhali, Sayyid Muhammad Taqi Marashi, Sayyid 'Izz al-Din Bahr al-'Ulum and others.

Conclusions

In conclusion, certain aspects of the century-long life of al-Kho'i, one of the most prominent *marja'* for the Shi'i Muslims, may be highlighted:

1. Despite his humble parentage, and the fact that he was a newcomer to the *hawza* of Najaf, he rose to the highest religious position, and surpassed most of his peers.

2. His life is a portrait of an exemplary religious scholar dedicated to the promotion and propagation of Islamic studies and to the consolidation of Islamic faith and practise among the followers of the House of the Prophet (the Ahl al-Bayt) throughout the world. His writings, teaching methods and spirituality were dedicated exclusively to this noble end. His published works, the institutions he established worldwide, his attitude to political activity, the number of graduate students who flocked to his seminars all illustrate his commitment to the role which he believed Almighty God had entrusted to him as a protector of the Islamic faith. Al-Kho'i became the *marja'* at a critical time for Shi'i Muslims and for the Iraqi Shi'ites in particular. By demonstrating great composure in the face of horrific events, he undoubtedly averted what would have been a massacre of the Iraqi Shi'ites. In effect, he preserved Najaf as the traditional centre of Shi'i learning: his self-possession and pragmatic attitude combined to safeguard the historical status and role of the city which the overwhelming majority of Shi'ites regard as the centre of grand religious authority. The fact that the great majority of *marja' taqlid* today, who are emulated by the majority of Shi'ites throughout the world, had been students of al-Kho'i, is an indication that the school of Sayyid al-Kho'i will not only be maintained, but will continue to exert a marked influence within Imami Twelver Shi'ism for generations to come.

CHAPTER FIFTEEN

The Political Theory of Muhammad Baqir Sadr

Talib Aziz

Few would consider Muhammad Baqir al-Sadr to be one of the pioneering leaders of the Islamic movements that have overwhelmed the landscape of the World of Islam. His brief rise in 1979–80, followed by his execution in April 1980, left him alive in the hearts of a close circle of admirers, yet in the shadow of the sweeping events of the Iranian Revolution and the giant figure of its leader, Ayatollah Khomeini. Those who revered Sadr are touched by his intellectual contribution to the Islamic discourses, which were overwhelmed by other thinkers such as Said Qutb of Egypt, Abu al-'Ala al-Mawdudi of Pakistan and Shari'ati of Iran. Others claim that he is the precursor of the whole Shi'i Islamic movement that existed outside the borders of Iran. However, Sadr's contribution is gaining some notice in many academic and religious circles, where his writings and thought are being revisited and analysed. This paper concentrates on a review of his political theory and thought in three major areas: (i) the legitimation of modern party politics in Shi'i jurisprudence; (ii) the reformation of the Shi'i religious authority (*marja'ism*); and (iii) his elaboration of the constitutional framework of the envisaged Islamic polity.

Political Party

Sadr's introduction into politics appears to have been purely accidental. Devoting much of his time to theological and juristic studies in the *hawza* of Najaf, he was no different to his peers and mentors in the age-old religious institution. To succeed in *hawza*, a cleric has to excel in jurisprudence and Islamic laws. It was his friend, Talib al-Rifa'i, a political activist and ex-member of Islamic Liberation party, Hizb al-Tahrir (HT), who introduced Sadr to political activism after the July 1958 revolution.¹ Rifaʿi and his collaborators, Mahdi al-Hakim and Sahib Dakhil, engaged Sadr in forming the first cell of the Islamic Daʿwa Party in Iraq to counter the activities and influence of the widespread Communist Party. By dint of his ideological input, Sadr later gained prominence in the leadership of the organization, helping the obscure founders to gain legitimacy within the conservative jurists and traditional environment of the religious establishment in Najaf.

Sadr envisaged a Leninist type party, a dominant model in the Middle East. Most socialist, nationalist, and communist parties were replicas of the Bolshevik Communist Party. This organization consisted of centralized political leadership, ideologically committed members grouped in small cells and functioning in clandestine operational networks in order to avert police crackdowns. Such organizational concepts influenced the formation of the Daʿwa party and other Islamic organizations which operated under authoritarian Middle Eastern political systems. Sadr and his colleagues, who founded the Daʿwa Party, were acquainted with the operation and structure of the Baʿth, Communist and the HT parties in Iraq. Their political organization predictably evolved into a small, cell-structured party of devotees who work towards a defined political plan aimed at seizing political power.

The first task for the Daʿwa was to recruit its membership from the masses, and indoctrinate them in small cells for long periods to ensure loyalty, cohesiveness and total devotion to the goals of the party. Sadr's job was to outline the basic principles and mission of the party, its political doctrine and programme of action. He was credited with choosing the name of the party, al-Daʿwa al-Islamiyya, and helping to recruit jurists and activists from the *hawza* of Najaf and Karbala. He used his credentials within the religious establishment to gain approval for the formation and operation of the Daʿwa Islamic party in an environment that has long been politically submissive.

Sadr argued that the type of people to be recruited to the Daʿwa should be 'committed Muslim personalities' who possess the necessary abilities and energies to achieve its goal. According to his thinking, the process of struggle entails hardship and suffering, both of which require deep commitment to the party's goals and sincere devotion to God. Without a reserve army of such individuals, the struggle for the cause of God will eventually fail, whether because of government oppression or the apathy of party members. In Sadr's vision, committed Muslims in the party must work towards the achievement of a socio-historical goal: such an endeavour would distinguish them from ordinary Muslims. While the latter might have deep beliefs and an understanding of religion, and might coordinate their behaviour according to the laws of Islam, they live on the edge of history and have no social role to play: they are, therefore, insignificant as factors in the historical progress of humanity. It is the political goal that gives a meaning to life, 'for the value of man's life is equal to the ideas which he believes in and contends to achieve'.[2]

Therefore, *al-Insan al-Hadif* (man-of-purpose, i.e., party member) would strive to create that environment most suitable for his creed.[3] Simultaneously, the Islamic movement should work to increase the number of committed Muslims among its ranks, and discover those among them who are 'objective,' i.e with leadership qualities, because these are the individuals upon whom 'the umma . . . depends to achieve its expectations . . . '[4]

Political Means

To make Islam the doctrinal basis of society that dictates the rules of behaviour for both the ruler and the ruled, planned political action is required to synchronize the efforts of the 'objective' committed Muslims under a specific political program. Although the random activities of dedicated Muslims are sincere, they will not produce tangible results in the political life of the Muslim society, as they lack coherence and rationality.[5] The need for coherence stems from the task that Sadr has assumed: to radically reshape society and polity on the basis of Islam rather than introduce reforms. In this connection, he called his political plan a 'revolutionary movement'. This differs from any 'reform movement' which aims to achieve a reform of the system, while disregarding other fundamental aspects.[6] The goals of the revolutionary movement, however, are to change the very pillars of the social system, because these conflict with the basic fundamentals of its beliefs, and to restructure human life and the social order accordingly.[7] The existing secular and authoritarian political regimes in the Middle East, Sadr argues, do not permit peaceful change or political dialogue with the Islamic movement. These regimes have inherited from western colonial and superpowers the tendency to eradicate religious sentiment among Muslims. As a result of this, the Muslim umma lost its inherent political and social structures; its religious values and Islamic principles were also supplanted by western value systems. Hence, the umma forsook its religious message and surrendered to the colonizing masters not only politically, but ideologically as well.[8] Sadr exuberantly exclaims:

> The problem – O Brothers . . . is not a matter of the young being corrupted by schools, and not of a group that needs sermons and guidance, and not of an environment that needs to be cleaned and purified from immorality and

rottenness; but an umma that must be emancipated according to the principles of Islam so as to be fortunate in this world and the hereafter.[9]

The solution for this 'predicament', therefore, would not come from efforts aimed at partial reform of the social order, but from comprehensive change in the whole structure. Restructuring the social system according to Islam can only be realized through the systematic Islamic action organized into a unified purpose.[10] The best possible way to achieve this is to create a political organization, a modern, disciplined party. To Sadr, this form is more progressive than other types of movements. In his view, '[Historical] experience of various international movements ascertains that organization is a successful means in changing the society in the direction either of righteousness or of wickedness'.[11] He adds,

> Of course there are differences between Islamic party activities and that of other parties of different ideology, and these differences stem from the fact that activists in an Islamic party strive for the message of God, . . . obey the laws of God, . . . and take their rewards from God, not from people.[12]

The concept of modern party politics created some problems relevant to obedience: God or leaders in the party. The hierarchy in the Islamic party, Sadr states, is not based on the position or status within the party structure, but rather according to closeness to God. This implies that members obey God's laws only and not the laws of those in the upper echelon of the party. However, such a spiritual hierarchy will cause chaos and disorganization, where a political party is institutionalized on the basis of members disciplined to comply with the commands of the leadership. To overcome this problem, Sadr explains that party directives should either be in agreement with God's law, or have a religious connotation that makes it obligatory for Muslims to follow and obey its dictates. This may be achieved either: (i) through a religious oath that the member voluntarily takes to follow the guidance of the party in its efforts to serve the interests of Islam; or (ii) through recognizing the necessity of achieving Islamic goals by the combined efforts of Muslims;[13] or (iii) through a decree by a Muslim jurist (*faqih*) requiring obedience to the orders of the party.[14]

According to Sadr, the organization of an Islamic political party is consistent with the teaching of Islam, and the obedience of party commands can have religious connotations. Furthermore, Islamic *Shari'a*, Sadr holds, . . . does not specify the means to be followed by the Muslims in endeavour for [social] change, therefore, it is religiously permissible for us to adopt any suitable way to spread the teachings of Islam and its commands, and to change the society as long as the way will not entail a violation which is religiously forbidden.[15]

Since a political party is an effective means by which to achieve the goal of Islam, and does not cause Muslim members to violate any religious laws, it can be utilized for Islamic purposes. Not every western or non-Islamic means should be rejected.[16] If party organization is the common means of political activities in the west, it does not mean that it should not be utilized as a political tool by Muslims. In fact, such a type of political organization is not alien to Islamic heritage. According to Sadr, if the Prophet had lived in our age, he would have, as a result of his wisdom, used the suitable modern means of propagation and communication. The truth is that his means of propagation was not far different from the cellular organization.[17]

Sadr concludes that from a juristic point of view, the organization of an Islamic political party is a legitimate political activity and an indispensable task. It can mobilize committed Muslims, utilize their efforts, and organize their activities to accomplish the goal of establishing an Islamic political state. Simultaneously, Muslims who become members of the party must coordinate their activities with that of the party and should not deviate from its general line. In fact, a party member should always refer to the party for guidance to see if his political activities are in harmony with the general goal of the party 'so that all political brooks would flow into one stream'.[18]

Currently, members of the party must execute the edicts and fulfil the duties delegated to them by the party. Sadr concludes that the activities of the political party can only be endured and sustained by committed cadre who dedicate their whole lives towards the achievement of the common goal.[19]

Stages of the Political Process

Sadr identifies four stages that the Daw'a party should go through in its development to achieve the political goal of its mission: (i) party formation; (ii) political opposition; (iii) control of the state apparatus and the establishment of the Islamic political order; (iv) serving and protecting the interests of Islam and the umma.[20]

In the first stage the party wages a campaign for what Sadr calls 'ideological change' to spread 'radical thought among the general public of the umma, and to create and teach the revolutionary masses'.[21]

The 'ideological stage' is not only confined to recruitment; it also encompasses a social dimension and aims to influence individual behaviour and the collective mind of the umma, and strengthen its attachment to the teachings of Islam.[22] It is through their behaviour, deeds, and words that these 'intellectuals' (as Lenin liked to call them) would affect the general behaviour and thinking of the umma. Here Sadr tries to emulate Lenin's concept of the intelligentsia as the main force that actually carries and transfers consciousness for revolutionary change in society. Without such an ideological foundation, the Islamic party will stray from its divine principle. This concept focused the recruiting endeavours of the party on educated groups such as professionals and college and university students. Recently, Muhammad Husayn Fadhl Allah, the spiritual leader of the Shi'ites in Lebanon, stated that 'without the Iraqi Islamic movement we would not have had any Islamist-minded college graduate and post graduate'.[23]

Sadr thought the ideological stage of the party should continue indefinitely until certain changes in the political environment favoured direct political action. He saw the potential for change within the international political environment which could have a significant impact on the domestic behaviour of the regime. Increasing world pressure on the regime for its human rights abuses, for example, might relax some of the suppressive measures, which in turn could help opposition to be more vocal. On this subject he said:

> When we live in a democratic country which respects its people and their opinion, the authority would neither be unaccountable and illegitimate, nor confront them with massacre and deportation. In this case, one can assume that any party can begin its activities underground to establish itself and then launch its political opposition in its attempt to mobilize the umma along its own line and drive it to adopt its political positions. But the condition in [a place like] Iraq is far away from such a reality. When the oppressive authority feels the existence of any organized Islamic party functioning according to such [planned] stages, it starts killing, deporting, imprisoning, torturing and suppressing the activists in the country before they fully achieve the goal of making the umma sympathize with it [Islamic party] . . . Unless there was a change in the world arena that can overrun [domestic regime] stability, it was not possible for the [Islamic] party to move from its initial stage to the next.[24]

There are no detailed characterizations of the other political stages envisaged by Sadr, at least in his published works, except for some comments about the structure of the Islamic state, which were published only after the success of the Islamic revolution in Iran.[25] In this commentary, Sadr outlines the role of the *marja'* and the umma in the structure of the state, in what can be considered as his views on the envisaged third and, partially, fourth stages of struggle. Suffice it to say that Sadr places great emphasis on the role of the *marja'* in leading both the political struggle and the Islamic political state. The *marja'* would assume the role of pedagogue left by the occultation of the *ma'sum* leader, i.e., Imam

Mahdi (the twelfth Imam) while the party would assume the role of the umma in Sadr's political programme.

Marja'ism

The role of *marja'* in Sadr's theory stems from his view that man would always have a constant need for some sort of divine intervention to protect him from corruption and guide him towards salvation. Without such intervention, man's potential for progress and emancipation will be hindered.[26] Accordingly, God established the role of *shahid* (witness) – the one who would take the responsibility of conveying divine guidance to mankind. Prophets were first commissioned to this function. Since the role of *shahid* is of vital importance to the communal role of vicar, while prophethood is limited to transmission of the divine message to mankind, men other than the prophets are appointed by Providence to continue the guidance of man in order to safeguard him against corruption.

> Surely we sent down the Torah, wherein is guidance and light; thereby the Prophets who had surrendered themselves gave judgment for those of Jewry, as did the master and the rabbis, following such portion of God's Book as they were given to keep and were witness to. (5:44)

According to Sadr, the Qur'an designated the Imams, and then the scholars of religious laws (*faqih* or what the Shi'ites refer to as *marja'*), to succeed the prophets in the role of shahid. Since the Imams and religious jurists understand divine laws and revelations, they will take the responsibility of safeguarding the message of God, convey it to mankind, and take on the active role of guiding man in his historical mission.[27]

The shahid [witness], from an ideological perspective, is the authority on [matters relevant to] creed and legislation who oversees social life and its congruence, ideologically, with the divine message. He is also responsible for getting [human] life back on its right course in case of any deviation that might occur during the application [of the message].[28]

The only difference between the three types of *shahid* is that the prophet and imams are divinely chosen; hence they are infallible leaders, while the *marja'* [*faqih*] is considered the most suitable candidate for the leadership due to his religious training and knowledge. According to Sadr, 'The *marja'*, through his personal dedication and long period of diligent training, understands Islam from its original sources, while his deep piety disciplines him to control himself, thus his conduct ensures his deep Islamic consciousness and safeguards him from sinful environment'.[29]

The *marja'* thus becomes the successor of the prophets and Imams for the Islamic umma in respect of his being a source of guidance and centre of leadership. The man who possesses the ordained qualifications (knowledge of divine laws, *'ilm*; and self-control of conducts justice, *'adala)* shall take the responsibility of *shahid*. However, the *marja'iyya* is not assigned to any particular person as is the role of prophets or Imams. Hence, the role of the *shahid* becomes more important than the individual who assumes the role himself. In other words, Sadr wants to define the duties of the office and then search for the most qualified office holder. So not every jurist is qualified to hold the role of *shahid*. The post of *marja'iyya* can only be assumed by a qualified jurist able to fit the role of the *shahid*.

Sadr's thesis on *al-marja'iyya al-mawdhu'iyya* (objective authority) is a political plan to reconstruct the leadership of the Islamic community that would replace, in the long run, the *marja'iyya al-thatiyya* (individual authority). In order to achieve the change, Sadr outlined five duties for the *marja'iyya*:

1. The dissemination of the teachings of Islam as broadly as possible among the Muslims.
2. Founding a wide-spread ideological movement from the umma, which embraces Islamic teaching and uses efficient means to consolidate its goal.
3. Meeting the needs of Islamic education, by commissioning sufficient Islamic studies in various economic and social fields, and expanding the scope of Islamic fiqh (jurisprudence) to provide Islamic legislation and direction for all aspects of life.
4. Taking the responsibility of guardianship of the Islamic movement; supervising its activities; and supporting every such proper move and rectifying what is improper.
5. Ensuring that the *'ulama* at the summit of authority of the umma work to safeguard its interests and are involved in the affairs of the people.[30]

Sadr realized that the current process of *marja'iyya* is centred on the *marja'* himself. Each and every *marja'* establishes his own authority and starts his activities from scratch with no reference to the preceding accomplishment of other marja's and no follow up with its accomplishment or evaluation of its failures. Each *marja'iyya* is linked to the *marja'* himself, and begins when he establishes his credentials within the *hawza*, and concludes with his death. Another chronic ailment of long-established traditional *marja'iyya* is the random selection of the individual who ascends to the rank of *marja'iyya*. There are no defined qualifications for the position, save those of religious knowledge and conduct. Although these qualifications might be considered as a basic requirement for eligible candidacy for the role of shahid, for Sadr they are not sufficient to carry out the responsibility of guiding and leading the umma in its historical mission. Such a socio-political task needs additional skills that go beyond mere religious knowledge and righteous behaviour. It requires an understanding of the social, political and economic conditions, developed insight and a will to guide people, in order to safeguard their religious duties and interests. For these reasons, Sadr contemplates a revolutionary process in the way the *marja'iyya* should administer its business.

To bring about these changes, Sadr proposes two types of structure for the *marja'iyya*: the executive office, which acts as the central administration; and the 'representatives', which act as the consultative body.

Central administration consists of six departments that carry out the planning and executive activities of the *marja'iyya*, and in which the *marja'iyya* is managed by qualified professionals. The tasks of each office are differentiated in order to better manage things and achieve goals.[31] The *marja'iyya* may further develop these offices as tasks and responsibilities expand, to include the whole spectrum of the umma affairs. These departments will 'replace the private court [of the *marja'*] which is made up of individuals arbitrarily grouped to fulfil some immediate needs although they exhibit superficial qualifications to achieve no defined or clear objectives'.[32] Sadr, therefore, specifies some of the tasks of the above proposed departments.

1. A committee to administer educational affairs, which regulates curricula, assigns the texts; gradually develops the education process of *hawza* to the level that allows it to participate in achieving the goals of the objective *marja'iyya*;
2. A research committee to found research centres to conduct studies and follow up its advancement; manage the affairs of the *hawza*; and follow up the intellectual discourse worldwide and produce publications;
3. A committee responsible for the affairs of *'ulama* to keep records of their names, places, and congregation; follow up their activities, behaviour and relationships; meet their needs and fill up their vacancies;
4. A foreign relations committee responsible for opening new links in areas where *marja'iyya* has no contacts, surveying the areas and the possibilities of making relationships, sending envoys, and utilizing religious and ritual ceremonies such as the event of pilgrimage to Mecca;
5. A committee to sponsor the Islamic movement and its activities worldwide, evaluate [of their activities], give guidance and support when needed;
6. A financial committee to keep records of capital and sources; appoint financial representatives; search for investing the regular resources of bayt al-mal (central treasury); and pay for the necessary expenses of *marja'iyya*.[33]

Sadr also wanted to create a hierarchical structure at the helm of which the *marja'* represents an institution. The *marja'* has been traditionally represented by *'ulama* in various parts of the world who serve the religious needs of Muslims and act as liaison officers for the *marja'*, who transmit his *fatwas* or collect religious taxes, donations and charities. However, such a relationship between the *marja'* and his parochial representatives has been 'in most cases, fictitious and formal relationship which does not have any chain of command or central order'.[34]

A more centralized structure becomes necessary in situations when the *marja'* ought to assume the leadership role of the people, and guide them toward their freedom and spiritual salvation. Sadr's political plan aims at making the local representatives more active participants in the process of *marja'iyya* and accountable to it. He proposes a consultative council that drafts policies and gives advice on courses of action for *marja'*. In addition to the heads of the above six committees of the central administration, the council will include representatives and high-ranking *'ulama*. The whole religious establishment becomes a full participant in the decision making process of the *marja'*, an arrangement which eventually would ensure commitment and participation. Such advisory and decision-making mechanisms will protect the *marja'iyya* from adopting naive policies that are driven by personal whim.[35] However, old traditional practices have some positive aspects, such as 'swift course of action, and high levels of secrecy that limit infiltration of unwanted individuals yet the proposed institutionalized structure will have much greater results and positive outcome'.[36]

The formation of the central administration and 'council of *marja'iyya*' will ensure continuity of *marja'iyya* beyond the life span of any individual jurist. The structural organization will provide expertise and long-term planning for achieving the defined goals. The succeeding *marja'* would not have to start from square one, but rather will depend on an institution to carry on the tasks of his predecessor. Moreover, the institution of *marja'iyya* will serve as a ground for selecting and training the future *marja'*.[37]

The Role of People

Although Sadr advocates the concept of *wilayat al-faqih*, by placing the grand jurist at the helm of the Islamic state, he also leaves a wide area of political power at the disposal of the people. He is foremost among contemporary radical Islamic jurists in his vision of the people playing an active role in politics, as opposed to purely revolting against unjust tyrants and supporting the Islamic states. Sadr based his views on the following verses from the Qur'an:

And the believers, the men and the women, are friends one of the other; enjoining good, and forbidding evil.[38]

Those who hearken to their Lord, and establish regular prayer, *who [conduct] their affairs by mutual consultation* (42:38).[39]

Sadr argues that Islam demands that we follow the opinions of the majority in matters where the *Shari'a* has not specified any rule. Thus, the door has been left open for people to conduct their affairs in a more meaningful and prudent way and follow the will of the majority. Politically speaking, in Sadr's Islamic political system the people should be put in charge of the executive and the legislative authority of the state. It is left to them to decide on any policy, and to take any course of action that does not violate the basic teachings of Islam. The marja's role, however, is to oversee the religious correctness of the people, acting as their spiritual and religious guide, advising them and showing them the right path to follow in order to avoid deviation. Needless to say, Sadr's argument seems to be based on linking the idea of *shura* (consultation among the believers) to his thesis about the role of vicar of God. Since man (as species) has rights and responsibilities that can be translated in political terms, the whole umma possesses these rights and responsibilities in the Islamic political system, although Sadr does not provide any logical basis from which to derive such a conclusion. The political process of his envisioned Islamic system is democratic, as policies are grounded in majority rule. However, if every man is considered a vicar of God, the majority rule principle implies that some vicars of God lose their rights and are forced to uphold the will of the majority. What theoretical or jurisprudential basis is there that justifies the tyranny of the majority? What religious claim does the majority have to impose its will on others who have similar rights to participate in the making of policies in the Islamic state? These questions are left unanswered by Sadr. Hence, the Islamic state that Sadr conceptualized would not, of course, be the ideal state, since the ideal state is led only by the *ma'sum*, the infallible Imam. The conceptualized polity is the best possible option during the absence of the *ma'sum*, where the *marja'* shares political power with the people. The *marja'* assumes the religious and guiding functions of the states, where he sanctions actions and legitimizes power; while the people would assume the executive and legislative powers of the state.[40]

Sadr argues that the supremacy of the *marja'* is not in any way to be considered a dictatorial rule but rather a leadership constrained by Islamic laws and the institutional process. In making decisions, however, the *marja'* should always refer to the 'council of *marja'iyya*' that consists of one hundred intellectual and religious scholars, as well as at least ten *mujtahids* of his peers.[41] It is through this council that the *marja'* should derive his policies and issue his religious decrees.

On the other hand, since man is the vicar of God, he must be responsible for conducting his social affairs in accordance with God's will. The umma should have the right to bear the divine trust and be eligible to form the executive and legislative branches of the government. Every member of the umma has an equal opportunity under the law to realize the potential of the vicarage role, i.e., to express his views and thoughts, carry out his political activities through any means, and conduct his religious or sectarian rites.[42] The umma, according to Sadr, should:

1. elect the head of the executive branch who has the right to select his cabinet;
2. vote, in general suffrage, to elect members of the legislative council who have the power to: (i) approve of the cabinet; (ii) choose between the different alternative policies that are not contradictory to Islam; (iii) make new legislation in areas where no definite regulations are defined by Islam; (iv) overrule the executive branch's implementation of law.[43]

Thus, in Sadr's Islamic state, management and administration are shaped and run by the people. The *marja'*, theoretically speaking, is limited to the role of the *shahid*, i.e., watching over the implementation of Islam by the umma and safeguarding religion from the corruption of its enemies.[44] The umma, by conducting its political activities, would be aware of its mission as vicar of God on earth, and take full responsibility for its behaviour. That is 'because even the umma is not the source of authority, but rather it is responsible before God, the most Exulted and High, to uphold the trust and carry on its duties'.[45]

The creation of an Islamic state is one of the means whereby man's role as vicar of God is realized.

Conclusion

Sadr was a forerunner in advocating an active role for the people in the political sphere both before and after the establishment of an Islamic state. In his political programme outlining the struggle for an Islamic political system, jurists co-operate with intellectuals in guiding and leading the Islamic movement; when they have achieved their goal of establishing an Islamic state, the grand jurist shares power with the people.

Sadr advocated the organization of an ideological political party to mobilize the masses in their struggle. He also participated in the formation of the Da'wa Party in Iraq, and later became the head jurist and sole ideologue of that organization, setting its political agenda, and supervising its activities. With the success of the Islamic revolution in Iran, he drafted six treatises that outlined his vision of the structure of the Islamic states. He visualized his proposed political system as a modified parliamentary democratic state, in which the people elect their representatives to the legislative branch that would form the government. The leading *marja'* will be the head of the state, sanctioning laws for their religious coherency, overseeing the government agenda and guiding the people towards their salvation.

Notes

1. See my 'The Role of Muhammad Baqir al-Sadr in Shi'i Political Activism in Iraq from 1958–1980', *International Journal of Islamic Studies*, Spring 1994.
2. Sadr, *Min Fikr al-Da'wah,* (n. p., n. d.): 21.
3. Ibid.: 24.
4. Ibid.
5. Ibid.: 26.
6. Ibid.: 35.
7. Ibid.
8. Ibid.: 36–7.
9. Ibid.: 37.
10. Ibid.: 26.
11. Ibid.: 10.
12. Ibid.: 10.
13. Ibid.: 11.
14. Ibid.: 10–11.
15. Ibid.: 9.
16. Sadr, *Risalatuna*, Beirut, 1981: 52–3.
17. Sadr, *Min Fikr al-Da'wa*: 10.
18. Ibid.: 27.
19. Ibid.: 26.
20. Ha'iri, Kazim, *Mabahith al-usul*, Qum, 1407 H, vol. 1.: 90.
21. Sadr, *Min Fikr al-Da'wa*: 31.
22. Ibid.: 31.
23. Muhammad Husayn Fadhl Allah, *al-Bayanat*, Beirut, December, 1979.
24. Ha'iri, *Mabahith*, op. cit.: 91.
25. Six political treatises compiled (by the Islamic government in Iran) in one publication under the title, *al-Islam Yaqud al-Hayat* (Islam Leads Life), Qum, Khayyam Press, 1979. The six treatises are: *1–Lamhah Fiqhiyya 'an Dustur al-Jumhuriyya al-Islamiyyah; 2–Sura 'an Iqtisad al-Mujtama' al-Islami; 3–Khutut Tafsiliyya 'an Iqtisad*

al-Mujtama' al-Islami; 4–Khilafat al-Insan wa shahadat al-anbiya'; 5–Manabi' al-Qudra fi al-Dawla al-Islamiyya; 6–al-Usus al-'amma li al-bank fi al-mujtama' al-islami.

26. Sadr, *Khilafat al-Insan*: 143.
27. Ibid.: 144–5.
28. Ibid.: 145.
29. Ibid.
30. Sadr, *al-Marja'iyya al-Saliha*, in Ha'iri, *Mabahith*: 92–3.
31. Ibid.: 94.
32. Ibid.: 94.
33. Ibid.: 94–5.
34. Ibid.: 96.
35. Ibid.: 96.
36. Ibid.: 96.
37. Ibid.: 97.
38. The Qur'an, vol. 1: 215.
39. The Holy Qur'an, translation and commentary by A. Yousif 'Ali, London, The Islamic Foundation, 1975: 1316–1317.
40. Sadr, *Lamha Fiqhiyya 'an Dustur al-Jumhuriyya al-Islamiyyah*: 12.
41. Ibid.: 13.
42. Ibid.: 16.
43. Ibid.: 11–12.
44. Sadr, *Khilafat al-Insan*: 170–1.
45. Sadr, *Lamha*: 11.

CHAPTER SIXTEEN

The School of Najaf

Jawdat al-Qazwini

With the arrival of the British armies in Iraq after the outbreak of the First World War, the religious institution in Najaf had to face a new challenge. Despite the earlier fanatically anti-Shi'i character of Ottoman rule, the British occupation of Basra on 22 November 1914 prompted the Arab Shi'i leaders to tone down their grievances against the Ottomans and issue *fatwas* supporting the Turks.

The Ottomans had adopted an oppressive policy against the Shi'is during the previous two centuries of their rule, as many incidents clearly demonstrated. Among these were the invasion of the holy city of Karbala by Najib Pasha in 1258/1842, and the invasion of the holy city of Najaf by Salim Pasha in 1268/1852.[1]

Prior to British intervention in 1914, relations between Ottomans and Shi'is may justly be described as bad. However, the Ottomans understood the danger presented by the occupation of Basra by British troops, and they therefore attempted to curry favour with the Shi'i *fuqaha'* in order to mobilize the Iraqi tribes. The Ottoman government sent envoys to the *mujtahids*, emphasizing the necessity of defending Muslim land against non-Muslims. A rapprochement took place between the two sides, and some *mujtahids* even devoted themselves to bringing together the tribes and creating paramilitary troops.[2]

The mobilization extended to all the Shi'i regions, including the middle Euphrates and the cities of Baghdad and Kazimiyya. Some of the *fatwas* focused at one time on fighting the British, and at others on defending Muslim land.[3] Some leading *fuqaha'*, among whom were Muhammad Sa'id al-Habubi (1266–1333/1850–1915) and Mahdi al-Haydari (d. 1336/1917), actually led the Iraqi tribes on the Ottoman side in armed confrontations with the British.

Nevertheless, the Shi'i tribes were against any support of the Ottomans because of the oppression their community had endured and the high taxes which
had been imposed on them by the Turks. But *'ulama* exerted strong efforts to
persuade the Shi'i leaders to support the Ottomans, who they believed would
emerge victorious after the war. This thinking lay behind the comment of one of
the Arab tribal leaders to the Turkish commander that the Ottomans had betrayed Islam 'because you had been treating the Arabs oppressively and we have
supported you because of our *'ulamas' fatwas'*.[4]

Relations between the Ottomans and the Shi'is reverted to their original
hostility soon after the Turkish defeat at Shu'ayba in 12–15 April 1915. The tribes
withdrew their support for the Turkish armies and set about asking for independence in an attempt to get rid of both the Ottoman and the British occupations.[5]

The Turkish government replied by launching repressive campaigns against
several Shi'i cities, where official centres had been attacked by the inhabitants.
In this way, the rift between both sides became wider than before, thus putting
an end to the first stage of *jihad*, which was characterized by close collaboration.

In April 1915 the Ottomans sent troops to regain control of the city of Najaf,
but the inhabitants resisted the forces and after a three-day fight, the Turks surrendered. As a result, the Najafis decided to take over the entire administration of
the city and dismissed the Turkish officials. The leading figures in the city administered its affairs until the revolution of Najaf (*thawrat al-Najaf*), brought
about by purely internal pressures in Najaf in March 1336/1918.[6]

Similarly, the inhabitants of Karbala rose up against the Ottomans in June
1915, dismissing the Turkish officials and administering the affairs of the city
themselves.

In November 1916 the inhabitants of Hilla revolted against the Ottomans,
who sent between 4,000 and 6,000 troops to occupy the city under the leadership of 'Akif Beg. When the troops arrived near Hilla, the inhabitants forbade
them to enter. The Ottomans claimed that they wanted to cross the city to get to
Nasiriyya. They requested a meeting with the prominent people of the community to negotiate with them for permission. When the leaders of the city, such as
Muhammad 'Ali al-Qazwini (d. 1356/1937) and others, met them, the Ottomans
detained them and declared to the inhabitants of the city that if their crossing
through the city to al-Nasiriyya was opposed, they would kill their hostages. The
inhabitants believed them and thought that the Ottomans would abide by their
promise and cross the city peacefully. The town was then occupied and much
damage was done. A number of leading citizens were hanged and their women
carried off.[7]

This event led to a big outcry within the Shi'i community. Al-Sayyid Hadi al-

Qazwini (d. 1347/1928) had already mobilised the Shi'i tribes and moved towards the city to fight the Ottomans.[8] He did not manage to catch up with them, however, because they had already left.

The British jeopardised their international reputation when they lost the battle in Kut against the Ottomans (from December 1915 to the end of April 1916). They decided to mass their troops to achieve victory in order to retain their well-known international standing which had suffered through their defeat. Under the leadership of Lieutenant-General F. S. Maude, British troops managed to invade Baghdad on 11 March 1917 after besieging it, and effected the eventual withdrawal of Turkish troops from the city, thus putting an end to Ottoman rule in Iraq.[9]

After the British had completed their invasion of Iraq, they resolved to pursue a course of friendly co-operation towards the Shi'is, because of the oppression which had been suffered under the Ottomans. So in 1917, after entering Baghdad, Sir Percy Cox held a meeting with the *mujtahid* Shaykh Muhammad Taqi al-Shirazi, in Kazimiyya, and suggested to him that he should take over the administration of the country's religious affairs. He told al-Shirazi that the British had not come to Iraq as conquerors, but as liberators. Cox decided on this approach despite the fact that the Shi'is had resisted the British invasion. Mirza Muhammad Hadi al-Khurasani (d. 1366/1947), one of Shirazi's disciples and later one of the prominent *mujtahids*, attended that meeting, later noting that Sunni *'ulama* began attending Shi'i ceremonies and festivals in an attempt to show their allegiance to the Shi'i *'ulama*. The same Sunni *'ulama* had long been accustomed to defaming the Shi'i *'ulama* and saying anything that might injure their reputations.[10] A movement preaching for the return of Turkish rule appeared, trying to use Sunni *'ulama* for this purpose. For this reason, Ibrahim al-Rawi (d. 1365/1946), one of the Sunni *'ulama*, wrote a book entitled *Da'i al-rashad ila sabil al-ittihad* (The summons of divine guidance to the path of unity). In its introduction, he claimed that the reason behind writing the book was the setback the Islamic state had suffered after the collapse of the Ottoman Caliphate.[11]

General Maude died on 18 November 1917. Four months after his death serious disturbances took place in Najaf. These were initiated by the oligarchs of the town who wanted to take over the administration of its affairs. They had sensed, after the arrival of Captain W. M. Marshall, that the British were further entrenching their power in the city by infiltrating society disguised as *Shabana* (local police); they attacked 'Atiyya's Khan and killed Captain Marshall. The British, on the orders of General Sanders, acted swiftly and blockaded the city with a brigade led by Sanders himself. The following conditions were proclaimed:

1. The unconditional surrender of certain individuals known to be the ring-leaders and believed to be among the attacking party
2. A fine of 1,000 rifles
3. A fine of 50,000 Rupees
4. Deportation of 100 people to India as prisoners of war
5. Pending fulfilment of the above conditions the town is to be blockaded and the food and water supply cut off.[12]

The blockade was lifted on 4th May, after the surrender of the prominent named persons. On 25 May 1918 the eleven men who were behind the attack were hanged in public.[13]

The siege of the holy city of Najaf and the mistreatment of its inhabitants led to a worsening in the relationship between the Najafis and the British. Al-Nafisi has attributed the failure of the British administration to avoid the siege of the city and the ensuing bloodshed to the lack of suitable advisers, who could have counselled the occupying forces as to the reality of the situation confronting them. The British had relied on information from local traders whose interests in the affair were purely personal.[14]

Complex as the events may have been, the Shi'i institution maintained its independence as closely as possible, and constantly resisted any occupation by foreign troops. This negative response reached its peak with the revolution of Najaf in 1918 and the great revolution of 1920.

After moving to Karbala on February 23 1918, Shaykh Muhammad Taqi al-Shirazi became a distinguished leader who engaged in political activities and played a great role in the initial stages of the revolution of 1920, of which he later assumed the leadership. He died on 17 August 1920 before the war had ended. Shaykh Fath Allah al-Isfahani, known as 'Shaykh al-Shari'a', assumed the leadership but died soon after on 18 December. There were three prominent Mujtahids who were candidates to succeed Shaykh al-Shari'a; two of them living in Najaf, Abu al-Hasan al-Isfahani (1277–1365/1860–1946) and Husayn al-Na'ini (d. 1355/1936), and the third, Mahdi al-Khalisi (1276–1343/1859–1924–5), in the region of Kazimiyya.[15]

The main reasons for the spread of resistance are related to the British failure to keep the promises they undertook when they occupied Baghdad (1917) claiming to be liberators, not conquerors; in addition, the repressive policies pursued by some of the British governors subdued the residents.[16] Regarding the resentment Iraqis bore against the British, some historians argue that most of the people welcomed the occupation at first, having suffered at the hands of the Turks during the First World War. Two or three years later, they turned to opposition for several reasons:

1. The Ottoman rule in Iraq was not very well organised, and when the British conquered Iraq, they introduced an administration which was unfamiliar to the Iraqi people and transformed the evolution of Iraqi society by placing too much reliance on unrepresentative social classes which were unacceptable to the majority of people.

2. Inflation, which resulted in overspending by the British on many new projects, caused the creation of a self-interested class whose monopolising methods disregarded the interests of the Iraqi people. The situation worsened and Iraq was almost struck by a famine.

3. Some of the political chiefs and their British collaborators, in charge of remote regions, were not fully aware of the tribal nature of Iraqi society.[17]

After the failure of the revolution of 1920, the British government undertook to set up an authority in Iraq which would be closely identified with it, and obtained international legitimacy in the shape of a mandate conferred by the League of the Nations.[18] This stipulated that people under mandate could not secede to self government without the help of advanced states.

Among the after-effects of Great Britain's designation as a mandatory power, were the accession of Faisal b. al-Husayn (1341–1352/1921–1933) to the throne of Iraq, the settlement of the Anglo-Iraqi treaty by the Provisional Government, and the confirmation of the Mandate according to the decisions of the conference held at San Remo by the Allies on 25 April 1920.[19] Imposition of the terms of the treaty resulted in violent reactions among the *'ulama*; Mahdi al-Khalisi stood against it and issued a *fatwa* prohibiting any collaboration with the official institutions. Abu al-Hasan al-Isfahani, al-Na'ini and al-Khalisi declared the proposed elections unacceptable.[20]

At the same time, the religious institution and the state indulged in propaganda warfare which ended with the deportation to Iran of the religious maraji', Abu al-Hasan al-Isfahani, Husayn al-Na'ini, and Muhammad Jawad al-Jawahiri. They were obliged to refrain from meddling in internal Iraqi affairs. However, this step appeared to have threatened British interests in Iran and the British decided to cancel the deportations, arranging the return of the exiles to Iraq. The *mujtahids* came back in April 1924, after they had agreed to keep out of politics, and fulfil a purely cultural role as part of their religious duties. For the next 25 years, no events of importance were to be recorded. Under the leadership of Muhsin al-Hakim (1306–1390/1889–1970), the religious institution was given a new political start, with the Islamic parties ultimately developing in Iraq in the 1950s.

The Emergence of the Islamic Parties

After the drastic political changes which took place in Iraq at the end of the First World War, the religious institution remained under the control of distinguished *mujtahids*. Some, such as al-Na'ini, played an outstanding role in the dispute between *mashruta* (constitutional) and *mustabidda* (monarchical) trends over opposition to the British occupation; others disassociated themselves from political activity, taking no definite stance towards the events. Dhiya' al-Din al-'Iraqi (d. 1361/1942), for example, abandoned religious leadership and distanced himself from public affairs, devoting his time to religious studies.[21]

After Abu al-Hasan al-Isfahani's death in 1365/1946, two *fuqaha'* appeared as religious leaders: Muhsin al-Hakim in Najaf and Husayn Brujerdi (1292–1380/ 1875–1961) in Iran. This was the period when several parties of various political persuasions, such as the Iraqi Communist Party and the nationalist parties, dominated the Iraqi scene.

In the early 1950s, the first two Islamic parties came into being: Harakat al-Shabab al-Muslim (Muslim Youth Movement) (1953) and Munazamat al-Muslimin al-'Aqa'idiyyin (Doctrinal Muslims Organization) (1954), led by 'Izz al-Din al-Jaza'iri, son of Shaykh Muhammad Jawad al-Jaza'iri. They attempted to unite the Najaf youth in organized action geared towards the renewal of Islam. According to 'Izz al-Din, whom we met in the summer of 1988 in Beirut, the lethargy of the religious institution and its passiveness vis-a-vis the evolution of events and society, incited him to search for a new, clearly defined basis for the efforts of the new generation.

Al-Jaza'iri's positions towards the spiritual leaders – and vice versa – led both parties to act independently of each other: they therefore failed to achieve the rejuvenation that might have been expected, especially with the appearance of a new Islamic party, Hizb al-Da'wa al-Islamiyya (The Islamic Call Party).

Through this renewal, a great *mujtahid*, Murtadha Al Yasin (1311–1397/1893–1977), founded *Jama'at al-'ulama* in Najaf, soon after the revolution of 14 July 1958 led to the monarchy being replaced with a republican system of governance. The *Jama'a* dedicated itself to cultural work, organizing religious ceremonies and publishing the journal *al-Adhwa'* (from 1960).[22] Hizb al-Da'wa was officially founded in 1959[23] on the initiative of a group of fervent young Muslims who believed that there was a need for organised efforts which might be influential in educating people and enabling them to adhere to Islam. Among these were Hadi al-Subayti, Talib[24] al-Rifa'i and Mahdi al-Hakim (assassinated 1408/1988). Later, the party was directed by Muhammad Baqir al-Sadr, and came under his influence.

This new movement followed the *marja'iyya* of Imam Muhsin al-Hakim, which it considered, according to one of the founders[25] of the Iraqi Islamic movement, as the most appropriate: it was Arabic and seemed to have a clear conception of the current political struggle and the intellectual invasion by western ideologies that Islamic thought was undergoing, especially in Iraq.

The new formulation of Islamic political thought met a favourable echo within the religious circles, where Sadr's writings represented great progress in juristic political thought, after its restriction, since al-Na'ini's work, to the general forms of Islamic government.[26] Sadr's activity developed during this period, and he set down the regulations for Hizb al-Da'wa, which some students of his group joined due to his personal influence.[27]

Imam Muhsin al-Hakim did not oppose the movement,[28] possibly considering it as a necessary step in the prevailing circumstances. Yet he declined to assume any leading responsibility for himself or any of his relatives, on the basis that *marja'iyya* was not to be limited to party leadership. In his view, *marja'iyya* had to reach out and include all the reform movements, whether institutionalised or not.

The Islamic Movement which took shape in 1960 developed in two main directions:

1. It confronted political power through supervising the religious ceremonies and other occasions of worship, as well as choosing speakers to expound the political situation and the social demands of the *marja'iyya* .
2. It trained educated people to fulfil leading roles in order to act upon the Iraqi scene. This consisted of encouraging students to go to Najaf to study religion; creating Islamic courses which would provide the students with modern education, so that most of the graduates would become *wukala* (representatives) for the *marja'iyya* in most cities of Iraq; encouraging the intellectual movement by offering people educational facilities such as public libraries; establishing schools and universities, such as the Faculty of Fiqh in Najaf and the Faculty of Usul al-Din in Baghdad.[29]

The *marja'iyya* of al-Hakim and the Islamic movement went through three phases under the Republican Regime:

1. The rule of President 'Abd al-Karim Qassim (1958–1963) is characterized by increasing conflicts between the Nationalists and Communists. The Communists had emerged as a political force hostile to Qassim, whose rule was showing worrying weakness. At first, al-Hakim supported the government, but he quickly came to oppose it on various matters, especially after the growth of Communist activity. He then issued a *fatwa* describing Communism

as atheism, an opportunity which was seized upon by all the opponents of Qassim. After the July Revolution in 1958, the Communists played an outstanding role, showing an effective presence among the people: Qassim, whose power derived from a coup d'etat, was unable to limit their influence.[30] Qassim tried to avoid the inevitable clash with al-Hakim, who was pressed by numerous forces to bring down the government.[31] But the religious leader continued to oppose the government, tackling it on its legislation against the *Shari'a*, right up to the fall of Qassim on 8 February 1963.

2. The rule of 'Abd al-Salam and 'Abd al-Rahman 'Arif (1963–1968) is characterized by general cultural activity which the Islamic Movement took advantage of, extending their influence significantly among the educated classes, particularly under the weak rule of 'Abd al-Rahman 'Arif.

3. The period from the Ba'th Party's assumption of power (1968) to the death of al-Hakim (1970): during these years, the confrontation between the holders of political power and the religious institution became direct and violent. One of the priorities of the government was to stand against the religious current and to strike at the *marja'iyya*, which was represented by al-Hakim. Many supporters of the Islamic movement were put under arrest, together with important Shi'i personalities, some of whom were executed ('Abd al-Husayn Jita and 'Abd al-Hadi al-Bachchari).[32] The government also expelled non-Arab students from Najaf.

In 1969, al-Hakim decided to move to Baghdad to demonstrate to the government his disappointment with its vicious practices against the Iraqi people, and to give those in power an impression of his strong position among the people. His representatives, *wukala*, and the leading members of the Da'wa Party, mobilised a wide range of Iraqi people from many difference parts of the country to visit him in Kazimiyya and pay their respects, showing the authorities the broad popular support which the *marja'iyya* could rely on.

He made a list of demands to the government which included the following:

1. No detention or imprisonment of any citizen without proper legal proceedings.
2. The cessation of all activities aimed at those of Iranian origin, the majority of whom were religious students.
3. The release of all political prisoners.
4. The cessation of corporal punishment.

Noting that none of the government officials had come forward for negotiation, al-Hakim chose to hold a popular meeting which gathered all the *'ulama* and representatives from the Shi'i cities in a show of force.

The plan was abortive. The official media had meanwhile accused al-Hakim's son, Mahdi, of being a spy. The attack weakened the mobilization.[33] But it was not the end of the matter. Al-Hakim saw that action was necessary and that, all things considered, it was better for the *marja'iyya* to be seen to be 'in action' than 'silent and inactive'. This was the first political confrontation between the authorities and the religious institution, resulting in the latter being temporarily defeated.

The Political Programme of Imam al-Hakim

Muhsin al-Hakim decided to move on two fronts, political and military:

1. He tried to attract and make connections with a large group of Shi'i military leaders and politicians, in order to take the lead in any Islamic move. The military was led by a well-known Shi'i, Rashid al-Janabi, a brigadier commander respected by the southern Iraqi tribes. The politicians were headed by Shaykh Muhammad Ridha al-Shabibi (d. 1384/1964), a well-known Iraqi personality.
2. He thought of creating academic and educational institutions. He was supportive of the funding of the Kufa University project and backed the existing Fiqh Faculty in Najaf and the Usul al-Din Faculty in Baghdad both financially and morally.
3. He set up contacts with Muslim and Arab governments and personalities, including Shah Muhammad Reza of Iran, President Jamal 'Abd al-Nasser of Egypt, King Husayn of Jordan, Lebanese political leaders and King Faisal of Saudi Arabia. The Egyptian Azhar accepted the Shi'i doctrine as one further contribution to Islam, relieving the pressure on the Shi'is in Saudi Arabia, and urging the Shah to release the imprisoned *'ulama* and encourage the *hawza al-'ilmiyya*.[34]
4. He showed a serious interest in Arabic affairs and expressed his support in matters such as the situations in Palestine, Algeria and Morocco. He also backed Egypt during the 1956 Suez Canal crisis and held festivals in celebration of these issues.

The military leader, Rashid al-Janabi, was arrested as soon as the Ba'th Party came to power in 1968. He was executed in 1970 along with 45 other people.[35]

Al-Hakim's failure may be attributed to two reasons:

1. The leaders of the Islamic movements had conflicting opinions regarding

the conduct of political struggle, because there were many different trends operating. The first was represented by the Da'wa Party, whose leadership insisted on organised strategy and action. The second tendency, of which al-Hakim was the main supporter, had decreed that the religious institutions should not become involved in political activities. The third trend attempted a compromise between political struggle and education, as represented by Muhammad Baqir al-Sadr.

2. The religious leadership decided to take action alone, which resulted in the isolation of popular political parties from the struggle against the authorities.[36]

Al-Kho'i's Political Leadership

With al-Hakim's death (1390/1970), the candidacy for the office of the *marja'iyya* was disputed by two *fuqaha'*: Mahmud al-Shahrudi (d. 1396/1976) and Abu al-Qasim al-Kho'i (1413/1992). Al-Shahrudi's leadership did not exercise any important influence in the Arab area, unlike al-Kho'i's. The latter emerged among the other *fuqaha'* as the founder of a rational school that created several *mujtahids*, who developed his way of thinking in both fiqh and usul studies. Some of them, including Muhammad Baqir al-Sadr in Iraq, Muhammad Husayn Fadl Allah in Lebanon, and Muhammad Sarwar Wa'iz during the war in Afghanistan, also played outstanding political roles.[37]

Before his accession to the religious leadership, al-Kho'i had opposed the policy of the Shah, as is noted in some of his statements made in 1382/1962.[38] Al-Kho'i was considered the most prominent scholar of the *hawza*[39] and known as its head, then as Imam. In al-Kho'i's lifetime, intellectual investigations in fiqh and usul flourished as much under al-Muhaqqiq al-Hilli (seventh/eleventh century) and al-Ansari (late thirteenth/nineteenth century).

In his early years, al-Kho'i is known to have had reforming views regarding the religious institution, and he thought of raising its status by establishing teaching circles under his supervision. He moved to Karbala in the 1940s, but had to return to Najaf when his project did not meet enough encouragement.[40]

Since the early 1970s, al-Kho'i had been living through a critical period of Iraqi history, with the success of the Iranian Islamic revolution led by Ruhallah Khomeini (d. 1409/1989), and the huge political changes in Iraq. When the Iran-Iraq war broke out in 1980, the Iraqi government sought public support against Khomeini from the religious leadership represented by al-Kho'i. Al-Kho'i, however, did not encourage the Iraqi government to assume that he would have any involvement in this conflict, upholding non-political principles of the *hawza*.

This attitude can be compared to that of al-Qatifi, a *mujtahid* who caused a rift within the Shi'i religious circles by taking up a particular position against al-Karki in the tenth/sixteenth century during the Safavid period; to a lesser degree, a contrast can be seen between al-Kho'i's stance and that of al-Yazdi's towards al-Khurasani in the fourteenth/twentieth century during the constitutional dispute.

Kho'i's refusal to attack the Iranian government openly led to the execution of some of his disciples. However, he maintained his position, refusing to condemn the Iranian revolution and its leader, or even to pass any *fatwa* relating to the conflict. This rebuff may in itself perhaps be seen as indicative of a political position dictated by the circumstances.[41]

Meanwhile, some of the political powers in Iran were trying to restrict the religious leadership to Imam Khomeini, considering the position to be both a political and spiritual one, thus diminishing the importance of the other *marja'*. But this did not affect al-Kho'i's popularity in Iran; nor did it persuade him to have new thoughts on his support for the revolution. In the earliest days, he sent a congratulatory message to Khomeini on the occasion of the birth of the Islamic Republic. He also held ceremonies to commemorate the assassination of Murtadha Mutahhari in 1399/1979,[42] – not because he was a member of the council administering the revolution, but because he was a religious scholar.

Al-Sadr's Leadership

Muhammad Baqir Sadr (1353–1400/1935–1980) became a prominent scholar, though al-Kho'i remained the absolute *marja'* for the Shi'is. Sadr would have assumed the leadership of the Shi'i had he not been murdered in 1980. His purpose was to establish the guiding Shi'i leadership (*al-Marja'iyya al-Rashida*) which is competent to handle and deal with current Islamic affairs, and can rely on popular support.

Al-Sadr lived in a very remarkable era in the history of the *marja'iyya*, which began in the early 1950s and continued until his murder after the Iranian Revolution. His role and contributions may be seen as comprising three stages:

1. During the leadership of al-Hakim (1960–1970)
2. During the leadership of al-Kho'i
3. During his leadership in the struggle against the ruling Ba'th Party (1979–1980).

During al-Hakim's leadership, Sadr's activities were limited to participation in the constitution of the Da'wa Party, and writings to refute Communism and capitalism and to assert the validity of Islamic laws. His work mainly focused on philosophical and economic issues.

The Role of al-Sadr during the Leadership of al-Kho'i

After the death of al-Hakim, al-Kho'i did not adopt the same firm positions towards the ruling Ba'th party as his predecessor. He preferred to distance himself from any confrontation, possibly due to al-Hakim's failure, or because he feared that some of his non-Iraqi entourage might be expelled from the country if they became involved in political activities. But the time was so critical that religious leadership was needed to tackle the current issues wisely.

Kho'i showed himself to prefer religious matters over any involvement in politics. This caused a sense of vacuum inside the *marja'iyya*.

In the first six years of al-Kho'i's *marja'iyya*, Sadr devoted himself to his studies and research, writing on *fiqh* and *usul*, teaching and keeping the *hawza* united. Among his works was his book *al-Fatawa al-Wadhiha*, a simplified version of Islamic laws. He also wrote commentaries on matters of fiqh in al-Hakim's *Minhaj al-Salihin*.

Sadr's activity has sometimes been described as being opposed to the high *marja'iyya* which was led by his master, al-Kho'i. Therefore, in order to attenuate the strong and hostile protests reaching al-Kho'i's ears, he emphasised 'the distinction (to be made) between *fatwas* on religious matters, which each *mujtahid* is entitled to issue, and the engagements (to be observed) towards the *marja'iyya* which are within the competence of a sole *mujtahid*', as he assumed that 'it is not allowed to divide the parties united within the high *marja'iyya* and to create divisions inside it'. In this way, Sadr was trying to silence the prominent personalities in his master's entourage and to dissuade them from creating frictions between himself and his master.[43]

Sadr did not try to claim the position of *marja'* at this time for the following reasons :

1. The regime took several coercive measures to control his widespread popularity among the Iraqis, and adopted a policy of exercising pressure on his disciples. He was detained on three occasions.
2. The position of those who were members of al-Kho'i's administrative circle was very isolated and discouraging because their interests might have been affected had Sadr assumed the leadership of the *marja'iyya*. The situation worsened and this forced al-Sadr to put a stop to his lectures in 1975. He

resumed after a direct request from al-Kho'i. By this time, Sadr had sent an indirect message to those around al-Kho'i to stop spreading rumours that his disciples had engaged in politics.

Sadr did not oppose the religious leadership during this period, because of the obstacles put in his way by the government, preventing him from disseminating his views and opinions. He was arrested on many occasions, and his disciples were threatened.[44]

By 1397/1977, Sadr had realised that al-Kho'i was not politically competent to deal with Iraqi affairs because of his total involvement in religious matters, and the position of those around him was not in compliance with Shi'i community interests and the Muslim Umma in general. Sadr therefore decided to take the lead and disregard al-Kho'i's authority. From 1978 he began to take independent decisions, and his popularity soared to new heights. His followers were society intelligentsia.[45]

A comparison between the characters and background of al-Kho'i and Sadr shows the following differences:

1. While Sadr is a descendant of a distinguished family, many of whom held positions of leadership, both religious and political, al-Kho'i came from a family with no historical background.
2. Sadr was renowned for his intellectual writings before he became famous as a religious *marja'*, while al-Kho'i was not very well known outside the religious organisation and circles of religious studies in the Najaf, before he became the High *Marja'*.
3. Sadr was in possession of a complete 'Islamic Project'. His intellectual interests were varied, covering philosophy, economics and sociology. He also employed *fiqh* in a modern manner from which he developed the Non Profit-making Islamic Bank, *al-Bank al-La rabawi fi al-Islam*. In politics Sadr was instrumental in the formation of the Islamic Da'wa Party, after the Communist Party had managed to infiltrate the major classes of Iraqi society, particularly amongst the Shi'is and in the town of Najaf. His opinion of party politics later underwent a change and in 1974 he issued a directive prohibiting students of theology from participating in the work of Islamic parties.
4. Sadr had access to different cultures and was well informed about the different intellectual schools in the west and the writings of philosophers, and had challenged their theories.[46] In addition he specialised in *fiqh* and *usul*, instructing students of higher education to prepare them for *ijtihad*. His understanding of modern western arguments was reflected in his use of those

theories in his different studies of *usul, kalam*, and *fiqh*, for example in 'Calculations of Probability', which he used in deducing legal judgements.

Kho'i, on the other hand, had concentrated all his efforts on his specialist subjects of the traditional sciences in the school of Najaf and he never showed any interest in modern methods.

The Emergence of the Islamic Revolution in Iran

The Iraqi people followed the progress of the Iranian revolution with great interest. This re-emphasised the importance of the religious institution and its competence in leading the political struggle. A great number of people began showing their support for the revolution by visiting Sadr as if he were an official *marja'*. The Iraqi regime, in order to ease the pressures put on it by the people, had appointed mosque Imams to preach in accordance with its system. It had also directed its efforts towards guaranteeing the support of the Iraqi tribes – either by bribing them, or through promises of social and educational reforms. Although events moved with unprecedented swiftness, the regime did not abandon its vicious intention to destroy its strongest opponent, the *marja'iyya* of al-Sadr. Al-Sadr felt that the regime's reprisals would certainly be directed towards him and his disciples. He therefore decided to take the initiative and issued his *fatwa* which forbade affiliation to the Ba'th Party as well as adherence to the mosque Imams whom the government had appointed. He decided to manipulate the resources available to him and adopt new measures to face the current situation. Internally, he sent his representatives to different cities and towns in Iraq, and got in touch with the Da'wa Party as well. He also made contacts with the Lebanese Shi'i jurists in order to exert strong pressures on the Iraqi regime through the media.

Why, then, did Sadr take the serious decision of opposing the regime, despite the limited prospects deriving from such a course of action?

There are two main reasons:

1. His strong position would force the regime to negotiate with him. He stressed his demands in his call to the Iraqi people on 20 Rajab 1399/1979. These were as follows:

    a. Freedom of practice in religious activities and rites;
    b. To refrain from exerting pressures on ordinary Iraqis to join the Ba'th Party;
    c. To release all those who had been arrested and imprisoned without any charges or proper court proceedings; and

d. To hold a general plebiscite to decide on a free council to represent the people.

2. To persuade the regime to adopt his point of view that the *marja'iyya* must not be attacked and destroyed while it was inactive. On the contrary, the *marja'iyya* must prove to be dynamic and, if it was to be destroyed should be seen in action first. His point of view runs in parallel to al-Hakim's, expressed in the late 1960s against the ruling regime.

When Sadr realised that the regime would not respond to his demands because of its uncompromising attitude, he had no alternative but to make a move in which he prophesied that he would be the first sacrifice. His political action rested upon theoretical views which he derived from his 14 lectures on the meaning of history in the Qur'an, *Muhadharat fi al-tafsir al-mawdhu'i li-l Qur'an* (lectures on the objective exegesis of the Qur'an) which he addressed to his disciples, who numbered around 150 students. Al-Sadr started these lectures two months after the success of the Islamic Revolution and ended them on 1 June 1399/ 1979.[47]

A call was broadcast from Tehran Radio (Arabic Section), claiming to be dictated by Khomeini himself, in which Khomeini requested Sadr not to leave Najaf[48] in order not to create a vacuum which would lead to the collapse of the *marja'iyya*. The message had to be understood as political and moral support for al-Sadr, but the call came during very critical circumstances when none would ever have thought of its seriousness to his life. Moreover, those who informed Khomeini of the story of Sadr's intentions to leave Najaf had ulterior motives. Strangely enough, the language used to address Sadr did not conform with his status and the responsibilities placed on him to protect the *hawza*.

However, in reply to Khomeini's request, a recorded message from Muhammad Baqir Sadr was broadcast on Tehran Radio (Arabic Section) (1 June 1979) in which he congratulated Khomeini on his victory and gave the direct impression that he would stay in Najaf, regardless of the difficult circumstances.

The influences of these exchanges between the two were felt by every section of Iraqi society and delegates paid their tributes to al-Sadr. These delegates reflected two undeniable facts:

1. The popularity of Sadr among the Shi'i community.
2. A change of nationality, i.e, Sadr was the first *marja'* who did not have any non-Arab family affiliations, and these delegates were considered by the regime to herald the beginnings of a real Islamic threat to the regime.

The regime had to take into consideration three factors:

1. The victory which Khomeini achieved in Iran underlined the fact that a similar success might be achieved in Iraq under the leadership of Sadr.
2. All other political parties and opponents had been eliminated by the regime. The Islamic threat was the only one which had any real influence.
3. The regime found itself in a very awkward situation and decided to act ruthlessly against anyone who might show any allegiance to Islam. It took fresh measures to justify its actions: among them was the issue of a decree[49] which made joining any Islamic party, and particularly al-Daʿwa, parallel to committing a serious crime, the punishment for which would be nothing but execution. By this the regime created the first concrete grounds for accusing Sadr of treason and getting rid of him. Immediately afterwards, the regime arrested Sadr on 16 Rajab 1399/12 June 1979 and held him in secret detention under the control of the General Security Department in Baghdad. However, when the news of his arrest broke, many uprisings and demonstrations took place in almost every Arab, Shiʿi city in Iraq, and the regime was forced to release him the same night. The government adopted a new policy and began directing its efforts towards eliminating his supporters, especially his representatives, while he was held under a house arrest which lasted nearly eight months.

During the intervening period (between 16 Rajab and mid-Shaʿban) there were signs that the deterioration in the relationship between the *marjaʿiyya* and the regime was about to be resolved. In a telephone conversation to al-Sadr, the head of the Iraqi Security, Fadhil al-Barrak, expressed his willingness to end the tension. Strangely enough, this proposition was made to Sadr after the regime had in fact executed a large number of his supporters. The regime intended to intimidate and corner him by reiterating their own demands, among which was to force him either to issue a *fatwa* against the Daʿwa Party or to legitimize joining the Baʿth Party, while condemning the revolution in Iran.[50]

As these demands were contradictory to Sadr's beliefs and principles, he refused to yield, after which he issued an urgent call to the Iraqi people encouraging them to rise up and overthrow the regime. He prophesied at the close of his call the inevitable end which he had to face for settling his scores with the regime.[51] When the regime was sure of its strong position through the elimination of his supporters, it detained al-Sadr in a secret camp in Baghdad on 5 April 1980 and after five days he died under physical torture. His sister, Amina, known as Bint al-Huda, died in the same way.

There were many important reasons underlying Sadr's murder. He was the only religious leader who had built bridges with non-religious parties in Iraqi society: his objective analyses and discussions with the members of the new generation won their respect. There had been a search for an intellectual basis for their future support after their experiences with the Nationalists and Communists proved to be a fiasco. Al-Sadr's writings satisfied such needs and attention was turned towards Islam as the answer to man's social and economic problems. He was also seen as a kind of deterrent against the regime's decision to go to war against Iran.[52] His death created a vacuum in the political and intellectual life of the Shi'is of Iraq, in particular, and the Shi'is of the world in general.

Notes

1. Al-Nafisi, 'Abdullah Fahd, *Dawr al-Shi'a fi tatawur al-'Iraq al-siyasi al-hadith*, Beirut, 1973: 81.

2. Al-'Alawi, Hasan, *al-Shi'a wal-dawla al-qawmiyya fi al-'Iraq* (1914–1990), London, 1990: 60.

3. Al-Faqih, Muhammad Taqi, *Jabal 'Amil fi al-Tarikh*, Beirut, 1986: 53.

4. 'Atiyya, Ghassan, *al-'Iraq, nash'at al-dawla*, Beirut, 1988: 120–60.

5. Al-Nafisi, op. cit.: 82.

6. Ibid.: 91.

7. *Personalities, Iraq* (Exclusive of Baghdad and Kazimain), confidential, Baghdad, 1920: 76.

8. Ibid.

9. Burne, A. H., *Mesopotamia: The Last Phase*, London, 1936: 5–10; Silverfarb, Daniel, *Britain's Informal Empire in the Middle East: A Case Study of Iraq, 1929–41*, New York, 1986: 5.

10. *Al-Sahwa*, no. 4, London, 1995: 21–3.

11. Al-Rawi, Ibrahim, *Da'i al-rashad ila sabil al-Ittihad*, Baghdad, 1929: 5.

12. Wilson, Sir Arnold T., *Loyalties: Mesopotamia, 1914–1917*, Oxford, 1930: 74.

13. Ibid.: 75.

14. Al-Nafisi, op. cit.: 64.

15. Al-Wardi, 'Ali, *Lamahat Ijtima'iyya*, Baghdad, vol. 2: 42.

16. Mahbuba, *Madhi al-Najaf wa hadhiruha*, Beirut, 1984, vol. 1: 344.

17. Al-Nafisi, op. cit.: 151–160.

18. Countries under the mandate had been classified into three categories, according to their degree of development. Being in the first one, the Arab countries were to be temporarily supervised by the mandatory states, up to their independence, see Foster, Henry A., *The Making of Modern Iraq*, London, 1936: 96–103.

19. Foster, op. cit.: 93.

20. Al-Wardi, op. cit., vol. 6: 43.

21. Hirz al-Din, Muhammad, *Ma'arif al-Rijal*, Najaf, 1965, vol. 1: 386.

22. Wiley, Joyce N., *The Islamic Movement of Iraqi Shi'as*, Boulder, 1992: 33–4; Sheikh Farzana, *Islam and Islamic Groups: A Worldwide Reference Guide*, London, 1992: 115.

23. The exact date is uncertain. Talib al-Rifa'i stressed that it was founded in the middle of 1959 according to his: *Mudhakarat al-sayyid Talib al-Rifa'i*, vol. 48, compiled by Jawdat al-Qazwini (unpublished manuscript). Others put the date as early as 1957, as in: *Mudhakarat al-sayyid Muhammad Bahr al-'Ulum*, vol. 2.

24. Hadi al-Subayti was a pioneer in the Sunni al-Tahrir (liberation party). He later became a member of al-Da'wa, then left Iraq for Jordan in 1974. During the Iran-Iraq war in 1982, he was extradited to Iraq and no information is available on him. Hizb al-Tahrir originated in Jordan in 1953, then some party members moved to Iraq and began preaching their thoughts. Because of the pan-Islamic views of the party, some Shi'i elements joined it, but when the party leader, Taqi al-Din al-Nabhani (d. 1398/1978) expressed anti-Shi'i views in his book, *al-Khilafa al-Islamiyya* (Jerusalem, 1956), the Shi'i members suspended their membership and then joined the Da'wa party when it came into existence.

25. Interview with Sayyid Murtadha al-'Askari, London, summer of 1991.

26. Al-Qabanji, Sadr al-Din, *al-jihad al-siyasi li-l-Shahid al-Sadr*, Tehran, 1981: 27.

27. Al-'Askari, interview.

28. There were four active groups around al-Hakim; each of them represented a certain authority, but with conflicting interests. Ibrahim al-Yazdi, his son-in-law (still living in Najaf in 1995) represented Iranian interests. His son, Muhammad Ridha al-Hakim, was to entertain the Nationalist interests under the leadership of Jamal Abdul Nasser of Egypt; while his other son, Yousif al-Hakim, (d. 1991) used to insist on not involving the religious leadership in unimportant affairs. His son, Mahdi al-Hakim (assassinated in the Sudan in 1988) and Muhammad Baqir al-Hakim (the Islamic leader who has been living in Iran since 1980), together with Muhammad Baqir al-Sadr, insisted on a new approach to applying Islamic tenets to social and economic life.

29. Bahr al-'Ulum, Muhammad, *Mudhakkarat*, op. cit., vol. 10.

30. Sadiq Hadi al-Bassam (d. on 18 August 1995), interview, London, 1991.

31. The exploitation of al-Hakim's status was reflected in the activities of the nationalists who misled him into taking steps to create internal disorder. The Sunnis also made made use of his status to worsen the internal disturbances when his photos began to appear in Sunni mosques in the 'Azamiyya district. In spite of this, Qassim used to have Shi'i inclinations and had deep respect for Shi'i jurists. I was told by Diya' Ishkara (d. 1409/1989), the civilian private escort to Qassim (in Baghdad in the summer of 1975) that Qassim used to secretly go with him to visit the shrine of Imam Musa al-Kazim in the early morning.

32. Bahr al-'Ulum, Muhammad, *Mudhakkarat*, op. cit. vol. 16.

33. Ibid., vol. 18.

34. Ibid., vol. 31.

35. According to Sadiq al-Bassam, al-Janabi's movement actually aimed at restoring monarchy in Iraq; it considered al-Hakim as a force susceptible to be used to achieve this end, by mobilizing tribes against the central power. Besides, the movement was supported at first by the Shah of Iran and King Husayn of Jordan, but it failed due to British opposition to such a restoration (interview with Sadiq al-Bassam, London, 1991).

36. Bahr al-'Ulum, Muhammad, *Mudhakkarat*, op. cit., vol. 26.

37. One of the leaders of the Afghan resistance, he was held under arrest by the Soviet expeditionary force from the very first days of the occupation and disappeared without a trace, leaving valuable writings on his master's research on *usul*. These had been edited in two volumes entitled *Misbah al-Usul*, published in Najaf in 1376/1957.

38. *Mudhakkarat 'Abbas al-Kho'i* [Memoirs of Abbas al-Kho'i], compiled and re-examined by Jawdat al-Qazwini, unpublished manuscript.

39. The *hawza* is a group of *mujtahids* under whose authority and sponsorship teaching circles are held. The *mujtahid* is responsible for the financial sponsorship of the teaching circles that are under his authority. He assigns a monthly salary to each disciple, guiding him in his studies and research.

40. *Mudhakkarat 'Abbas al-Kho'i*, op. cit., vol. 15.

41. Interview with Muhammad Taqi al-Kho'i (the son of Imam al-Kho'i), London, 5 November 1988. He died in suspicious circumstances in Iraq on 21 July 1994, age 36.

42. Ibid.

43. We are in possession of the letter written by Muhammad Baqir al-Sadr in the presence of his master, Abu al-Qasim al-Kho'i, in reply to a question he put to his attendants about his relationship with his master. He answered the question himself (1396/1976).

44. We were present at a public assembly held in al-Sadr's residence in Najaf, where Shaykh Muhammad Jawad Mughniyya, a well-known Lebanese Islamic author, asked him not to interrupt his lectures; but al-Sadr insisted upon settling the problems which he and his disciples had been facing, particularly the accusations made against them by some religious men. From al-Sadr's point of view, these accusations would lead to fragmentation of the *marja'iyya* and the institution might implode, especially now that the government was also trying to carry things to this conclusion

45. Following the rebellion of Sufar (1397/1977) caused by the prohibition of the Shi'i religious decrees, the government gave permission to some journalists accredited in Iraq to interview al-Kho'i. He declared that the Shi'is enjoyed quite a good situation in Iraq, provoking the anger of Sadr, who had suffered torture and aggression, and that of most Iraqis, whatever their social class or culture may have been. This statement is thought to be one of the main reasons for the severance.

46. In a letter to the writer (Jawdat al-Qazwini) on 21 May 1983 from the Egyptian philosopher Zaki Najib Mahmud.

45. The intellectual form which Muhammad Baqir Sadr presented in his writings,

after he had inspected the western cultures, demonstrates that there are things that may agree or disagree with these cultures. In my opinion the correct thing is to plait the two together.

46. Mahmud died in Cairo in 1993.

47. Sadr, Muhammad Baqir, *Muhadharat fi al-tafsir al-mawdhu'i li-l-Qur'an*, Beirut, 1982. In these lectures, Sadr proposed a prospective vision of the movement of history, interpreting some extracts from Islamic history to explain the current events.

48. This is a translation of the original request broadcast on Tehran Radio in the name of Khomeini to Sadr: 'We have heard of your intention of leaving Iraq because of some events [pressures from the Ba'th regime]. I feel that it is not of interest to leave Najaf, the centre of the Islamic scholarship. I am worried about your decision [of leaving Najaf]. I hope that God wills to dissipate your worries. Peace be upon you and God's mercy and blessings.'

49. Decree no. 461, issued on 31 March 1980.

50. Informal discussion with Husayn Sadr, London, 1 February 1990.

51. Najaf, 'Ala', *al-Shahid al-Shahid,*(n. p., n. d.): 129.

52. For Sadr's role in the Islamic history of Iraq, see Mallat, Chibli, 'Religious Militancy in Contemporary Iraq: Muhammad Baqir al-Sadr and the Sunni-Shi'i Paradigm', *Third World Quarterly*, vol. 10, no. 2, April 1988: 699–729.

CHAPTER SEVENTEEN

The School of Qum

Jawdat al-Qazwini

Historical Background

Qum was one of several villages scattered around the plain just south of Tehran. There are no real remains which may throw light on the history of the city and its early inhabitants. However, it is known that it was inhabited in the year 83/702 by an Arab family, al-Ash'ariyyun, who had been in opposition to the Umayyads at the end of the first century of the Hijra.[1]

Al-Ash'ariyyun came from al-Kufa after their chief Muhammad ibn Sa'ib al-Ash'ari had been put to death by al-Hajjaj ibn Yousif al-Thaqafi (d. 95/714), who was governor of Iraq under the later Umayyads. The whole tribe left Iraq for Iran and settled at Qum, which was at that time a small village. They protected it from attacks by the Daylamis. Throughout time, peace and settlement were behind the expansions of these villages and their integration.

Qum began to grow after the death in the year 201/816 of Fatima, the daughter of the eighth Shi'i Imam, Musa ibn Ja'far al-Sadiq, and her burial there. She was on her way to visit her brother the Imam al-Ridha (the ninth Imam), who was at Marw, after his recent appointment as representative in Khurasan of the 'Abbasid caliph, al-Ma'mun.

The Ash'ariyyun reached the peak of their influence when they became the leaders of the city of Qum and its surrounding villages. The Sunni rulers subjected them to brutal persecution, their influence declined and they disappeared in the middle of the fourth/tenth century.[2]

Qum was renowned in the Seljuk period for its madrasas, for the sanctuary of Fatima, and for its religious foundations. Many *'ulama* were known by the title of al-Qummi, i.e. born in Qum. At the time of the Mongol conquest in 621/1224, its inhabitants were massacred, possibly at the instigation of the Sunnis. It seems, however, that there was an attempt at reviving the region under the Ilkhans, as evidenced by some important hydraulic constructions. It appears that the Timurides demonstrated respect and favour to this holy city. In any case, from the ninth/fourteenth century onwards, the town began to enjoy definite royal patronage. The Turkoman Sultans used it as a kind of winter capital for hunting, and this tradition was continued under the Safavids, Isma'il I and Tahmasip I. Above all, however, it was the religious policy of Shah 'Abbas I which endowed Qum with an unprecedented glamour. The sanctuary was embellished, and two of its four khans, lodging, were transformed into a madrasa with a hostel for visitors. Many 'ulama came to Qum to study, men such as Mulla Muhsin al-Fay', and Mulla Sadra al-Shirazi.[3]

At the start of the Qajar dynasty (1193/1779) a new intellectual resurgence began in Qum: it remained local in its effects until the advent of the fourteenth/twentieth century, when the Qum scholarly centre advanced under the guidance of al-Shaykh 'Abd al-Karim al-Ha'iri al-Yazdi (1276–1355/1860–1936), whose name became associated with the resurgence.

Al-Shaykh al-Ha'iri

Al-Ha'iri was known among Iranians as an authoritative *mujtahid* to be consulted on legal decisions. He concentrated his efforts on organizing studies and supporting a group of renowned religious figures. One of these students, who subsequently became very well-known, was Ayatollah al-Khomeini (1320–1410/1902–1989); another was Ayatollah Muhammad Reza al-Gulbaykni, who limited his activities to Qum and died there in 1412/1993.

Although al-Ha'iri lived through a difficult time in Iranian history, after the fall of the Qajar regime with the coup of Reza Pahlawi, he did manage to shield the religious establishment in Qum and maintain its independence. He would not permit men of religion to become government officials, even in their own field of law.

Al-Ha'iri's efforts to protect the religious establishment in Qum and his high qualifications in religious knowledge and traditional scientific methods enabled him to bring about revitalization to the city after a long period of stagnation. His name lives on as the initiator of the modern scholarly renaissance of Qum.

The movement associated with him produced a group of *mujtahids* who followed in his path. Although al-Ha'iri was not known to have indulged in politics or opposition to the regime, some of his students were open in their objections to the government and, under Ayatollah al-Khomeini, finally succeeded in bringing down the Iranian regime after 50 years of opposition to it.

After the death of al-Ha'iri, Sadr al-Din al-Sadr (1296–1373/1879–1954) became the leader in Qum. He was active in several fields. He built many mosques and religious schools and kept religious education flourishing in a number of Iranian cities. He wanted Qum to become a centre of religious education to which students would converge from all over the country. Under his leadership, the number of students in Qum reached 5000; in al-Ha'iri's time there were only 300 or so.[4]

On the death of Sadr al-Din al-Sadr, Sayyid Husayn Brujerdi (d. 1380/1961) took over the leadership at a time when Sayyid Muhsin al-Hakim was supreme in Najaf.

Brujerdi followed in the footsteps of the *fuqaha'* before him, and took part in a project to compile the Twelver Shi'i Hadiths [oral traditions] into a corpus, fourteen volumes of which were printed and given the title *Jami' al-Hadith al-Shi'a*. He formed a committee to re-arrange Hadiths in a thematic way.

Although Brujerdi did not attempt to compile a comprehensive collection to rid the Twelver Shi'i Hadiths of weak, untraceable material, as the Shaykh Hasan Ibn al-Shahid al-Thani had done in the 11th/17th century in his book *Muntaqa al-Juman fi al-ahadith al-Sihah wa-l-Hisan*, his work was a major advance in the development of Hadith studies. These two attempts were much appreciated by Shi'i scholars as they freed the Imami Hadiths of weak material which was difficult to verify.

The Mujtahids of Qum

After the death of Brujerdi in 1380/1961, the leadership in Qum was shared by more than one *mujtahid*. The most prominent were Muhammad Kazim Shari'at Madari (1322–1407/1904–1987), Shihab al-Din al-Mar'ashi (1318–1410/1900–1990), and Muhammad Reza al-Gulbaykni (1316–1412/1898–1993). In Najaf, the Sayyid Muhsin al-Hakim was still the undisputed leader, his authority having gained strength after the death of Brujerdi.

The *mujtahids* of Qum took part in very important educational projects. Shari'at Madari initiated a Shi'i information centre which helped in publishing Shi'i books through a specialized publishing group. Shihab al-Din al-Mar'ashi founded a large library which was filled with a magnificent collection of texts (70,000 volumes, including 15,000 manuscripts) making it one of the best-known libraries in the Muslim world.[5]

After the death of al-Hakim in 1390/1970 none of the *mujtahids* from Qum attained the eminence of Abu al-Qasim al-Kho'i, who became the undisputed leader in Najaf. The leadership in Qum remained a more localized matter.

Ayatollah al-Khomeini

Alongside the religious leadership that emerged following the death of Brujerdi, a political leadership also appeared in the person of Ayatollah Ruhallah al-Khomeini, who was known as an anti-Royalist and the initiator of a movement against Shah Muhammad Reza Pahlawi. This ended in a crackdown by the government on the movement in 1383/1963, resulting in the death of a number of the students of the religious school in Qum.

Al-Khomeini was exiled to Turkey after his arrest, and finally settled in Najaf in the year 1385/1964, where he taught and at the same time intensified his opposition to the Iranian regime. He was forced to leave Iraq for Kuwait at a time when the political climate was hot and demonstrations against the Shah had reached their peak, but Kuwait refused to receive him. The troubles which convulsed the whole of Iran in 1978 began in Qum between the 7th and 9th of January 1978. In October 1978 al-Khomeini took refuge in France, at Neauphle-le-Chateau, from where he led the opposition which caused the Shah's departure from Iran.[6] Al-Khomeini returned to Tehran (1 February 1399/1979) when the revolution against the Shah succeeded and he became leader and founder of the Islamic Republic of Iran. Al-Khomeini implemented his theory of *wilayat al-faqih* by forming a type of government in which both religious and political leadership remained in his hands until his death in 1410/1989.

The revolution of Imam al-Khomeini evokes memories of the struggle of the *fuqaha'* establishment in the person of al-Karki against some of the official Safavid trends in the tenth/sixth century, and the continuation of this struggle in various forms until the time of the Pahlawis. It was as if al-Khomeini had adopted al-Karki's methods of struggle in order to impose the will of the *fuqaha'* on the political arena and to keep a hold on the reins of government. More than four centuries elapsed between al-Karki's initiation of the struggle and its successful conclusion at the hands of al-Khomeini.

With the success of the Islamic Revolution in Iran two things became apparent :

1. The duty of the *faqih* had changed, with his line of activity running parallel to the line of the government. In times of disagreement he had been considered only as a counselling and guiding influence: he assumed a more positive role after al-Khomeini became head of government. In other words, in their struggle against the despised regime before the rise of al-Khomeini, the religious *marja'iyya* had not aspired to become a replacement for the political forces. Al-Khomeini became at the same time a religious and political leader, a new development in the history of the *fuqaha'* in general and in the history

of Iran in particular. The political and religious leaderships became identical.

2. The theory of *wilayat al-faqih* was a natural outcome of the struggle between the political authority and the *fuqaha'* establishment and was developed because of the change that took place in the religious duties of the *faqih* and his active role in political life. Both the religious and the political authority were in the *faqih*'s hands and this was paralleled by subsequent developments within the Iranian community.

Wilayat al-faqih

After the success of the Iranian Revolution in 1979, al-Khomeini put *wilayat al-faqih* into practice. He was the first *faqih* to publicise it.

During his exile in Iraq (1964–1979), Imam al-Khomeini examined the theory of *wilayat al-faqih* in a series of lectures which were published in Najaf in 1969 under the title *al-Hukuma al-Islamiyya* (The Islamic government). In these lectures he persuaded his disciples to carry out their religious duties to establish the foundations for the development of the Islamic state.

Some scholars claimed that the theory of *wilayat al-faqih* was originated by Shaykh Murtaza al-Ansari (d. 1281/1864).[7] In fact, al-Shaykh Ahmad al-Naraqi (d. 1245/1829) is considered the pioneer jurist, having written about the theory in his *'Awa'id al-Ayyam*.[8] According to al-Naraqi the *wilayat al-faqih* is as unrestricted as the prophets and as infallible as the Imams' *wilaya* on the Islamic umma, because in his opinion, the *faqih* is the representative of the hidden Imam at his occultation, and he acts in the Muslims' interest.[9] Khomeini adopted the same opinion.[10]

According to the Iranian constitution, the leader (*wali al-amr*) must possess the following necessary qualifications: scholarship, piety, political and social perspicacity, courage, strength and the necessary administrative abilities for leadership. If there is no such a person, the position may be occupied by a leading council (*majlis qiyada*) whose members should not be less than three or more than five.

The constitution has authorised the leader (*wali al-amr*) or the leading council to carry out the following duties:

1. Appointment of the *fuqaha'* to the Guardian Council (*Majlis Siyanat al-Dustur*).
2. Appointment of the Supreme Judicial Authority (*Majlis al-Qada' al-A'la*) of the country.

3. Supreme command of the armed forces, exercised in the following manner:
   a. appointment and dismissal of the Chief of the Joint Staff;
   b. appointment and dismissal of the Chief Commander of the Islamic Revolution Guards Corps (*Haras al-Thawra al-Islamiyya*).
   c. formation of the Supreme National Defence Council, composed of the following seven members:
      - the President.
      - the Prime Minister.
      - the Minister of Defence.
      - the Chief of the Joint Staff.
      - the Chief Commander of the Islamic Revolution Guards Corps.
      - two advisers appointed by the leader.
   d. appointment of the supreme commanders of the three wings of the armed forces, on the recommendation of the Supreme National Defence Council.
   e. the declaration of war and peace, and the mobilisation of the armed forces, on the recommendation of the Supreme National Defence Council.
4. Signing the decree formalising the election of the President of the Republic by the people.

   The suitability of candidates for the presidency of the Republic, with respect to the qualifications specified in the Constitution, must be confirmed before elections take place by the Guardian Council and, in the case of the first term (of the Presidency), by the Leadership.
5. Dismissal of the President of the Republic, with due regard for the interests of the country, after the Supreme Court holds him guilty of the violation of his constitutional duties, or after a vote of the National Consultative Assembly testifying to his political incompetence.
6. Pardoning or reducing the sentences of convicted persons, within the framework of Islamic criteria, on a recommendation (to that effect) from the Supreme Court.

It is worth mentioning that the ordinary Iranian, according to the constitution, has the right to elect the Majlis members who will empower the qualified candidate to be the leader (*wali al-amr*). This process will give the leader the divine legitimacy for his appointment through endorsement by the people.[11]

As for the status of the religious establishment in Qum after the success of the Islamic Revolution in Iran in 1979, two of the most senior clergy, Muhammad Reza al-Gulbaykni and Shihab al-Din al-Marʿashi, fully supported the revolution, whereas another *mujtahid*, Kazim Shariʿat Madari protested at the involvement of *ʿulama* in any role in the administration, and he deplored the practices of some of his fellow *ʿulama*.

The Iranian government, for its part, responded by encouraging those who supported it, while weakening those who opposed it by using methods of suppression and trying to isolate them from the popular masses of the people.

After the death of Imam al-Khomeini, the policy of the Islamic Republic underwent great changes, the first being a shift from a revolutionary state to a state of stable government. While maintaining the spiritual line of succession, Sayyid 'Ali Khamenei, then President of the Republic, took over Khomeini's position as Imam; while Shaykh Hashimi Rafsanjani, who was speaker of the House of Shura, became President.

The new trend had started to develop within the group known as the *hawza* in the mid-1950s. Known later as *al-Hujjatiyya*[12] it tried to bring its rejection of the government's policy into the open, relying on religious interpretations prohibiting the setting up of an Islamic government until the re-emergence of the twelfth Imam.

In the beginning the Hujjatiyya was unclear in its aims: however, as a dissenting movement from the core of the religious *hawza* itself, it was somewhat similar to the Akhbari movements which surfaced in the last years of the Safavids.

The Hujjatiyya movement did not rely on a particular religious outlook but fell back on slogans which were religious in appearance, but were actually an excuse to oppose the political authority. However, the movement could not keep up its momentum and started to weaken when faced with the strength of the government.

The Hujjatiyya began to emerge in the 1950s as an organising educational party opposed to the Baha'i activities in Iran. In order to understand the Hujjatiyya, it is important to look at its origin and background. This investigation will start with the Shaykhiyya, and covers the intervening years up until the time of the Hujjatiyya.

The Shaykhiyya

The term Shaykhiyya came into use during the life of Shaykh Ahmad al-Ahsa'i (d. 1241/1826), when his views gave rise to doubts among the Shi'i community.

Al-Ahsa'i was preoccupied with Greek philosophy and Illuminationist ideas on the one hand, and the hadiths narrated by Shi'i transmitters but not authenticated, on the other. His philosophy was not compatible with Shi'i traditions regarding the Ithna ashari Imams, such as on the extreme veneration paid to the Imams, on God, on the Hidden Imam, on eschatology, on the nature of the world and many other subjects.[13] These ideas caused a great deal of argument between his supporters and opponents in the Shi'i centres in Iraq (Karbala and

Najaf) and in most Iranian cities. In some instances, these disputes culminated in bloodshed, as happened frequently in Tabriz. The conflict was led by two groups:

1. The Shaykhiyya or al-Kashfiyya, those who followed al-Ahsa'i.
2. The Mutasharri'a, those who adhered to Islamic law.[14]

After al-Ahsa'i's death, his disciple, Sayyid Kazim al-Rashti (d. 1259/1843), assumed the leadership of the movement and followed the example of his tutor by defending the ideas of his master and refuting charges targeting them both.[15] He, like his master, took advantage of the concept of the Hidden Imam and claimed to be the representative who received his directives from him. Both of them made use of this to enhance their status among their followers. Al-Rashti died without appointing a successor, and the movement was split up into many factions, each taking a different direction, though all agreed on the concept of the Hidden Imam and the possibility of communicating with him.

The main factions were:

1. The Shaykhiyya al-Rukniyya. They were the followers of Karim Khan al-Qajari (d. 1288/1871), a descendant of the Qajar family who believed that the *mujtahid* can communicate without any intermediary with the Hidden Imam and receive his directions. This concept was considered the fourth principle of *usul al-Din*, and their name was derived from this. They are mainly found in the city of Kirman.[16] After Karim Khan's death, the Rukniyya branched into two: one group was headed by his son, Muhammad Khan (d. 1324/1906), called Natiqiyya or Nawatiq; the other was headed by al-Mirza Muhammad Baqir Hamadani (d. 1319/1901), whose followers were known as al-Baqiriyya. His followers are to be found in the Iranian cities of Isfahan and Na'in. After the death of Muhammad Khan, his brother Zayn al-'Abidin Khan (d. 1360/1941) became the leader of the Nawatiq, succeeded by his son, Abu al-Qasim Khan al-Ibrahimi (d. 1389/1969), and grandson, 'Abd al-Riza Khan al-Ibrahimi (killed during the Iranian Revolution in 1979).[17]
2. The Shaykhiyya al-Kashfiyya. These are the followers of al-Mirza Muhammad Baqir al-Usku'i (d. 1301/1883), who believed that communication between the Hidden Imam and his deputy is achieved through *kashf* (conceptualising of the revelation): hence the name Kashfiyya. This movement was started in Karbala by al-Mirza Hasan Gawhar (d. 1261/1845), who was a disciple of al-Rashti. It spread from Karbala, through the efforts of al-Usku'i, to Tabriz, then to Usku. The leadership has become hereditary, with Hasan's son, Mirza Musa al-Usk'i al-Ha'ir'i taking over after his death. During al-Mirza

Muhammad Baqir's stay in Karbala, some Ahsa'is were attracted to his ideas and through them the Shaykhiyya has spread to al-Ahsa', Kuwait, Bahrain and Suq al-Shuyukh in the south of Iraq.[18] The leader of the sect now is al-Mirza Hasan al-Usku'i (born in 1900) and his son al-Mirza 'Abd al-Rasul, who resides in Kuwait. The Shaykhis are now found in several Iranian cities, Pakistan, the Gulf and Iraq, and number about half a million.[19]

3. The last faction of the Shaykhiyya was a group led by Sayyid 'Ali Muhammad al-Shirazi, or al-Bab (the Gate). The Babis and, later, Baha'is belong to this group.

The Babi Movement

The Babis were closely associated with the Shaykhiyya school up until the death of Sayyid Kazim al-Rashti. They took advantage of a dispensation of the Prophet Muhammad, namely, 'I am the city of knowledge and 'Ali is the Gate', for their leader to call himself, first the Bab (Gate) to the Hidden Imam, then the Hidden Imam himself. 'Ali Muhammad al-Shirazi (executed 1267/1850) declared in 1260/1844 that he was the Bab to the Imam, then advanced his claim of being the Twelfth Imam, who had come to proclaim a new prophetic cycle. There are still a few Babis nowadays, but they mostly became Baha'is, as will be shown.[20]

The Baha'i Religion

After the death in 1267/1850 of al-Mirza 'Ali Muhammad al-Shirazi (al-Bab) by firing squad, the Babis were split into three factions:

1. Original Babis
2. Azali Babis
3. Baha'is.

The second faction are followers of al-Mirza Yahya Subh al-Azal, who was appointed by the Bab as his successor. Then the Babis were accused of the attempted assassination of Shah Nasir al-Din al-Qajari, and were repressed by the government. Zirin Taj, whose popular name was *Qurrat al-'Ayn* 'Coolness of the eye', was put to death with many others, while al-Mirza Yahya fled to Baghdad.

Subh al-Azal's leadership was challenged by al-Mirza Husayn 'Ali Nuri (d. 1310/1892) who claimed in 1866 to be the messianic figure foretold by the Bab, took the title of Baha'allah (Glory of God) and managed to win over the majority of the Babis.

At the request of the Persian government, the Ottomans imprisoned both leaders in 1280/1863, first at Edirne; they then sent Subh al-Azal to Cyprus and Baha'allah to 'Akka in Palestine.[21]

The Azalis disappeared after the death of their leader, while the Baha'is prospered. Baha'allah died in confinement in 1310/1892. His son 'Abbas Afandi (d. 1340/1921) took over the leadership and his grandson, Shawqi Afandi (d. 1377/1957), succeeded him. Since 1280/1863, however, an elected body has been in control.

The Baha'i faith is now an independent religion separate from Shi'ism and Islam. It has its own holy books, teachings, laws and prophets. They consider al-Bab and Baha'allah to be equal in status to the Prophet Muhammad, bearing new revelations from God, while Baha'ism replaces all other religions; Islam, Christianity, Judaism and Zoroastrianism.[22]

The Hujjatiyya Movement

At the beginning of the 20th century, the Baha'is became very lively in Iran. This activity was met with concerted opposition from the Shi'i religious establishment. One of their measures was to set up a charitable society called Anjuman Khairiyya Hujjatiyya Mahdawiyya, 'The Hujjatiyya Mahdawiyya Charity', which was established at the beginning of the 1950s by Shaykh Mahmud Dhakir Zadah Tawalla'i, also known as Muhammad Halabi.

Halabi was a student at Mashhad of al-Mirza Mahdi al-Isfahani, who was a declared devotee of the Hidden Imam. Halabi noticed that some of the other students were attracted to the Baha'i faith: he argued with them and managed to convince them against joining. He then moved to Tehran and started preaching against the Baha'is, supported morally and financially by the religious establishment.

The Hujjatiyya movement was based on belief in the Hidden Imam, its members considering themselves soldiers in his army and ready for his appearance from occultation. To them, neither political nor military organisations were permitted to oppose oppressive regimes before the Imam's appearance. Their activities would be limited to cultural and religious education. Their work was centred on the conservation of human resources, in order to be in readiness for the Imam, whom they consider to be commander of all forces. They show their sorrow for his absence and pray for his safety.

Their movement was contemporaneous with another, the Revolutionary Islamic Movement of Iran (headed by Nawwab Safawi, executed in 1956), calling for armed struggle against the regime of the Shah.

The Hujjatiyya was, however, in a quandary after the advent of the Islamic Revolution in 1979, as there were differences between its religious beliefs and those of the Revolution. These may be summarized as follows:

1. The Hujjatiyya slogans had become different from those of the Islamic Revolution since the outbreak of the Iran-Iraq war in 1980. They were calling, for example, for the conservation of assets and forces, until the appearance of the Imam to give his command for Holy War, *jihad*, as he is, to them, the commander-in-chief. The Iranian Revolution on the other hand, considered al-Khomeini to be commander of all forces in the country. The Hujjatiyya used to call al-Khomeini the deputy of the Imam, reserving the latter title for the Hidden Imam, the one who is infallible, *ma'sum*. The Iranian Revolution, however, countered with one of their slogans, which said, 'You cannot love al-Mahdi if you do not love al-Khomeini', *Bi 'ishq Khomeini natawan 'ashiq Mahdi shud*.

   During this time, the Hujjatiyya considered Communism as the real enemy, and Marxism as the inheritor of the Baha'i mantle, while the Iranian Revolution's greatest enemy was America, which was labelled 'Great Satan'.

   The enemies of the Hujjatiyya accused it of trying to become involved in unnecessary skirmishes with no serious threat to the Revolution at present. At the beginning of its emergence, its members worked hard at creating enemies of the Baha'is instead of concentrating on the struggle against the regime of the Shah. That is why its opponents used to call it *Hizba qa'idin* (the effete Party).[23]

2. Shaykh Mahmud Halabi was opposed to philosophy and philosophers. He thought that the essence of all divine religions is alien to Greek philosophy and philosophical ideas in general, and so he advocated adherence to the ideas of the *fuqaha'* and the narrators of the *hadith*. Al-Khomeini, on the other hand, was in opposition to that, giving philosophy a great deal of attention and writing a number of books on the subject. His disciples have also followed the same path, as is apparent in the writings of the martyr Shaykh Murtaza Mutahhari (who was subsequently assassinated a few months after the success of the Revolution).

3. Interpretation of religious utterances, upon which the Hujjatiyya society based their ideas, was taken up by other groups opposed to the revolution and its leader. The Society, for example, generally followed the Imam al-Kho'i, who was at Najaf, and considered him to be the highest *marja'* of the Shi'ites, because his approach was wholly religious, and involved no interference in politics, in contrast to al-Khomeini's. The Society also adopted the writings of Sayyid Murtaza al-'Askari because of his close relationship with Shaykh

Mahmud al-Halabi. Al-'Askari was considered one of the leaders of the Da'wa Party in Iraq during the sixties.[24]

4. On the 12 Shawwal 1403/1983 al-Khomeini warned members of the Society, indirectly, not to act against the Islamic Revolution's aims. He said: 'Do not make any move against this surge [meaning the Islamic nation in Iran], otherwise you will be crushed'.

After this, the Society issued the following statement: 'Now that it has become certain that Imam Khomeini meant the Society in his speech, and that the opinion of 'The Great Founder of the society', Hujjat al-Islam Halabi, has been taken, he has ordered that all activities and programmes should be suspended'. The activities of the individual members are now limited to privately held religious meetings.

The Shi'i Leadership after al-Gulbaykni

A number of *fuqaha'*, some of the most prominent of whom are listed below, are mentioned as *marja'* to their followers:

1. Sayyid 'Ali al-Sistani (Najaf).
2. Sayyid Muhammad al-Sadr (Najaf).
3. Sayyid 'Ali Khamenei (Tehran, the spiritual leader of the Islamic Republic of Iran).
4. Sayyid Muhammad al-Ruhani. He is one of the outstanding *fuqaha'* and has a large number of followers in some of the Gulf countries and in cities in the north of Iran. He was not on good terms with the Islamic Revolution in Iran. He was under house arrest in Qum.
5. Shaykh Muhammad 'Ali al-Araki. He lived in Qum, and was nominated by the Iranian government. He died on 29 November 1994, at the age of 100 years.
6. Sayyid Muhammad al–Shirazi. He was born in Iraq in 1928. After the death of his father, Mirza Mahdi, in 1380/1960, he put himself forward as *marja'* and has some followers in Karbala, the Gulf countries and eastern parts of Saudi Arabia. He left for Kuwait when the Ba'th came to power. After the Islamic Revolution, he left for Iran. He was not on good terms with the Iranian regime and, to make matters worse, he was in opposition to the Khomeini concept of *wilayat al-faqih*. He has been very active and has attracted a great number of ordinary people to him. He has been under house arrest in Qum.

The Marja'iyya in Najaf

On the other hand, in Najaf a decline in its influence that began in the mid 1970s continued because of the vicious attacks by the Iraqi regime on this centre of learning.

Najaf, in spite of the presence there of the highest *marja'iyya*, has become a centre in name only, especially after the military attacks carried out by Iraq on this ancient Shi'i city, the bombing of the Holy places with missiles, and the arrest of a large number of religious men after the uprising this city witnessed in the aftermath of the defeat of the Iraqi regime by the allied forces of the United Nations in 1991, following Iraq's invasion of Kuwait and 'Desert Storm'.

At end of the Iran-Iraq war in 1988, the government of Iraq realised its mistake in suppressing the *marja'* and changed its way of dealing with it by trying to control it and by supporting the nomination of Sayyid Muhammad al-Sadr as leader, after the death of Imam al-Kho'i.[25] It assigned to him the responsibility of running the affairs of the foreign students who come to Najaf. Its aims were, in the first instance, to establish an Arab *marja'*, in opposition to an Iranian one, and secondly, to admit after a decade to an error on the part of the regime in executing Muhammad Baqir al-Sadr. The nominee was a student of him and a relative.

Sayyid 'Ali al-Sistan was one of the brightest students of al-Kho'i. He studied first at Mashhad, then at Qum and finally migrated to Najaf in 1950, where he was a regular participant in al-Kho'i's circles. His *marja'iyya* began after the death of al-Sabzawari and was strengthened after the death of al-Gulbaykani. Al-Sistani's character and leanings are similar to those of his master al-Kho'i, and it could be said that his *marja'iyya* could be a continuation of al-Kho'i's.

Support for al-Sistani comes from three sides:

1. The agents of al-Kho'i and those running the cultural centres and charitable organisations all over the world.
2. The conservative Shi'is, such as the Khoja community headed by Mulla Asghar 'Ali Muhammad Ja'far, whose headquarters are in London.[26] They believe that al-Sistani is the best and the most qualified leader at present. They represent the Shi'i groupings in Africa, India, Pakistan and other countries, and some of the merchants in the Gulf also adhere to it.
3. Those who oppose the policies of the Iranian government in nominating the *marja'iyya*.

The Marjaʻiyya in Iran

The religious organisation in Iran exists in a country where the government was established by the efforts of a *faqih*, al-Khomeini; after he passed away, his place was taken by the former President, Sayyid ʻAli Khamenei. And just as al-Khomeini succeeded in heading both the religious and the political establishments, his successor is trying to emulate him.

From the above it may be noted that, after the death of al-Gulbaykani, the *marjaʻiyya* was divided between Sayyid al-Sistani, considered to be an independent *faqih*, and Shaykh Muhammad ʻAli al-Araki, who was favoured by Iran. Al-Araki's leadership, before his death, was considered to be of a temporary nature because of his age and, consequently, as paving the way for Sayyid Khamenei.

Muhammad al-Ruhani, despite having some followers in the northern cities of Iran and the Gulf, and Muhammad al-Shirazi, who has disciples in the Gulf, Iraq and Pakistan, have been unable to communicate with the Iranian masses because of the restrictions imposed on them.

After Shaykh al-Araki many questions about the *marjaʻiyya* were put forward because of the relatively large number of marjaʻs who have influence over people. Some official groups, however, nominated ʻAli Khamenei to be the successor of al-Araki, in addition to his existing position as *wali amr al-Muslimin*, for the following reasons:

1. Unification of political leadership and religious *marjaʻiyya* (represented by Imam al-Khomeini) had taken place in 1979.
2. Not to allow the *marjaʻiyya* to be located outside Iran because the *hawza* in Iraq had come under the control of the regime after Abu al-Qasim al-Khoʼi, and the size of the Shiʻi community in Iran is about one third of the total number of the world-wide Shiʻi community.

There is disagreement among some *mujtahids* about the appointment of Khamenei as a *marjaʻ* for the community because the choice and the position of the *marjaʻ* cannot be made and assigned by the state. The Shiʻi *marjaʻ* comes to the notice of the community not because of any propaganda, but because of his high achievements in religious studies.

Proposing Khamenei for *marjaʻiyya* resulted from pragmatic needs of the Iranians rather than the whole Shiʻi community for the following reasons:

1. Politically, he is the head of a religious country.
2. According to the Islamic Shiʻi theory, the leadership of the Shiʻi community at the time of occultation should be with the *fuqahaʼ*. This was enshrined in

the Islamic constitution of 1906 during the rule of the Qajar dynasty. The Islamic Revolution was not satisfied with that and put a bigger emphasis on the role of the *marja'* in ruling the government through the theory of *wilayat al-faqih.*

3. During al-Khomeini's time the religious and political leadership were unified. This appears in the Iranian constitution under Article 5, which says that the political leadership should be in the hands of the *faqih* who is known and acceptable to the majority of the people.

4. Following the withdrawal of Shaykh Husayn al-Muntazari of the succession in 27 March 1989 and a few months before his death, al-Khomeini sent a letter on 29 April 1989 to the chairman of the Committee for the Revision of the Constitution. In it he said that there was no requirement for the political leader to be a *marja'* also, but it sufficed for him simply to be a *faqih*. This made it possible for Khamenei to be appointed leader of the Islamic Revolution of Iran.

5. The appointment of Khamenei as a *marja'* in addition to the political leadership is a new phenomenon in the selection procedure, in two respects:

   a. A *marja'* becomes so because of his extensive knowledge of *fiqh* and *usul.*

   b. Khamenei's appointment happened during a period where there was an Islamic Shi'i government, and since a *faqih* is not necessarily knowledgeable in the running of a country's government, a new theory was developed for the appointment of a *marja'*. This says that it is not necessary for a leader to be the most knowledgeable in religious studies.

And so, on account of the special needs of the Iranian regime, Khamenei was nominated for both leadership and *marja'iyya*, so that no disagreement would arise were they to be split. This new practice of not taking knowledgeability into consideration has become a trend, encouraging others like Muhammad Husayn Fadhl Allah in the Lebanon, who possesses both political and religious knowledge as a *faqih*, to nominate themselves for the *marja'iyya*. And it might open the doors for other contenders in the future.

Notes

1. Al-Qummi, al-Hasan ibn Muhammad, *Kitab Qum*, Tehran, 1935, (ed.) Jalal al-Din al-Muhaddith: 242; Muhammad ibn Hashim, *Khulasat al-Buldan*, Qum, 1975, (ed.) Husayn al-Mudarissi: 172.

2. Calmard, J., 'Kum', Encyclopaedia of Islam, vol. V, Leiden, 1986: 369–72.

3. Calmard, op. cit.: 371.

4. Interview with Sayyid Rida al-Sadr, London 1990, one of the *faqih*'s sons who was also a *mujtahid* in his own right and a philosophy lecturer in Qum. Another son was the Imam Musa Sadr who was active in politics in the Lebanon and disappeared during a visit. Sayyid Rida Sadr died on 1 November 1994.

5. See Husayni Ahmad, *Fihrist Nuskhabay Khatti Kitab Khana 'Umumi Hadrat Ayat Allah al-'Uzma Najafi Mar'ashi*, 18 volumes, Qum, 1975; Calmard, op. cit.: 371.

6. Calmard, op. cit.: 372.

7. Calder, Norman, 'Accommodation and Revolution in Imami Shi'i Jurisprudence: Khomeini and the Classical Tradition', *Middle Eastern Studies*, 18, 1982: 16.

8. See Dabashi, Hamid, 'Mulla Ahmad al-Naraqi and the Question of the Guardianship of the Jurisconsult Wilayat al-Faqih', in Nasr (ed.), *Expectations of the Millennium: Shi'ism in History*, New York, 1989: 287–300.

9. Al-Naraqi, Ahmad, *'Awa'id al-Ayyam min Muhimmat Adillat al-Ahkam*, Tehran, Lithograph, 1849, and reprinted by offset in Qum, 1982.

10. Al-Khomeini, Ruh Allah, *al-Hukuma al-Islamiyya*, Beirut, 1972: 116.

11. *Dustur al-Jumhuriyya al-Islamiyya*, (ed.) by Ali Ansariyan, Beirut, 1985: 104–5.

12. The name Hujjatiyya is related to the title of the twelfth Imam, al-Hujja (the proof).

13. Momen, *An Introduction to Shi'i Islam*: 226–9.

14. Kizrawi, Ahmad, *Baha'ikri*, Tehran, 1944: 12–15.

15. Al-Rashti wrote a comprehensive biography for his master al-Ahsa'i in his book *Dalil al-Mutahayyirin*, Kuwait, 1978.

16. Al-Fadli, Abd al-Hadi, *Fi dhikra Abi*, manuscript in the writer's possession: 90

17. Momen, op. cit.: 229.

18. Al-Fadli, op. cit.: 90.

19. Momen, op. cit.: 231.

20. The Concise Encyclopaedia of Islam, Leiden, 1913–1936: 61.

21. Balyuzi, H. M., Baha'ullah: *The King of Glory*, translated from the German by Antonia Nevill, Oxford, 1995: 72–7; The Concise Encyclopaedia of Islam: 61.

22. Momen, op. cit.: 232.

23. Baqi, A., *Dar Shanakhtaya Hizba Qa'idina Zaman* (in Persian), Qum, 1983.

24. Murtadha al-'Askari was very active in the cultural field at the beginning of the sixties. He had a big hand in establishing many schools and cultural projects, one of which was the College of Usul al-Din in Baghdad, and he became its first principal. After 1968, when the Ba'th party came to power, he fled to Iran where he now lives. Al-'Askari wrote many books, such as *Khamsun wa-Mi'at Sahabi Mukhtalalq*, (The Unreal 150 Companions); *Ma'alim al-Madrasatayn* (The differences between the Sunni and Shi'i Schools of Thought), in three volumes, and many others. His writings deal exclusively with Shi'i issues, otherwise he would have been one of the leading intellectuals of the present time. He is now over eighty years old.

25. In Najaf, two of the names mentioned above were real candidates for the *marja'iyya*: Sayyid Muhammad Baqir al-Sadr and Sayyid Ali al-Sistani.

26. Al-Khoja derives from a group of Hindu African tribes in Tanzania which were

converted from Hinduism to Islam. Some of its members became *Ithna 'asharis* in the middle of the nineteenth century. In 1946 the Federation of Khoja Shi'a Ithna 'asharis' *Jama'at* of Africa was founded in Tanzania. Later in 1967 the World Federation of Khoja Shi'a Ithna 'ashari Muslim Community was founded in London. See, Sachedina, Abdul Aziz, A., *Haji Naji, the Great Religious Educator of the Khoja Shi'a Ithna 'Ashari Community*, Canada, (n. p.), 1992; Asghar Ali and M. M. Ja'ffer, *An Outline History of Khoja Shi'a Ithna 'Ashari in Eastern Africa*, London, 1983. The Khoja community number around 125,000. Some of them are well-known traders and businessmen. They live in many different countries, such as America, Africa, and Great Britain. Mulla Asghar Muhammad Ja'far has been the President of the Community since 1965. He was born in 1936.

Contributors

Faleh Abdul-Jabar, PhD Sociology, London University, Birkbeck College. Visiting Fellow at the School of Politics and Sociology, Birbeck College, London University. His works in Arabic include *Religious Thought in Iraq* and *State and Civil Society in Iraq* . His most recent publication in English (ed.) is *Post-Marxism and the Middle East.*

Basim al-'Azami, a lawyer and author of many essays on Islamist movements in Iraq. Based in the UK.

Talib Aziz, PhD, Utah University, author of many essays and papers based on his dissertation on the life and works of Ayatollah Muhammad Baqir al-Sadr.

Ali Babakhan, PhD, Paris, author of *L'Irak: 1970–1990; Déportations des Chiites; Les Kurdes d'Irak, leur historie et leur déportation par le régime de Saddam Hussein.* He contributed to many academic publications in France. He died in 1999.

Helkot Hakim, PhD, Paris, Lecturer at the Institut National des Langues et Civilisations Orientales, Paris; author of many essays and papers on the culture, history and religion of Iraqi Kurds.

Ibrahim Haydari, PhD, Berlin, lectured at various universities in Berlin, Baghdad and 'Annaba, Algeria. His works in Arabic on culture and society include *The Karbala Tragedy* and *The Sociology of the Shi'i Discourse.* He is currently based in London.

Peter Heine, a professor at Berlin University, a leading German scholar on modern Iraq and Middle East History. Editor of *al-Rafidayn,* an annual review on the history and culture of Iraq.

Yousif al-Kho'i, a director of the Kho'i Charitable Foundation in London, author of several papers on Shi'i classical and modern history; founder of *Dialogue* review.

Pierre-Jean Luizard, PhD, a leading French author and scholar on Shi'ism in general and Shi'ism in Iraq in particular. His works include *La formation de l'Irak contemporain: Le rôle politique des ulema chiites à la fin de la domination ottomane et au moment de la construction de l'état irakien.*

Yitzhak Nakkash, a professor at Brandeis University; author of *The Shi'is of Iraq*, and a host of published papers on Shi'ism and Shi'i rituals.

Jawdat al-Qazwini, PhD, SOAS, (London), scholar and author of several historical studies in Arabic on classical Shi'i authors and thinkers; his *The Scientific and Political Development of the Shi'i Institution* is forthcoming.

Jens-Uwe Rahe, MA, Bonn University, Germany. His contribution is based on his MA dissertation, *Shi'is in Exile*. Works at present for the Deutsche Welle Television Network, Berlin.

Abdul Halim al-Ruhaimi, MA, The Lebanese Univeristy, Beirut. Author of *The History of the Islamic Movement in Iraq: The Ideological Roots, 1900–1921; A Short History of Iraq, 1921–1958.* Based in London.

Sami Shourush, MA, SOAS, London, a prominent writer and commentator on modern Iraq politics and society. Based in London and Prague.

Index